SONS OF THE WAVES

THE COMMON SEAMAN IN THE HEROIC AGE OF SAIL 1740-1840

STEPHEN TAYLOR

YALE UNIVERSITY PRESS
NEW HAVEN AND LONDON

Published with assistance from the Annie Burr Lewis Fund.

For information about this and other Yale University Press publications, please contact:
U.S. Office: sales.press@yale.edu   yalebooks.com
Europe Office: sales@yaleup.co.uk   yalebooks.co.uk

Set in Adobe Garamond Pro by IDSUK (DataConnection) Ltd
Printed in Great Britain by Clays Ltd, Elcograf S.p.A

Library of Congress Control Number: 2019954649

ISBN 978-0-300-24571-4 (hbk)
ISBN 978-0-300-25751-9 (pbk)

A catalogue record for this book is available from the British Library.

10 9 8 7 6 5 4 3 2 1

To Caroline, again and always

Your trade is the mother and nurse of your seamen; your seamen are the life of your fleet, and your fleet is the security and protection of your trade, and both together are the wealth, strength, security and glory of Britain.

Lord Haversham to the House of Lords, 1707

CONTENTS

CONTENTS

ILLUSTRATIONS

IN THE TEXT

PLATES

ILLUSTRATIONS

4. *Tom Allen (1771–1838), a Greenwich Pensioner*, by John Burnet, 1832. National Maritime Museum, Greenwich, London, Caird Collection.

5. *The Shipwreck*, by Joseph Mallord William Turner, exhibited 1805. © Tate/CC-BY-NC-ND 3.0/www.tate.org.uk.

6. *The Grosvenor East Indiaman, Capt Coxon Commander Wrecked Augst 4th 1782, on that Part of the Eastern Coast of Africa, Inhabited by the Caffrees . . .*, by Robert Smirke, 1784. National Maritime Museum, Greenwich, London.

7. *Sailors*, by John Augustus Atkinson, 1807. National Maritime Museum, Greenwich, London.

8. *A View Taken in the Bay of Oaite Peha [Vaitepiha] Otaheite [Tahiti]*, by William Hodges, 1776. National Maritime Museum, Greenwich, London.

9. *The Landing at Tanna [Tana], one of the New Hebrides*, by William Hodges, 1775–6. National Maritime Museum, Greenwich, London, Caird Fund.

10. *A Sailor Bringing Up His Hammock, Pallas, Jany 75*, by Gabriel Bray, 1775. National Maritime Museum, Greenwich, London. Purchased with the assistance of the Society for Nautical Research Macpherson Fund.

11. *Seaman Leaning on a Gun on the 'Pallas'*, by Gabriel Bray, 1775. National Maritime Museum, Greenwich, London. Purchased with the assistance of the Society for Nautical Research Macpherson Fund.

12. *The Point of Honour*, by George Cruikshank, 1825. National Maritime Museum, Greenwich, London.

13. *Portsmouth Point*, by Thomas Rowlandson, 1811. National Maritime Museum, Greenwich, London.

14. *The Delegates in Counsel or Beggars on Horseback*, by S. W. Fores, 1797. National Maritime Museum, Greenwich, London.

15. A death mask of Richard Parker. Baldovio/Hunterian Museum, London/CC-BY-SA-4.0.

16. *Duncan Receiving the Surrender of de Winter at the Battle of Camperdown, 11 October 1797*, by Daniel Orme, 1797. National Maritime Museum, Greenwich, London.

17. *British Sailors Boarding a Man of War*, by John Augustus Atkinson, 1815. National Maritime Museum, Greenwich, London.

PREFACE

THE precise span of his long and turbulent life is a matter of some dispute. Some say he is to be seen as early as 1577, among the 166 seamen who circumnavigated the globe with Francis Drake on the *Golden Hind*. He was certainly recognizable by the 1650s when Britain went to war at sea against the Dutch as well as the Spaniards. At Trafalgar, he emerged fully formed: the common man as national hero. What concerns us here, however, is an era – the century from 1740, when Foremast Jack, the man who went aloft under the British flag, established his country's command of the oceans.

Also known as Jack Tar, his very name proclaimed him a man of the people – Jack being a generic term for the common man. Yet among them he was an outsider, almost another species. At a time when others of his class might never stir beyond their native valley, he roamed the world like one of the exotic creatures he encountered on his travels, returning home bearing fabulous tales – some of them actually true – as well as curious objects and even stranger beasts. Although while at sea he was as poor as any rustic labourer, ashore he knew spells of brief wealth. Then, fired up with back pay and prize money, he would eat, drink, cavort and fornicate like a lord. Habitually profligate and with a terrifying thirst for alcohol, he was loyal to his ship, his country and his king, roughly in that order. Most of all, though, he was loyal to his mates, and it was this kinship, as of a tribe, that made him capable of the endeavour and boldness that marked him in his golden age, under Horatio Nelson.

He was, simply, the most successful fighting man ever produced by his native land which, with its taste for booty, pugilism and foreign adventure, is saying quite something. So profoundly did he believe in himself, and so deeply did he awe the enemy, that defeat was never contemplated and rarely experienced. His spirit earned him the respect, the admiration, and sometimes even the love, of his officers.

It was not only in action that he was tested. Voyages of exploration, of trade and of imperial expansion took him to the farthest reaches of the globe. Jack was with Captain Cook in charting the South Seas. He joined in the discovery of a Pacific idyll, and helped to cast Captain Bligh adrift when the dream turned to nightmare. He went aloft in the East India Company's ships, venturing to lands of outlandish peoples and mystifying customs. Among the cargoes he shipped were humans – African slaves to the Caribbean and convicts banished to the ends of the earth. In doing so he encountered perils every bit as dire as those he faced in battle; for if one thing about his existence is plain, it is that he was far more likely to be carried off by disease or shipwreck than by a cannonball.

The dangers and hardships – even sufferings – of his life are well known, and were certainly enough to deter most of his compatriots. Samuel Johnson spoke for baffled landlubbers in general when he declared: 'No man will be a sailor who has contrivance enough to get himself into a gaol; for being in a ship is being in a gaol, with the chance of being drowned.' One clergyman who joined a man-of-war – and fled as soon as he was able – could not fathom how human beings dwelt 'in a prison within whose narrow limits were to be found Constraint, Disease, Ignorance, Insensibility, Tyranny, Sameness, Dirt and Foul air: and in addition, the dangers of Ocean, Fire, Mutiny, Pestilence, Battle and Exile'.

Still, we do well to challenge received truisms that are confined to the wretchedness of existence below decks, most notably that glib old chestnut about rum, sodomy and the lash. While obviously there was a great deal of rum, many hands went years at sea without being flogged, and sodomy was a capital crime scorned by almost the entire tribe. The bleak monograph that portrays Jack as a hapless sufferer does no justice to his individuality. He might be a press-ganged hostage, yet he could also be an enthusiastic volunteer; as often as he was a noble simpleton he was a cunning devil; the drunken dolt was sometimes a thoughtful and, yes, literate, traveller. And at a perilous moment in Britain's history, he showed a capacity for rebellion and defiance that utterly terrified his superiors and countrymen.

What might be termed the miserabilist school prevailed for most of the last century. John Masefield was a key influence on it and one might be forgiven for wondering why on earth the poet laureate, who spent part of his early life on windjammers, ever – in the elegiac words of 'Sea Fever' – wanted to go down to the sea again.

The truisms of another age have been overtaken by the subtler work of modern historians. In the past decade particularly, Britain's maritime past has been chewed over and contested from a range of perspectives. What might be termed a revisionist school has challenged long-received attitudes about matters ranging from the press gang to discipline and social history, provoking vigorous debate among academics not only in home waters but across the Atlantic.

While addressing recent scholarship, this book will attempt to advance a different form of narrative. It will do so by confining itself to the lives and experiences of common seamen, as related in their own tales and memoirs and through maritime records; and it will argue that the notion of victimhood falls down, not only because of Jack's achievements, but because of his spirit. One characteristic stands out above all others in his storytelling, and it is self-respect. These reminiscences, it has been argued, are not invariably to be trusted: on top of his tendency to be carried away by a good yarn, Jack's memoirs are said to have been used as a vehicle for polemical axe-grinding in a time of reform. But the records are there for us to test his accounts, and to a remarkable degree they stand up to scrutiny.

Over the century to be examined, the seafaring man became a crucial figure in almost every aspect of Britain's endeavours. He was the essence of its defence – its guard against invasions as well as the key to its victories – and the means by which it acquired wealth and new possessions. Without him there could have been neither the trade nor the exploration that made Britain a mighty power. The fact that he stood out among his less adventurous compatriots – that he dressed differently, talked differently, even walked differently – conferred further distinction on him. For his part, the simple truth is that he rather looked down on anyone who was not a seaman.

Among the biggest myths is that he lacked a voice. Jack's story was neglected by generations of naval historians, perhaps because of a mistaken belief that he had failed to tell it. The unearthing, and dusting off, of many texts over the past thirty years has amply disproved that. In fact, it is now plain that the Trafalgar moment gave rise to a spate of lower-deck memoirs, including one magnificent fantasy, *The Life and Surprising Adventures of Mary Anne Talbot, Related by Herself*, purportedly by the illegitimate daughter of an aristocrat who followed her seducer to war, joined the Navy disguised as a man, was wounded at the guns on the Glorious First of June, and, unsurprisingly, created the publishing sensation of 1809.

Of genuine full-length accounts by plain tars there are at least a dozen. One of the earliest was the work of William Spavens, who signed on almost fifty years before Trafalgar as an unlettered orphan, and towards the end of his life – disabled by the loss of a leg, living on the charity of benefactors, but self-educated to a level little short of erudition – produced a memoir that is as gripping as it is moving.

Subsequent accounts extend to the Napoleonic Wars and beyond. One of the most thoughtful is by John Nicol, a shrewd observer and traveller, who fought at the Nile but was also an incurable romantic and fell hopelessly in love with a female convict on their voyage to New South Wales. Another romantic, the dashing Jacob Nagle, was an American who took up arms for his country's independence before crossing over to the former enemy by volunteering for the Royal Navy; he also sailed with the East India Company, survived shipwreck and being cast away, and kept a vivid, carefree diary covering forty years at sea. A contrast to the usual heroics is provided by William Robinson, who was at Trafalgar and wrote a sour account of navy life under the *nom de plume* Jack Nastyface that is more in line with the Masefield perspective and was long accepted as a valuable record; interestingly, Robinson's record shows him to have been a failure as a seaman.

The best sailors' memoirs are about more than the sea. Robert Hay, William Richardson, Samuel Leech and Robert Wilson, like Spavens and Nagle, cast real light on their times. Olaudah Equiano, renowned as the former slave who campaigned for abolition and wrote a celebrated autobiography, was also a sailor. Famous as a thespian, Charles Pemberton was another hopeless seaman but wrote eloquently. Others were less fluent but still had stories to relate – John Wetherell, Daniel Goodall and James Choyce among them. Their chronicles are supplemented by many shorter accounts encompassing a century of seafaring to 1840, by which time the age of sail was drawing to a close.

This is not a book about naval policy, strategy, tactics or the political designs that shaped maritime history – for in general Jack would appear to have had little awareness of or interest in any of these; and, if he did, they are not matters that figure in his writings.

Nor is it about the beautiful machines, compounds of wood, canvas, hemp and a small amount of iron in which he lived and fought. Crucial though ships are to this story, the emphasis is on how seamen saw them – often as living things imbued with human qualities – rather than how they were made, or the technical process of sailing them, the mystery by which they were summoned to motion by the raising of sails, set for the far side of the world and, despite storm, navigational error and other disasters, reaching it more often than not.

In telling Jack's story, I have been at pains to confine myself to his own voice, turning to the writings of his officers and other contemporaries only when they touch on his character and his world. Extracts from Admiralty records, including ships' logs and court-martial proceedings, are used to provide context and an overview for individual accounts.

The man who emerges bears a surprisingly strong resemblance to the Jack of folklore. He did, whenever he could, drink, dance, fiddle and sing. He was indeed as impulsive and headstrong as he was improvident – and often pugnacious with it. And he really did lollop along like a sturdy little vessel on a rolling sea (although this arose from his habitual need to balance on a heeling deck, rather than, as was sometimes said, because his body had actually been deformed by living in the confined space of the lower deck). By his own account, he was no put-upon sufferer but a proud soul with robust opinions, and learned in his own fashion, even when his phonetic way with words needs some deciphering.

But while he was crucial to a great national enterprise, he was no national stereotype. He came from every corner of the British Isles and sometimes very much farther off. Quite often, like Jacob Nagle, he was an American (although the assumption by the naval establishment, long after the War of Independence, that former colonists still owed allegiance to the king was a constant source of trouble). He could be from Scandinavia, from a range of European states – hostile as well as friendly – and, surprisingly often, from Africa or India.

There is a further paradox to Jack, and it helps to explain his sense of self-worth. He may have been part of a great and powerful tribe, yet he retained a degree of independence almost unknown to his class at the time. He was mobile. If he disliked his ship, he would find another. A press gang might cut short his liberty, but it could not stop him deserting at the next port and signing on with a new captain. A spirit bold enough to embark for the far side of the world, a man with the strength and skill to clamber aloft in choppy seas and wrestle canvas while a wind blasted through the rigging – he was always a rare commodity. As long as ships went to sea, an able hand was never short of a place to stow his chest.

By the time sail gave way to steam, Britain had gained an imperial hold on the globe. In this Jack had been a critical factor, for neither naval supremacy nor mercantile prosperity could have been achieved without him. He would have been the last to see it that way, but it is reasonable to suggest that the engine of national success up to the Industrial Revolution was the common seaman.

PROLOGUE

UNTIL the buccaneering appearance of Francis Drake in the 1570s what is represented as the great English seafaring tradition was actually more a policy of stout isolationism. While Norsemen and Spaniards advanced across the Atlantic, and the Portuguese launched astonishing voyages of navigation and exploration around the globe, Britons mainly rested in their isles. As the naval historian N. A. M. Rodger has written, in 1558 there was probably not one Englishman capable unaided of navigating a ship to the West Indies. It took a ruthless pirate to set the nation on its course with destiny.

Plainly though, one quite small island – with a coastline of 11,070 miles and in which no one is more than 70 miles distant from the sea – had bred a familiarity with the encircling element. Coastal dwellers had engaged in fishing since time immemorial and gradually – because poor roads often made it easier to shift goods around the country by boat than by cart – evolved into what might be termed shallow-water sailors. Coal, iron, timber and crops in effect kept our early seafarers afloat. To start with, however, Britons were slow to set sail for distant profit, and they were signally unable to prevent a series of invasions during the first millennium. So, as a defensive response, they used the sea as a means of preserving their security, while launching occasional forays across the Channel.

Talk of the Royal Navy would have been premature before Tudor times, but as early as the fourteenth century, officers in the king's service known as admirals could forcibly recruit men – a process known as impressment – to fight on their ships (or, rather, to manoeuvre the vessels so that the actual fighting could be done by men at arms and archers). This power was a royal prerogative and not confined to the sea service, for soldiers and a range of craftsmen such as masons could be recruited in the same way. But, interestingly, the prevailing wisdom was that a volunteer sailor did better service than a pressed one, with the result that ships' captains tended to take on willing men from their own communities. A Devon vessel spoke with a West Country accent, a Norfolk ship with an East Anglian voice and so on.

Drake's exploit in the *Golden Hind* was a watershed. It was, first and foremost, a great voyage. He became the first seafarer to follow Magellan's 1519 circumnavigation of the globe, and did better still than the Portuguese pioneer by surviving and bringing home 59 of the 166 men who sailed with him, whereas Magellan was murdered in the Philippines and just 18 of his 237 men returned. But the *Golden Hind* also succeeded in plundering a Spanish treasure galleon of booty, creating for Britons a vision of mountains made of gold and silver beyond the horizon.

A decade later Drake wrote a further epic by sweeping into Cadiz and torching twenty-four of the Don's ships. As if it were not enough for an upstart seafaring nation to 'singe the King of Spain's beard', Drake and Lord Howard of Effingham were ready and waiting for the Armada that set out on an invasion in 1588 and was destroyed by a combination of English gunnery, Atlantic gales and abundant bad luck. (Men on the *Revenge* had so perfected loading and firing her cannon that they could get off a round every hour, compared with the Spaniards' one every day.[1] It would take another two centuries for these skills to be refined to the point that a gun crew could fire one round almost every minute.)

But if Drake captured the nation's imagination and gave appeal to the idea of seafaring for those tough or desperate enough to follow in his wake, resources remained limited. The Navy of the day mustered fewer than 200 sailing vessels, including light pinnaces, and some 7,600 men. In the entire British Isles there were an estimated 16,255 seamen of all kinds.[2]

Why, it may be asked, did they go at all? What induced men to leave a relatively secure if rude hearth for the discomforts and dangers of the sea? Seafaring was a young man's business, and few lived to become ancient mariners. In 1598 the geographer Richard Hakluyt wrote of seamen: 'No kind of men of any profession pass their years in so great and continual hazard . . . and of so many so few grow to grey hairs.' But from fishing and coastal trading, mercantile interests were starting to reach out to distant parts of the world – none more avidly than the East India Company, founded in 1600. And it is hard to escape the conclusion that while Jack signed on for different reasons – family tradition, regular food and pay, even curiosity – the lure of prize money was always in the background, and with it the various forms of piracy and privateering that became bound up in English seafaring.

If the timid were discouraged by risk and hardship, these very elements honed Jack's spirit. Already he was notorious for making drunken mayhem in port, and wilful independence at sea. A little verse from Drake's time casts the seaman in contemporary perspective:

> *You live at sea a lawless life, for murther and piracy,*
> *Which on the land you do consume on whores and jollity.*[3]

Daniel Defoe was of much the same opinion. 'They swear violently, whore violently, drink punch violently,' he wrote, 'in short, they are violent fellows and ought to be encouraged to go to sea.'[4] In creating *Robinson Crusoe* he got many others to do just that – as we shall discover.

Piracy was a formative school. Desperate bands operated under William Kidd in the Indian Ocean, and in the Caribbean under Edward Teach. Paradoxically, however, fewer British sailors actually became pirates at this time than fell victim to them. Ships did not have to venture far from home waters to encounter Barbary corsairs who enslaved an estimated 10,000 British seamen. Among them was Thomas Pellow, born near Falmouth in 1704 into a prominent Cornish seafaring clan and aged eleven when his uncle's ship was taken off Cape Finisterre. Thomas spent the next twenty-three years a captive in Barbary, converting to Islam, joining the Sultan's army of European rene-gades, marrying and finally escaping. On returning to Cornwall and writing a best-selling narrative, he tended naturally to pass over these ambiguities while making much of his sufferings under the Moors and 'the aftonifhing *Tyranny* and *Cruelty* of their Emperors'.

British seamen had by then become participants in slavery themselves. From the colonization of Jamaica in 1655, British dominance in the Caribbean ensured the regular passage of two commodities across the Atlantic – black bodies out to the West Indies, and sugar homeward to Liverpool. The number of Jacks involved in transporting up to three million Africans into slavery grew from a matter of hundreds in the 1650s to some 5,000 annually by the 1770s.[5] While it may be said that the slave trade was a nursery for seamen, it was a desperate business all round. Merchant seamen in home waters suffered a death rate of 1 per cent annually. Of those who transported the East India Company's merchandise, 10 per cent died. Crew mortality on slave ships was between 20 and 25 per cent.[6]

Among those who traversed the Atlantic and Indian oceans in these early days were the first two hands to record their experiences. Each was an archetypal character – Edward (Ned) Coxere, the born adventurer whose boisterous scrapes never found him short of spirit; and Edward Barlow, the disciple of gloomy miserabilism.

Coxere started as a ship's boy in Dover and crammed enough excitement into his thirty-four years at sea – including a spell of service on an enemy ship and another as a slave in a Barbary galley – to fill a volume by Robert Louis Stevenson. A pithy overview of his career showed, moreover, how a seaman's trade could transcend nationalism:

I served the Spaniards against the French, then the Hollanders against the English; then I was taken by the English out of a Dunkirker; and then I served the English against the Hollanders; and last I was taken by the Turks, where I was forced to serve against English, French, Dutch, and Spaniards, and all Christendom. When I was released from them, I was got in a man-of-war against the Spaniards, till at last I was taken prisoner by the Spaniards.[7]

Often Coxere served in small merchantmen, vessels of around 100 tons with crews of about thirty, armed with perhaps a dozen cannon and shifting anything from fish out of Newfoundland to raisins from Malaga. His record speaks plainly of the risks, but he was used to earning twice as much as a navy hand and, despite learning his trade under a series of crazed or drunken captains, once came swaggering home with almost £45 in his pockets.

Coxere married a Dover lass named Mary and seven weeks later was bound for the Mediterranean. When he returned again, nine months later, it was to find her cradling a baby. We shall encounter other episodes of the sailor's unheralded homecoming, a subject fondly portrayed in paint and song; but Coxere's simple description, from 1656, is as poignant as any:

> She, being surprised, could hardly speak to me, for she knew not before whether I was dead or alive. I laid down my pack and rested myself, and had my relations come about me with joy.[8]

Ned would often be gone for a year, sometimes disappearing into captivity, as occurred on his next voyage when his ship was seized by an English renegado turned Barbary pirate and taken to Tunis; Coxere was lucky in being enslaved for just a few months before the Navy launched one of its periodic rescue expeditions to Barbary. Soon he was bound for the Canaries on a ship laden with beeswax, almonds and goat skins – only to be taken captive again, by a Spanish man-of-war, beaten and told: 'Cromwell is dead. There is a feast in Hell.' Rounding off what he called 'this troublesome voyage', he managed to escape in Malaga, getting on board a Dutchman and ultimately reaching home in 1659.

Ned became a Quaker because 'the Lord gave me a glimmering of the unlawfulness [of] striving to kill men who I never saw nor had any prejudice against'. His pacifist faith earned him three spells in jail, once after rebuking a judge at Southwark in ringing terms: 'I was among several nations [at sea] and did wish I might find as much kindness here as I did among them.'[9] He returned from his last voyage to find Mary had been buried two days earlier. He outlived her by thirteen years, dying at Scarborough in 1694.

Edward Barlow, like Coxere, left a vivid account of his life and times, but could scarcely have been a more different character. In the modern idiom,

Coxere had a glass-half-full view of life; Barlow was a decidedly glass-half-empty fellow.

He was born into a Lancashire farming family around 1642. Hearing tales of 'travels and strange things in other countries', young Edward set himself against 'ploughing and sowing and such Drudgery' and set off to sea aged seventeen with scarcely a backward glance at folk who, he scoffed, 'would not venture a day's journey out of the smoke of their chimneys'.[10]

Over four decades Barlow voyaged the world – in navy and merchant ships, in East Indiamen and West Indiamen. Six times he sailed to India, four times to China. He was shipwrecked on the Goodwin Sands and witnessed one of the early major fleet actions – the Four Days' Battle of 1666 which ended in a British defeat at Dutch hands, with ten ships and more than 4,000 men lost. Like Coxere, he drew political radicalism and religious zeal from his experiences. It is fair to add, however, that the same disdain he felt for tyrannical captains, exploitative merchants and stay-at-home rustics was extended to a good deal else besides, including his own kind. 'Many seamen,' he wrote, 'are of that lazy, idle temper that, let them alone, they never care for doing anything they should do, and when they do anything it is with a grumbling unwilling mind.'[11]

A morose ingrate perhaps, but Barlow left the most vivid early description of men going aloft:

> . . . half awake and half asleep, with one shoe on and the other off . . . always sleeping in our clothes for readiness; and in stormy weather, when the ship rolled and tumbled as though some great millstone were rolling up one hill and down another, we had much ado to hold ourselves fast by the small ropes from falling by the board; and being gotten up into the tops, there we must heave and pull to make fast the sail, seeing nothing but air above us and water beneath us, and that as raging as though every wave would make a grave; and many times in night so dark that we could not see one another, and blowing so hard that we could not hear one another speak.[12]

This was the talent, it bears repeating, of a farmer's son of the seventeenth century. Here is his description of doctors attending to a patient:

. . . feeling his pulse when he is half dead, asking him when he was at stool, and then giving him some of their medicines upon the point of a knife, which doth as much good to him as a blow upon the pate with a stick. And when he is dead, then they did not think that he had been so bad as he was, nor so near his end.[13]

Coxere and Barlow – both Edwards, yet as opposites as bow to stern. What makes this noteworthy is that at sea they would have repeatedly encountered those of the other type and, in crushingly close proximity, still managed to rub along most of the time. As to how, well, it may have had something to with a deeper, shared identity. A captain of the time could write of his men as 'a sort of people that, if they have justice done them, a good word now and then, and be permitted their little forecastle jests and songs with freedom, they will run through fire and water for their commander, and do their work with the utmost satisfaction and alacrity'.[14]

The tribe was expanding constantly. The fleet sent against the Armada in 1588 had 7,600 men among a total estimated seagoing population of 16,255. By the time Edward Barlow left the sea, more than 40,000 seamen were borne on navy ships and 50,000 on merchantmen.[15] And the interdependence of these two maritime worlds had become inescapable. A French philosopher living at Covent Garden in 1728 observed that trade had enriched the English, contributed to their freedom and extended their commerce, 'whence arose the grandeur of the State':

Posterity will very probably be surprised to hear that an island whose only produce is a little lead, tin, fuller's-earth and coarse wool, should become so powerful by its commerce as to be able to send three fleets at the same time to three and far distanced parts of the globe.[16]

Soon after Voltaire's essay was published, Britain set its sights on another distant part of the globe in what was to be one of the most ambitious, harrowing and epic voyages in all seafaring. The year was 1740 and it was a landmark in the shaping of Jack.

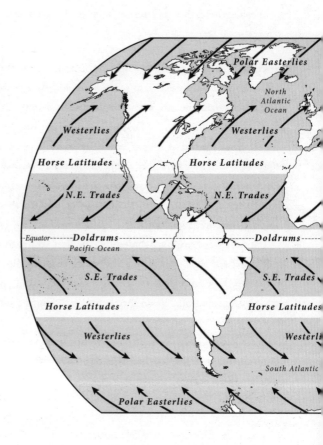

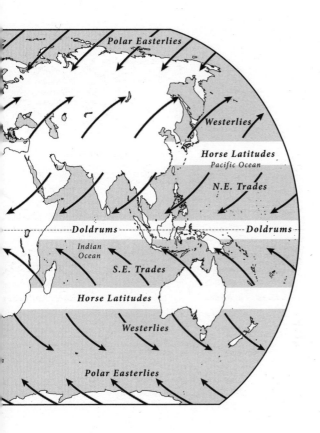

PART ONE
RISING

1

ORDEAL WITH ANSON
1740-44

~~~~~~~~~~~~~~~~~~~~~~~~~~~~

THERE were almost fifteen hundred of them to start with. They shared a heritage and inhabited a communal world. They were bound together by fate and a joint purpose, but as to their origins and why they were in Spithead at all in the summer of 1740, every man was an island.

That is as much as we can say with confidence of the common seamen involved in one of the most daring enterprises of British naval history. In all other respects it must be acknowledged that the epic of Commodore George Anson's voyage to the Pacific is sadly lacking in personal details.

In part this was down to the sheer scale of the undertaking. Early that year, Anson, a forty-two-year-old navy captain of no signal achievement, had been ordered to take a squadron with an army across the world to parts of the South Seas almost unknown to British seafarers and there invade Spanish colonies and seize treasure galleons. This was an instinctive attempt to relive what the English regarded as their greatest seafaring exploit, a buccaneering voyage around the world more than 150 years earlier when Drake put the wind up the Dons, plundered richly laden vessels and returned home with a fortune in gold and silver, charts and spices.

As was invariably the case in naval operations, however, there was a shortage of one critical article – seamen: which is to say Jacks with the variety of skills required to handle ships to far-off seas, and once there to defeat an enemy in battle. And as so often when they were hastily assembled, only the barest information had been entered in the ships' muster books which were supposed to show, among other things, a man's age and where he came from. The upshot is that virtually all we know of them is their names and, all too often, the approximate dates of their deaths.[1] None would set down the events of which he became a part.* In all likelihood none had any idea of making history. Even so, there is evidence to ascribe personality to a handful of individuals; and to bring them to mind, in their dwelling below decks, over those summer months of 1740.

Most had come aboard at Deptford, a marshy, smelly, muddy blend of shipyard and farmyard, storehouse and bawdyhouse, on the Thames east of London. For months they remained there at anchor, with forays ashore that tended to end in the Gun Tavern rather than the noble baroque church of St Paul – completed just a decade earlier to nourish the spiritual welfare of seamen. As spring turned to summer, five ships at anchor slipped their cables and worked their way down river and round to Spithead, a sheltered anchorage off Portsmouth and the nucleus of naval operations in the Channel.

While plenty has been written about its hardships, a seaman's life also involved a great deal of routine, as well as random pleasures. And so, while their sailing orders were awaited from London, the men were divided into watches and messes, groups of eight who would share their meals at tables between guns on the lower deck and become, as one tar put it, like 'so many families'.[2] The more experienced hands – those rated Ordinary and Able – were carrying out tasks with which they were familiar and that were recorded in the ships' logs: 'Fixing new Trysail trees at the Main Top mastheads, staying the lower masts, fixing the topmast rigging.' All this being utterly incomprehensible to the newcomers – the Landsmen – they were engaged in mundane business, such as storing provisions and holystoning decks.

At leisure they fiddled, danced and drank, though there was some grumbling from the older men about a new regulation, stipulating that their tradi-

---

* The contentious and exculpatory version of their actions by John Bulkeley, a gunner, and John Cummins, a carpenter, is not included here among lower-deck accounts.

tional spirits be watered down into an innovative concoction that had been dubbed 'grog'.* Being at Spithead, ready to depart, they were not allowed visits ashore; but, because little restriction was placed on the toing and froing of boats, they were joined in recreation by women from the port, and fornication went on relatively discreetly, screened by the carriages of 24-pounders.

While their dress could not be called a uniform it was sufficiently regular to distinguish these men from other commoners. To take one of their number as fairly typical, Charles Bubb of the *Severn* wore the loose canvas breeches known by the nautical term trowsers, a white checked linen shirt with a brightly knotted handkerchief at the neck, and leather shoes with no stockings. Like many of his kind, Bubb was a dab hand with a needle, and his blue double-breasted jacket was decorated with coloured ribbon. Another jacket, stowed in his chest below, was coated with tar for waterproofing in foul weather. This distinctive garment had earned the English seaman his popular name, Jack Tar. He wore his hair long, plaited or pigtailed, but was usually clean-shaven, at least insofar as a razor and cold water permitted.[3]

Bubb was among the older hands, nearing fifty, with years of seafaring in his wake and a skin as rough as his canvas trowsers. His hands were leather hard, numbed by handling coarse rope and sail alike without protection and in all conditions. His forearms were still wiry, his shoulders broad, but he was ailing after a severe winter ashore when food became scarce and he had been as ready to sign on for the regular rations as for any prospect of prize money. He was a shadow of his former self – of the seaman in his prime described by another hand:

Jack had been at sea ever since he was the height of a marlinspike, and a better practical sailor was not to be found from stem to stern. From the knotting of a rope yarn to the steering of a ship under bare poles in a tiffoon [typhoon], Jack excelled in all. No one could surpass him at the manoeu-vring of a thirty-two pounder, and he could hit a mark with it as well as any.

* Vice-Admiral Edward Vernon had become so concerned about alcoholism in the Navy that he ordered the dilution of the brandy or rum served to the men twice a day. His nickname was Old Grogam, for the coat of grogam that he wore, and the name attached itself to the drink that he instituted.

He was an excellent sail-maker too, and there was not a sail aboard, from the windsail to the spanker, but what he could shape and make . . . What may seem strange, Jack with all his acquirements, did not known the alphabet! 'I have frequently begun,' said he, 'with that fellow at the stem head (meaning A) but I never could get so far aft as that crooked gentleman (Z) that is at the helm.'[4]

At this stage Bubb and his fellows knew little of the mission on which they had embarked, other than what was spoken of in the taverns – that it would take them to the far side of the world, and that treasure was in the offing. Many hands would have been making their first real voyage, and it is reasonable to speculate that a substantial number – just how many is not known, again because of silences in the musters – fell into that unhappy category of men seized by press gangs.[*]

A few names stand out among the hundreds listed on each ship's muster, like the faceless dead on a war memorial.

John Duck was among those known to have been pressed, probably in Wapping, the seaman's habitat in London. He had spent weeks in utter squalor, imprisoned with dozens of others below the grating of a supply vessel known as a tender, awaiting his fate, before being sent on to the frigate *Wager* in June. Duck was rated Ordinary, which indicated some previous time at sea. What set him apart from most of his fellows, however, was his race. At a time when black seamen were still relatively uncommon, Duck was noted as 'a Mullato [sic], born in London'.[5]

Samuel Cooper was among Duck's shipmates, an Ipswich fellow and an experienced seafarer, rated Able. He entered the *Wager* as a volunteer, had second thoughts on hearing where they were bound, and ran, only to return four weeks later. So pleased were his officers to see a useful hand come back

---

[*] Each muster book was supposed to record not only a seaman's name, his age, place of origin and the date of his entry but whether he had volunteered or been pressed. It was also supposed to state the circumstances of his leaving the ship, whether by discharge (marked with a D) or because of death (DD) or desertion (R for 'run'). These details are almost entirely absent in the musters of Anson's five ships.

that, deserter or not, he escaped a flogging. Cooper would prove to be a lucky fellow in more ways than one.

Another of their shipmates, Robinson Crusoe, was even luckier as well as apparently being literate. Daniel Defoe's novel, first published in 1719 and based on the true adventures of a Scottish tar named Alexander Selkirk who was cast away after a dispute with his captain, proved (somewhat perversely) influential in attracting young men to the sea. Whether or not this whimsical choice of name indicated a premonition of what lay ahead, the individual named in the *Wager*'s muster as William Robinson Crusoe – also Cruzoe – deserted three weeks after entering, not to be seen again and thereby avoiding the entire ordeal.[6]

Pseudonyms were quite common, usually being adopted by men who had 'run', or deserted from other ships, and signed on under false names to avoid identification. Anson's venture, with its hint of Spanish gold, attracted hands who had drunk of the legends of Drake's plunder, and whose anticipation of prize money gave rise to a wry wit in their choice of names. The *Centurion* could boast not only her very own Francis Drake, but also a George Million and a Thomas Richman. The *Gloucester* had a Jacob Blackbeard, who was evidently hoping to emulate the fearsome pirate Edward Teach. Of these men, sadly, little is known besides their spirit and insouciant optimism.[7]

Anson's squadron consisted of five men-of-war and a sloop. The flagship, *Centurion*, had sixty guns, the *Gloucester* and *Severn* fifty guns, the *Pearl* forty guns and the *Wager* twenty-four guns. These were not ships of the line, those vessels of seventy-five guns or more, large enough to join the line of battle in a fleet action; Anson's ships had been chosen for speed and mobility as well as a degree of firepower, and they were joined by a dashing outrider, the sloop *Tryal*, of eight guns.

Whatever her armament and tonnage, each was a creaking hugger-mugger, a habitat dank, dark and cramped, sandwiched between tiers of timber, where sea air blended with rank smells and shouting, murmuring and grumbling voices. Those coming on board were entering both an enterprise and a home, an inescapable dwelling for what would clearly be years to come. And the more experienced among them would have had their senses alert to these surroundings, for it was an accepted fact that each ship acquired a reputation, one that encompassed her disposition – not only her sailing qualities and comforts, good or ill, but a curious blend of common experience, folklore and superstition by which she became defined. Her captain, crucially, shaped her character as a happy or an unhappy place in which to serve; but she had a nature of her own. One Jack, with an eloquence less rare than might be expected, wrote: 'The qualities of a ship are to a seaman what the charms of a mistress are to a poet.'[8] Just like a mistress, however, allure could bring anguish; seamen trapped in the embrace of an unhappy ship knew a special kind of suffering – would rue their encounter as bitterly as any lover.

This sense of identification with a ship was strong among tars. Unlike officers and warrant officers, Jack did not join the Navy, he signed on to a ship; and, until being paid off, he was known collectively by her name, so the 400 hands on Anson's flagship were called Centurions. Those preparing to sail also included some 300 Gloucesters, 300 Severns, 250 Pearls, 120 Wagers and 70 Tryals.[9] By late summer their wait was nearly over. Just before they sailed, however, an event occurred that, while it attracted little attention at the time, has resonated down the centuries.

On 1 August a succession of coaches drew up at Cliveden, a mansion on a hill overlooking the Thames west of London. To mark the occasion – it was the anniversary of George I's accession – Thomas Arne had composed music to a patriotic masque entitled *Alfred*, and although the work as a whole met with only polite applause from the guests in Cliveden gardens that evening, one song, to a poem by James Thomson, won immediate acclaim. No connection with Anson's mission was intended, but Thomson and Arne had captured a mood of the nation's ambition:

> *When Britain first, at heaven's command,*
> *Arose from out the azure main,*
> *This was the charter of the land,*
> *And guardian angels sang this strain:*

Rule, Britannia! Britannia rule the waves!
Britons never, never, never shall be slaves.

It is salutary now to look back on that first performance of 'Rule, Britannia!', before it became virtually a second national anthem, then a jingoistic paean, because in the months that followed it would echo with hollow mockery: Anson's voyage demonstrated that Britons could indeed be slaves; and as to the notion that *any* seafaring people were capable of ruling the waves – well, such hubris invited nemesis.

———

The Anson expedition holds a unique and terrible place in British maritime history. In his grimly authoritative account, Glyn Williams describes the combination of dithering and misfortune that set disaster in train.[10] Firstly, the Admiralty held up Anson's sailing while his orders were finalized, then a pattern of contrary winds delayed departure for another month, until late September, which was ill-timed for the prevailing winds across the Atlantic.

As the vessels battled down the Channel against westerly gales, Joseph Burchill of the *Severn* became the first seaman to die. His body was sewn up in a hammock and – as a precautionary measure, to ensure he really was dead – a final stitch was passed through his nose. Weighted with shot, he was then dropped over the side with a few appropriate words. A day later two more men, John Orr and George Derry, followed him to the bottom.

On 7 October the old hand Charles Bubb died. His embroidered blue jacket and the remaining contents of his chest – including two silver shoe buckles which were all he had to show for a lifetime at sea – were auctioned among his shipmates according to custom.[11] Within two weeks of sailing, four men had died on a single ship.

In an age when life was usually cheap, the loss of a seaman mattered – less on a human level, though his messmates might regret his passing, than in the way it could affect the smooth running of his ship. As one hand described their world:

A vessel of war contains a little community of human beings, isolated, for the time being, from the rest of mankind. This community is governed by laws peculiar to itself . . . Each task has its man, and each man his place. A ship contains a set of human machinery, in which every man is a wheel, a band or a crank, all moving with wonderful regularity and precision to the will of its machinist – the all-powerful captain.[12]

Jack's primary task was, of course, to shift the giant wooden beasts across the seas. In the simplest terms that meant care and maintenance of the ship, and raising and spreading the maximum amount of canvas from the yards of each mast when the wind was favourable, and adjusting the same canvas – often in peril or great haste – to suit changing conditions. There were a variety of associated skills, involving the knotting and splicing of rope, stitching canvas, and manning the helm. But setting and stowing the sails was paramount. That

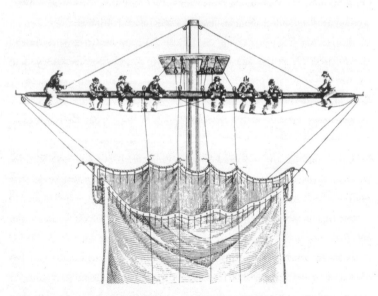

The topman's duties aloft, bending and reefing sails, often in perilous conditions, made him the most valued and respected of seamen.

required men of vigour, agility and strength: vigour to race up the ratlines; agility to shrug out along a yardarm with the support of just a footrope; and strength to balance there, swaying aloft in all conditions, while setting the sails to gather up the wind's momentum, hauling them in when the wind became excessive, and bending new ones when it shredded the canvas (which was all too often).

Because of their late departure, Anson's hands were always struggling against countervailing winds. The passage to Madeira, ten days in reasonable conditions, took five weeks. Having barely cleared the European mainland when they might have been across the Atlantic, their health began to suffer. After the early deaths of Bubb and his shipmates on the *Severn*, typhus broke out and took violent hold of the *Gloucester*.

Conditions in any man-of-war were cramped. Anson's squadron had the further burden of carrying what was supposedly an army of invasion, but which in fact amounted to a pathetically decrepit cohort of military invalids. On a 50-gun ship such as the *Severn* the 300 hands and fifty marines were berthed on the gundeck, roughly 150ft by 40ft. Each hammock was allocated a width of 14 inches – although because of the rotational watch system the men had a theoretical 28 inches in which to rest. At least they would have had but for the presence of about seventy soldiers quartered below as well.

By the time they reached the coast of Brazil, most of the soldiers and many of the hands were too sick to leave their hammocks. As a result, they could not make their way forward to the 'heads', where men squatted over the bows and defecated into the sea; so instead they made do with makeshift pots. In these atrocious quarters – damp, stinking with disease and bodily effusions – a man's death had the compensation of creating a little more space for his fellows.

But it was not until they approached Cape Horn that the ordeal really began. Now the full consequences of having sailed so late became evident as they battled into the teeth of ferocious westerly gales and seas that seemed as high as the looming heights of Tierra del Fuego. Winds shrieked in the rigging and 'caused the immense masts to vibrate and bend like the boughs of a tree. The sea broke over the forecastle, flooding the lower deck.'[13]

Beating into the wind meant that a ship would tack, or alter course in zigzag manoeuvres, in an effort to advance. Each time she came round, those hands manning the deck had to clap on to ropes attached to the sails to prevent her going too far towards the wind as the canvas filled. Each rope had at least one man clapping on, hauling on it or letting it go as necessary, and any error could wipe out the small progress made over hours of labour. But demands were greatest on the topmen, the elite among any crew and the true Foremast Jacks. Though ailing, they forced themselves again and again up the ratlines and out on to the yards, in snow and sleet, to bend or reef sails, only to see the canvas split and shred, so that it had to be cut away and new sails bent. Some, manoeuvring themselves along footropes, slipped and plunged to their deaths. Others lost fingers and toes to frostbite.

After no less than a month of this desperate struggle, and while still trying to round the Horn into the Pacific, the men started to show symptoms of another, more pernicious, disease – scurvy.

The plague of the sea, as it was also known, was as old as seafaring itself, a constant and deadly companion to long voyages. Its cause, understood even at this time, was poor diet – rations of salted meat and biscuit unrelieved by fresh produce for months on end. Its best remedy, citrus fruit, was as yet unknown. Its outcome, fatal without an improved diet, was a ghastly combination of physical and mental disintegration. Scorbutics literally dried up, to the point that their bodies began to 'rattle and creak when they moved', while their behaviour swung between melancholy and ebullience. A German botanist of the time observed how 'people's minds became as loose and unsteady as their teeth'.

In May, eight months after their departure from England, one officer wrote:

> The weather was stormy with huge deep, hollow seas that frequently broke quite over us, with constant rain, frost or snow. Our decks were always full of water, and our men constantly falling ill with scurvy; and the allowance of water being but small reduced us to a deplorable condition.[14]

In the midst of an especially violent storm, the ships were dispersed. Two of those that came together again, *Severn* and *Pearl*, were believed by their captains to have been the sole survivors and turned back for England. That did not stop further attrition through scurvy and by the time these ships reached home, the majority of their hands had died. One captain, who paid tribute to 'the resolution not to be met with in any but English seamen', noted that they:

> . . . became so dejected as to lay themselves down in despair, bewailing their misfortunes, wishing for death as the only relief from their miseries, and could not be induced by threats or entreaties to go aloft.[15]

Separately, the other three ships and the sloop continued to battle their way south-west and, after an utterly hellish three months, each managed to make her way around the Horn. But the scurvy – among the worst outbreaks in recorded maritime history – continued to rage on *Centurion, Gloucester, Wager* and *Tryal*. In the face of unrelenting winds, their progress was pathetic, as little as 16 miles in a day. And there were now barely enough men fit to go aloft.

Another of the captains noted the effects of scurvy on his men in grimly clinical style:

> Some lost their senses, some had their sinews contracted in such a manner as to draw their limbs close up to their thighs, and some rotted away . . . Most of their insides were decayed intirely and no blood [was] in any of their vessels, but clear water.[16]

An officer on the *Wager* observed another phenomenon: 'Some hours before they die, they are taken light-headed, and fall a joking and laughing; and in this humour they expire.'[17]

Thus reduced, the *Wager* was wrecked in the Gulf of Troubles of south-east Chile on 14 May. For the survivors, a different kind of ordeal had begun. One group of about thirty men, under a ruthless but capable gunner named John Bulkeley, made an open-boat voyage of some 2,500 miles back around the

Horn to reach safety at the Río de la Plata early in 1742. Another party, consisting of eight men abandoned by Bulkeley, foraged along the coast of what is now Argentina for almost a year – 'comforting each other with imaginary hopes', as one of them put it – until they were attacked by Indian nomads who left four dead: 'We buried 'em in the best manner we could, scraping away the light sand with our hands two feet deep.'[18] The others – including John Duck, the 'Mullato born in London', and Samuel Cooper from Ipswich – were found by a tribe who treated them humanely but used them as bearers and foragers. *Pace* the bravado of 'Rule, Britannia!'; as one admitted, 'We were their slaves.'[19]

For months they wandered with the nomads across Patagonia, covering more than a thousand miles on foot and being regularly traded between tribes. Yet the tars found much to admire in their captors, and noted that although the Indians were hardened, disciplined and respectful to their chiefs, they were ruled without a lash.[20] Late in 1743, Cooper and two of his fellows were handed over to a British trader in Buenos Aires. An exception was John Duck, whose darker skin, it was noted, rendered him 'too near of a complexion with the Indians'. He was sold to another tribe.[21] His shipmates never saw him again.

The sufferings on land of the Wagers were matched by the hell on water of the other ships. By the time she rounded the Horn and entered the Pacific, the *Gloucester* had lost well over 200 of her company and had just ninety-two men and boys left alive, most of them sickly. 'Words cannot express the misery that [they] died in,' her captain wrote.[22] Nor, presumably, the way their bodies were left to wash about on deck, there being no one fit enough to heave them overboard. On the flagship, *Centurion*, about half of the 400 men were dead. A similar proportion were gone from the *Tryal*. It was not lost on Anson that the island where they had come together, Juan Fernández, had a dubious place in seafaring legend as the site where Alexander Selkirk had been marooned. It is a testimony to the doughty commodore that he seemingly gave no thought to abandoning his mission.

The natural resources of Juan Fernández – sea lions, seals, fish and vegetables – restored the survivors, but the squadron was plainly incapable of carrying out its original orders, to invade the territories of Peru and Chile. Instead, Anson managed to reach Canton where he recruited more hands and replenished stores before returning to his orders, to 'annoy and distress the Spaniards . . . by taking, sinking, burning or otherwise destroying all their ships that you shall meet with'.[23] Six merchant ships were captured. Thus fortified, Anson began to plan for taking the biggest prize of all – the annual treasure galleon that sailed from Acapulco to Manila laden with silver, by which Spain sustained her regional trade.

Amid these high hopes, scurvy made a sudden return. All the more terrifying this time for being unexpected, it rapidly reduced the number of hands from around 320 to about 200 – insufficient to work all three vessels. First the *Tryal* had to be scuttled, then the *Gloucester*.

It was in this state, and having set sail homewards, that at sunrise on 20 June 1743 the *Centurion* came in sight of a large ship south-east of the Philippines. At that time and in that place, she could only be the Acapulco galleon, the *Nuestra Señora de Covadonga*.

Among those Centurions still able to climb the ratlines, still holding fast to the dreams of riches for which they had signed on, were George Million, Tom Richman and Jacob Blackbeard. They gave three cheers and, 'mad with joy' as one officer put it, raced aloft.

As history was to witness over the next century, the Navy would fight many battles more epic as well as more bloody or strategically significant. As a feat of endurance in the face of almost inconceivable obstacles, however, the 90-minute action fought by Jack that day is fit to rank with any. Thirty men went into the tops with muskets, from where they rained death down on the Spanish decks while Anson brought his ship into a position from which her cannon fire was simply more effective than the *Covadonga*'s. Sixty-seven Spaniards were killed and more than eighty wounded before their colours were struck. An English officer came on board to find 'carcasses, entrails and dismembered limbs'.[24]

The English dead numbered three. Among them was Tom Richman. The young fellow who had dreamed of Drake's treasure survived his wounds for two days – long enough to know that although he would not live to savour his *nom de guerre*, his shipmates would.[25]

For them the rewards were to be immense. From the *Covadonga* were taken 1,313,843 pieces of eight and 35,682 ounces of silver – all contained in almost 300 chests. For once the piratical notion of trunks overflowing with coins was no mere fantasy.

The 188 hands left alive on the *Centurion* could not have failed to note one macabre aspect to their plunder: they would get a very much larger share of the prize money because so many of their shipmates were dead; they were the last survivors of three ships with an original complement of 770 men. In all, of 1,900 men who sailed from Spithead in 1740 with the original squadron, fewer than 550 returned.[26]

On a high summer's day in July 1744, a procession of thirty-two horse-drawn carts set out from Portsmouth, accompanied by a curious escort of armed men whose exuberance and rolling gait set them apart from the baffled countryside folk watching them pass. Crossing the Hampshire Downs – pastures blooming, woodlands billowing and lilac scenting the chalky hills – they paused to gambol and jig to the strain of fiddles on their 50-mile parade to London.[27] For sheer contrast, there was little to match the world from which the Centurions had passed to this rustic idyll.

The value of the treasure born by their triumphant cavalcade was the subject of fantastic speculation in the newspapers and ranged from £500,000 to £1,300,000. Though it would take some months for this question to be resolved and for their portion of the prize money to be distributed, the tars who had returned from the South Seas were already being marked – and doubtless regarded themselves – as commoner kings. Granted three months' leave and an advance instalment of more than £100 each, they accompanied the booty to the Tower of London and, once it was deposited, dispersed into the nearby lanes and taverns of Wapping to embark on an extended bout of drinking, wenching and all-round mayhem.

Anson's voyage is remembered, the historian N. A. M. Rodger has noted, as a classic tale of endurance and leadership in the face of frightful disasters; but for the British public, the victorious parade of Spanish treasure through the streets of London provided a moment of national self-esteem.[28] It also established an image of seafaring as a means by which simple men of the towns and shires could make fortunes utterly beyond imagination.

To what extent Jack's enduring reputation for profligacy was forged by subsequent events is not clear. What can be said is that the tales that appeared in the press over the summer certainly enhanced it. From the £355,324 realized in prize money, each of the 188 Centurions involved in capturing the *Covadonga* received about £300 – more than twenty years' pay and the equivalent today of about £90,000. This might seem small beer compared with Anson's £91,000 (£27 million today), which he spent on the noble estate and mansion at Shugborough in Staffordshire and another magnificent house, Moor Park, but it was money of an order quite unknown to men of their class and it gave rise to a communal outpouring of excess. For the first time, as the author Glyn Williams put it, men of the lower deck became prominently visible in public, 'celebrating, fighting and dying in the streets of London, prize money in pocket, and all too often knife in hand'.[29] One man, it was reported, had been robbed of his fortune by a gang near Bow. Another, his pockets full of guineas, fell into the Thames and was drowned. Yet another got into a fight with a soldier, stabbed him and was probably hanged.[30]

There has ever been a tendency for the press to sniff at the excesses of the nouveau riche and other upstarts, yet among the surviving Jacks were also a handful of prudent men who made much of their windfall. John Maddox married a widow possessed of an even greater fortune at a ceremony that was attended by forty of his shipmates. An Essex man, James Stewart, is recorded as dying in 1768 at South Benfleet Hall, an address that indicates that his riches were not wasted either.

There were also those who went back to the sea, because that was all they knew. Both George Million and Jacob Blackbeard were old hands – gamblers and adventurers. Fanciful it may be, but in the absence of evidence to the contrary, we can imagine them, their riches spent, signing on again for the sea – Jacks going aloft once more to discover where the wind of fortune might take them.

2

A LINCOLNSHIRE LAD
1755-59

FOR all the suffering it entailed, Anson's mission symbolized a transformation in Britain's destiny. The country had embarked on a voyage that would carry her not just to naval power but mercantile dominance. The two were intimately connected, and together they would be the making of modern Britain – for while great fleet battles established supremacy in European waters, merchant ships were instrumental in exerting a more subtle form of dominion in the Atlantic and Indian oceans. Of this period in both endeavours, one man from the lower deck provides a unique perspective.

We first glimpse William Spavens some ten years after Anson's return, standing on a rope 80 feet above the sea off Portsmouth. Why Spavens should have felt pride that summer's day in 1755, even he could not explain. He was there on sufferance, a young fellow who had gone to sea in the hope of seeing the world. It was no concern of his that Britain was on the verge of war with France. Seized by a press gang, he had been confined in a floating prison with dozens of others like himself in conditions so foul they had considered rising against their captors in violent insurrection.

Yet here he was, a few weeks later, out on a yardarm and taking in a spectacle that made his heart leap. Portsmouth beach was lined with spectators as the

Royal Barge put out, followed by another barge carrying the great Anson, now First Lord of the Admiralty, and a swarm of pinnaces, yawls and cutters. From his perch Spavens counted thirty-five men-of-war at anchor, 'a long train of gallant ships,' he wrote, each with hundreds of men clustered along the yards like pegs on a line.[1] A slight breeze did no more than ruffle the sleeves of those aloft and the sun was resplendent – so the ships' logs of 4 July inform us – casting this pageant of power in dazzling shades of blue – of jackets, sky and sea.[2]

Aged about nineteen, Spavens had been a navy hand for just a few weeks since being impressed. Brought to Portsmouth, he was given his first lesson by a bosun's mate who told him, 'I must become a sky-lark and mount up aloft'. Now he found that while his vantage point gave a thrilling perspective, staying upright in so precarious a position for hours on end – belly resting on the yard, legs pushing back against the footrope – was uncomfortable. It was also dangerous. Amid the review by Anson, as each ship thundered out a 21-gun salute, a platform high on *Medway*'s main top cracked and gave way, casting a dozen men onto the deck or into the sea – 'by which,' Spavens wrote, 'some lost their lives, and others were very much hurt'.[3]

In most respects this Lincolnshire lad was an unremarkable fellow. He was lithe as well as young, and attractive enough to the girls of Gosport (at least once he had been paid off), but the same could be said for thousands of other young, fit and freeborn Britons who had been forcibly recruited amid rising tension with France that year. Yet of the more than 80,000 Jacks who would serve in the Seven Years War and live to see Britain's emergence as the first global power, William Spavens was almost unique in leaving a memoir of his experiences. He wrote, moreover, about a life of adventure, adversity and achievement with the clarity and candour of a self-educated man.

At this stage a humble country boy like Spavens would have seemed an unlikely chronicler of any kind. His start in life had been pure flint – born in rural poverty about 20 miles south of Grimsby to a couple of farm labourers, both of whom died while he was an infant. His first gift was to be taken in by the farmer and given a rudimentary schooling; the second was his own spirit and a questing imagination. The sight of ships passing up the Humber while he was toiling on the land fired what he called 'the curiosity that seemed implanted in my nature'. So, in 1754, he signed up for the sea in the hope of 'beholding the wonderful works of the Creator in the remote regions of the Earth' – while being perfectly convinced at this time that the Earth was flat.[4]

Like the great majority of seafarers, he first signed on a merchantman and his early ventures contained nothing of the exotic. Spavens had voyaged in a two-masted snow to Russia and Sweden and was homeward bound from the Baltic when his ship was intercepted off Hull by the press gang that changed his life. On board the tender carrying them down the coast to Spithead, the impressed men considered how they might 'take the ship from the crew [and] run her on shore to regain [our] liberty'. Fortunately the scheme was discovered, for the outcome would almost certainly have been disastrous, and instead the guard was doubled 'with orders to fire amongst us if we attempted to mutiny'.[5] And so, in the summer of 1755, shouldering a small chest with the meagre treasure of a seaman's possessions, Spavens entered the dark, fetid space some 120 feet in length that he would share with more than 100 other men on the frigate *Blandford*.

Young Spavens and his fellows may have had little awareness of themselves as a vital national resource, but such they had become. In 1740, at the time of Anson's voyage, the prime minister Sir Robert Walpole had been given to lament the shortage of a particular article, crying: 'Oh! Seamen, seamen, seamen!'[6] By 1755, just months before the declaration of war with France, the manning crisis was the most acute in the Navy's history. Its peacetime strength had been reduced to a mere 10,000 hands and the Admiralty was wont to say of the ships lying imposingly at anchor that they were 'as useless as if they did not exist'.[7]

Navy recruiters moved inland for the first time, to cities and the rural heartland. Coastal dwellers – men from Dorset, Kent, Devon and Hampshire in England, from Fife and Midlothian in Scotland, and Cork in Ireland – had always featured prominently in the musters. Now volunteers were sought among miners, tinkers, farmers, labourers and other working-class folk willing to learn the ropes. At the same time, the Admiralty began impressment on an unprecedented scale, among those who already 'used the sea'. In all, 29,278 seamen were recruited by the end of that year, the majority of them forcibly.[8] Press operations had been extended from the seafaring centres of Plymouth and Portsmouth to seven more ports across the country, and subsequently another three ports and six inland towns.[9] Among the new ports was Hull, where William Spavens was taken.

Naval history has no more controversial aspect than the press gang. As a subject, it continues to excite debate, giving rise to challenging studies claiming, on the one hand, that it was a significant factor in the American Revolution of 1775–83, and, on the other, that its role in raising naval manpower between 1793 and 1801 has been grossly exaggerated.[10] As a theme, it will recur throughout this narrative. For now it may be noted that as a form of conscription it was not only arbitrary but often detested by those in charge of it – 'repugnant to one's nature and temperment [sic]', as one officer wrote.[11] That it went against the grain of the very men it sought to recruit is apparent from regular instances of resistance.

One case that year, much celebrated by Jacks, involved the *Deepsey Brigantine* which was nearing Portsmouth when a navy tender intercepted her. As a press gang tried to come on board, the fourteen-man crew first opened fire and then raced ashore in the ship's boat before disappearing into the Sussex countryside.[12] A few months later, also off Portsmouth, a boarding party came alongside the whaleship *Britannia* to be met this time by men brandishing harpoons and hatchets. Although they were within their rights because whalers were exempt from the press, the Britannias came under fire and three were killed.[13]

Yet we do well to remember that the human spirit is nothing if not adaptable and the circumstances of most commoners in the mid-eighteenth century allowed of less freedom than we may appreciate. Forcible recruitment, or impressment, had been going on for 400 years.* At this point in our chronicle,

---

* The power of impressment was a royal prerogative and not confined to the sea service. Soldiers and a range of craftsmen could be recruited in the same way.

the men taken by the Navy were already professional sailors; the caricatures by James Gillray and Thomas Rowlandson, of club-wielding brutes pulling hapless civilian victims off the streets, lay in the future.

Evidence suggests that pressed seamen tended to put their loss of liberty aside briskly. As a freeborn Englishman, William Spavens disliked the press – 'a hardship which nothing but absolute necessity can reconcile [with] our boasted freedom,' he thought.[14] But as a seaman he saw it as part of the natural order – to be avoided, but inevitable – and he would serve in press gangs himself. Another old hand, John Nicol, also recognized Britain's dependence on its seamen. 'Necessity has no law,' he wrote – adding, with a touch of conceit: 'Could the government make perfect seamen as easily as they make soldiers there would be no such thing as pressing.'[15] Some Jacks were even blithe. 'I was young, did not fret much, and was willing to go to any part of the world,' wrote William Richardson.[16]

A sense of value, then, of playing a role in a great national enterprise, was evolving and would add to Jack's self-esteem. Walpole's cry of need – 'Oh! Seamen, seamen, seamen!' – became increasingly insistent, and endured to the end of the Napoleonic era.

In the tops that summer's day in Portsmouth, Spavens had seen ships of every rate and type below. From the shore, a landlubber observing these same vessels for the first time would have noted certain common features, notably that most had three masts and square-rigged sails. It was plain, too, that they rose in levels of oak, bristling with cannon, and it was in the number of these levels, or decks, that they became distinctive. Our landsman, on being joined by a seaman, would soon have had pointed out to him what else it was that set a single-deck frigate apart from a two- or three-deck ship of the line.

A 24-gun frigate like Spavens's *Blandford* might be compared with a giant seabird, her crew of 150 officers and men likened to the muscles and sinews that brought her to an optimum state of grace in flight, an object caught between air and water, part of both but not fully of either. Whether as a scout, raider or escort, she was the eyes and ears of a fleet. For a true topman, a frigate under the right captain was potentially the best of berths – and not just for the sense of activity and pride it might bring. Here he could be part of an elite team who could emerge from action with pockets swollen by prize money.

The ships of the line that constituted the Navy's fighting power were better compared with floating castles. These were the mobile but ponderous artillery units that formed up in line of battle, the 'wooden walls' as they were known, that defended Britain. The complement of such a ship was based not on the number of men required to sail her, but the number needed to fight her guns, so these island fortresses were also large individual communities, with their inhabitants dwelling on different levels within the citadel. Ships of the line mounted upwards of 64 guns. The most common, the foundation of the great fleet actions to come, had 74 guns and required about 750 officers, petty officers, seamen and marines, who would be housed over two decks less than 170 feet in length. The largest of the day was the 100-gun *Royal George*, with a crew of about 1,000 across her three decks. Having a spread of canvas that would have covered acres, and guns ranging from thundering great 42-pounders on her bottom deck to 24-pounders on the middle deck and 18-pounders on the upper deck, the flagship was also a mobile headquarters for the admiral, with a suite of accommodation in the stern that would not have disgraced a country estate.

Jack dwelt forward and on the lower deck, but even here and among those defined as common seamen a hierarchy was to be found. At the bottom were Landsmen – lubberly volunteers straight off the quay without skills. Men having a working knowledge of the ropes and seafaring were rated Ordinary. Those rated Able were experienced, adept and strong enough to go aloft or sufficiently skilled to be entrusted with, say, manning the helm. The rates of pay for these three categories, established in 1653, remained unchanged for almost 150 years: Landsmen received 18s a month; Ordinary seamen were paid 19s; Able hands 24s. That annual pay for the best men of £12 did not hold up well against £27 or so received by labourers and £40 by solid tradesmen, but then again Jack had a place to lay his head, was provided with food and drink, even medical care of a sort; and there remained the possibility that he might swagger home like Anson's survivors with £300 in his pocket.

Spavens, aged about nineteen and with scarce a year's experience as a deckhand on a merchantman, was rated Ordinary. Almost directly he went aloft. The *Blandford* was bound for the West Indies, where French privateers were playing havoc with British trade, and even new hands would be needed in the tops.[17]

Of the 150 men on a small frigate like the *Blandford*, five including the captain were commissioned officers. Another ten fell into the category of warrant officers – men of specialized skills, among them the master, or navigator, the surgeon, the carpenter and gunner. Lower down the order were up to twenty petty officers, including the bosun, the coxswain, quartermaster and sailmaker. In a category of their own were about thirty-five marines, who

John Glover's sketch of seafarers in pensive mood is among the few attempts to represent sailors in any other than caricature form.

enforced the captain's orders and whose red jackets and military bearing could give rise to tensions. That left about eighty who fell into the category of common hands – whether Able, Ordinary or Landsmen – the men known as the 'people', otherwise jacks, ratings or bluejackets.

Jack's working dress was of a kind, marked by a jerkin and loose breeches, the canvas rough against the skin. But for men of few possessions and little domestic life, clothing was a matter of importance, and the means by which he presented himself ashore would be carefully preserved in his chest. He slept in a transportable bed pioneered by the Portuguese called a hammock. Since the 1650s he had lived by a code known as the Articles of War that would be read to ships' companies on Sundays and that, indeed, assumed greater significance among an impious band of men than the Bible. The Articles of War were the Ten Commandments of sea life, although there were thirty-six of them, and they proscribed activities ranging from mutinous assembly and sleeping on watch to fighting and sodomy 'with man or beast'.

Set against a dramatic narrative – of battles, mutinies and storms – it is easy to forget how much of Jack's life was defined by routine. But it was routine of a most uncommon kind. For one thing, the day as defined by the ship's log began at noon; and for another, no rating enjoyed more than four hours' sleep at a stretch.

Spavens was introduced to the rotational system that divided men into the larboard or starboard watch, one of which was on duty at any time. So he might have four hours in his hammock from midnight before being roused by a shrill blast from the bosun's pipe. In the gloom, one old hand wrote, 'rough, uncouth forms are seen tumbling out of their hammocks on all sides'. Slackers were dealt with by the bosun and his mates, 'each armed with a rope's end with which they belabor the shoulders of any luckless wight whose slow-moving limbs show him to be but half awake . . . With a rapidity which would surprise a landsman, the crew dress themselves, lash their hammocks and carry them on deck where they are stowed for the day.'[18] At the same time, the watch coming off duty would sling their hammocks from the beams and sleep, from 4 a.m. to 8 a.m.

Captains were keen to keep Jack employed, especially when time hung heavily, and the start of the day was marked by cleaning the decks with blocks the size of bibles, known as holystones. With their trowsers rolled above the knee, 'the men suffer from being obliged to kneel upon the wetted deck and a gravelly sort of sand strewn over it'.[19]

Another pipe from the bosun at 8 a.m. summoned all hands to breakfast, an oatmeal porridge called burgoo, before a further change in the watch. Midday meant dinner and was 'the pleasantest part of the day', wrote a hand named William Robinson:

> The fifer is called to play *Nancy Dawson* or some other lively tune, a signal that the grog is ready to be served. It is the duty of the cook from each mess to fetch and serve it to his messmates, of which every man and boy is allowed a pint, that is one gill of rum and three of water . . . [The cook] reserves to himself an extra portion of grog. Thus he can . . . take upon himself to be the man of consequence, for he has the opportunity to invite a friend to partake of a glass, or of paying any little debt. It is grog which pays debts, and not money, in a man of war.[20]

After dinner, it was the turn of the other watch to go up, 'working the ship, pointing the ropes or doing any duty that may be required'. Again it was the bosun's pipe that called the men to supper – 'half a pint of wine or a pint of grog, with biscuit and cheese with butter'.

A watch system that allowed roughly half of every twenty-four hours for leisure and sleep gave rise to activities that included music-making and story-telling – and a domestic expertise noted by a hand named Robert Wilson that might have been thought somewhat incongruous:

> It's curious to see a tar lay hold of a piece of fine white linen (to make himself a go-ashore shirt as he terms it) and a black cinder and mark where he wishes to cut the linen. Then to see him take into his hand – which is like a shoulder of mutton – a fine small needle and sew away, and that

not slow. And you could not but give him credit when he has finished his shirt.

Those who are not employed sewing or mending, you'll see them either learning to read or write, or cyphering or instructing others. Some are playing the violin, flute or fife, while others dance or sing thereto. Others are relating awful stories of what happened in awful times, while their hearers are listening with respectful silence, especially the young.[21]

Victuals were almost as important to harmony on a ship as grog. Not that standards were high, far from it; but the men were outspoken in requiring quantity and a certain variety. When fresh produce was not available, which was most of the time, they would – ideally speaking – receive two pounds of salt beef on Tuesdays and Saturdays; one pound of salt pork on Sundays and Thursdays; and cheese, butter and burgoo on Mondays, Wednesdays and Fridays. A pound of biscuit was issued daily and mashed peas four times a week.[22] On relatively small ships like the *Blandford* messes consisted of four rather than eight men, and Spavens found himself taking his victuals with an enigmatic character who had evidently wished to conceal something in his past when he signed on as Madera Wyne.[23]

Rules of conduct were of course defined by the Articles of War. But each ship had an additional regime. It was peculiar to her captain and, in effect, an extension of his character and foibles. He made rules that extended into every aspect of Jack's life – from punishment to shore leave and from standards of cleanliness to the presence or absence of women on board. Constraints on his power – he was not supposed to give any man more than a dozen lashes without reference to a court martial – meant little once they were at sea. Robert Wilson put it thus: 'Every commanding officer of a vessel of war is like unto a prince in his own state and his crew may be considered his subjects, for his word is law.'[24]

Or, as another man observed:

No creature existing has it so much in his power [as a navy captain] to render the lives of those under his command either miserable or happy.[25]

The captain of the *Blandford* fell into the first category. Penhallow Cuming was a moody tartar who, in black fits, would rouse the men from their hammocks purely to make an example of the tardy. Spavens recalled: 'If we were not all on deck in five minutes, he would place a petty officer at every hatchway to stop those who remained below and would order each man a dozen lashes.'[26] Cuming had also what seemed to his men a loathing for their pleasure, their grog, which he would withhold for petty misdemeanours.

He was also, however, an excellent seaman. The Caribbean swarmed with small French privateers and letters of marque (ships licensed by the state to act against the enemy) which sheltered among the inlets and coves of islands like Martinique before setting out on forays to seize British cargoes of sugar, tobacco and cotton. They were an elusive foe, yet in a few months of cruising between Barbados and Antigua the *Blandford* took five of them, from the 16-gun schooner *Pacific* to the 10-gun sloop *Minerve*. The frigate also captured eight merchantmen, mainly Dutch, bound for French ports. To top it off, she twice encountered and survived hurricanes.

It was a heady time for a young hand, and Spavens responded to the thrill of each challenge, dashing up the ratlines to set and adjust sails, feeling the wind and sun on his skin. He revelled in physical activity and the camaraderie of the foretop, from where he surveyed his new world. Once they pursued a French privateer from ten in the morning to three the following afternoon, firing more than 100 nine-pound balls from their bow-chasers, before she outstripped them.

Within a few months of sailing from England, Spavens was rated Able.[27] It had been a rapid rise and when he reflected on the life he had left behind, as a farmhand with prospects of neither advancement nor adventure, it is not surprising that his pride grew along with his pay. He might have reflected on other benefits too: companionship and a diet – certainly in the Caribbean with its fresh produce – he could never have enjoyed at home.

Above all, he had discovered the wonder and power of a ship under sail, moving through the air like a god. Barely into his twenties, he had become a 'thoroughbred seaman' – one who could:

. . . not only hand and reef [sails] and steer, but is likewise capable of heaving the lead [to establish the sea's depth] in the darkest night as well as in daytime; who can use the palm and needle of a sailmaker; and is versed in every part of a ship's rigging, and the stowage of the hold [distributing the contents to maintain optimum sailing], and in the exercise of the great guns.[28]

His literacy apart, Spavens was a typical enough member of the tribe – improvident, fond of grog and a yarn, and occasionally turbulent. Like most, he was a poor swimmer: 'Sometimes above and at others below the water,' he joked. Along with a robust spirit, he had a questing intelligence. William Spavens may have believed that the world was flat, but that did not stop him reaching out for the mysteries beyond the horizon.

Even at this time he had a keen interest in the world beyond his ship, and a gift for observations on geography and natural history. Predators fascinated him in a morbid sort of way – sharks: 'a rapacious kind of fish . . . which bit one of our men in two' – and alligators: 'the shape of a newt but large and voracious, so as to kill and eat a man in a very short time'. He had, too, a broad humanity. At a time when many seamen were directly involved in the slave trade, he noted the contrast between an idealized Barbados – 'not to be exceeded for beauty or fruitfulness' – and the iniquitous treatment of its slave inhabitants:

Some of these people are of as bright a genius as those that rule over them. They suppose they are to return to their native country when they die, and from such a delusion they rejoice at the funerals of their deceased friends, dancing, singing . . . and using other expressions of joy.[29]

Of Spavens's appearance we know nothing, but a typical seaman of the time was spare in build and about 5 feet 6 inches in height.[30] Nor can much be said about his disciplinary record, because the *Blandford*'s log for his Caribbean service has been lost; but it is fair to surmise that under a captain like Cuming he knew what it was to be ordered to strip to the waist, tied to a grating by his wrists and feel the lacerating bite of a knotted cat.

Spavens was a topman, one of a relatively small group of the most active hands who scrambled out along the yards to bend and reef sails and who were the true Foremast Jacks. Daring, acrobatic and with a *sang froid* that won the respect of their fellows, these were the elite of the lower deck. Whether Spavens ever joined the aristocracy – the Captains of the Tops, who were generally selected by their peers and who would represent the views of the lower deck to officers in any protest, or, indeed, mutiny – is not known. But cutting a dash aloft was demanding enough: 'The duty requires alertness [to] shorten or reduce sails in sudden squall,' wrote one of their number, 'and courage, to ascend in a manner sky-high when stormy winds do blow.'[31]

It was also, self-evidently, dangerous. Ships' logs often record men falling to their deaths, both on deck and into the sea. Samuel Leech thought it astonishing that not more were killed, especially in the long hours of a night watch:

Often have I stood . . . hours on the royal yard or the top-gallant yard . . . Here, overcome with fatigue and want of sleep, I have fallen into a dreamy, dozy state, from which I was roused by a lee lurch of the ship. Starting up, my hair has stood on end with amazement at the danger I had so narrowly escaped. But, notwithstanding this sudden fright, a few minutes had scarcely elapsed before I would be nodding again.[32]

In a society ordained by hierarchy it is not to be wondered that Jacks had their own pecking order. Below the topmen – literally, for they operated on deck – came the forecastlemen, the afterguard and the waisters. Forecastlemen, who included Able hands no longer youthful enough to work aloft, attended to the lower rigging and bowsprit, to weighing and anchoring. The afterguard, at the rear on the quarterdeck, consisted of less skilled hands, rated Ordinary or Landsmen, who trimmed the after yards and sails. Lowest in this ranking were the waisters, stationed amidships – the most inexperienced Landsmen plus the old men and boys – who were fit for no more than clapping on ropes and drudgery. When it came to battle, however, all were expected to serve at the guns in one way or another.

The pay of 24s per lunar month for an able hand like Spavens was reduced to 22s 6d after deductions for Greenwich Hospital and the Chatham Chest – pension and insurance contributions respectively. That rate had been unchanged for more than a century now, and payment was made only on return to a home port. While on board the men's basic needs for food and drink were met. But for casual spending in port, they often depended on the system of prize money by which they received a quarter of the value of any captured prize.[33]

Trouble arose on the *Blandford* when she put into St Johns at Barbados and prize money due to the men was not forthcoming. A gang of barefoot seamen went ashore and set off, without permission, on a thoroughly risky endeavour to 'procure payment by forcible means' from the local prize agent. Spavens left a bucolic account of what followed:

It was unanimously agreed not to separate nor abandon each other, whatever might be the result. We then marched forward. The unusual appearance of so many men on the road excited astonishment in the Negroes in the plantations and when we came on St Johns green we put to flight a number of privateer's men who were playing at cricket, they taking us for a press gang.[34]

At length, the barefoot men were brought not to the agent, but to Admiral Thomas Frankland, who might have had them seized on the spot and flogged for their 'forwardness'. Instead, he pardoned them, and then sought an explanation:

Being asked what we intended to do with the Agent, we told him we would pull his house down if he would give us leave; but he advised us not to offer any violence, but choose two men from amongst us who should go and tell Colonel Lasley from him that he insisted on him making us some payment in a few days, as he saw our necessity; there being 27 out of 30 of us bare-foot.[35]

Returning to the ship tired and hungry, Spavens found that the messmates for whom he had put himself in danger had been entertaining 'Negro girls' on board. He also went to his hammock hungry because the girls had been given his beef and pudding. Of the outcome he noted ruefully: 'In a few days we were paid about £6 which made some amends; but the remainder, about £30, was never paid.'

Naval discipline is seen here in an unexpectedly mild light. Spavens and his fellows had technically deserted from the *Blandford* when they went ashore, which was a capital offence. Even so, they had gone to the admiral, not grovelling and forelock-touching, but as self-respecting fellows seeking their rightful dues. Such forwardness was not, in fact, so unusual at the time. As a leading historian has noted, the discipline of the mid-eighteenth century Navy would have appeared to a later generation lax to the point of anarchy.

Take the case of John Dowick. On a winter's night at Spithead in 1765, Dowick entered the officers' wardroom on the *Augusta* yacht where a midshipman named Hugh Tonken and others were seated and on being asked what he had come for replied: 'You may ask my arse.' Presumably unable to credit what he had heard, Tonken asked him to repeat himself, to which Dowick said again, 'Ask my arse.' Allowing for the fact that midshipmen were not quite officers, a seaman who went out of his way to spell out his contempt for a superior might have been thought lucky to escape with fifty lashes.[36] Perhaps, however, it reflected a stability of English society. At this time there was an understanding of interdependence between officers and men, and the latter 'assumed that officers in general would support their legitimate grievances'.[37]

On the *Blandford*'s quarterdeck, meanwhile, Captain Cuming had started to show symptoms of a kind of mania not uncommon in men isolated by command. Increasingly irrational and arbitrary, he took mistresses on board and when one displeased him had her stripped, and tarred and feathered. Matters came to a head at his court martial for conduct unbecoming an officer.

It turned out he had been not merely cruel but corrupt. While supposedly stopping the men's rum for neglect of duty, he had been selling it privately. He had also been behind the withholding of prize money. Cuming was dismissed from the service.[38]

If discipline was more even-handed then, some offences were always beyond the pale. One case in particular would have been the talk of Spavens and other Blandfords.

———

The sloop *Stork* was cruising west of the *Blandford* in the Caribbean when she fell in with a French vessel and took her. Captain Peter Carteret went aboard with seventeen men and a boy to sail her to Jamaica. He was asleep on the night of 17 September 1758, when a petty officer woke him to say 'that the people were up in arms'.

Coming on deck, Carteret heard a general cry, 'Liberty for one and all, by God.' He approached a man named Patrick O'Hara, who responded by threatening him with a spike and said: 'God damn you, keep off. Who are you?' O'Hara was plainly drunk and, on being advised from the dark by an uneasy shipmate that he was speaking to the captain, meekly handed over the spike. Carteret told the subsequent court martial:

> I asked him the meaning of this riotous behaviour. In reply I heard many voices declare [that] as they were most of them pressed men, they were determined never to go on a man of war again.[39]

It transpired that the mutineers had a grievance against a lieutenant who carried a cane with which he beat them to their stations – a practice known as 'starting', detested by all upright men. Though respectful to the captain, they said they had seized the ship so that once they reached Jamaica they could go ashore and disappear, as free men again.

Carteret appears to have had some sympathy with them. A hand named Thomas Halsey approached him and while the other mutineers got so drunk 'there was a general riot the whole night', Halsey engaged him earnestly in conversation:

> He [Halsey] said they didn't want to harm any officer, but they were deter-
> mined to have their liberty and would stand by one another to the last man.
> I [Carteret] warned him of the consequences, but he said he'd given his
> word, and that was his bond. From that night [the mutineers] followed his
> every direction.[40]

They succeeded to the extent of landing in a quiet bay in Jamaica. What happened after that is not clear. No more was heard of thirteen men and the boy. But four of them, including Halsey and O'Hara, were caught and, after a trial in Port Royal, hanged.

Violent mutiny invariably attracted a capital sentence, even when real culpability was open to question – as in 1748 when Lieutenant Samuel Couchman, a drunken lunatic, announced to the crew of the 44-gun *Chesterfield* while the captain was ashore at the Cape of Good Hope that they would all be better off starting a colony in the West Indies. On reaching Barbados they met the sword of authority. Couchman and a lieutenant of marines were executed. Although they had been acting in response to their officers' authority, thirteen able hands were tried and seven sentenced to death. Ultimately, as the nooses were being placed around their necks, all but two were reprieved.[41]

Desertion was also a hanging offence, but at this time execution for it was rare – largely because it wasted manpower. In 1756, Hugh Holland deserted from the *Falkland* while in port visiting his family, a fact he stated openly on being apprehended in Bristol. A Welshman 'who scarcely understood a sentence of English', he explained through an interpreter that 'he thought there was no harm in what he did and never desired to desert'. Three hundred lashes was usual in such cases, but the court recommended sixty for Holland, then on further reflection lowered it to fifty.[42] Hundreds of known deserters had a blind eye turned to their offences on re-enlisting. Of twenty-six men sentenced to hang for desertion during the Seven Years War, probably no more than five were executed, the rest being pardoned.[43]

By 1759, there was still no easing in the demand for men. Having returned to England in the *Blandford*, Spavens was among forty-five hands sent into another frigate, *Vengeance*. Momentous events were in the making off France and *Vengeance* had orders to assist with recruitment. William Spavens, the pressed man, was about to join a press gang.

3

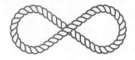

MAN AND BOY
1756-59

THE *Vengeance*'s orders that summer of 1759 were unusual and discomforting for the crew of a 28-gun frigate. No scouting or cruising as the eyes of the fleet this time. She was, William Spavens recalled, to prowl the west coast of the British Isles intercepting vessels homeward bound and 'procure men for the service'.[1] The *Vengeance* had been commissioned as a seaborne press gang.

The story of what followed is told only in part by the ship's log. Sailing between Cork, Dublin and Liverpool in June and July she stopped and boarded four English and American letters of marque – in effect licensed privateers.[2] How many men were pressed is not stated in the captain's record, which also passes lightly over the resistance that was offered; but Spavens pulled no punches in describing these events and his part in them, although his every instinct rebelled against the whole business. What particularly rankled was the seizing of men when they were in sight of home. Spavens declared it 'shocking to the feelings of humanity' for a sailor 'after a long voyage [and] innumerable hardships . . . returning to his native land with the pleasing hope of shortly beholding a beloved wife and children, to be forced away to fight, perhaps to fall'.[3]

Yet, like others having to carry out orders they all detested, he was pragmatic too – and tough. One American ship offered resistance and was boarded:

We fired down amongst them, while they kept firing up at us. After having shot one of our men through the head, and another through both thighs, they submitted and we got 16 brave fellows.[4]

Among the American hands was one William Budd.[5] That Herman Melville should have entitled his novella about an impressed topman *Billy Budd* is doubtless coincidental. Even so, the case of Budd and his shipmates symbolized the resentment already starting to develop among colonists at the British habit of treating American seamen as their own. In time this would be felt so keenly across the Atlantic that it contributed to war.

Whatever the number of men taken off the four privateers – perhaps seventy or so – it was not enough. Sailing off Liverpool, the *Vengeance* intercepted a whaler, *Golden Lion*, returning from Greenland. This time the boarding party were met by men 'with lances and flinching-knives' who drove them off. Under fire, the *Golden Lion* managed to make port; and that posed an awkward dilemma.

Resistance to press gangs from seamen was natural and common. By now, however, it was also to be encountered from their outraged relatives and other civilians. Among the port towns where Press Service operations had been extended, Newcastle and Bristol were notably hostile.[6] But none was more renowned for offering violence than Liverpool. The regulating officer there, Captain John Fortescue, in charge of recruiting and press gangs, was often in despair. Every seaman, he reported, was 'fought hard for, there being a number of men in town continually armed to defend themselves against my gangs, and to rescue what men they can from us'.[7] As Spavens put it: 'Pressing on shore at Liverpool had been deemed impracticable.'[8]

In the event, a party of eighty from the *Vengeance* was sent ashore, where they surprised the *Lion*'s crew in the process of renewing their protections from impressment:

We secured 17 of them, guarding them along the streets. Several hundreds of old men, women and boys flocked after us, well provided with stones and brickbats, and commenced a general attack. Not wishing to hurt them, we fired our pistols over their heads; but the women proved very daring, and followed us down to low water mark, almost up to the knees in mud.[9]

Spavens's experiences in press gangs left him to reflect sourly: 'Such are the methods frequently made use of to obtain seamen for service in this land of liberty.' Yet even now he would add his caveat: 'It is a hardship which nothing but absolute necessity can reconcile to our boasted freedom.'[10]

By 1759, the number of seamen in naval service had risen from 10,100 at the start of the Seven Years War, and 33,600 at the end of the first year, to some 84,400.[11] Such rapid recruitment had clearly involved rough practice. As Spavens also shows, however, the law confining impressment to men aged between eighteen and fifty-five who 'used the sea' was still, by and large, respected. In one foray from the *Vengeance*, 'we picked up 16 men but only one of them being a seaman, the rest we set free'.[12] Where the law was bent it tended to be on inland waterways: men had been taken from rivers and beside them, off barges, lighters and wherries. We are still some way from the violations that occurred during the frantic remanning after 1803, when known instances occurred of civilians with no seafaring experience at all being seized. But opposition to impressment was already finding a voice, as heard in an anonymous forty-two-page polemic, *The Sailors Advocate*, which cited the rights of Magna Carta and went through seven editions by 1777:

> Oppression certainly debases the mind, and what can be a greater Oppression than forcing men as prisoners on a man of war without necessaries, without allowing them time to order their affairs, or to take leave of their families. How can it be expected that a man should fight for the Liberty of others whilst he himself feels the pangs of Slavery.[13]

How many of the Navy's 84,000 hands had been pressed since the onset of war it is not possible to say. Ships' musters are incomplete and unreliable and many of the sailors listed as Able or Ordinary and described as volunteers had doubtless taken the sensible course when confronted by a press gang and accepted the alternative, usually offered at this point, of a bounty for those who signed on willingly – £2 10s for an Ordinary hand, £5 for an Able man. One study concludes: 'At most one can only speculate that a majority were pressed.'[14]

Those listed as Landsmen did, however, include a substantial number of volunteers from a source experiencing its own revolution. Farming communities had previously provided sturdy types during hard times for agriculture. Over the next fifty years a quarter of the entire farmed area of the country became privately owned and as the old cooperative ways of working the land were killed off, a process of rapid urbanization began.[15] London's population doubled between 1750 and 1770, unemployment was rising, and the urban poor were also presenting themselves – and receiving Landsmen's £1 10s bounty – at the six inland recruitment centres of Leeds, Leicester, Gloucester, Reading, Winchester and Shrewsbury.

Not all were white Britons. One of the best-known Africans in English history went to sea at this time. A former slave, Francis Barber, actually volunteered in preference to service in Samuel Johnson's household. For all the doctor's lofty pronouncements on the ghastliness of a sailor's life, his Gough Square home was itself not a happy place, being composed of 'morose, taciturn, argumentative individuals'.[16] And Barber, as we shall see, only came ashore again – with obvious reluctance – because of Johnson's insistence.

On more distant shores, meanwhile, men were recruited in Italy and Greece, while in India local seamen, known as lascars, began serving on British merchant ships.[17]

The need for new hands had also given rise to a most extraordinary and innovative social experiment.

As a solution to that intractable problem the idea had much to recommend it. The Navy never had enough seamen, yet city backstreets were alive with urchins – ragged, unemployed and disorderly. Taking the ragamuffins off the streets and putting them to the sea would resolve a social problem while breeding a new generation of top hands. In our cynical age, the creation of the Marine Society would be seen as the exploitative brainchild of some Admiralty hardnose. In its time, it was the inspiration of a philanthropist.

Ships' boys are part of maritime lore, familiar figures in a seascape. There we espy the powder monkey – a nimble, barefoot scamp wriggling his way between the guns with a cartridge of gunpowder; and there in the aftermath of battle – a solemn, wide-eyed fellow squatting at the feet of a genial elder who is spinning tales. He can be seen with his bowl among the men at a mess table, and gambolling with friends amid the fug of tobacco on the focsle. One lad wrote of their fellowship: 'We were always together, and a great part of our time was spent in play.'[18] This same child would nevertheless be a combatant – witness to the ghastly spectacle of war and subject to all its dangers. Yet, so the theory went, innocence and vulnerability would be lost, skill and fortitude gained. Ships' boys would grow into seamen.[19]

The Marine Society was formed in 1756, early in the Seven Years War and as a direct result of the old manpower shortage. But there was another factor. The process of urbanization had spawned a body of outcast youth – 'distressed orphans who wander about like forsaken dogs', as the society's founders put it.[20] In London especially, abandoned children survived on the streets as 'shop-lifters, pilferers and pickpockets' and were seen as a threat to order.

Jonas Hanway, a merchant with seafaring connections, brought pragmatism to bear, combining his own humanitarian ideals with practical considerations. As well as boys, the Marine Society would recruit adult volunteers off the street for the Navy. But, as Hanway declared, it was 'those who are bred to the sea from the earliest part of life [who] generally become the ablest mariners'.[21] The society's primary objective was always to channel the energies of those boys wandering London's streets 'like forsaken dogs'.

What gave the concept resonance, and contributed to its success, was Hanway's recognition that society's hostility towards homeless urchins closely matched its suspicion of seamen. A delinquent's prospects were never good in an era when miscreants, generally deemed beyond salvation, were liable to be put to death or sent to a penal colony in America. As outcasts, however, there was a possibility that they might assimilate with another group of outsiders. They were, as one navy official put it, of an age 'when their *bodies* or *minds* may be formed to any thing'. Hanway's welcome came with a sermon:

> You are the sons of freemen. Though poor, you are the sons of Britons, who
> are born to liberty; but remember that true liberty consists in doing well; in
> defending each other, in obeying your superiors and in fighting for your
> King and Country to the last drop of your blood.[22]

The first 4,000 Marine Society boys were aged between thirteen and fifteen. They were provided with 'slops', a basic outfit for going to sea that included bedding, and designated in the musters as servants – usually to captains or other officers. In addition, they were expected to act as powder monkeys in action. Initially they would be among the idlers or waisters, while they learnt the ropes and rose in time to the tops.

As well as removing from the streets 'those who by extreme *poverty* and *ignorance* are pernicious to the community', the Marine Society aimed 'to encourage the *industrious poor*' to send their children to sea. By 1760 it was advertising for recruits in the press:

> Wanted to serve on His Majesty's Ships of War, thirty or forty stout lads not
> under fourteen years of age, and of the stature of four feet and four inches,
> that go with their own and friends consent, and are no apprentices.[23]

However boisterous a figure he might have cut in Gin Lane, the Marine Society recruit took a step back on entering his first ship. One lad wondered in awe whether he was 'among spirits or devils ... All seemed strange; different language and strange expressions of tongue, that I thought myself always asleep, and never properly awake.'[24] The babble was confusing enough – a new dialect embracing words and phrases that have since become part of common usage but at the time would have had a novel ring to any lubber: from 'ship-shape' to 'plain sailing', 'loose cannon' to 'broad in the beam', or 'pushing the boat out' to 'short-handed' and 'copper-bottomed'.

Still at anchor, although by now all at sea, the young recruit would have gazed at the spider's web of ropes above. Though probably none the wiser as to the function of the folded bales of canvas, let alone the difference between a staysail and a studdingsail, he would be given a quick run-through by an experienced man:

> When the [anchor] cable is up and down, the order is given to loose sails. The men stationed to loose them go up on the different yards; when the word is given to trice up and lay out, they lay along the yards and cast off the gaskets and keep the sails snug up in their arms until the word is given to let fall. The topsails are then sheeted home by those on deck, viz. the whole of the larboard watch forward on the forecastle to the fore topsail sheets, the starboard watch on the main deck to the main topsail sheets, the boys and idlers on the quarterdeck to the mizzen topsail sheets, those in the tops overhauling every rope that has any connection with the sail. Then the topsail halyards are manned by the same who haul home the sheets and the yards are run up. The topgallant sheets are then hauled home and the yards hoisted up. The capstan is again manned, the anchor is hove up, the sails are trimmed according to the point it [the wind] blows from, the ship gets to sea, the ropes are coiled up and the watch is set.[25]

A boy's first sensation in this new world was nausea. The phenomenon of seasickness rarely features in sailor's writings but everyone experienced it to start with. On coming aboard his first vessel aged fourteen, Samuel Kelly 'lay about in holes or corners, unable to eat or scarcely crawl' for weeks; Kelly remained in the Packet Service – based at Falmouth and carrying mail, despatches and passengers to British colonies and outposts – despite suffering seasickness at the start of every voyage for seven years.[26]

The newcomer would also receive an early lesson in shipboard hierarchy. For every genial patriarch on the lower deck there was a tough nut. Samuel Leech, an orphan from Essex who joined at the unusually young age of twelve, wrote that the unruly lad would 'be kicked and cuffed by all':

He will be made miserable. Sailors, being treated as inferiors themselves, love to find opportunity to act the superior over some one. They do this over the boys, and if they find a saucy, insolent one, they show him no mercy.[27]

Worse than bullying, Leech thought, was the depravity. His memoir, coloured by the fact that he had embraced a spirit of evangelical mission, concluded that few worse places existed than a ship for instilling morality in a boy. It started with 'beastly intoxication', which led to 'singing libidinous or bacchanalian songs' before, ultimately, ships' boys were exposed to vice 'in the worst of its Proteus-like shapes . . . the meshes of temptation spread about his path in every direction'. And, bad as things were at sea, 'they are worse in port'.[28]

With due respect to Leech, it is unlikely that children raised in the poorest households, living cheek by jowl with their parents, were ever shielded from adult ways. But he brings into focus two particular aspects of life at sea – alcohol and sexuality.

Drink played a central part in Jack's world. It was his comfort and his scourge, and not just for health reasons. Depending on where his ship was stationed, he received a daily ration of a gallon of beer, a pint of wine, or a half-pint of rum. That created a habit, and once acquired a real imbiber would go to great lengths to satisfy it. He would trade for the rations of more abstemious shipmates, and he would commit crimes that put his life at risk. Not that his habitual daily offence went unpunished. By far the greatest proportion of floggings noted in ships' logs were for drunkenness. One study has found that it accounted for almost 30 per cent of punishments, followed by 23 per cent for neglect of duty, 11 per cent for insolence, 10 per cent for disobedience, with single figures for theft, fighting and desertion.[29] A modern perspective might conclude that the Navy first institutionalized alcoholism, then punished it.*

Sex was more rare, for obvious reasons. Insofar as boys are concerned, however, another form of sexuality came into play. While the fond attachment between a boy and an old hand is a theme of the age of sail, the fatherly figure has an ugly yet unavoidable associate – the sexual predator.

Indexes to court-martial records between 1750 and 1800 show just two men from the lower deck being found guilty of serial paedophilia, so either the authorities turned a blind eye to offenders or this form of crime must have later gained significant momentum. The former seems more likely. Henry Bicks of the *Royal William* was convicted in 1757 of 'the detestable crime of sodomy upon the body of a boy', and despite testimony from the victim, John Booth, that the accused had buggered him six times previously, Bicks was given the relatively moderate punishment of 500 lashes before being towed to Portsmouth Point with a halter around his neck and a note declaring his crime.[30] Forty years then passed before another man was convicted of the same offence, although this time David Jenness, who had sodomized three boys on the *Prince*, was hanged off Cadiz in 1798. At his trial, one of the victims testified that he had once driven Jenness away with a knife but did not report him, 'being ashamed to mention what had passed'.[31]

Michael Berry was more fortunate. Although accused of attempting to sodomize five boys under the age of thirteen, one of whom testified that Berry 'wanted me to take his prick in my hand and told me he would give me a shilling or six pence to shake it about', he was acquitted at his trial.[32] One study has concluded that the testimony of boys at such hearings was treated with

* A criminal trial of 1763 is an example of the consequences ashore. James Chapman and Richard Forsit came to London with pay of 45 and 13 guineas respectively, and the anticipation of more in prize money. It was not forthcoming and after two months at the taverns of St Giles they were penniless. They were convicted of robbing a man of his shoes, a pair of silver-plated buckles, a hat and 7/6 in coins, and were executed at Tyburn on 15 June. They declined to join a priest in prayer, Forsit saying: 'There is but one God but many ways to worship him.' Instead they formed a circle with a third man on the gallows in their own quiet prayer. (Old Bailey online)

suspicion, especially when made against officers, who made up the great majority of defendants.[33]

The harrowing case in the summer of 1761 of George Newton and Thomas Finlay, a boy on the *Ocean*, provides a slice of social history all its own. Before their joint trial on charges of sodomy could begin, the court had to consider an objection that a black seaman, Charles Ferret, could not testify against Christians – a claim it rejected after hearing that Ferret had been baptized and that his godfather was Captain Augustus Keppel, the son of an earl. Ferret went on to testify that he had been awakened at about 3 a.m. by 'hearing somebody blowing and puffing alongside of me'. It was Newton lying on top of the boy Finlay:

> I got hold of both his stones fast. The other part was in the body of the Boy.
> I asked him what he had got there. He said Cunt.[34]

Finlay was aged fifteen and had been on the ship for just two weeks. Why he had been brought to trial was not spelled out, but the testimony of one officer was recorded:

> Q: Do you remember to have heard the Boy declare he had been guilty of this before, or had been accustomed to suffer men to commit sodomy with him?
> A: He said he had run away from his friends and had been accustomed to run about the Birdcage Walk in St James's Park, but on what account he did not say. His confession was made freely and voluntarily.[35]

A confession of sorts it was deemed, because the tree-lined avenue of Bird Cage Walk had acquired notoriety as a homosexual meeting point in London. Why the boy had not tried to conceal this activity, whether he might have been oblivious to any wrongdoing, the court seems not to have considered. And despite his father's plea for mercy, testimony that he had been a dutiful lad and did butcher's work in London before going to sea, fifteen-year-old Thomas

Finlay joined the man who had sodomized him in being hanged from a yardarm.[*]

What then of homosexuality in general?

Sodomy always attracted opprobrium but was also – whatever Winston Churchill thought – rare.[36] Admiralty indexes record only fourteen cases involving seamen over an entire half-century up to 1806, four of which led to acquittals.[37] There were only three convictions for attempts to commit sodomy. An interesting example of legal punctilio involved John Ware and John Douglas, who were found naked and 'in great motion' in a hammock. They were obviously guilty of conduct 'infamous, scandalous, unmanly and unworthy of British seamen'; but because it could not be stated emphatically 'that the one's privates were in the body of the other', both were acquitted.[38] In another case where penetration could not be proved, George Reed and Thomas Tattershall were convicted only of 'a most scandalous Action & abominable Uncleanliness'.[39]

There was doubtless an element of self-regulation behind these figures, a degree of tolerance in some instances, and a tendency to overlook uncomfortable truths in others. No charges appear to have been brought between 1762 and 1797 and, perhaps typical of the period, one captain, rather than prosecute a case of attempted sodomy, had the accused flogged and turned ashore; Graham Moore of the sloop *Bonetta* admitted he had no right to avoid enforcing naval law, but his company 'could not brook such a man remaining amongst them' and he wanted to spare them shame. His own opinion was that 'morality suffers by such practices becoming notorious'.[40]

Yet making due allowance for exceptions, an incidence of one case every four years hardly suggests that homosexual practice was widespread. When

---

[*] ADM 12/21. A larger proportion of offenders came from the higher ranks, mainly warrant officers such as Robert Paton, bosun on the *Volage*, who preyed on four boys aged between fifteen and seventeen. 'He made a practice of getting these boys into corners, handling their private parts & taking them into his mouth & thrusting his finger up their fundaments, blowing into them and with a wonderfully capricious and brutal depravity, making themselves in his hands.' Paton was flogged around the fleet and drummed ashore with a halter around his neck (ff. 211/2). See also B. R. Burg, *Boys at Sea: Sodomy, Indecency and Courts Martial in Nelson's Navy* (Basingstoke, 2007).

discovered, it could produce on the lower deck a kind of ribald horror – as when Martin Billin and James Brian were found with their breeches down between a gun and a chest on the *Newark* in 1762.

A witness told their trial that he had 'laid hold of Brian's yard, pulled it out of Billin's fundament, held it in his hand and called out to the bystanders to observe what a posture they were in'. Asked how he could be sure that penetration had taken place, he said: 'Because Brian's yard came out with a spring, as if a cork had been drawn out of a bottle.' The two men were sentenced to receive 1,000 lashes each.[41]

When it came to buggery, the Navy made no distinction between man and beast. In one especially pitiful case, John Blake of the *Rippon* was convicted in 1757 of 'the unnatural Sin of buggery on the body of a goat'. A marine testified that he had observed Blake beside a cannon, 'with a goat between his legs, kneeling upon his left knee and standing on his right leg, in motion the same as if a man was with a woman'. Asked whether he had anything to say in his defence, Blake, shamed and terrified, replied he could only remember 'offering the goat a piece of bread'. It did no good. He was sentenced to hang.[42]

The Marine Society continued to play a part in recruiting the seamen of the future. It won the support of such benefactors as the composer George Friderich Handel and the actor David Garrick, and its scope shifted from saving boys from the streets to providing those already in trades with alternative opportunities. Apprentice boys suffering under tyrannical masters or unhappy in their line of work were taken on, including, for example, nineteen apprentice chimney sweeps found in 1773 in circumstances that amounted to little more than slavery.[43] And just as Jack's status grew during the final quarter of the eighteenth century, so did the number of boys coming from simple backgrounds for whom a life of opportunity and adventure had appeal. By the end of the Napoleonic Wars in 1815, the Marine Society had equipped around 25,000 boys for the Navy and sent thousands more to sea in merchant ships and coastal vessels.[44]

Far from all ships' boys were protégés of the society, however. A great many were the sons of seafarers, particularly those engaged in the traditional trade of the east coast, the colliers of Newcastle, regarded as the finest nursery for seamen. Others came by more random routes, and one individual of special interest made his appearance at this time.

Olaudah Equiano was among those who found life at sea a genuine release. But then he had been a slave until he was purchased at the age of nine from a Virginia plantation by a naval officer, Lieutenant Michael Pascal, who wanted a servant. Equiano never regretted it. 'I had sails to lie on and plenty of good

Olaudah Equiano, or Gustavus Vassa, in an engraving of 1789 when his seafaring days had given way to campaigning.

victuals to eat; and every body on board used me very kindly, quite contrary to what I had seen of any white people before.'[45] More than comfort and kindness, however, life at sea brought Equiano friendship, education and ultimately the opportunity to redefine himself.

His first companion was Dick Baker, an American lad five years his senior who seemed blind to Equiano's race, having 'a mind superior to prejudice; and who was not ashamed to notice, to associate with, and to be the friend and instructor of one who was ignorant, a stranger, of a different complexion, and a slave!' They shared duties as Pascal's steward which, as Equiano's biographer has pointed out, gave him the status of other ship's boys, rather than a slave. They received no pay, but officers were given an allowance for a steward's keep and during his navy service Equiano was entered in ships' musters as Gustavus Vassa or Vasser, a volunteer and captain's servant.

Equiano's arrival in England aged ten coincided with the start of the Seven Years War and active duty appears to have given him a certain swagger. On the 40-gun *Roebuck* cruising off France he learnt to box, 'the first time I ever fought with a white boy'. His next ship was the pride of the Navy, the 100-gun *Royal George*, where at anchor in a home port the quarters forward resembled a crowded village with

> men, women and children of every denomination . . . Here were also shops or stalls of every kind of goods, and people crying their different commodities about the ship as in a town.[46]

The 90-gun *Namur* was another castle, with a complement of 780 men, and she marked the high point of Equiano's seafaring life, even if his memory of the voyage transporting General James Wolfe's army across the Atlantic to Quebec has a hint of embellishment. 'The good and gallant general,' he wrote:

> . . . often honoured me, as well as other young boys, with marks of his notice; and saved me once a flogging for fighting with a young gentleman.[47]

It was in the *Namur* that Equiano finally saw action. He was fourteen and after four years at sea felt himself 'a stranger to terror of any kind and, in that respect at least, almost an Englishman', when the war took a historic turn. Olaudah Equiano and William Spavens were at the two battles that would define Britain's future as a naval power.

4

HEART OF OAK
1759-61

THE *Vengeance* weighed anchor in Plymouth Sound on 22 September, a hazy day with a fresh wind blowing down the Channel. On the foremast lift, Spavens heard the cry below: 'Trice up and lay out.' He and his mates shrugged their way along the yards and cast off the gasket ropes while enfolding the furled topsail in their arms until the order came to let it fall. As they did so it flapped briefly before snapping taut and, in slow motion, billowed with the breeze as the forecastlemen below sheeted it home.

At first imperceptibly, then with a slow hastening of the air that men aloft could feel on their faces, she started to slide forward; and, in a vision that one old topman recalled with a leap of the heart many years after his seafaring days were over, 'in a few minutes the ship, from appearance as naked as a tree, would be as a cloud'.[1]

Mess tables that day had the buzz of any new commission. That they were bound for France, they knew. How much they had been told about what awaited them is not clear. But the *Vengeance* under Captain Gamaliel Nightingale was a far more contented ship than the *Blandford*. Nightingale was no flogger – months passed without the cat being unsheathed – but a strong, direct captain of the old school, supportive of his men, even in pay disputes with the Admiralty.[2]

So it is fair to suppose that he did not leave them in the dark for rumour and gossip to reign as it so often did on a ship, in one tar's words, 'like a Barber's shop or Pott house in London'.[3] If nothing else, they had a fair idea of what was at stake. For months, there had been talk of little else but the French invasion.

The war at sea was going badly. Off Minorca in 1756, the Navy had offered feeble resistance to a French fleet and the strategic island was lost – leading to a timid Admiral Byng being put before a firing squad, 'pour encourager les autres', in Voltaire's words. Byng's death sent a rare signal to all hands that it was not only the lower orders who might be executed for failing in their duty; yet the Navy was left demoralized and, for the time being, the Army was in the ascendant. Robert Clive's victory at Plassey in India in 1757 had been followed by the taking of Guadeloupe and, the ultimate coup, James Wolfe's scaling of the heights at Quebec.

Dispirited or not, the Navy was now all that stood between Britain and calamity.

Events that year foreshadowed those of 1805. Then too a grand French army was mustered to cross the Channel; then too the French navy was preparing to escort the invasion; and then too a British fleet had mounted a blockade to prevent the two combining. This time, however, the admiral with orders to contain the enemy troops on their own shore was not Horatio Nelson, but Sir Edward Hawke with the Western Squadron. The *Vengeance* with Spavens was about to join them.

One item of glad tidings reached Plymouth shortly before they sailed. A squadron of eleven ships had just fought an epic battle with seven French vessels off Lagos, taking three and driving two more ashore. Among the British ships in the thick of it had been the *Namur*, with Olaudah Equiano.

Blockading was based on the very proper principle that to confine the enemy's ships in port was to prevent him doing harm to British interests, and as a consequence it became the cornerstone of naval strategy.[4] For a true Foremast Jack, however, it was close to misery. The thrill of blue water sailing, the challenge of keeping the right spread of sail – crowding on enough to take full advantage of the wind, yet not so much as to tear the canvas or threaten to bring down spars or masts – were lost. The athlete of the tops became just another landsman, a maintenance lackey whose tasks were carrying and stitching, while awaiting an enemy breakout. Lack of activity bred boredom, disaffection and drunkenness.

Blockading, moreover, could last for months and because large numbers of ships were involved, the logistics were formidable. In Hawke's fleet, anchored off the main French port of Brest, his flagship alone, the 100-gun *Royal George*, had a crew of almost 1,000. In all, the thirty-two ships of the line contained some 14,000 men. This population – the equivalent of a substantial town yet living at sea more than 200 miles from friendly soil – had to be supplied not only with food of a quality and quantity to keep them healthy, but fresh water. By the time Spavens's *Vengeance* joined them, outbreaks of scurvy had obliged Hawke to send ships home periodically for revictualling, leaving the blockade porous and vulnerable to attack.

At least it could be said that since Anson's time a good deal more had become known about how seamen might best be kept healthy. The naval physician James Lind, noting that the number of hands who died in battle or shipwreck was negligible compared with those 'destroyed by ship diseases and the maladies of intemperate climates', had recently published his land-mark *Treatise of the Scurvy*. While it would take decades for his observations about the antiscorbutic qualities of citrus to be fully accepted by the Admiralty, his views on the significance of fresh produce had come to the attention of Hawke. At that officer's insistence, the Navy was now attempting a bold experiment. Spavens's ship was escorting to the island of Ushant just off Brest a fleet of vessels laden with live cattle and sheep, along with fresh vegetables and beer, to keep the squadron in health. Nothing like it had been attempted before.[5]

Twice in September and October, *Vengeance* escorted deep-keeled vessels resembling agricultural stalls to Hawke's squadron, where yardarm cranes lifted cattle and sheep, vegetable crates and water butts onto men-of-war. Fresh beer was also provided to replace the men's grog. It was a painfully slow and difficult procedure that entailed considerable dangers: moving barrels of water on a shifting deck was a risky business, as many seamen including Spavens discovered to their cost.

But the benefits of this unprecedented operation that began in the spring had become plain by the autumn. There had been not a single case of scurvy. Lind celebrated that many thousands of men

> . . . pent up in ships should continue for six or seven months to enjoy a
> better state of health upon the watery element than it can well be imagined
> so great a number of people would enjoy on the most healthful spot of
> ground in the world.[6]

At the end of 1759 the French fleet remained bottled up in Brest while the French Army was quartered more than 100 miles to the south-east at Quiberon Bay. The threat of invasion had seemingly receded when Hawke was suddenly driven up the Channel by a gale. On returning to resume the blockade, intelligence reached him on 16 November that the French fleet was out of Brest and making for Quiberon Bay to launch the invasion.

Spavens's dreams of adventure – of 'beholding the wonderful works of the Creator in the remote regions of the Earth' – were dimming. By the end of 1759 he had spent five years at sea, had crossed the Atlantic and risen in his trade. Yet there had been little to stimulate him since the privateer actions in the Caribbean, so to exercise a lively intelligence he had begun to improve his rudimentary schooling by spending off-duty hours in the company of a book.

On 18 November he came down at noon, wet and chilled from a buffeting by the gales typical in Biscay, where the *Vengeance* was cruising with two other frigates. The hands were still at dinner when a sloop was sighted and a boat came across with news.[7] Nightingale, good captain that he was, addressed the company from the quarterdeck in the evening. Their orders, he said, were to make speed to Quiberon Bay and alert the few British ships there, for the French fleet was in all likelihood about to descend.

Spavens's account of events breathes with the excitement that he still felt as he wrote it many years later. He had doubtless told his story often enough. It is highly coloured in places as well as being out by the odd day here and there, yet is broadly matched by the more prosaic language of the *Vengeance*'s log.

'We applied ourselves to the dangerous task assigned us, carrying a press of sail all that night and the next day,' he wrote, 'and in the night of the 17th, we discovered ourselves almost in the midst of the enemy's fleet, twenty-one sail of the line and four frigates.' It was 10 p.m. and the Vengeances could make out toplights on the French ships all around. 'But the wind blowing hard and being very dark we soon cleared them undiscovered.'[8]

Having overtaken the French, they were approaching Quiberon Bay where Captain Nightingale's log picks up the story:

Nov 19: Moderate gales & cloudy with rain. At 10am being in sight of our ships in Quiberon Bay made the signal of an enemy of superior force & fired minute guns.

Nov 20: Mod & clear. Continued firing guns. At 3pm saw Capn Duff's squadron coming out. At half past 7am, saw the French fleet, consisting of 26 sail, bearing SSW abt 2 leagues. Some of their ships chac'd [chased] us.[9]

Just at this point, Hawke's fleet was spotted to windward, coming down under full sail. Spavens, high in the tops, marvelled at this 'grand and awful sight':

A powerful French fleet drawn up in fighting position, ready for action; and a British fleet . . . bearing down on it with crowded sail, and each breast glowing with ardour to decide the grand dispute between the two nations, which should have sovereignty of the seas.[10]

And as *Vengeance* raised her colours, he joined in a salute that became customary when British seamen went into battle: 'We gave three cheers, took a reef in our topsails and stood for the fleet, which we joined with gladness.' Thereafter, all was thunder and smoke.

On the 74s and other ships of the line, a standard battle procedure was followed. Port-lids were flung open, flooding the lower decks with light, and the guns trundled forward. A hand named Robert Wilson wrote of the dispersal of Jacks to their positions:

> The drummer beats to Quarters. Every person in the ship, from the captain to the smallest boy, repairs to their stations. At Quarters there are three divisions of men . . . There is a captain, a sponger and a boarder, a fireman and a sail trimmer to each gun. The captain of the gun has to fire her off; the sponger and boarder (one person) has to sponge the gun in action and to be ready to board an enemy's vessel; the fireman with his bucket is to attend in case of fire; the sail trimmers are to trim the sails when required . . . The powder men or boys supply the guns with powder; there are also some on the lower deck who pass along the powder from the magazine.[11]

Among those to have served as powder monkeys, Olaudah Equiano's account from the *Namur* is as vivid as any:

> My station during the engagement was on the middle deck, where I was quartered with another boy, to bring powder to the aftermost gun; and here I was a witness to the dreadful fate of many of my companions who, in the twinkling of an eye, were dashed to pieces and launched into eternity. Happily I escaped unhurt, though shot and splinters flew thick around me during the whole fight.
>
> Towards the latter part of it my master was wounded, and I saw him carried down to the surgeon; but though I was much alarmed for him, and

wished to assist him, I dared not leave my post. At this station my gun-mate and I ran a very great risk . . . for when we had taken the cartridges out of the boxes, the bottoms of them proving rotten, the powder ran all about the deck, near the match tub . . .

We were also very much exposed to the enemy's shots; for we had to go through nearly the whole length of the ship to bring the powder. I expected therefore every minute to be my last, especially when I saw the men fall so thick around me . . . At first I thought it would be safest not to go for the powder till the Frenchmen had fired their broadside . . . But immediately afterwards I thought this caution was fruitless; and cheering myself with the reflection that there was a time allotted for me to die as well as to be born, I cast off all thought of death and went through my duty with alacrity.[12]

Battles dominate the imagery of seafaring life in art and prose. Yet they occupied a fragment – hours within years – of the time a ship spent at sea. They were usually shorter than those fought on land, but marked by still greater confusion. 'The lower deck,' one participant wrote, 'becomes so completely filled with smoke that no one can see two yards before him.'[13] Spavens, however, remained aloft and had an unusually clear view of events.

The French admiral, the Comte de Conflans, found himself confronted by a superior force – his twenty-one ships of the line against Hawke's twenty-three – and he tried to gain the shelter of Quiberon Bay. He had the advantage of pilots with intimate knowledge of the coast and, as Spavens noted, 'many of the [British] ships being far astern, could not get up'. But Conflans, initially complacent, did not form his ships into a line of battle – reasoning that Hawke would not dare to take his fleet into a treacherous, unfamiliar bay late in the day and with darkness descending. Heavy seas were rising with a gale. Despite the awesome risk, Hawke gave no sign of hesitation, racing in after the retreating enemy and pounding the hindmost ships.

Confusion passed through the French. On the 74-gun *Thésée* an order was given to open the lower-deck gun ports, a fatal error in the deteriorating weather. She was promptly flooded and went straight down.

Hawke's *Royal George*, that mighty cathedral of a ship, came up alongside the 70-gun third-rate *Superbe* and in two broadsides from her 32-pounders utterly shattered the Frenchman. No one lived to describe the scene on *Superbe*'s lower deck, but accounts of the frightful injuries done to the human body by a 32-pound ball, and the flying fragments of timber it created, are legion; tales of men having their heads taken off by cannonballs became so common as to have an apocryphal edge. More chilling is the matter-of-fact account by a man named Robert Hay of a shot that 'went through two upper decks and dashed a young Irishman, a messmate of my own, into a dozen pieces. His flesh, as I collected the scattered fragments of it, creeped to my hand as if unwilling to part.'[14]

As a frigate, the *Vengeance* had no business exchanging fire with a ship of the line, but she had been in the thick of the action. And in the confusion and gathering dark, Spavens noted a terrible sight. The *Superbe*, her rigging shot to pieces and her hull everywhere fractured, was struck by a heavy sea. She broke up and followed *Thésée* to the bottom.

The special perils of sea life bred a kinship that, in extremis, transcended enmity. English boats were hoisted out to save French lives and Spavens was relieved to see two other enemy ships, *Héros* and *Formidable*, strike their colours 'having displayed the greatest bravery' while being savagely reduced by gunfire. But visions of *Superbe* and *Thésée*, which had both gone down in 15 fathoms, haunted him:

> Only their mast heads were to be seen; and we could perceive several of their dead men in the tops, and hanging amongst the shrouds and rigging . . . our boat took up four of the men belonging to the *Thesee*; the rest, together with the *Superbe*'s crew, amounting to 1615, perished.[15]

Ten hours of murderous gunfire wrought an immortal victory. Quiberon Bay was one of the most dramatic events in the Navy's history and quite comparable in its way to Trafalgar. Six French ships, including Conflans' *Soleil Royal*, were wrecked or sunk, and another was taken. Two British ships were lost, but their crews were saved. Coming on top of the action off Lagos, the French Navy was destroyed as a rival force.

For France herself the damage went wider and deeper. An invasion of Britain was now out of the question. Canada would soon be lost. Designs on America and India had been severely damaged. While the Seven Years War continued until 1763, Britain's naval superiority was now unquestioned. What the historian N. A. M. Rodger has described as a prevailing national myth, of Britain as a great sea power, had at last been made reality.[16]

As a fast-sailing frigate, *Vengeance* was given Hawke's despatches to carry the glad tidings home, and she reached Plymouth early on 28 November, a moment with echoes of the homecoming rituals related by Robert Hay after similarly dramatic events, when Jacks took sand from the seabed to mix with grog 'as if to imbue it with the soil of our native land', and toasted Happiness and Prosperity: 'All our favourite national songs was . . . chorused and encored until the decks were made to ring.'[17] The Vengeances were home for Christmas.

There was just one disappointment. They were given shore leave but sworn to secrecy while the news was carried to London. 'Should any body ask us from whence we came, we were instructed to say from sea; and if they enquired what news to say good news and not to answer any further enquiries.' They duly made their way to taverns and bawdy houses, where they found that the locals 'knew almost as much of the affair as we did'.[18]

And so ended a year on the *Vengeance*. Spavens and his fellows had gone aloft as a matter of routine on 364 days and had fired the great guns in anger and passion on just one. They had eaten fresh beef or mutton on roughly half of those days, and savoured women's company during thirty-four nights in port. They had heard the Articles of War read by Captain Nightingale fifty-two times and probably knew them as well as he. And in all that time just one Jack and two marines had been flogged.[19] There are plenty of accounts of unhappy ships. The *Vengeance* was a proud one.

Anson's voyage had provided the context for 'Rule, Britannia!' The Battle of Quiberon Bay inspired a Drury Lane production, *Harlequin's Invasion*, with another song that would echo down the centuries – one, indeed, that was taken up by Jack himself, who adopted David Garrick's lyrics and William Boyce's melody as his own anthem:

> *Come cheer up my lads, 'tis to glory we steer,*
> *To add something more to this wonderful year.*
> *To honour we call you, not press you like slaves,*
> *For who are so free as we sons of the waves?*
>
> *Heart of oak are our ships, jolly tars are our men;*
> *We always are ready – steady, boys, steady –*
> *We'll fight and we'll conquer again and again.*

Thus did Jack emerge fully formed – recognizable from the observations of a navy surgeon, Dr Thomas Trotter, who had years to study those in his care and described them thus:

'Saturday Night at Sea.' A seaman's mess, the communal table where hands ate, shared stories and sang, as seen by Cruikshank.

The[ir] mind, by custom and example, is trained to brave the fury of the elements with a degree of contempt for danger and death that is to be met with nowhere else. Excluded by the employment they have chosen from all society, the deficiencies of education are not felt and information on general affairs is not courted. Their pride consists in being reputed a thoroughbred seaman, and they look on all landsmen as beings of inferior order.[20]

Olaudah Equiano did not remain among them. Though he would have been happy to stay in the service, with the prospect of rising in time, perhaps to a clerical post, he was betrayed by his master when they came ashore in 1762. Lieutenant Pascal still evidently regarded Equiano as his property and although shipmates 'strove to cheer me and told me he could not sell me, and that they would stand by me', Pascal passed him on to another officer who in turn sold him to a Philadelphia merchant.[21] Yet Equiano had acquired abilities that eventually enabled him to obtain his freedom and return to Britain, and he was careful to acknowledge the part naval life had played in shaping him, providing friendship, the education he received at sea from a schoolmaster, and the care of a shipmate. Daniel Quin, he wrote, was 'like a father to me and took very great pains to instruct me in many things . . . to shave and dress hair and also to read in the Bible'.[22] All these contributed to the other life for which Equiano is remembered – as an entrepreneur, author and anti-slavery campaigner.

Another former slave who served in the war came ashore as well. Francis Barber's two years on the frigate *Stag* and sloop *Raven* had been comparatively uneventful and he was still a Landsman when he left to resume his place as Samuel Johnson's servant; but Barber had no desire to quit the sea either and seems to have rather resented Johnson's interference at the Admiralty to obtain his discharge, telling James Boswell it had been done 'without any wish of his own'.*

---

* Barber was ultimately the beneficiary of the doctor's actions. Having served Johnson until his

Johnson, mystified that the servant to whom he was devoted preferred being on a ship, persisted in his hostile pronouncements on a sailor's life. His view that a man was better off in prison than at sea, 'for being in a ship is being in a gaol with the chance of being drowned', is famous. Less well known is his declaration that 'men go to sea before they know the unhappiness of that way of life; and when they have come to know it, they cannot escape from it, because it is then too late to choose another profession'.[23] All of which was at variance with his servant's experience.

In fact, Barber and Equiano were not alone among black Englishmen in being drawn to a sailor's life. Prejudice was far less common in the Navy – where black men shared the same food, the same quarters, the same duties and the same pay as their white shipmates – than on the streets of London. The number of black British seamen in the age of sail has been the subject of much study and some dispute: by a conservative estimate, however, between 6 and 8 per cent of navy seamen in the era covered by this narrative were black, a considerably larger proportion than in the population as a whole.[24]

Spavens spent another two years in the *Vengeance*. He was off Quebec when the war for Canada came to a climax, and again brought despatches home in a cruise that he recalled as perhaps the most exhilarating of his life, twelve days from Newfoundland to Land's End with a stiff following wind all the way, 'and never could bear more sail . . . sometimes running 272 and never less than 240 miles a day'.

He was in the ship when news came of George II's death and the accession of George III, upon which 'we hoisted our colours quite up again, and our mourning was at an end' – opening an era as important as any in British history, in which the young king came to be associated by seamen with their endeavours. And he was in her for a sharp engagement with *Entreprenant*, a heavily armed letter of marque, after an overnight chase off Ushant that ended

---

death, Barber was his principal heir with a legacy that left him an independent married man able to start up his own school.

with a broadside-to-broadside action in which twenty men were killed and the French surrendered.

Of all the ships in which Spavens served, it was the *Vengeance* under Captain Nightingale that he remembered with the most pride. When he deserted, it was also a matter of pride.

Nightingale had been given command of a bigger frigate, the *Flora*, much to the dismay of the Vengeances, who wrote to him, declaring their firm intention to join him. The letter has not been found but its flavour may be gathered from an evocative note to the captain of the *Sunderland* from hands similarly placed two years earlier:

> Hif your honer would be Cind A Nuf to Right to the Lords of the Admirlte to get your Ould Ships Compeney We All Would be glad to go A Long With you honer A gain.[25]

In both cases, the Admiralty bowed to the men's wishes. At bottom, while the Navy was run by coercion it depended on cooperation, and at this time their lordships were still sensible of the sentiments expressed by another captain for his men: 'Their good behaviour has been such as to gain my affection, and I do believe that I have not less of theirs, which makes us very unwilling to part with each other.'[26]

Despite his respect for Nightingale, Spavens did not settle in the *Flora*. It took time for ship's companies to gel, for men to find their feet in a new command, and it was at points of transition that they were most inclined to become restive. Spavens had been highly rated in the *Vengeance*, but did not get on with his new lieutenant, finding him 'haughty'. When other hands were promoted to petty officer rank – though in Spavens's view, 'neither so good seamen, nor of so long duration in the service as myself' – he decided to desert.[27]

It was perfectly easy. He went ashore at Plymouth, bought landsman's clothes, gave away his seaman's trowsers, and set off on foot to London on a passage through the countryside that might have come from the pages of *Tom Jones*. Though affecting to be a simple rustic, he was a distinct enough figure to be identified as a seaman, probably from his rolling gait, by an old woman as he passed through Honiton. Still, he managed to avoid press gangs as well as the odd highwayman in his progress around southern England, and struck up a fond acquaintance with a serving maid at an inn in Guildford before reaching London.

Pride had something to do with it, but Spavens's desertion may have been influenced by another factor too. Experienced hands were never more in demand than in wartime, when private ship-owners were obliged to pay well above navy rates; tens of thousands of Jacks besides Spavens deserted between 1755 and 1762, mainly to serve in merchantmen or privateers.[28]

At Deptford he signed on a merchantman bound for Guadeloupe, and after pocketing the advance of £2 15s promptly deserted again. This too was not unusual, but the use to which he put the money certainly was. Spavens's reading had become avid and, rather than strumpets or drink, his ill-gotten gains were spent on books.

Next he signed on the East Indiaman *Elizabeth,* sailing for Java. At last, Spavens was bound for the Indies and the 'remote regions of the Earth' of which he had long dreamt.

5

TO THE EASTERN SEAS
1760-70

VICTORY at sea ushered in a new era, one that saw British ships voyaging farther, in greater numbers, and in a wider quest for knowledge and possessions as well as trade. Whether, as one historian has put it, 1759 was the year Britain became master of the world, it was certainly the year in which she became master of the seas. The rest followed, for, as Adam Smith wrote, the sea was 'the great high road of communication to the different nations of the world'.[1] China and the Far East were becoming theatres for British enterprise, but of all the destinations visited by her ships now, none was more crucial to the national interest than India.

The instrument of this traffic was the East India Company. From 1760 the barons of Leadenhall Street embarked on a process of deepening commercial, military and political expansion in the Orient, and their ships, the East Indiamen, introduced to Britain consumer products ranging from tea to cotton, spices to coffee, and textiles of bewildering variety. A threefold increase in the number of Indiamen, from some thirty to ninety sail by 1772, brought with it a corresponding growth in the need for the finest oak to build ships and experienced hands to man them.[2] Given that a large Indiaman was roughly the size of a frigate, took some 740 mature trees to build and needed seventy hands to sail, it is not surprising that Company and Navy found themselves in ferocious competition for both.

One consequence of this growth was a further increase in the number of men using the sea. Another was the rise of practices by which unscrupulous individuals made a living from exploiting them.

By the time William Spavens signed on an Indiaman, an industry had grown up around Wapping and other seafarers' haunts where those known as crimps – often publicans and harlots, acting as agents for merchantmen and privateers – lured hands into deserting the Navy by 'first debauching them with drink, then bribing them with money'.[3] Seamen themselves were not above exploiting their own by crimping. A letter in the crabbed hand of a tar named John Davis was received by the Admiralty in 1766, imploring 'For the Good of All Sailors' that a stop be put 'to a most vilonous profeeding' involving two brothers named Latchman, a gunner and a carpenter, who would welcome hands arriving at Woolwich and 'decoy them into bad houses with Loose women in order to run them up reckonings and then at pay day they will have writs against them'.[4]

A constant theme in such tales of woe is the naivety of Jacks who, whatever their self-assurance at sea, showed an almost childlike simplicity ashore. As the author of *Tom Jones*, Henry Fielding knew a thing or two about picaresque adventure. On a voyage to Portugal he was able to admire seamen in their element – 'They submit to every difficulty which attends their calling with cheerfulness, patience and fortitude' – while noting their vulnerability: 'All these good qualities they leave behind on shipboard; the sailor out of water is, indeed, as wretched an animal as the fish out of water.'[5]

The naval surgeon Thomas Trotter observed: 'Having little intercourse with the world, they are easily defrauded, and dupes to the deceitful wherever they go; their money is lavished with the most thoughtful profusion; fine clothes for his girl, a silver watch and silver buckles for himself are often the sole return for years of labour and hardship.' All of which, as Trotter saw it, was part of the sailor's innate generosity:

His charity makes no conditions to its object, but yields to the faithful impulse of an honest heart ... Was I ever to be reduced to the utmost poverty, I would shun the cold threshold of fashionable charity [and] beg among seamen, where my afflictions would never be insulted by being asked through what follies or misfortunes I had been reduced to penury.[6]

Spavens was as profligate as most, but joining the *Elizabeth*, an Indiaman of 800 tons, seemed to make good financial sense. While navy pay had remained fixed for a century, the Company was more flexible. It could afford to lure good men with wages of up to 70s a month, almost three times the navy rate, and other benefits, including two months' pay in advance to provide for families or settle domestic affairs.[7] This generosity evaporated when sailors were abundant, usually in peacetime, and when Spavens signed on late in 1761 it was for just 45s a month. Still, he received his two months' pay in advance and bought more books to occupy his increasingly questing mind on what he anticipated as a voyage of two to three years to Java and China.

As Spavens no doubt reasoned, too, it was prudent for him to go as far away as possible; being a deserter, he could expect punishment of up to 500 lashes if he was picked up. The Indian Ocean, moreover, held out the prospect of those strange and colourful places that would satisfy 'the curiosity that seemed implanted in my nature'. A fascination with the Far East and the South Seas had already been roused among seamen; and it would flourish, thanks to episodes as disparate as those involving James Cook and William Bligh.

Prior to sailing, Spavens lodged in Wapping, a habitat on the Thames to which seafarers were drawn and where, at inns clustered beside the river's inky ooze, they would find drink and women, company and gossip. Here was a network providing news of old shipmates, information about sailings and what passed for intelligence about a prospective captain, his regime, his whims and crimes. Along the half-mile of Ratcliffe Highway, north of the riverside, were almost forty taverns, stores, pawnshops and billets for hands newly returned or preparing to sail.[8] Wapping was the closest many old seadogs would come to feel at home on land, a place where a lubberly Londoner was 'apt to think himself in another country' among these outlandish fellows with their ways of 'living, speaking, acting, dressing and behaving so very peculiar to themselves'.[9] Samuel Johnson, despite his hostility to seafaring life, thought the place exemplified 'the wonderful extent and variety of London' and urged Boswell: '*Explore Wapping*'.[10]

While staying at an inn Spavens had a couple of close calls. Despite having been warned by his new captain to stay indoors because press gangs were operating in the area, he was out browsing at a bookstall on Tower Hill when he spotted a lieutenant from the *Vengeance*, who fortunately failed to see him. Days later, as his new ship was working down from Deptford, another naval officer came on board, 'saying he had received information of some deserters'. Again Spavens escaped detection.

There was a curious paradox about navy and merchant ships. While tars took a special pride in the king's service, and regarded themselves as a cut above other seamen, men in Company ships had to work harder, which often made them better hands. A navy ship's complement, as we have seen, was based on the number needed to fight her guns, while an Indiaman took on just enough to sail her, which the Company saw to it was as few as possible. Whereas the *Vengeance* had a crew of about 200, the *Elizabeth* – of similar dimensions and rigging – had 120, and they had to take her through some of the most turbulent seas. In other respects the ships were not dissimilar. Indiamen resembled frigates, with up to twenty-six cannon, and were run along naval lines, albeit with a lighter hand.[11] Spavens had served one model captain and one tartar and was pleased to find that Captain George Stuart of the *Elizabeth* had more in common with Nightingale than Cuming.

The *Elizabeth* was making her first voyage. She proved a prime sailer and, as the bows cleaved towards the sunshine of the Canaries, the topmen had repeatedly to shorten sail to prevent her racing ahead of others in the convoy. Early on, Spavens struck up a friendship with one of his messmates, Stewart Gray, a lively, reckless fellow with a scheme he said could make them rich in

India. At what stage Spavens started to fall in with Gray's designs is not clear, but during months of voyaging the subject came up repeatedly.

They were plying a route that had been followed by Indiamen since the Company's founding 150 years earlier, south-west across the Atlantic, almost as far as Brazil, where they might collect the south-east trades. After four weeks they reached the Equator, an occasion marked in the case of hands like Spavens who had not previously crossed the Line, by a ceremonial ducking from the yardarm and sundry other frolics. Soon afterwards they picked up the trades, which meant reinforcing masts and rigging so the *Elizabeth* could carry a heavy press of sail to make the most of the conditions.

Passing below Lat 40°S, they entered what were, in every sense, new waters – a latitudinal band where the westerly winds known with good reason as the Roaring Forties blew around the globe without the obstacle of land, testing topmen and sweeping ships in mighty seas around the Cape of Good Hope, into the Indian Ocean. This was the kind of challenge that thrilled true Jacks, and Spavens – lightly dressed in a cotton shirt, skin darkened by the sun – was among those aloft, balanced at arms' length from one another on the yards, wrestling with rope and canvas as the wind shrilled and timbers groaned in their ears. With the night came a sense of awe and wonder, and the extreme smallness of humankind, as he stood alone in darkness beneath the stars.

Off duty, Spavens was almost alone in spending an hour or so reading while slung in his hammock; by now he was on to Anson's account of his expedition, which was duly devoured.[12] He and Gray would also fish for albacore, bonito and dolphin, finding them excellent eating – and all the better now the *Elizabeth* had been at sea for more than two months, with neither pause nor sight of land for fresh rations. On seeing albatrosses as they neared the Cape, they jested about the superstition that the birds were inhabited by dead seamen's spirits. 'We used to say they were old transmigrated pursers,' Spavens recalled.[13]

Somewhere around this point, as they passed into the Eastern Seas and set a course east-by-north-east across a sun rising pinkly across the starboard quarter, Gray's scheme was taking shape and had drawn into its compass two other men. As Gray explained it to William Oliver and Robert Sims, there were opportunities in India where experienced Jacks like them might gain the captaincy of a country ship – a vessel involved in the coastal trade – and so engage in sailing that would bring wild riches. All they had to do was get to Calcutta.

This notion passed lightly over the awkward fact that the *Elizabeth* was bound not for Calcutta in the Bay of Bengal but Canton in the South China Sea – and the distance between the two was roughly equivalent to crossing the Atlantic. She would also pass through the dauntingly unfamiliar and prolific maze of islands that constituted the Dutch East Indies. Gray's madcap plan had, nonetheless – as Spavens declared ruefully in his later years – 'presented us with a view of accumulating fortunes and being great'.[14]

The *Elizabeth* came to anchor in the Sunda Strait, between Sumatra and Java, on 27 July 1762. She had covered about 13,900 miles in 119 days, passing through all the seasons while never once coming in sight of land. Naturally, the men burst with a kind of elemental energy at the possibility of release from their little wooden island.

Jack's wildness is well charted. We are less familiar with its paradox – his self-control, at least at sea. Despite cramped quarters and miserable rations, even prolonged voyages might pass off without serious friction on the lower deck. There were fights, naturally, but it is remarkable that available evidence does not indicate a great many more. Admiralty indexes show a mere three ratings being tried for 'assault on board ship' in the twelve years prior to 1777, including the most serious case, an Irishman named Murphy who slashed a shipmate on the *Torbay* with a bottle 'which he had broke for the purpose', earning himself 200 lashes.[15] Clearly, all this shows with certainty is that men were adept in keeping ordinary fisticuffs out of sight: one seaman, John Nicol, wrote of a scrap between a sailor and a marine that, 'they went forward on the deck to be out of sight of the officers, we forming a ring and screening them from observation'.[16]

Nevertheless, the implication is clear: Jack might be quick to use his fists ashore, but at sea he signed up to another code, one of tolerance, enabling coexistence with even the most awkward members of the tribe. On the one hand, this is all the more unexpected for taking place in a hugger-mugger inhabited purely by males, where large quantities of alcohol were drunk and from which there was no escape besides jumping overboard. On the other, it is arguable that only such a code made their existence possible at all.*

By the end of a voyage, visions of liberty unleashed the kind of wayward-ness that had one officer write in despair of his men: 'They will run every risk to satisfy the caprice of the moment.'[17] For Spavens, the spur was going ashore for the first time in four months. Here, on a lush corner of south Sumatra, he found 'wigwams or huts, built of bamboos' and traded trinkets for fruit. The next day, he and his three mates took the ship's yawl and deserted. They left behind not only four months' pay but all their worldly possessions – in Spavens's case, 'a chest of clothing, bedding and books, which cost me above eighteen pounds in England'.[18] In time, he would look back on this act of premeditated madness as the turning point of his life.

Their intention was to reach Batavia and take ship to Calcutta where, it followed, they would join the country trade and become as rich as nabobs. No sooner had they gone over the side, however, than they found themselves hopelessly adrift.

The four men appear to have had little idea how to negotiate the straits up the west coast of Java to Batavia, the Dutch capital in the East Indies. Nor had they paused to consider that they would be in an open boat, exposed to the tropical sun with only a little bread and water. At first they were reluctant to approach the natives, being fearful of their 'scimitars', until Spavens made the point that 'we had as good perish by their hands as by thirst'. In the event, the

* These cases of fighting do not take into account the trials of seamen for killing fellow hands, but these too were comparatively rare and convictions even more so: Of thirty-six men tried between 1755 and 1800 for murder, twenty-seven were acquitted, usually due to findings that death was accidental because blows had been exchanged by both parties. Most of the eight seamen hanged over those forty-five years had wielded knives. In another case worthy of note, a marine named Rae was sentenced to death in 1780, 'for beating a Negro to death in St Lucia'. See ADM 12/24.

Sumatrans turned out to be friendly, and gave them water and melons as well as guidance on navigating to Batavia. After rowing and sailing more than 100 miles, they reached it in a week. But their next calculation, that they would find an English ship at anchor bound for Calcutta, proved as erroneous as the rest.

By now thoroughly regretting their rashness, they were in a strange land and without money. A Dutch official offered work, with a promise that in a month they could take passage home. This turned out to be a ruse to entrap and enslave them. Spavens was shipped to a fever-ridden offshore prison. What became of Oliver and Sims he never found out; but Gray somehow got back to England and turned up as third mate on a merchantman, so, Spavens noted wryly, 'He who brought us into the snare, fared the best.'

Left to his own devices on the island, Spavens gathered bamboo and rope to build a raft – 'meaning to make a sail of my hammock and put off in the night and make the Java shore [to] get among the Malays and abide with them' – when, without explanation, he was taken back to Batavia. His captivity ended in a way as randomly whimsical as it had begun. Allowed into town one day, he spotted an English seaman ashore on leave:

> I said, what ship, brother? He answered the *Panther*. I said do you belong [to] the long-boat? He replied, yes. I said, Oh! That's right. I want to go off with you.[19]

Spavens gained the *Panther* and was brought aft to tell his story to an officer, who said, 'You are now safe', to which he replied, 'Sir, I am sensible of it.' And because it was Sunday they had chickpeas and pork for dinner.

Spavens returned to the Navy's bosom with gratitude, reflecting that 'His Majesty's service is, in many respects, preferable to any other.'[20] It was a hard-won lesson, though. He had come full circle – back where he had started before deserting the *Flora* a year earlier, and having lost everything. Still, as he discovered, his misfortune might have been infinitely greater had he remained on the *Elizabeth*. She had reached Macao where a drunken sail-maker dropped a candle, starting a fire that took her down to the bottom along with Captain Stuart and thirty-five men.[21]

In another sense, Spavens's ordeal was just beginning. Soon after joining the *Panther*, he was loading water into a longboat when his right leg was crushed between a cask and the ship's side. He was left lame. No longer able to go aloft, he had first to join the idlers – older men given deck duties – then, as it became clear his disability was long-term, he was ordered home from Madras an invalid. William Spavens's seafaring career was near its end.

Of all the foreign places where Jack served, India was the strangest and the deadliest. The West Indies might be unhealthy, but it had a pleasant climate and was endowed with willing girls and punch houses, and if a man had a sudden longing for home it was easy enough to desert and sign on for Liverpool, with 'high wages and thirty gallons of rum'.[22] A great many hands did.

India, on the other hand, was about as far from home as any ordinary Briton could then find himself, both in distance and customs, and the chances of quitting it in health were not good. Four in five of the Company's servants in India died there.[23] Attrition was especially severe among the soldiery – a species pitied even by hands like Spavens, who might have suffered impressment yet thought the troops 'poor fellows . . . generally kidnapped'. In fact, the prospects for sailors were little better.

Jacks died at such a rate in the Bay of Bengal that the East Indies Squadron could not be sustained without constant injections of men – for which the only source was newly arrived Indiamen. There existed a sour interdependence between Company and Navy: the Company needed the Navy to protect its ships from French raiders in the Indian Ocean; the Navy depended on the Company for seamen. Over the next fifty years, until Napoleon's defeat, many thousands of Indiamen hands would have the experience of coming in sight of Madras, Bengal or Bombay – only to be met by a navy longboat. Here was the impress at its cruel and capricious worst, dividing men who would be home in a few months from those destined to stay, until either the Admiralty recalled their ship or death intervened.

Statistics tell their own story: roughly 1 per cent of seamen died sailing in home waters or to North America. Among those voyaging to South America or the West Indies the rate increased to between 2 and 3 per cent. On East Indiamen, it was about 10 per cent.[24]

Risk was only part of the reason Jack became an even wilder fellow in the East than at home. Distance from regulating institutions made India a hedonistic and disorderly place for Europeans generally and, as the exploits of Spavens and his fellow deserters showed, seamen picked up an exhilarating sense of possibility, that in this feverishly outrageous world so far from the familiar, they too might grow – might become different beings. The Eastern Seas was a theatre for reckless adventurism.

In this remoteness, too, Jack felt able to assert himself in unusual ways. Take the case of John Carter of the *Tyger*. Aged eighteen but rated Able, Carter was a fellow of unknown origin but rare character on a man-of-war which had more than its share of curiosities, notably a cabal of Romans named in the muster as Julius Caesar, Mark Anthony and Henry Bacchus. (Anthony and Bacchus were, rather prosaically, rated Able, while Caesar was at least a carpenter's mate.[25] The likelihood is that all were deserters from other navy ships.)

Although the *Tyger*'s log gives no indication of simmering insurrectionism on board, soon after she arrived in India pamphlets started to appear on walls around Calcutta 'of a seditious nature' denouncing the naval authorities. These pamphlets, supposedly authored by Carter, are actually less remarkable for any revolutionary intent than for puritanical fervour, a fire-and-brimstone righteousness. What was described at Carter's trial as Paper No 1 addressed 'the principal officers of the East Indies Squadron' and began by declaring that seamen were 'not such Fools as you make us, but free born People'. It went on:

Knowing the consequences of your Arbitrary Power, we are not Allowed the Use of our Tongues to speak before your faces, we have thought Proper to take this Method to acquaint you that tis you alone that is the Instigation of all these Outrages that are committed on the Natives [of India] . . . Pray look at the unhappy people you make row up & down the river Naked every day.[26]

In Carter's other pamphlets, the teenage firebrand turned from the natives' troubles to those of his own tribe. Navy commanders, he wrote, ought to be ashamed of 'draining our Blood to enrich your Bodies'. He listed seven grievances, including the withholding of prize money and neglect of the sick and wounded. Respectful touches – 'be kind enough to Comply with what we ask for' – were rather spoilt by one last thunderbolt: 'Remember Delays are Dangerous.'

An investigation led to Carter being brought to court martial on the *Tyger* in August 1757. Not surprisingly, his confession was couched in more emollient terms:

I wrote those papers not being in the least apprehensive of any ill that might come thereby. My intent was that they might come to your honours' hands, thinking you would be pleased to enquire into the truth, which if you should find it so, I believed from your equity we should find redress.

The officers, finding it hard to believe that one so young could have been the source of such uncommon ideas, asked whether he had been put up to it. 'No person whatever advised me in writing the papers,' he replied. We may still wonder whether other disgruntled hands – the cabal of Romans, say – may have been at the bottom of it all; a lingering doubt among the officers perhaps, and Carter's youth, were reflected in his sentence. While an older man convicted of mutinous practices would have been run up from the nearest yardarm, Carter was given six dozen lashes.[27]

What became of him, we can only surmise. Rear-Admiral George Pocock was not inclined to forgive so zealous a troublemaker, whatever his age, and dismissed him from the service a month later.[28] Pocock probably did the young agitator a favour. Carter was spared a pestilential service and would have had no difficulty signing on a homeward-bound Indiaman.

John Newson took a more direct form of opposition to authority. Off Cuddalore in 1760, he came onto the *Norfolk*'s quarterdeck, grabbed a lieutenant named Bone and flattened him with a single punch. Newson, too, might have been hanged, but naval justice was not merciless. A court martial found he was 'a melancholy, irrational man who could only be considered a lunatic' and discharged him.[29]

It was true, as Adam Smith wrote in 1759, that the sea was the great highway to the nations of the world, and it followed that Jack was the first of his countrymen to visit those places. In coming ashore his eyes were opened to the strange folk and curious creatures that would become a staple of the yarns with which he regaled listeners back home.

In Indian ports, earthy urban quarters evolved where seamen might encounter sword-swallowers, jugglers and holy men. Chief among these cultural stewpots was Blacktown, outside Fort St George in Madras, where Jacks mingled with Hindus, Muslims, Portuguese, Armenians, Persians and Arabs. At anchor in the Bay of Bengal, men given leave might venture up the Hooghly to Calcutta and observe local customs like the practice of suttee, described by a hand named William Richardson:

> One caste has the custom of burning the living widow with her deceased husband, and our carpenter told us he had seen it done. We asked if she cried out much, but he could not tell, for immediately the torch was put to the pyre it was instantly in a blaze, and the Brahmins made so much noise at the time it was impossible to hear her.

While in Calcutta, Richardson observed too how 'the English gentry live high and nearly burn their livers up with curry'. It might have served for nabobs, but Indian food did not find immediate favour with British seamen, one of whom declared the hot spices 'very disagreeable to uninitiated palates'.[30]

There were no such reservations when it came to the local women, who were not only extremely lovely but 'wear very little covering on their bodies'. One Jack wrote:

Their features are pleasing and expressive; their hair long and, colour excepted, they come pretty near European ideas of beauty.[31]

Spavens had much the same opinion. 'The Gentoos [Hindus],' he wrote, 'are very ingenious and industrious, and many of their women would be exquisite beauties if they were not black, as they have handsome features and excellent hair.'[32] Their intercourse was sexual, social and commercial. A seaman named Robert Hay left a detailed description of a 'shampoo' – a manicure, haircut and massage – by a youth which concluded:

I was about to pay but he had not yet done with me. He seized my fingers, one after another, and jerked them until he extracted a crack from each; gave my ears a few gentle pulls, by way of securing a better adjustment of their position, seized my head between his knees and after fingering the veins in my neck, gave my head such a jerk as made it ring. I had now got shampoo-ed, and on paying my single fanam received a Nabob salaam to the bargain.[33]

Spavens was departing from the Eastern Seas after three years. With time on his hands as a result of his injury, he had begun to make notes of his observations: Indian holy men were 'Bramines, a sort of magicians or prognosticators [who] pay adoration to a voracious kite'; the local means of transport was 'a nice machine called a palenkeen which is slung and carried on a bamboo on the shoulders of two men when gentlemen and ladies are disposed to indulge themselves with an easy ride'. Of the Chinese he could write: 'They are an industrious, lively, and active people, notwithstanding the delicacy of their constitutions, and exceedingly ingenious in many useful manufactures.' These pithy and discerning notes from Spavens's *Brief Description of Several Countries* are the first recorded observations of the Orient and its people by a common seaman.[34]

Spavens emerged from Haslar hospital in Spithead on crutches in the winter of 1765, his life as a seaman over. Aged thirty, he had lost more than his livelihood. 'How much I now differed from that gay and sprightly youth who used to trip along the streets of Gosport,' he recalled, when girls had looked envious on seeing him 'with another lass in tow'.

And, quoting from John Dryden's *The State of Innocence, and Fall of Man*, he went on: 'If thou art he, but ah! how fall'n':[35]

> The contrast seemed as great as that between the bright-sided *Neptune* with all ataunt and her colours streaming in the wind, and the old *Blenheim* hospital ship with pieces of plaister and poultice-clothes sticking to her wales, having nothing standing except her ensign staff.[36]

He was in his late fifties when he wrote that, and though there is regret, it is without self-pity. Spavens believed he had much to be grateful for, and he had acquired a gentle and simple faith. All this, along with a knowledge of Dryden and a gift for literary imagery, is as touching as it is remarkable – coming from a man who had once believed the Earth to be flat.

Of vicissitudes he knew a good deal, having been left not just, in the idiom of the time, a cripple, but (the ever-improvident Jack) fleeced of his entire pay and prize money, to the tune of £281, by a fraudster who ended up in Fleet prison. Spavens got by, initially on a pension of £6 a year, renewable every three years at a Greenwich review when he joined '500 other mutilated creatures, some clean and decently apparelled, some dirty and almost naked. Some have lost an eye, others both; some have a hand, some an arm off, some both, some with wooden legs . . .'

Grotesque as these parades might appear, they demonstrated a care that the Navy had begun to provide for its seafarers – and that far exceeded anything available for the civilian poor. The Royal Hospital for Seamen at Greenwich was, Spavens averred:

> . . . not to be equalled in the world . . . close by the fine river Thames, where ships pass; the air is salubrious, the park delightful, the chapel elegant, the clothing for the pensioners comfortable, and the provision wholesome and plentiful; all which conspire to render life, loaded with infirmities, tolerable if not happy in its decline, 'when safe moor'd in Greenwich tier'.[37]

Not for Spavens though. He returned to Lincolnshire, married, and had hopes of becoming a teacher, but was 'diffident of my abilities because I could not write well'. Instead he turned to glove-making, while continuing to read – poetry, natural history, travel accounts, almost anything. In the meantime his seafaring tales won audiences at taverns in his native Louth and, encouraged by this reception, he started to set some of them down. Although his bad leg troubled him grievously and had finally to be amputated when he was fifty-eight, he lived another six years and earned a little immortality as the author of *The Narrative of William Spavens, Pensioner on the Naval Chest at Chatham*, published in 1796. As a lower-deck memoir of the mid-eighteenth century, it is unique. As an attempt to emulate the other travel volumes then enjoying a vogue, it is somewhat dry. As a testimony to the human spirit, it is a triumph.

It is also a relic of a more innocent age. Spavens and his fellows had been witness to Britain's advance across the Indian Ocean. What lay beyond that horizon was still more fantastic, alluring and dangerous.

6

FARTHER STILL AND FARTHER
1768–88

JACK the servant of science – the idea sounded ludicrous. Pursuit of earthly treasures, that was natural. But transporting the botanist Joseph Banks to the far side of the world in order to discover new plants and animal life? And what did these bemused hands of the bark *Endeavour* make of the geographical aspect of their mission – to observe the Transit of Venus and explore the existence of a Great Southern Continent?

Nothing so ambitious in pure seafaring terms had been attempted by British mariners since Anson's expedition; yet it was as a scientific enterprise of the Enlightenment that the first of Lieutenant James Cook's three voyages gained resonance, and had a profound effect on Britain's view of the world. The Pacific was the final frontier. Thanks to Cook's discoveries, Edmund Burke could declare: 'The great map of mankind is unrolled at once.'[1]

But while the biggest ocean excited the imagination of intellectuals, what has been called 'the age of wonder' also introduced currents into life at sea that would challenge the natural order. For Jack the Pacific was utopia; it could also be dystopia.

A journey to the far side of the world took a long time in 1768 – but thanks to the *Endeavour*'s nimble sailing qualities, and fair weather off Cape Horn, less than eight months – just 230 days to be precise – passed from her Portsmouth departure to reaching Tahiti. Another 146 days then went by before the ship's boy, Young Nick, piped up from the masthead that he could see the Ends of the Earth. At the time it was believed he had found the Great Southern Continent – a mistake, it turned out, because no such land mass existed; but it ensured Young Nick was not forgotten.*

Forty-two hands had sailed in the *Endeavour*. They witnessed wonders, experienced sensual delights, and, on a sturdy tub not even 100 feet long, were the constant companions of Cook and Banks. They celebrated three Christmases with those great men, when, as Banks recalled, 'all good Christians, that is to say all hands, got abominably drunk . . . Wind, thank God, very moderate or the Lord knows what would have come of us.'[2] Their deeds are unknown, their names forgotten. The only one who did gain a kind of immortality was Young Nick. His keen sight earned him a gallon of rum and his name being entered on Cook's first chart. And so it is that Young Nick's Head is found on maps of New Zealand to this day.

Thirteen out of the crew of forty-two left their bones in the South Seas, including the remarkable figure of John Ravenhill, a sailmaker from Hull, thought by Cook to be aged between seventy and eighty and who was 'generally more or less drunk every day'.[3] So too did John Thurman, a New Yorker, and Jeho Dozey from Brazil.[4] There was also the melancholy figure of a young marine described by Banks as 'remarkably quiet and industrious' who jumped overboard after being accused of stealing a sealskin tobacco pouch from Cook's cabin; Banks cited this as an example of 'the powerful effects shame can work

---

* Young Nick is an enigma. Various suggestions have been made as to his identity – that he was part of Banks's entourage, that he was a stowaway. In fact, his origin is unknown. The muster shows only that he was taken on at Tahiti in April 1769 as a supernumerary, then designated as surgeon's servant (ADM 36/8569, muster of the *Endeavour*). He was clearly unknown to Banks, who wrote of his sighting of New Zealand on 7 October: 'At half past one a small boy who was at the mast head called out Land.' While named in the muster as Nicholas Young, he was universally known as Young Nick and, having joined at Tahiti, the likelihood is he was an islander, adopted by the crew, given a name that would define him as a ship's boy, and encouraged to show activity aloft.

upon young minds', though it may equally speak to the effect of close confinement experienced on a ship.*

By the time England was sighted again in July 1771 – by Young Nick, once more at the masthead – three years had passed, and everyone had suffered from the malaise Banks described as 'the longing for home which the Physicians have gone so far as to esteem a disease under the name of Nostalgia'.[5] Yet returning to the land they had despaired of seeing again released complex emotions too, and memories were apt to haunt those who had dwelt all too briefly in Paradise.

Coming ashore, the surviving Jacks experienced a sensation known to everyone who had spent months at sea. So conditioned were they to the sense of a rolling deck that the land felt as if it were moving under their feet. They were paid off, said their farewells, and departed for homes in Scotland, Cornwall, Northumberland and, in one case, Venice. Among them was William Dawson, who had left his Deptford home a teenage boy and returned a messenger from Xanadu, bearing tales at which his family and friends could only gawp in disbelief.

From its earliest days seafaring had been a process that explored prevailing myths and imagined realms. Jonathan Swift's *Gulliver's Travels*, published in 1726, with the voyaging of its protagonist to 'several remote nations of the world' and the unnerving inhabitants who dwelt there, was almost as much a reflection of these fables as it was a satire. Fear of monsters lurking beyond the horizon was one strand rooted deep in the contemporary psyche. Another was

---

* *The Endeavour Journal of Joseph Banks*, entry for 25 March 1769. Other instances of jumping overboard as a form of suicide are recorded. However, a more common cause of the phenomenon was a condition known as calenture, associated with tropical climates and vitamin deficiency, which was common enough to be defined in Johnson's *Dictionary* as 'a distemper curious to sailors in hot climates; wherein they imagine the sea to be green fields and will throw themselves into it if not restrained'. In one recorded case in 1780, 'a very fine young fellow' named Lloyd, suffering from a fever in terrible heat, leapt from the gangway of the frigate *Sybil* 'in a raving insane fitt . . . supposing the Sea [to be] a green field' (Pasley, pp. 70–1).

a legendary land of milk and honey. Never did these elements combine quite as they did in the greatest of all oceans, the Pacific.

On the island called Otaheiti, or Tahiti, the Endeavours had engaged with a raw landscape – beaches, volcanoes, gorges – and people of dark, naked beauty who, despite a poverty not unlike their own, lived lives of bewitching abandon out in the sun, who rode giant waves on wooden boards, painted their bodies and roasted animals over open fires. Otherwise the natives' food fell from trees and, as Cook wrote, 'benevolent Nature hath not only Supply'd them with necessarys, but with abundance of Superfluities'.

But what really enchanted the seamen about the New Island of Love, as the French had called Tahiti, was its open sensuality. Amid the breaking surf, palm-fringed beaches and volcanic peaks, Cook noted how nubile young

A woman of Eua, one of the Friendly Islands as Tonga was known. Beauty, nudity and innocence in the South Seas revealed a new world to seafarers.

women would display themselves in a ceremonial celebration of nudity, 'with as much innocence as one could possibly conceive [while] exposed entirely naked from the waist down'.[6] Another early English seafarer wrote:

> All the sailors swore they neaver saw handsomer made women in their lives and declard they would all live on two thirds allowance rather [than] lose an opportunity of getting a Girl apiece.[7]

Sexual favours did not come exactly free, but a small piece of metal was enough: 'One ship's nail for one ordinary fuck,' as Richard Holmes put it.[8] The plainest seaman was transformed into a swaggering rake, while the ship's carpenter fulminated at the disappearance of entire sackfulls of nails. Cook, indeed, noted with exasperation in his journal that a hand named Archibald Wolf had been given two dozen lashes for stealing 'a large quantity of spike nails'.[9] While Banks and the other learned gentlemen were off making their astronomical observations, the men were disappearing into huts set among coconut and breadfruit groves, having 'procured temporary wives amongst the natives, with whom they cohabited'. (When Banks did find time to consort with a local woman it was in a more formal manner, after she had been paraded before him to cast off her robe and display 'her naked beauties to me'.)

Paradise was not for eternity, however, just a few months. From Tahiti and observing the Transit of Venus, the *Endeavour* was set on a course south-west in search of a Great Southern Continent. What they found was New Zealand, where the natives, far from the sensuous welcome extended in Tahiti, came alongside in canoes displaying human heads 'with the hair on and flesh very green'. Francis Wilkinson, an able seaman, wrote in horror: 'Saw one of the Indians with the arm bone of a man, eating the flesh from it.'[10]

For the next six months they kept a healthy distance from the locals while charting the coast of New Zealand, before heading west. Just weeks later land was sighted again and the *Endeavour* started north, passing up the eastern shore of this fresh discovery, which Cook named New South Wales. Their first landing was at a sheltered spot he called Botany Bay where the natives again turned out to be unwelcoming, if less menacing. When, a few days later, an able seaman named Forby Sutherland, who hailed from Orkney, became the first Briton to die in Australia, the cause was consumption rather than any act of hostility.

The real trouble only started after they rounded the northern tip of Terra Australis and found Batavia, the Dutch outpost on Java, in the grip of a bloody flux, or dysentery. Death ran the length of *Endeavour*, carrying off an even higher proportion of gentlemen and petty officers than seamen; most of Banks's entourage died here.

Overall, however, the health regime established by Cook was ground-breaking – particularly in what it showed about preventing scurvy. The Endeavours were the healthiest body of seamen yet to reach the Antipodes, thanks to a diet of salted cabbage and lemons. They did not particularly take to the sauerkraut until Cook made a point of treating it as a luxury, because, as he said: 'Such are the tempers and dispositions of seamen in general that what-ever you give them out of the common way – altho' it be ever so much for their good – it will not go down, and you will hear nothing but murmurings against the Man that invented it; but the moment they see their superiors set a value upon it, it becomes the first stuff in the world and the inventor an honest fellow.'[11] Not one man died of scurvy in three years. (Of the ninety-five personnel to have sailed on the *Endeavour*, thirty-one succumbed to dysentery, three from consumption, three drowned, two froze to death and one died of alcohol poisoning.)[12]

A second legacy of the voyage – one adopted by seamen to the point that it became as distinctive a mark of their identity as dress or gait – was a Tahitian custom of body painting known as Tattowing, which involved 'inlaying the colour of black under their skins in such a manner as to be indelible', although the operation, with shards of bone or shell, was painful, 'especially the Tattowing of the Buttocks'.[13]

Along with tattoos, venereal disease and tales they would be able to relate for the rest of their lives, the Endeavours returned with Cook's praises for having 'gone through the fatigues and dangers of the voyage with that Cheerfulness and Allertness that will always do honour to British Seamen'. But also, perhaps, there was a sense of dislocation.

Encounters between the islanders of the North and South Seas altered perspectives on both sides. Cook's next expedition came back with a Tahitian named Omai, who was presented at court by Banks and took to English society as if born to it; Dr Johnson and Fanny Burney were among those to perceive the virtues of a 'noble savage', though Omai's views on fidelity – 'two wives, very good; three wives, very, very good' – were closer to Jack's than to those of the literati. Once he went home, Omai appeared out of sorts with island life and never fully assimilated with his own people again. As an English youth who had been of that little company on *Endeavour* to stare in bewilderment at the far side of the world, taking in the magic and mysterious diversity of our planet, William Dawson, who now found himself back in Deptford and still aged only twenty-two, may have understood why.

The romanticism of the early Pacific visits could not endure. Just as the scientific aspects of Cook's first voyage quickly gave way to imperial and commercial designs, so the fragile innocence of those initial encounters was lost. In 1776, in the *Resolution*, Cook left England for the last time to explore the North-West Passage – the corridor linking the North Atlantic and the Pacific. He did not find it, but became the first European to land on an archipelago he called the Sandwich Islands. There a spate of thefts by the islanders provoked him to a fatal over-reaction; in a confrontation on the beach, Cook was clubbed and stabbed – dying in the surf of what is now Hawaii.

The South Seas came to occupy a haunting place in the seaman's psyche – partly because of their remoteness, but also because they seethed with unpredictability. The island on a pink horizon could just as easily be inhabited by demonic cannibals brandishing green-skinned skulls as by half-dressed nymphs offering their favours; and it could turn seamen no less than Polynesians or Melanesians into savages and sensualists. Among Cook's officers on his fatal voyage was William Bligh, whose return to these waters eight years later would precipitate events more turbulent still.

The first common seaman to leave an account of sailing the Pacific, the next of our Jacks to record his adventures in detail, came from a world starkly different in its austerity. John Nicol lost his mother as a child and was raised near Edinburgh by a strict Presbyterian father who was determined that he should be educated and learn a respectable trade. 'But my unsteady propensities did not allow me to make the most of the schooling I got,' Nicol recalled, adding, tellingly: 'I had read *Robinson Crusoe* many times over and longed to be at sea.'[14]

John Nicol signed on at the age of twenty-one in 1776, ten years after William Spavens came ashore for the last time. While Spavens had seen the emergence of British naval power, Nicol would be witness to its consolidation and he was still at sea twenty-two years later, serving at the Battle of the Nile. He was no foremast cavalier, however, but a romantic wanderer. Forever in thrall to the horizon, Nicol suffered from a condition identified by Norse seafarers as *aefintyr* – a spirit of adventure brought on by restless curiosity. His other quest was for love, which he found only once, and that with a woman convict on a transport ship to Australia. She bore his child and after they were parted he spent years crossing the oceans in a tireless mission to trace her.

Of Nicol's appearance we have no record before he was sighted – in 1822, when he was sixty-seven, tottering feebly around Edinburgh while trying to scavenge coal for warmth – by the chronicler who set down his life story. Even then, reduced as he was, his memory and spirit were intact.[15]

As an idealistic volunteer, he found himself on a navy tender with pressed men and was rudely surprised to discover they were not going to sea for the love of it, and shocked by their cursing and 'loose talk'. His daily prayers were soon abandoned and he became 'a sailor like the rest', but Nicol was never less than reflective. Like Spavens before him, he shipped to the West Indies and like Spavens was horrified by the treatment of slaves (a natural sensitivity among seamen to bondage, it might be thought) while noting: 'No sound of woe is to be heard in this land of oppression [only] wild music and song, the shout of mirth and dancing, resounded along the beach and from the valleys.'[16] And if he was soon seaman enough to appreciate the slave women brought on board to serve the hands' sexual needs, he felt guilt and pity too: 'poor things! And all to obtain a bellyful of victuals.'[17]

Like Spavens, Nicol may have had a limited education but he was a natural storyteller. Take his description of the rafts of frontier folk on the St Lawrence:

> They were covered with turf, and wood huts upon them, smoke curling from the roofs, and children playing before the doors and the stately matron on her seat, sewing or following her domestic occupations, while the husband sat upon the front with his long pole . . . They had floated thus down the majestic St Lawrence hundreds of miles. It looked like magic and reminded me of the fairies I had often heard of, to see the children sporting and singing in chorus on these floating masses.[18]

Nicol's first great enterprise was to join 'a voyage of discovery and trade' under Captain Nathaniel Portlock to the Pacific. Portlock was a navy officer who had sailed with Cook and was a natural choice to lead an expedition exploring opportunities for trading fur between Alaska and China. In 1785 the *King George* and *Queen Charlotte* set south-west into the Atlantic. These two taut little vessels, of 320 and 200 tons respectively, would spend the next three years on another grand circumnavigation of the globe.

Nicol is sparing in detail of life among the fifty-nine-man crew over the interminable months they spent proceeding south-west across the Atlantic before rounding the Horn into the Pacific. Crossing the Line involved the usual capers for first-timers such as Nicol – duckings from the yardarm or shaving – rituals that would have seemed almost quaint by the time they saw England again, having by then passed over the Equator five times. In her global trawl the *King George* would leave something like 35,000 miles in her wake, at rates that ranged from the purely static, becalmed under a tropical sky and slack canvas, to languid balmy airs that shifted her on at 5 miles an hour or so before brisking up to around 10 miles, but which could never attain the unimaginable 20 miles an hour.

Nicol's greater gift is for describing the images that are set within the detail of the log kept by Captain Portlock – like his account of catching a shark off Hawaii which was found to be 19 feet in length and to contain four pigs, four turtles and forty-eight baby sharks – with which his narrative chimes remarkably in content.[19]

They anchored off Hawaii on 16 November, sighting dolphins, flying fish and tropical birds as they did so. These were the first ships to visit Hawaii since Cook's death six years earlier and Portlock was naturally wary of allowing men ashore. When islanders came on board, bearing gifts of pigs, yams and breadfruit, an elderly bosun shook with terror, convinced a massacre must follow. Once more half-naked Polynesian women helped to ease the tension. As Nicol put it in his rather prim way, 'almost every man on board took a native wife' – including the gunner, whose choice was so enormous she had to be hoisted on board like cargo.[20] A pattern was established: in the evening, the women would come up the side, 'calling for their husbands by name'; in the morning, they would go ashore with presents. It was no longer a single nail for a fuck; beads and buttons had become the currency of love.

Whether for its sexual abundance, or because 'the people [were] so kind and obliging, the climate so fine and provisions so abundant', Nicol would reflect on the Hawaiian archipelago as an elysium – 'the best country I ever was in'. From the island of Kauai he retained a tender memory of the friendship struck up between the chief and a hand named Dickson. The chief, according to Nicol, loved Dickson better than any other man in the ship, and was taught by him to sing 'Rule, Britannia!' They would perform it in duet, the chief with eyes popping to mimic Dickson's squint and being cheered on as he grappled with the English lyrics that come out something like 'Tule Billicany, Billicany tule . . .'

Christmas that year was spent under a tropical sun off Oahu, near modernday Honolulu, where they feasted on roasted hogs and Portlock dispensed a carefully hoarded cask of wine. Two of the islanders were evidently so taken with the festivities they declared a determination 'to go to England with us' until canoes came out with their mothers, who 'wept continually until they left the ship'.[21]

The ship's company were still reflecting happily when they reached America, where the natives presented a more forbidding aspect. Off Vancouver Island, the ship was blasted by furious winter gales while pelts were traded with Indians who turned violent 'if any of our men were found with their women'. Not that these particular females were thought very desirable, being 'much disfigured by slitting their lips and placing large pieces of wood in them shaped like a saucer'. After 'a good deal of hardship on this coast', Nicol and his mates were delighted to return to Hawaii where they again embraced and touched noses with the islanders, and 'our deck was one continued scene of joy'.[22]

Polynesia filled Nicol's heart but another land captured his imagination. Tales about China had fascinated him even before the *King George* and *Queen Charlotte* set a course due west for Canton to trade their fur cargoes. By the time they came in sight of this fantasy land, on 17 November 1787, he was at a pitch of excitement:

> I scarcely believed I was so fortunate as really to be in China. As we sailed up the river I would cast my eyes from side to side. The thoughts and ideas I had pictured in my mind of it were not lessened in brilliancy, rather increased. The immense number of buildings that extended as far as the eye could reach, their fantastic shapes and gaudy colours, their trees and flowers so like their paintings . . . all serve to fix the mind of a stranger upon his first arrival.[23]

His hosts tried to constrain his curiosity. Going ashore at Canton, Nicol was frustrated to find that outsiders were not admitted to the city and although he managed to reach the gates a number of times, 'all my ingenuity could not enable me to cross the bar'. He was rare among visitors, however, in being invited into a Chinese home, after saving a child from drowning. To start with he was apprehensive about what he might be fed, having traded rats caught by his dog, Neptune, to the locals: 'The Chinese, I really believe, eat anything there is life in,' he declared; but they presented meals in grand style:

> I like their manner of setting out the table at dinner. All that is to be eaten is placed upon the table at once, and all the liquors at the same time. You have all before you and may make your choice.[24]

Two centuries on, Nicol's observations retain their enthusiasm and authenticity, whether he is talking about Polynesian sensuality or Chinese food. (Not all contacts were conducted in so blithe a spirit, and the ship's log indicates a frisson of tension on Christmas Day when 'the Chinese stopped all fresh provisions for the English ships in port'.)[25]

All this took place against the background of a voyage into uncharted waters. No British ship had sailed to China from Hawaii before and Portlock had hired a local pilot in the Marianas Islands midway across the Pacific to guide their way to Canton. In parts of the East China and South China Seas, islands littered the water like reefs and shoals, and just as an unexpected land mass could be a haven of hospitality, food and water, it might as easily destroy a ship and all those on board of her. Finding a way through them here was more a matter of observation and the taking of soundings than navigation. Portlock appears to have come close to being overwhelmed. Anxious to collect as much data as possible, he made constant entries of readings and sightings in the ship's log, so that in places it resembles the scratchings of an unhinged mathematician.

Even in the Indian Ocean, British ships were navigated at this stage by a blend of experience, intuition and luck rather than by the accuracy of their charts.[26] When the *King George* and *Queen Charlotte* departed from China, homeward bound with a cargo of tea, they were in relatively familiar waters as they passed south through the Sunda Strait and into the Indian Ocean in April 1788. Yet still they remained dependent on data collected by East India Company ships. And this was all too fallible, as recent events had demonstrated.

The *Grosvenor* was a typical Indiaman of her day – 800 tons, built to transport passengers in relative comfort as well as cargo. Homeward bound from Calcutta in 1782, she was packed with both as she followed the route across the Indian Ocean known as the Outer Passage, passing east of Mauritius and south of Madagascar before tacking west to southern Africa.

The dangers of this shore were well known. Mariners had recently been reminded of this by the fate of the *Dodington*, an Indiaman wrecked with great loss of life in Algoa Bay because erroneous Company charts showed the coast of south-east Africa some degrees west of its true position. Navigators had been urged to 'be very cautious not to haul to the northward too soon'. The admonition was wasted on Captain John Coxon of the *Grosvenor* and on the night of 4 August she went aground.

The wreck of the *Grosvenor* has a special place in seafaring folklore. For one thing, it illustrated what might happen when rich but vulnerable passengers were cast away with seamen. There was another dimension to the disaster, however, for it landed rich and poor alike – and women and children – among tribal people they regarded with dread. Thanks to a Venetian hand named Francisco Feancon who swam through the waves with a rope, thirty-four passengers and ninety crew reached safety; but once they were ashore, order disintegrated.

It is possible that the sailors would have abandoned the gentlefolk anyway. They were more than 400 miles from the Dutch settlement at the Cape, and the appearance of half-naked Pondo tribesmen, with high conical hairstyles and daubed with red mud, unnerved the castaways. Still, the Pondo were not hostile to start with. Their interest was in metal from the wreck. What the situation cried out for was leadership. Unfortunately, Captain Coxon proved no more capable ashore than he was at sea. When he ordered the hands to offer no resistance as the Pondo started to plunder their belongings, they decided he was not to be trusted. Having elected the second mate their leader, the sailors started away, leaving Company nabobs and their families with senior members of the crew. From this point a pattern noted by a hand named John Hynes during the wreck would recur: 'All hands [did] the best they could for themselves.'[27]

The surest instinct was demonstrated early on by Joshua Glover, a topman who went off on his own to join the Pondo. Glover was dismissed as a loon, 'disturbed in his mind', but on the contrary had had the sense to salvage from the wreck a chisel and tools with which he carved wooden figures – and so fashioned a new life for himself. Glover was described as 'the carpenter' in Pondo oral history, and remained among his new tribe until his death.

The *Grosvenor* epitomized the horrors that might befall a ship's company when order was lost. Having been abandoned by the hands, the families were then left by the officers. Of those who had begun the voyage in the quarters reserved for gentry, none reached home. Instead, at least one of the women and three girls became African wives and mothers.

As for the crew, further separations took place as they made their way down the coast, trudging across dunes, clambering down gorges, swimming rivers, and leaving behind those too exhausted or feeble to go on. In the absence of food they ate grass, drank their own urine, and contemplated cannibalizing the bodies of dead shipmates. Almost all died.

Four months after the wreck, and having covered almost 400 miles on foot, a party of six men reached an outlying Dutch homestead. These survivors were distinguished by their youth and strength: Jeremiah Evans, born amid the lanes of Wapping, was aged eighteen, while Barney Leary was a young bullock of a fellow with 'very robust habit of body'.

The Cape authorities sent a rescue party up country where more hands were found, including William Habberley from Wapping, Thomas Lewis from Belfast, and Feancon from Venice, their saviour at the wreck – all living contentedly among tribal people. Only Evans, however, opted in the end to stay in Africa.

Pragmatism was of a part with self-preservation. Those who went to sea recognized that, in extremis, it really was a case of every man for himself. The Grosvenors were not unusual in abandoning the vulnerable. Their story became a subject of horrified fascination at home only because the women had been left, not to drown, but to the mercy of supposed savages. It took another famous shipwreck to refashion the survivalist tradition: the steamer *Birkenhead* also went down on the coast of southern Africa, when 445 men obeyed orders to sacrifice themselves so all fifty-six women and children could be brought safely off. However, the creation of that code, of 'Women and Children First', did not come until 1852.

The experience of living on the sea – within its moodiness, mystery, fury and unknowable majesty – left a mark on the most prosaic soul. Awe was never far away. And the utter unpredictability of what lay across the horizon explains much about the seafaring character, including those traits of impulsiveness and improvidence.

John Nicol was homeward bound in April 1788, midway across the Indian Ocean and in a region notorious for hurricanes – no fewer than seven Indiamen were dashed to eternity in one terrible season – yet the log of the *King George* shows they were under a following breeze and a comfortable press of sail. They passed around the coast of southern Africa – graveyard of the *Grosvenor* – without a sight of land. Over some 8,000 miles from the Sunda Strait to St Helena, day after day passed under soft skies with a sweet singing from the rigging, the untroubled continuity of blue-water sailing. The greatest mishap suffered by the men was eating albacore and bonito 'hung in the rigging to dry [where] the moon's rays have the effect of making them poisonous'. Nicol was alarmed to note that 'men's heads swelled twice their ordinary size' but could conclude: 'We all recovered.'[28]

They came to off Margate on 21 August. Three years had passed, but little else had changed, least of all the weather. Tropical skies were replaced by grey haze and heavy showers.[29] Their voyage of circumnavigation had accomplished no great feat of discovery, nor had the enterprise made a fortune for their employers, the King George's Sound Company. All that endures of another relatively minor epic is Nicol's account of it, and a less vivid one by Portlock published in 1789.[30]

Nicol went home to Scotland where at first he experienced 'a sensation of joy only to be felt by those who have been absent for some time. Every remembrance was rendered more dear, every scene was increased in beauty.' For a while he even considered settling down. Then a letter came with tidings that another voyage across the world was in the offing; and Nicol found 'my wandering propensities rekindled with as great vigour as ever'.[31]

HANDS ACROSS THE ATLANTIC
1775-83

THE North Atlantic was the maritime equivalent of Jack's backyard. He had been crossing that ocean for centuries and since the establishment of the North American colonies the flow of settlers and merchandise between Old England and New England had surged like a tide. Seamen on a transatlantic run were as familiar with Boston as with Bristol.

Unsurprisingly, therefore, America's War of Independence touched a rare nerve of uncertainty in Jack. Fighting a Frenchman or a Spaniard came naturally. This new foe was a quite different fish. Up to this point he had been not an enemy at all but a shipmate. He not only spoke the same language, he shared the same popular culture of folk tales and songs. He was part of a common history. Diversity on British ships may have reached a point that a mess could have among its number Danes, Swedes, Italians, Portuguese and Germans; but by far the largest proportion of hands from outside the British Isles hailed from the American colonies. This was a conflict that divided kith and kin across the Atlantic.

The outcome was always going to be decided on land, where the fighting started and brought early victories to a supposedly ill-disciplined rabble. No such outcome was ever likely at sea, where the Navy maintained an armada off New York with a combined firepower that exceeded all the American guns facing them from the shore.¹ The declaration by Congress of the colonies as free and independent states was followed by the formation of an embryonic US navy consisting of two ships, two brigs and a sloop. How their lordships at the Admiralty chortled at that. Then, in the summer of 1778, France joined in, sending a great fleet across the Atlantic to exploit the old enemy's difficulties.

There, stationed off Newfoundland, was John Nicol. Last glimpsed among orientals in China and cannibals in the Pacific, the young Scot was in a 28-gun frigate, the *Surprise*. He retained an eye for the quirks of humanity: Newfoundland he thought an unnervingly primitive place, from the vicious-ness of fishermen's feuds to the practice of incest in marriage; but the *Surprise* helped to knock any last semblance of faintness out of him. Her hands were mainly Irishmen, who 'fought like devils and the captain was fond of them on that account'. In fact, Captain Samuel Reeves was a tough disciplinarian, but one who gave his men latitude at anchor. Officers would go ashore at St John's, leaving the Irish to get drunk and turn pugnacious among themselves – and then with the English and Scots. Nicol tried to stay out of the way but once, when 'the crew were all fighting amongst each other in their drink, an Irishman came staggering up, crying "Erin go bragh!" ["Ireland forever"] and made a blow at me. My Scottish blood rose in a moment and I was as throng as the rest.'²

The *Surprise* was based at Newfoundland to deal with American privateers playing havoc with trade and was out cruising on 30 September when a strange sail was sighted. It was the *Jason*, one of the most active rebel privateers and an emblem of the gulf that now divided motherland and colony; her captain, a redoubtable character named John Manley, was an old Devon man who had crossed over and become a senior rebel officer. On being hailed and ordered to surrender, Manley shouted back: 'Fire away! I have as many guns as you.' Nicol was full of respect: 'He had heavier metal but fewer men than *Surprise*.'³

Single-ship actions were dramatic and noisy but rarely prolonged. Manley, however, stuck to his guns for more than two hours. On the *Surprise*, Nicol was 'serving powder as busy as I could, the shot and splinters flying in all directions', when he was mortified to see the warlike Irish tars put his anvil –

he was in the ship as a cooper – into the muzzle of a cannon and roar in triumph as it blasted a gaping hole in *Jason*'s side.

Off on the *Jason*, a young hand named Joshua Davis from Boston came up on deck after an exchange of broadsides to find it a shambles:

> . . . the ship reeling one way and the other. The helmsman was killed and no one to take the wheel. The rigging, sails, yards, &c. were spread all over the deck. The wounded men were carried to the cockpit, the dead men lying on the deck and no one to throw them overboard.[4]

By the time the *Jason* struck she had eighteen dead and twelve wounded, the *Surprise* seven dead. The colonists were taken to St John's and, as was routine practice, urged to submit once more to the Crown or face transportation to jail in England. Manley refused and was duly shipped off to the Old Mill prison in Plymouth.

The reaction of the nineteen-year-old Joshua Davis was more typical. He was brought before Captain Reeves, who said, 'if I behaved well he would give me a midshipman's pay'. Davis agreed, and was then rather aggrieved to find himself back on the lower deck 'as a gunners' boy, at 16 shillings 6 pence per month'.[5]

In later years Davis was understandably keener to emphasize his revolutionary role, writing as 'an American citizen who was pressed and served on board six ships of the British Navy, was in seven engagements, once wounded, five times confined in irons and obtained his liberty by desertion'. The truth is that he went from one side to the other repeatedly during the war, and by his own account seems to have sung ballads to England's glory with the same gusto as Yankee songs. His is a remarkable tale. Moreover, he and Nicol are a unique case of hands who were in action against each other, then, astonishingly, served in the same ship and went on to write lower-deck memoirs. (Neither made any mention of the other and they lost touch; both were by then elderly and down on their luck – Davis, living in Boston in 1811, lame after 'repeated misfortunes', and Nicol back in his native Edinburgh, aged sixty-seven, and living from hand to mouth.)

Davis soon fell foul of Captain Reeves, who decided he was an idle fellow and put him ashore as a prisoner. If Davis is to be believed – and it may be said that his tales in general have the ring of an old hand's mythologizing – he escaped to Boston with eighty-four other Americans and joined another privateer before being captured again. This time he was transported to England, exasperating his captors with a song that went:

> *Vain Britain, boast no longer with proud indignity –*
> *By land your conq'ring legions, your matchless strength by sea;*
> *Since we your braver sons incens'd, our swords have girded on.*
> *Huzza, huzza, huzza, huzza, for war and Washington.*

On landing in Plymouth, Davis and his fellows were incarcerated in the Old Mill, 'for rebellion, piracy and high treason on His Majesty's high seas'.[6] Again he was offered his liberty on condition of agreeing to serve in the Navy. Within weeks he was entered on another British man-of-war, the 64-gun *Anson*, bound for the West Indies and singing a quite different tune.

The ambivalence of men like Davis was only natural. As well as ties of language, culture and geography, the act of seafaring itself made the connection between Britain and North America almost umbilical. Migration had become relatively easy and in 'a world in motion', as the age has been described, about 125,000 people had left Britain and Ireland between 1760 and 1775 and settled across the Atlantic.[7]

Seamen on both sides found their loyalties divided. Just as there were colonists who adhered to the king, there were Britons drawn to the notion that a man might be a citizen rather than a subject. It would be unwise, however, to characterize the maritime aspect of the American Revolution in terms of ideals and beliefs. From the available evidence, when Jack switched allegiance from the Crown to the Yankees, or deserted from the Yankees to the Crown, it was usually with the same pragmatic blend of self-interest and impulsiveness with which he changed ships.

Sailors raising a flag. An eighteenth-century sketch by the Anglo-American artist
John Singleton Copley represents men of graceful, almost balletic, form.

Yet if there was expediency, there was also a libertarian streak among
American Jacks that sat ill with the rigour of naval tradition and above all with
impressment. The fact that Britain – and the Admiralty in particular – had
come to treat the colony as a source of manpower and, therefore, seamen, had
come to stick in American throats like rank salt pork. Andrew Sherburne,
another rebel hand, recalled growing up in New Hampshire where:

> . . . sailors and fishermen used to dread the sight of a man of war's boat as
> a flock of sheep would dread the appearance of a wolf.[8]

Fear of the press was one thing. Gradually in America, however, it had been replaced by systematic resistance. Decades before the revolution, anti-impressment riots had rendered Boston, New York and Newport dangerous ground for red-coated enforcers. While violence never reached the levels seen in British ports, press gangs ceased to operate on American soil.[9] They still took men out of American merchant ships, and one study has gone so far as to argue that American seamen's resentment played a primary role in fostering the revolution; naval impressment was cited in the Declaration of Independence among the grievances against British rule.[10]

On the other side, old habits died hard. Long after the king's troops had been driven from America, his ships would impress hands deemed 'colonists' almost wherever they were to be found. While this only deepened antagonism towards the old country, so far as their lordships at the Admiralty were concerned there was no avoiding those stormy waters in the eternal demand for manpower.

The consequences were felt in policies starting to take shape which would redefine procedures in the coming century. For now, the figures may be left to speak for themselves. At the height of the Seven Years War, it has been calculated, the number of seafarers employed in British ships was an unprecedented 130,000. By the time of the American war it had risen to 150,000, of whom 110,000 were mustered by the Navy.[11] How many were Americans is impossible to say. (Ships' musters do not cast much light on the subject because the column for a seaman's place of birth was frequently left blank; that said, where such entries were made, the number of Americans is significant – up to a third on some ships.) What we do know is that some 900 American privateers and merchant vessels were captured and their hands first invited, then coerced, to recognize the Crown.[12] Those born in Britain, known as 'old country men', plainly found this easier than most. There were still a significant number, like Joshua Davis, for whom the prospect of regular food and pay was sufficient to overcome any initial reluctance.

Those of stronger character and diehard rebels would be brought to Britain and committed to the Old Mill prison where again they were invited to acknowledge their duty to the king by serving in his Navy. Out of 631 Americans imprisoned in the Old Mill between 1777 and 1781, roughly one in eight sought a pardon and entered a navy ship.[13]

Another group of Americans who went over to the enemy did so not reluctantly but as a form of escape. Proclamations that 'all indentured Servants willing to bear Arms' against the rebels would be freed and that 'Negroes [are] free as soon as they set on English ground', started a movement by black slaves. Thousands went over to the British and served in the Army, including a 300-strong 'Ethiopian Regiment'.[14] As for the Navy, fanciful claims have been made about the number of former slaves who signed on and served as seamen when no reliable figures exist and the individuals are anonymous. An exception was Anthony Mingus, who was to be found on British men-of-war until the end of the war.*

Of the British seamen drawn to American republicanism we have a somewhat clearer picture. An analysis of naval records shows a sharp spike in courts martial for desertion over the course of the war – from twelve in 1775 to twenty-nine in 1778 and sixty-six in 1781.[15] Most of these incidents occurred off America, and at least four cases involved hands who enlisted with the rebels and were caught and hanged.[16] How many Britons actually went over to the rebels is impossible to say, because we know only of the very small number who were recognized and captured. It is reasonable to assume, however, that many deserters – and there were hundreds if not thousands who ran from British ships off America during the war – found the new country to their liking and stayed, even if they did not actually fight for it.

Among those clearly sympathetic to the rebels was Francis Roderick, who deserted from the *Rose* off Rhode Island in 1775 and was captured at the guns

---

* A study of American slaves who served willingly in British ships is found in *Unkle Sommerset's Freedom: Liberty in England for Black Sailors* by Charles R. Foy, *Journal for Maritime Research*, 13:1, 2011. No personal information about Mingus is included, other than his listing in the three men-of-war in which he served, and Foy notes that most eighteenth-century black mariners are unidentified; Olaudah Equiano and Francis Barber are exceptions.

of an American privateer, *Alfred*, three years later. As he was clapped in irons he was heard to shout defiantly that given the chance, he would do the same thing again. Roderick declined to explain himself more fully at his court martial and was sentenced to hang.[17]

William Pearce from Bristol seems to have been another genuine republican. Aged twenty-four, he ran from the *Solebay* near Charleston and disappeared from sight, only to be captured more than a year later, hundreds of miles away, a soldier in an American regiment serving under the name of William Powell. Pearce was brought to New York where he suffered the freakish misfortune of being recognized by a marine from his old ship. He too was hanged.[18]

Another Englishman, Charles White, was luckier. White bore a navy brand on his cheek, the mark of a serial deserter, when he was captured along with the rest of the company of an American privateer; but having realized his peril in the form of an approaching British ship, he had a shipmate cut his face with a razor, obscuring his features. He escaped detection and, having been identified as an American, subsequently regained his liberty in an exchange of prisoners.[19]

Who can say what was in the minds of Stanley Cooper and James Read when they swam from the *Centurion* off New York in January 1778? The officer who ordered a marine to open fire at them in the water believed they meant to go over to the Americans. However, the fact that a search party later found them concealed on a ship bound for Jamaica indicated that they were ordinary deserters, and when their captain gave them a good character, declaring that he had brought them to a court martial only to deter others from running, they were given the unusually light punishment of fifty lashes apiece.[20]

There was also some vagueness over what William Dominey of the *Fox* really intended after his ship was captured by rebels in June 1777. Dominey's shipmates thought that he had become too friendly with their captors, and when the *Fox* was retaken he was brought to trial for deserting to the enemy. The proceedings were full of pathos. Dominey was an unworldly outsider who fraternized with the Americans to prevent his possessions being stolen and was won over by their easygoing warmth. The question was whether he had actually 'entered' with them. Some of his fellows thought not, but the evidence of a surgeon who saw Dominey acting as a powder monkey in action proved decisive – along with his own statement to another hand that 'he was better used by the Yankees than he had been in the King's service'. In his defence, Dominey declared: 'I never had any intention of entering with the rebels. What I did was in return for their civil usage, and to protect my things from being plundered.' He was still sentenced to hang.[21]

The American Revolution may also account for a wider trend in Britons' resistance to authority. Within a year, three cases came to trial involving conspiracies to seize the king's ships and defect with them. In the most serious, eight men of the *Narcissus* tried to recruit their shipmates off New York 'to take command of her and carry her into some rebel port'. Six were sentenced to hang, one received 500 lashes and another 200.[22]

Were there other signs of assertiveness? Certainly there had never been defiance of the press in quite the same startling form it took off Sheerness in 1779 when Thomas Wood managed to get his hands on a substantial quantity of gunpowder and smuggled it aboard the tender *Speedwell*, 'for the purpose of blowing up the fore-part of the deck, to enable the pressed men on board to make their escape'.[23]

The Admiralty would draw its own conclusions from such cases, leading to a stricter punishment regime for offences of disobedience. Patterns are not invariably clear, however, and inconsistencies abound. Initially, there may even have been a tendency towards flexibility rather than severity. The gunpowder plotter Wood was given 300 lashes, a number often inflicted for plain desertion. Other cases that might have been expected to bring automatic death sentences included the mutiny by two men who plotted to seize the sloop *Savage* off Halifax in 1778 with the help of American prisoners and who received 500 lashes apiece.

What the Navy ought to have learned from this surge of libertarian spirit was that men worked better when they were not subjected to casual violence. The practice of 'starting', the beating of men to their stations with sticks by petty officers – always detested by all self-respecting hands – was being challenged, and Captain John Inglefield wrote approvingly of a new method of:

... dividing and quartering the officers with the men, and making them responsible for that portion of duty allotted them, without noise, or the brutal method of driving the sailors like cattle with sticks ... By a just proportion of labour falling to the lot of each man, instead of the management of it being entrusted to the partiality and brutality of boatswains' mates, the men were kept in better temper; and were less harassed and fatigued in their spirits, as well as in their bodies.[24]

Inglefield's conclusion, that during the war discipline was 'brought to as great a degree of perfection, almost, as it is capable of receiving', may sound too blithe; a considerate captain, he held to the traditional opinion that Jack would undertake any task cheerfully if he was allowed to 'enjoy the society of his mistress and be permitted to drink his skin full of liquor'. It remained the case, however, that the great majority of men were indeed dutiful as well as loyal, and a far cry from the pathetic creatures described by another captured American hand, Israel Potter, as 'an exceedingly oppressed and forlorn people'.*

Events on the sloop *Scorpion* in the summer of 1778 are a case in point.

The *Scorpion* was at anchor off New York when William Swift entered her on 4 July; the date is unlikely to have been coincidental for Swift and his accomplice, Edward Power, were rebel agents.[25] Swift, who had signed on as a volunteer, went about ingratiating himself with other new hands. 'He threw himself in my way,' said William Wilson, 'saying he had friends ashore with a fine purse of money.'

Nothing is known of the origins of Swift and Power. Even the names have the defiant ring of aliases, and Swift's only admission at his trial was that before volunteering for the *Scorpion* he had served on an American frigate. As an *agent provocateur* he was well out of his depth, however. His efforts had an air of desperation. Trying to impress another new hand, he claimed that:

---

* Israel Potter's colourful narrative of his capture and impressment was used by Hermann Melville as the basis for his novel of the same name. However, Potter was writing after his return home from years in Britain and was trying to obtain a pension as 'one of the few survivors who fought and bled for American independence'. As a historical source, the *Life and Remarkable Adventures of Israel R. Potter* is partisan and unreliable.

He could raise eight men in as many minutes to take away the cutter, that there was arms in the cutter and if he got clear he would bring a rebel frigate alongside and blow the ship out the water.[26]

When Swift urged George Turner to join him, he declined, saying: 'I was a deserter before, but was forgiven.' Meantime, Wilson had gone to the captain and exposed Swift and Power as 'agents employed to entice away the King's subjects'. The evidence against Power was not very compelling and he escaped with 100 lashes. Swift was consigned to the yardarm.[27]

Fear, dutifulness, bewilderment . . . all are to be seen in the lives caught on the edge of the war. And so too those other forces at work in Jack's life – elements akin to the tides and currents that shaped ships' movements and that might carry men off on a quite unexpected course – forces of the kind that help to explain the later career of Joshua Davis.

Davis never went into much detail about how he found himself back on a king's ship. Once independence was won, American seamen tended to emphasize the miseries of life in the Navy and in this Davis was no exception. Although writing in his memoir that he had been sent forcibly on the *Anson*, he probably volunteered in order to get out of the Old Mill prison in Plymouth.

The *Anson* sailed for the Caribbean late in 1781, just as news from across the Atlantic reached England. French intervention on the American side had altered the war at sea from small-ships actions to fleet battles, and when the Comte de Grasse prevented a British fleet entering Chesapeake Bay in September, the Army under Lord Cornwallis was cut off and surrendered. America had won its independence.

What remained was a new phase of the Anglo-French war for global domination, which for the time being turned on control of the West Indies and its commercial riches. Joshua Davis was in the *Anson* with Admiral George Rodney's fleet when it caught up with an equal French and Spanish squadron preparing to invade Jamaica.

The Battle of the Saintes was notable for its bloodiness, its unusually clear outcome and for the tactic known as 'breaking the line'. Joshua Davis, as so often in a view from the lower deck, does not touch on strategy, but he retained two especially vivid memories. The first was of the fleet's entire livestock being hove overboard to clear space before the battle, so 'cows, sheep, hogs, ducks, hencoops &c. were seen floating for miles around us'. The battle raged for the next four hours, by which time, Davis wrote, 'we could scarcely see for smoke'. During a lull the men were served raw salt pork and bread before battle was resumed and the 64-gun *Anson* found herself caught with an 84 on the larboard quarter and a 74 on the starboard bow. Davis was on the poop, helping the signal officers, when a ball:

> . . . struck Capt. Blair in the side, which cut him entirely in halves. The first Lieutenant ordered the men to take his remains, and throw them overboard. We continued fighting under the command of the first Lieutenant, until a shot took his leg off, and he was carried below.[28]

Ordered aloft to help repair the rigging, Davis heard a thunderous explosion as the 74-gun *César* blew up, before he was wounded in the leg. British casualties that day ran to more than 1,000 with 200 dead, but the French had some 3,000 killed and 5,000 taken. Five of their ships of the line were captured or sunk, including the 110-gun *Ville de Paris*.

The victorious tars had a new ballad in honour of this triumph and Davis, so recently singing 'huzza, huzza for war and Washington', now joined in a chorus to British glory:

> *Success to our good officers, Our seamen bold, and jolly tars,*
> *Who like brave daring sons of Mars, Take delight for to fight*
> *And vindicate Old England's right, or die for Britain's glory.**

---

* The words were set down by Davis on page 38 of his memoir. He stated that that song was 'sung by the officers', but the fact that he reproduced the entire twelve verses indicates a considerable degree of familiarity with it. The significance of song in Jack's life is examined in

Had Rodney followed up his victory, the entire French fleet might have been taken. As it was, Jamaica was saved and Britain had regained control of the Atlantic. While still lamenting the loss of the American colonies, its command of the oceans was once more secure.

There were other benefits, fresh insights. While the fleet was in the Caribbean, the physician Sir Gilbert Blane had experimented with a new regime of cleanliness and diet. 'A true seaman is in general cleanly,' he remarked, 'but the greater part of men in a ship of war require a degree of compulsion to make them so.' The rewards of rigorously enforcing Blane's regime – based on ventilation, clean clothes, and fresh fruit and vegetables – were astonishing. The death rate in one of the unhealthiest climates for seamen was reduced to 1.4 per cent a year – which, the historian N. A. M. Rodger has noted, made them probably the healthiest body of British subjects anywhere in the world.[29]

Joshua Davis was in the Navy for another five years before returning to his home town of Boston. By the time he sat down to pen his memoirs a further fifteen years had passed and, as he acknowledged, he wrote them only because he was in desperate need of money. The year was 1811, anti-British sentiment was on the rise again and Davis had quite a story to tell. To those of his countrymen 'anxious to know the fate of fathers, husbands or sweethearts' he offered little solace: 'Many are on board those hellish floating torments . . . the ships of his Brittanick Majesty.' Nor did he pull his punches in describing the treatment their loved ones might expect, outlining the procedures for hanging by the yardarm, flogging through the fleet and running the gauntlet. To any Yankee unfortunate enough to find himself on a British ship his advice was to mess with other Americans and stay out of the way

> . . . until an opportunity offers when you may make your escape to your native country, and finally get clear of these dens of horror, cruelty, confusion, and continual uproar.[30]

Singing for the Nation: Balladry, Naval Recruitment and the Language of Patriotism in Eighteenth-Century Britain by James Davey, in *The Mariner's Mirror*, 103:1, 2017.

Whether Davis's narrative helped to ease his final years financially is not recorded, but it was certainly prettily timed to touch a chord. A year later, in 1812, Britain and the United States went to war again, for reasons that had partly to do with the continued impressment of American seamen, and this time the conflict was fought largely at sea.

Not all Americans took so bleak a view of navy life; and one who spent a virtual lifetime at sea under the British flag had credentials that define him as a stand-out figure in Jack's story.

———

Jacob Nagle had fought for American independence on land and sea before signing on with the old enemy to serve in one of the king's ships. He would have the rare distinction of encountering both George Washington and Horatio Nelson in the flesh, and of sailing with the East India Company and the First Fleet to Botany Bay. He also survived shipwreck and being cast away, all the while keeping a journal that is in every sense an epic – the tale of an adventurer to rank with any from Joseph Conrad's imagination. Jacob Nagle was Foremast Jack writ large.

He was fifteen when he marched off to fight the king. His father served in Washington's army and in 1777 Jacob set out from home in Pennsylvania to join him, starting a warrior life on land and sea in which he always served with distinction while remaining on the lower deck. As the historian who brought Nagle's journal to light has observed, this was not due to lack of ability, but rather to an entire absence of ambition, combined with wiliness: 'He could drink, carouse, throw a punch, pick up a girl, and tell off an officer with the best of his shipmates, but he chose his moments for each of these activities carefully. There was a shrewd intelligence, a solid self-assurance . . . and an instinct for self-protection that explains his longevity.'* Nagle's military career

* Dann, pp. xviii–xix. As John C. Dann, the journal's editor has said, it appears almost too good to be true – a diary in the original hand, discovered almost 200 years on, vivid and accurate, and complete with heart-warmingly phonetic spellings. Reviewing it in *The Mariner's Mirror*, N. A. M. Rodger wrote: 'None has ever conveyed so much authentic and important evidence about the life of the common man at sea.'

was brief. An artilleryman, he was at the Battle of Brandywine when Washington rode up 'and enquired how we came on'. He might have been killed then but the shells that landed nearby 'never busted' and he joined the retreat to Philadelphia. After that Nagle found himself 'inclined for the see [sea]'.[31]

His first ship was the *Fair American*, a 16-gun privateer commanded by Stephen Decatur, father of the US naval hero. She took prize after prize, along with an English brig, the *Holker*, of twenty-six guns, and Nagle became a bit of a dandy, able to sport a silk handkerchief at his neck and buckles on his shoes, along with rings and a gold watch. Ideally set up for the sea, slim but strong and with a sprightliness that would still carry him into the rigging when he was well into his forties, Nagle had found his calling.

He was untroubled by serving in an English ship – but only after independence had been won. A series of Caribbean scrapes landed him in a French jail with British captives, so when they were handed over in a prisoner exchange, Nagle followed them up the side into a Royal Navy vessel. Peace brought him to Plymouth in the spring of 1783, and a crossroads in his life. He was paid off from the 64-gun *Ardent* and might have taken a ship home directly. Instead, 'the first English ground I ever stood on' led naturally 'to a publick house where we had sum beer'. Within hours Nagle was squaring up on a common to a gunner's mate who had refused to pay for his round, and whom he scolded with a thrashing before they adjourned again to 'a publick house and drank and treated our seconds and parted'.[32] On reaching Wapping, Nagle would see a good deal more of public houses until his money ran out and he signed on again.

Other navy ships were also slipping homeward across the Atlantic at the end of the war, among them the frigate *Surprise*. John Nicol had been away long enough to 'sigh for the verdant banks of the Forth'. Nicol suffered from a curious affliction: wanderlust, interspersed with bouts when he longed for a domestic hearth and a woman's love. These conditions could never be reconciled and, although a sensitive soul, he was not immune to outbursts of frustration. The *Surprise*'s log records three times when he was lashed, once for fighting.

John Nicol and Jacob Nagle were contemporaries. They would spend the next twenty years crossing the world and, although never serving on the same ship, are often to be found sailing in one another's wake – to the Eastern Seas, or transporting convicts to New South Wales. They could not have been more dissimilar: Nicol the thoughtful romantic, Nagle the devil-may-care blade; it is curiously typical of the age that transformed England in every respect into an imperial power, that one was a Scot and the other an American.

8

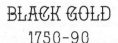

BLACK GOLD
1750-90

AMID the growth in trade from India, another cargo continued to proceed from Africa, no less profitably yet to mounting condemnation by men of conscience. Slavery did not sit comfortably with many seafarers either. Impressment and flogging may even have given some a degree of empathy with the victims. It is still an ugly truth that the slave trade was only possible because of Jack. The statistics are fairly plain. From an average of around 23,000 slaves shipped annually by British traders to the West Indies and North America in the 1750s, the number rose to 40,000 in the 1790s.[1]

Ghastly details proliferate: sailors used women slaves for sexual purposes; slaver crews were alert to uprisings by their cargoes and suppressed them mercilessly; and in one of the most infamous incidents in British maritime history, in 1783 Captain Luke Collingwood of the *Zong* ordered his men to throw overboard 133 sickly slaves as a precaution against insurance loss.[2] Seamen were obviously complicit in this stain on British history, though it may be added that their own toll was high. By one estimate between 2 and 3 per cent of hands died on transatlantic or European voyages, a rate that increased to one in ten in the East Indies. On slaveships, it rose to one in five. No branch of seafaring was deadlier.[3]

Britain's trade in Africa took place along the shoreline running from the Senegal to Congo rivers, with the ill-named port of Bonny at its centre. Forts had been garrisoned on the coast by soldiery of the Royal African Company since the mid-seventeenth century to protect trafficking – first of gold and silver, then slaves. From the company's demise in 1752, slavery fell into the hands of private ship-owners and consortiums operating largely out of Liverpool.[4]

Olaudah Equiano was unique in recording his experiences at sea as both slave and sailor. The latter began, as we have seen, with his purchase by a navy officer who used him as a servant. His passage to a Virginia plantation allegedly started, however, in the Gulf of Guinea – somewhere on the coast of what is now Nigeria.

Equiano claimed to have been born among the Igbo people, or the 'Eboe' as he termed them, in the 1740s although, as he acknowledged, 'the imperfect sketch my memory has furnished me with' can afford no certainty as to his

Britain's involvement in the slave trade was sustained by her sailors, but with a death rate of one in five no form of seafaring was deadlier.

origins.[5] He would have been about eight when he was kidnapped. Nothing of his parents is known and, as his most diligent biographer has pointed out, his recollection of African life 'in a charming fruitful vale named Essaka' is reminiscent of Oliver Goldsmith's nostalgic image of rural England in the 1770s. Equiano's *Interesting Narrative*, written when he had turned campaigning abolitionist, may actually have been based on a memory retrieved 'only with the help of others'.*

It is nonetheless appropriate that this description of a slave ship preparing to sail came from a former slave who became a sailor himself:

> Some of us had been permitted to stay on the deck for the fresh air; but now that the whole ship's cargo was confined together the stench of the hold became absolutely pestilential.
>
> The closeness of the place, and the heat of the climate added to the number in the ship, which was so crowded that each had scarcely room to turn himself, almost suffocated us. This produced copious perspirations, so that the air soon became unfit for respiration, from a variety of loathsome smells, and brought on a sickness among the slaves, of which many died, thus falling victims to the improvident avarice, as I may call it, of their purchasers.[6]

His first impression of the seafaring tribe among whom he would later find a welcoming berth was terrifying: 'White men with horrible looks, red faces and long hair.' Their customs were no less savage:

> I had never seen among any people such instances of brutal cruelty; and this not only shewn towards us blacks, but also to some of the whites themselves. One man in particular I saw, when we were permitted to be on deck,

---

* Carretta, pp. 10–14. In researching Equiano's early life, the author concluded that he had probably not been born in Africa but in South Carolina. The evidence shows that Equiano's account is factually flawed in places, that he used the writings and stories of others, including free black men in England, in presenting a campaigner's case. His story is none the less remarkable for that and the broad outlines are indisputable.

flogged so unmercifully with a large rope near the foremast that he died in consequence of it; and they tossed him over the side as they would have done a brute.[7]

It has been suggested that this vessel was the two-masted snow *Ogden*, and that Equiano was among the 243 slaves to have landed at Barbados after a two-month voyage in May 1754. No records of their passage exist but during the next voyage by the same vessel, 63 of the 343 slaves taken on board at Bonny did not survive to reach Jamaica. Nine of the 32-strong company had also died – an even higher proportion.[8] If not from scurvy, these losses would have been attributable to that other plague of the sea, the 'bloody flux', or amoebic dysentery.

About 80 per cent of British slaves remained in the West Indies where their labours produced the sugar and tobacco that made life more palatable for European consumers. Equiano, however, did not stay in Barbados. A brutal circus – gathering individuals into groups known as 'parcels' and establishing their fitness by jumping tests – saw the child, now aged nine or ten, herded off and shipped on to America. He had, it appears, been rejected by West Indian buyers.

So it was, Equiano related, that he washed up on a Virginia plantation, 'grieving and pining, and wishing for death'. He was fortunate to be taken into the household of the owner, a man named Campbell, and it was this domestic role that transformed his life for the second time that year. An associate of Campbell's, Lieutenant Michael Pascal of the Royal Navy, needed a servant and liked the boy well enough to pay a substantial sum to take him to sea, and the experiences of battle and friendship which we have already witnessed.

Free black men were becoming a familiar presence on British ships. Just as some hands sought refuge in America from impressment, blacks had been sailing in the opposite direction since the War of Independence. It started with the proclamation of 1775, welcoming 'Negroes willing to bear arms' for the king. Among them was Moses Johnson, who escaped from his Virginia plantation master, only to be captured on a British privateer off New Jersey and sold back into slavery.[9] An estimated 3,000 former slaves had still been evacuated to England and found a comparatively welcoming wooden world. No figures for black seamen are certain because ships' musters were colour blind (they listed men's ages and place of origin but not their race). But emergent black populations in such ports as Liverpool and Bristol, along with passing references in numerous texts, testify that black sailors were becoming quite common in British ships.

The existence of these free black communities arguably gave impetus to the rising tide of voices raised against slavery. So did the campaigning of a former slave-ship captain, John Newton, whose epiphany during a storm turned him to the Church, as author of such hymns as 'Amazing Grace', and, with his pamphlet of 1787, *Thoughts upon the African Slave Trade*, an abolitionist ally of William Wilberforce.

By then Equiano had joined London's circle of popular radicals himself.

Seven years in the Navy had shown him, in the words of his biographer, that the content of his character mattered more than the colour of his complexion; the paternal care of his messmate Daniel Quin had opened the door to reading, and he started to adopt English manners.[10] His respect for maritime society survived betrayal by Lieutenant Pascal, who sold him to a merchant captain who, in turn, traded him on to a Quaker merchant in Montserrat. Fortunately, Robert King was a generous master who paid a small wage, cared for slaves owned by others, and interceded on their behalf to stop floggings. At this point, the former slave turned slave trader himself.

By way of context, it was unremarkable for an ordinary man, whatever his colour, to be drawn into the trade. In a Caribbean economy that revolved around slavery there was virtually no escaping it and, as Equiano observed, some of those who used slaves, like King, 'found that benevolence was their true interest'.[11] With his seafaring experience, Equiano was allowed to serve on a local sloop carrying slaves between islands or on to America. He used the opportunity to benefit by some private trading on the side – mainly liquor, but also 'live cargo'. And he once joined in an enterprise 'to purchase some slaves to carry with us and cultivate a plantation; and I chose them all of my own countrymen'.[12] All the while, he was determined to 'return to Old England' and his success as an entrepreneur provided the opportunity. With profits of about £40, he bought his freedom in 1766.

Back in England, Equiano trained as a hairdresser in London's Haymarket until finding himself bridling against confinement ashore. His most extraordinary voyage was with the expedition led by Constantine Phipps to establish how far a vessel could be navigated towards the North Pole, the first step on what became the quest for a North-West Passage between the Atlantic and Pacific oceans. Olaudah Equiano, rated Able in the *Racehorse*, thus shared bone-chilling hardships and the peril of entrapment within icy wastes with a fourteen-year-old midshipman, Horatio Nelson, in the *Carcass*.

The two vessels, with crews of eighty to ninety, had special clothing for the conditions and victuals that included a new 'portable soup' of dried meat to be soaked and boiled. They left the North Sea in June 1773, passing east of Greenland into the Arctic Ocean, reaching the island of Spitsbergen in three weeks. Equiano was mesmerized while grappling vainly to describe this 'striking, grand and uncommon scene'. Another member of the expedition wrote of the setting sun's rays:

. . . sometimes they appeared of a bright blue, like sapphire, and sometimes like the variable colours of a prism, exceeding in lustre the richest gems in the world, disposed of in shapes wonderful to behold, all glittering with a lustre that dazzles the eye, and fills the air with astonishing brightness.[13]

Within this grandeur lurked extreme danger. Imprisonment by ice could crack a wooden ship like a nut, and at the beginning of August both *Racehorse* and *Carcass* were trapped. Days were spent hacking at the ice and hauling on ropes to free them. At one point Equiano fell into what he called 'a pond' and 'was very near being drowned' before being pulled out. He was not, it seems, a very able hand, and after starting a fire that came close to consuming his vessel and all in her was 'severely reprimanded and menaced'.[14] He was fortunate in not being flogged within an inch of his life, like many similarly culpable hands.

They returned safely home after four months. The expedition had reached 80° 48' N yet was deemed a failure, leaving the quest for a North-West Passage to be resumed a generation later. Sir Joseph Banks would have been disappointed too, having asked his friend Phipps to bring back a live polar bear. They did have plenty of skins, though, including one bear measuring 6 feet 9 inches from head to tail. 'We killed many animals,' Equiano wrote, 'among the rest, nine bears.'[15]

The former slave-child had thus sailed the extremes, from the Caribbean to the Arctic and Mediterranean, when he left the sea and began a new career. Nearing forty and switching between hairdressing and domestic service, Equiano embraced Christianity, and with it a sense of mission. As a seaman he had been entered in the musters as Gustavus Vassa; under this name he began his work on behalf of other blacks, both free and enslaved.

London in 1786, observed the philanthropist Granville Sharp, was full of 'unfortunate Negroes starving on our streets'. Some were refugee slaves from America, 'but most are seamen who have navigated the King's ships from the East and West Indies, or have served in the [American] war, and are thereby entitled to ample protection and a generous requital'.[16] Equiano, or Vassa, joined in the emerging campaign to resettle free blacks back in Africa, on the coast of Sierra Leone, working alongside Sharp and Jonas Hanway, whose last mission had been to found the Marine Society for boys.*

Three years later, having been accepted by London's intelligentsia and embraced by subscribers from 'the Nobility and Gentry', this fully self-made

---

* The first settlement of Sierra Leone was a disaster. Of about 400 men, women and children who set out, many died within a year and the survivors were dispersed when a local chief destroyed their town in December 1789.

black man published *The Interesting Narrative of the Life of Mr Olaudah Equiano, or Gustavus Vasa, the African, Written by Himself*. Its summary of slavery's contaminating influence is lucid and perceptive:

> I will not suppose that the dealers in slaves are born worse than other men. No! It is the fatality of this mistaken avarice, that it corrupts the milk of human kindness, and turns it into gall. And had the pursuits of those men been different, they might have been as generous, as tender-hearted and just, as they are unfeeling, rapacious and cruel.[17]

Equiano's marriage to Susannah Cullen, a woman of respectable family in Cambridgeshire, 'in the presence of a vast number of people', was announced in the London press. They had two daughters and lived a gentrified life in London and the country on the book's proceeds. It continued to earn, providing an estate of almost £1,000 on his death in 1797.

Slavery, unsurprisingly, is not a feature of seamen's writings. By the time publishers had started to take an interest in Jack's story, the slave trade had been abolished and that dark past was overlooked. There was an exception, however, William Richardson – and he one remarkably candid about the whole business. Or, as the editor of his papers put it, 'not so much ashamed of it as one would wish him to be'. But then few hands could own up to having participated in slavery while also having seen Bonaparte sail into exile after Waterloo.

Richardson came down to the quay at Whitby early in 1790 to see a ship with a copper-bottomed hull. This was rare for a merchantman at the time and word had it that the *Spy* was bound on a voyage of discovery, which made the young hand think 'how glad I should be to join her and see more of the world' rather than 'dragging about in a collier'.[18] He had done that for nine years, since he was a cabin boy of thirteen, mainly between Newcastle and London but also to the Baltic and Barbary.

As he found in calling on her captain, however, rather than discovery, she was bound for Guinea. To this 'land of heathens' they would be carrying brandy, muskets, swords and brass pots. Homeward, Richardson, the former collier, would go 'from a cargo of black coals to a cargo of black negroes'.*

A Yorkshireman, he was nothing if not plain-speaking.

They came to off the island of Bonny in the Bight of Benin, roughly where Equiano was said to have been taken off and the perils awaiting new arrivals were summed up thus:

> Beware, beware the Bight of Benin,
> For few come out, though many go in.

King Pepple of the Igbo was welcomed on board like an admiral, saluted by the guns, and presented with a blue suit trimmed in gold lace and a feathered cap. With formalities out of the way, the *Spy* started to receive her cargo. Some 200 men and women were brought out by pinnace over the next two months, each one traded individually. Richardson observed:

> People in England think that we hunt and catch the slaves ourselves but that is mistaken for we get them by barter as follows: their petty kings and traders get them not so much by wars as by trade and treachery and bring them to the coast and sell them. So many bars are given for each slave, and for a prime one perhaps a hundred bars [about £20].[19]

Richardson confirmed a phenomenon mentioned by Equiano: because none of the slaves ever returned, Africans believed that their captors were cannibals:[20]

> It was pitiful to see the distress they were in when first brought on board. Many of them think that we live on the sea and come here to buy them for

---

* Richardson's journal was edited for publication in 1908 by Spencer Childers, who abbreviated the text and altered it in places to make the writer's voice less stark. The original has been restored here where alterations were made. The unpublished journal is held at the National Maritime Museum, reference JOD/156.

food. Some of the females fainted and one of them went out of her mind; we endeavour'd all we could to console them, and by degrees they got more reconciled.[21]

Efforts to improve the efficiency of shipping slaves – in other words to keep more cargo alive – had led to some reforms. An Act of 1788 laid down a scale of human lading based on a vessel's tonnage and provided for the services of a surgeon on board.[22] Males were kept in shackles on the upper deck during the day. But with water scarce and temperatures ferociously high, they would have to beg with hands to their mouths for refreshment, saying 'Minee wantee'. When Richardson knew he was not observed, 'I have given the nearest at hand a can full':

> . . . and instead of guzling it up as many who call themselves Christians would do, they would fill their mouth, pass it to the next, who did the same, and so on until it was expended.[23]

He was often ashore among the Igbo, finding them civil and helpful. 'I never saw a quarrel among them; they were sober and industrious, and no more deserve the name of savages than in some countries where they call themselves Christians.' Humanity was set aside when he was sent to help suppress an uprising on a French vessel and joined in opening fire on about a hundred slaves as they wielded billets of wood. Fourteen were killed, including 'a fine young fellow I could not but admire who, though his partner in irons lay dead at his feet, would not surrender but fought until a ball finished his existence'.[24]

It took almost five months for the *Spy* to obtain her full cargo of 450 humans, roughly half of them women and boys. Two 'fine prime female slaves', as Richardson termed them, had been lost, having gone over the side to escape and been torn to pieces by sharks. Four crewmen had died of fever. Thus 'we left this island where the natives ought to be happy, if happiness exists in the world, and proceeded on our passage to the West Indies'.

Reformers of a later generation were apt to draw an analogy between sailors and slaves. Impressment became a natural cause for reform after the Abolition Act of 1807, and press gangs were caricatured in the same thuggish way as slave traders. (We may also recall that campaigning in these terms dated back to 1727, when *The Sailors Advocate* first posed the question: 'How can it be expected that a man should fight for the Liberty of others whilst he himself feels the pangs of Slavery?') The lash was another theme cited as being shared by both groups: naked backs flayed on the one hand by the cat, on the other the whip. American authors such as R. H. Dana and Herman Melville employed flogging as a theatrical device in their writings, complete with actors, victims and audiences.[25]

Direct comparisons between men, women and children who had been dragged from their cultures as well as homes and sent to a brutally alien planet with no hope of return, and men who had the skills and freedom to desert one ship for another, are patently absurd. Yet there were some echoes in these lives. The seaman Samuel Leech perceived song and dance as a common outlet for misery:

A casual visitor in a man of war, beholding the song, the dance, the revelry of the crew, might judge them to be happy. But I know that these things are often resorted to because they feel miserable, to drive away dull care. They do it on the same principle as the slave population of the South, to drown in sensual gratification the voice of misery that groans in the inner man – that lives within, speaking of the indignity offered to its high nature by the chain that eats beyond the flesh – discoursing of the rights of man, of liberty on the free hills of a happier clime.[26]

On the *Spy*, Richardson observed how the women would form a circle around one of their number, dressed in cloth and ribbons provided by the sailors, and 'dance around her, singing and clapping their hands':

One of our men was stationed with a cat to keep them in order, but he never used it except when running round and round the quarterdeck, and then he would give the hindmost one a light touch, which made the others laugh and her run faster: this was to keep their health and spirits, and it did so, for I cannot recollect a single female dying on the passage.[27]

The dividends of an unusually trouble-free voyage were reaped at Montego Bay. After 'letting the planters see what fine slaves we had got', the fittest males who had been bought for £20 were sold for up to £44 a head. Senior hands like Richardson were being paid £2 5s a month, so would receive roughly £25 for the voyage.[28]

Homeward, the *Spy* carried rum, sugar and mahogany. In May 1791, ten months after sailing from England, she was brought to off Beachy Head by the *Nemesis*. The frigate was aptly named, for she pressed all but four of *Spy*'s thirty-five hands.

Richardson did not remark on the irony of slavers being thus yoked themselves. Like most of his shipmates, he recognized abduction by the Navy as part and parcel of his trade, and was happy to go anywhere, 'except in a slave ship again'. He even made a joke: 'I was made a captain, only it was captain of the maintop – a great rise certainly, but with the same pay as I had before.'[29] But he drew a line between Britain's dependency on her seamen and the heartless methods by which they were obtained. At the end of a lifetime at sea in which he had observed the press at its worst – and been seized twice more himself – he concluded:

People may talk of negro slavery and the whip, but let them look nearer home and see a poor sailor arrived from a long voyage, exulting in the pleasure of soon being among his dearest friends and relations. Behold him just entering the door, when a press gang seizes him like a felon, drags him away and puts him into a tender's hold, and from thence he is sent on board a man-of-war, perhaps ready to sail to some foreign station, without seeing either his wife, friends or relations; if he complains he is likely to be seized up and flogged with a cat, much more severe than the negro driver's whip, and if he deserts he is flogged round the fleet nearly to death. It would be greater lenity to shoot a man at once!

It may be said that England cannot do without pressing. Be it so; but then let it be done in a more equitable manner, and let sailors arriving from long voyages have liberty a month or more to spend their money and enjoy themselves; then I will be bound to say they will endure pressing with more patience, be better satisfied and not so ready to desert.[30]

9

COMING HOME
1771-83

IT WAS said they could smell it before they saw it. On the air, moist and stinging with salt, came a hint of earth and another equally unfamiliar scent – of fresh, verdant growth. Then eyes would strain through the spray for shapes to confirm that heady whiff, spirits would burst, and there would commence a 'carousing on the quarterdeck and dansing and shouting and so great a noise it was thought there was a mutiny on board of us'.[1] Because if one thing about homecoming was sure, it was that landfall unleashed a surge of wild energy. What came after that was anyone's guess.

'She, being surprised, could hardly speak, for she knew not before whether I was dead or alive,' wrote Edward Coxere of an unheralded return to his cottage near Dover. 'I laid down my pack, and had my relations come about me with joy.'[2] Coxere was a sailor of another age but his account of a family reunion endures for ever. *The Sailor's Return* had become a standard theme for popular art – fond representations, idealized of course, but at their best, in the hands of a craftsman like Thomas Stothard, still poignant. Here is Jack, home unannounced – 'the true Sailor way' Jane Austen called it – back from the sea to a cosy cottage set among woodland: his wife and children are gathered around in love and awe; he is safe, the war is over and in this elysium we can imagine a wholesome if simple future; the rustic landscape hints at possible employment, as a forester perhaps, or a farm labourer.

The reality, naturally, was far more complex, and a good deal earthier. Sight of the English coast meant home and liberty to returning seamen. It also meant women. Landfall at Plymouth or Portsmouth produced an explosion of sexual energy. Men subject to having every movement dictated by a bosun's pipe came to anchor and would then be suspended, on the foreshore of freedom, waiting to be paid off. So it was perhaps not all that surprising that – after months if not years in close confinement – they might then sacrifice every-thing on a mad impulse, by running.

John Nicol put it eloquently:

> Did those on shore experience half the sensations of a sailor at perfect
> liberty after being seven years on board ship without a will of his own, they
> would not blame his eccentricities but wonder he was not more foolish.[3]

Time was when hands on a returning ship would have been allowed ashore directly to savour the delights of Portsmouth Point, a warren of taverns and bawdy houses so rum it might have daunted the inhabitants of Gin Lane. But, as Samuel Leech recalled, the 'riot, drunkenness and debauchery' that followed often ended 'in bringing poor Jack into difficulty; for once on shore he is like an uncaged bird, as gay and quite as thoughtless'.[4] Because so many men deserted, strategies were developed to restrain them. A hand given leave could, for example, be required to nominate a bondsman – a messmate who would be liable to take his punishment should he run.

Playing on loyalty in this way did not always work, as a note from William Bowman to his bondsman after deserting at Guernsey in 1781 shows:

> Dear George, I send you these few lines in hopes you will forgive me as I
> own meself as a Willainous Rascall for leaving you in the Risk. A frollick
> tempted me to stay till next morning along with Bill and afterward Good

Sailors Carousing. A Portsmouth tavern as seen by Cruikshank – the scene of liberty
erupting after the disciplines of life at sea.

opportunity offerd us a better fortune if we can only ride the Gale out.
I only hope that you wont be Hurtted on Account of me. For you may
depend on, dear George, that I will satisfy you for your favour if it lays in
my power till the day of my Death.[*]

Rather than allow men ashore, it became the custom for boats to come out to
the ship 'freighted with cargoes of ladies', as one hand, William Robinson,
wrote of Spithead. This was a gratifying sight, 'for our crew of six hundred,
nearly all young men, had seen but one woman on board for eighteen months'.
Hands 'flocked down pretty quick, one after the other, and brought their
choice up, so that in the afternoon we had about four hundred and fifty on

---

[*] In the event, Bowman was captured soon afterwards, so his bondsman was spared while he
was flogged around the fleet. The record of his court martial on 24 January 1782 is found in
ADM 1/5319, f. 439.

board'.[5] To fastidious eyes what followed resembled 'the lower kingdom set afloat', with 'brawling and uproar all day long';[6] but there was merriment too. Night after night – because once they were aboard women might spend weeks with the same man – there would be more than just grog to drink, and the lower deck hung heavy with smoke and resounded with jigs and reels. Other gambols took place between the carriages of the guns, and produced illegitimate offspring frequently enough to give rise to the term 'a son of a gun'.

The few Jacks who wrote about prostitutes, or Polls, tended to adopt a rather sanctimonious tone, especially when their literacy was combined with religious zeal. Samuel Leech's memoir, from his years as a ship's boy, reads in places like a priggish tract. His devoutness was not typical, still less his horror at the 'boat-loads of defiled and defiling women permitted to come alongside' for the men to select 'whoever best pleases [their] lustful fancy'. Despite thirty years at sea, which provided him with material for a substantial journal, Leech answered his own question – 'how can a boy be expected to escape pollution, surrounded by such works of darkness?' – with the incongruous conclusion that he would be 'better off in a house of correction'.[7]

William Robinson (not to be confused with William Richardson of the slaveship *Spy*) was a more pragmatic soul. Self-styled 'Jack Nastyface', he reserved his disapproval for the boatmen whose profits depended on securing partners for the Judies they ferried out to ships at anchor, and how 'it often happens that he refuses to take some of them, observing usually with some vulgar oath; to one that she is *too old*; to another that she is *too ugly*; and that he shall not be able to sell them . . . Thus these poor unfortunates are taken to market like cattle; and whilst this system is observed it cannot with truth be said that the slave-trade is abolished in England.'[8] Robinson, otherwise a hardbitten fellow, concluded regretfully that 'these unfortunately deluded victims to our passions might at one time have been destined to be the valuable companions and comforts of man':

We cannot reproach them for their abject condition, lest this startling question be asked of us – Who made us so?[9]

A similar compassion is evident in Robert Wilson's recollection of how a girl brought on board the frigate *Unite* by one of his messmates turned out to be not only pretty and educated but – under her cloak – large with child. Wilson tried to dissuade his friend from tupping her, 'which made him think I was anxious to possess her charms [and] more determined to satisfy his [lust]'. Once he had done with her, she went into labour. Wilson, by now half in love with this 'unfortunate fair one', organized a collection on her behalf and later 'I had the pleasure to hear that all went well and her friends had received her into their good graces'.[10]

In truth, though, the Portsmouth Polls, as they were known, had less in common with the likes of Wilson and Leech than they did with ordinary Jacks. This extended to a gamey appearance that reflected indomitable spirit – or at least 'a bold countenance [with] the warlike features of two wounded cheeks, a tumid nose, scarred and battered brows, and a pair of blackened eyes . . . a pair of brawny arms fit to encounter a Colossus, all set upon two ankles like the fixed supports of a gate'.[11] These were not women to be trifled with. A hand named Daniel Goodall was astonished by their ability to procure liquor in unlikely places, while 'smoking was quite a prevalent fashion and as for swearing, they seemed to take a peculiar delight in uttering the oldest oaths [in] the newest kind of ways'.[12] A loftier view held them to be 'inured to immorality from childhood, rotten with disease'.[13] There were certainly Polls and Judies who were not above contracting a hasty marriage with a seaman while his pocket was full, before resuming their old trade once he had gone back to sea. But there were far more genuine wives who found themselves without income for the long spells their men were away and who resorted to occasional prostitution to make ends meet. There were even those who, like the wife of a sailor of the *Active* who had not returned for five years, assumed their man to be dead and married again, only for her husband to arrive back in Portsmouth shortly afterwards. Their reunion was reported in the press:

The Tar pleaded his prior Right, and insisted on having his Wife back again, which the new Husband readily agreed to. The Sailor putting his hand into his pocket said, 'Here, friend, accept of a couple of guineas for the service you have done my Wife.'[14]

Seamen's women in general, like their Jacks, were sturdy spirits used to deploying their bodies, and to some extent their wits, to survive at the edge.

One of the Polls' earthy ditties is clear-sighted about who, in a choice between a sailor and a soldier, was the more suitable object for their favours:

> *Sailors, they get all the money, Soldiers, they get none but brass,*
> *I do love a jolly sailor, Soldiers, they may kiss my arse.*[15]

In his jaunts among these lively creatures, the American Jacob Nagle provides a refreshing contrast to the sanctimony of Leech.

Nagle's first English landing, at Plymouth in the summer of 1783, led to scrapes involving public houses, beer and fisticuffs before he made his way to London, and the dockland of Wapping. This enclave of taverns and boarding houses beside the Thames had continued its evolution as a seaman's habitat since the days of William Spavens and was – with the country at peace – the best place for Jack to find a ship, whether one bound for the East Indies, to return with a cargo of tea, china or pepper, or another with rum, sugar or coffee from the Caribbean. It had a dark side as well: the old gibbet at Execution Dock and the Tower at the top of the hill; but Nagle's picaresque adventures in Wapping might have come from the pen of Henry Fielding, and his strut is visible in the figure vividly described by a fellow seaman, wearing:

an elegant hat of straw, indicative of his recent return from a foreign station, cocked on one side; a head of hair reaching to his waistband; a smart switch made from the back bone of a shark under one arm, his doxy under the other, a huge chew of tobacco in his cheek, and a double stingo recently deposited within his belt by way of fending off care. Thus fitted out, in good sailing trim, as he himself styles it, he strides along with all the importance of an Indian Nabob.[16]

Swagger was important, dress a point of pride. A sailor named George Arnold, writing to a messmate after deserting on impulse one night, was obviously a dandy:

> Send my Blue Jacket and waistcoat, Four of my best shirts, Four pairs of stockings, my black velvet breeches, two linen waistcoats and the peice [sic] of nankeen. Tie them up in a red silk handkerchief that you'l find in my shirt bag and send them by any person you think proper. Take the remains of what things is in my chest amongst you messmates. God bless you all.
>
> My kind love to Kit Dalton and I wish he was along with me.[17]

Nagle would set out to impress the tavern lasses 'with about two guineas in my pocked [sic] and som silver to cut a flash with'. Once at Tower Hill he made his way to the long room of an inn, and a scene redolent of Cruikshank's cartoon 'Sailors Carousing' – a smoke-hung saloon, bare wooden floorboards heaving with fiddlers and dancers, gamblers and hussies, where he ordered a pot of flip and 'I let them see I had both gold and silver'. What followed was a game older than seafaring. Taken to her bed by one Judy, he was plied with liquor until:

> . . . she begin to hug me to see if I was sound, but having no life in me, she got up, overhalled my pockets and stowed away all she found.

Nagle felt no resentment, simply demanded his money back, and 'she said I was the best friend she ever fell in with. I have saived hur from the gallos or transportation.'[18] Another woman aroused his sympathy when she took her gown off, 'which was clean and deasent but hur shift was nothing but rags. It hurt me to see so lovely a young girl so much in distress for the want of some assistance, and I found by discourse it was to support hur poor mother':

> In the morning I gave her a half a guinea and told hur to get a couple of shifts. She cried and took me round the neck. I went down stairs and

the old ladie was there. I bid her good morning and she returned the complement with chearfulness. I presented hur a guinea and told hur it might be of service to hur. She seemed stagnated [astounded] and I told hur perhaps you may never see me any more and bid them both good morning. I always thought I never done a better job in my life for the good of my own soul.[19]

Wherever he went, and in twenty years of voyaging under British colours Nagle traversed every ocean and most of the seas, his enjoyment of women was based on generosity, fondness and, usually, simple commerce. In this respect he could not have been more unlike the yearning romantic John Nicol.

———

When the *Surprise* came in at Plymouth at the end of 1782, she had crossed the Atlantic four times since May – hard sailing that had certainly earned the men their frolic. Whether this took the form of shore leave or a visitation by the local women is unclear, but the news that awaited them was the talk of ports around the land and it had Nicol and his mates shaking their heads over their tankards.

Three months earlier, the mightiest navy ship afloat, the 100-gun *Royal George*, had been at Spithead for repairs with hundreds of seamen and their women aboard. The precise number was never established, as some men had been given shore leave, but estimates put it at around 700 hands and 200 women. What resembled a bagnio on parts of the lower deck was more like a compact village on others, with families of squalling children and wives, artisans plying their trades and vendors with their wares. Some late risers were still yawning and stretching after a night of hectic revelry when, at 7 a.m. on 28 August, the ship was heeled over for repairs below the water line. This was a common procedure that involved shifting all her cannon to one side, but on this occasion the officer in charge had failed to close the larboard lower gunports and, as the deck tilted, water poured through them and surged across the lower deck. Then, as if in slow motion but quite suddenly, she went right over. A seaman, James Ingram, noted with bewilderment: 'The starboard portholes were as upright [as] the top of a chimney', except that the men trying to clamber out had 'nothing for their legs and feet to act upon'. Ingram managed to drag one woman out through a porthole before fastening on to some rigging. She was swept off by the flow – to be picked up by a rescue boat, so becoming one of only 13 among the 200 women on board to have survived that night.[20] Just one child escaped, reportedly by holding on to a sheep.[21]

The loss of the *Royal George* was the *Titanic* of her day: a calamity shared by all classes of humanity on a single ship, where survival was a matter of chance. At least 800 lives were lost, among them Admiral Richard Kempenfelt and an unnamed woman who had just gone on board with her five children to see their seaman father. A hand named Samuel Kelly, who came into harbour a few days later on the Falmouth packet, was met by the sight of bodies floating on the tide. He joined in their retrieval, and years later was still haunted by the memory of bodies – tied to the shrouds of the *Royal George* to stop them being swept away – 'suspended several feet above the water' at low tide, their pockets turned out by scavengers.[22]

John Nicol, for all his love of the curious, was no devil-may-care adventurer, and had been longing for home even without this reminder of the sea's perils. For six weeks the *Surprise* remained at Plymouth, before she began to work her way up to the Nore – a clear sign at last that she was about to be paid off. On the day they came to anchor, Nicol was witness to a final grim vision of what he was leaving behind.

Soon after 10 a.m. on 15 January 1783 he was among the thousands of hands to be mustered across the fleet. It was a hoary day that had them stamping and rubbing their hands as drums rolled and two men were brought up on the *Greenwich*. While the Articles of War were read, Thomas Murray and John Haggiston had ropes fastened around their necks. At 11 a.m., on the firing of a cannon, fellow seamen took up the ropes' ends and began to haul, and very shortly, while the drums continued to hammer out, Murray and Haggiston were writhing convulsively from the foremast yardarm.

Coming on the eve of peace, the executions were controversial enough for the authorities to decide an explanation was warranted, and later that morning the dead men's crimes were read out to ships' companies.[23] Murray, an American, and Haggiston had been among seventeen hands, including some pressed from an Indiaman, who had seized the *Jackal* cutter. Any violent mutiny was serious but what really disturbed the Admiralty about this case were the revolutionary overtones. The mutineers had cried 'Liberty we want, and liberty we will have', before taking the cutter to France, and had been seen around Calais with cockades on their hats; the Gordon Riots in London three years earlier had established the cockade as a symbol of insurrection, a decade before the storming of the Bastille. There were also echoes of the rebellion in America, with sailors flying to the enemy, in this case one just across the Channel. Yet whatever their desire for liberty, it was not enough to keep the mutineers away from England. Murray and Haggiston slipped back, found work at a brewery, then a farm in Essex, and were wandering around London's Spitalfields when they were spotted by an old shipmate who reported them.[24] There was never much doubt over their fate after that.

How severe by comparison were the sentences passed on ten men of the *Raisonable* a few months later. While at Spithead, the company had assembled and given three cheers, a show of unity that often preceded mutinous action. They then announced that because they lived in the area, they 'had determined not to carry the ship to Chatham, but to be paid off at Portsmouth'. Their demand ought to have been negotiable: the peace had been signed and their petition insisted they had been 'strict in maintaining Lord Hervey's honour as our brave commander'; they were, moreover, acknowledged to be good men who had 'behaved very well previous'. Instead, this so-called mutiny was referred to the Admiralty. Of the ringleaders, seven were sentenced to death and three to receive 300 lashes.[25]

Most sailors witnessed hangings, many were participants, although the selective practice of sending men to another ship for execution meant their messmates could be spared having to haul them aloft. William Lenfield's hanging for seditious speech took place on his own ship, *Castor*.[26] It was watched by William Richardson, who had seen terrible things on a slave ship but nothing like this ghastly bungling, the knot having been placed under Lenfield's chin rather than under an ear:

> A few minutes after he was run up he began to groan, and soon after so loud he was heard some distance off. He then struggled and drew up his legs and arms; but as the latter were only fastened above the elbows, he made a shift with his hands to reach the noose and pulling it closer soon expired. Thus it may be said the poor fellow finished his own existence . . . It was a great shame [he] was not lowered down again to put the halter aright.[27]

Nicol initially thought himself well shot of the whole business. He was paid off on 16 February and boarded a coach for Newcastle, the first stage of his journey to Edinburgh and a long-awaited family reunion. Within a few hours, he had fallen in love.

Her name was Mary, and she was a farmer's daughter. As the coach trundled north she listened to Nicol's tales of distant lands with evident interest and soon, he 'began to think of how happy I might be with such a wife'. He had the barrel-making skill he had learnt at sea and nine guineas in his purse, and when she alighted to be met by her father, Nicol resolved to seek her hand once he had visited his family. 'I whispered Mary a promise to see her soon, and pressed her hand as we parted. She returned the pressure.'[28]

His first disappointment was reaching Edinburgh to find his father had died. A visit to the grave and a few days among friends – and he was on his way back to Mary. But dreams of a cosy hearth and his own trade were rapidly dispelled. A brief farmyard encounter with his sweetheart ended when her father emerged from the house and sent him packing. Within weeks of coming shore, he was in London again, scouring the wharfs of Wapping. Yet in a time of peace, 'seamen were so plenty there was great difficulty in getting a berth'. More weeks passed before he was hailed by a captain who recognized him.

And so 'my wandering propensities came as strong upon me as ever,' he wrote. 'No matter whither, only let me wander.'[29] Nicol signed on a whaler, bound for Greenland.

———

The Unknown Sailor – the only name by which he was ever identified – was also on his way to sea again as he walked southwards across Surrey on an afternoon late in the summer of 1786. His precise progress that day is another mystery, but he had already covered well over 30 miles since setting out from London so in all probability had spent at least one night on the coach road to Portsmouth, taking up whatever sleeping arrangements were at hand, when he came through farming countryside to the village of Thursley. There, feeling a thirst, he stepped into the Red Lion Inn.

The Unknown Sailor was that rarity – a hand going back to sea with coins still in his purse and, being a generous spirit on top of it, he extended the hand of hospitality to three fellow seamen he met at the inn. James Marshall, Michael Casey and Edward Lonegon had their food and drink paid for by the Unknown Sailor before the four of them left together and were last seen walking south towards Hindhead Hill. Patrons of the inn would recall that the liberal seaman had promised to further treat his fellows on the road to Portsmouth.

Later that day the Unknown Sailor's body was found, stripped of clothes and money, and with his head – if lurid newspaper reports are to be believed – virtually severed. Within hours the renegados were traced to another inn, the Sun in the village of Rake, where they were caught in the act of selling the dead man's clothes. Marshall, Casey and Lonegon were executed near to the murder scene six months later.

One of the striking aspects of this crime was the outrage it created. The murderers were not merely put to death but, as a mark of their depravity, hanged from the gibbet in chains; and a local worthy had a stone erected beside the road, in memory of 'a generous but unfortunate Sailor'. Both stone and crime acquired notoriety, being featured by Charles Dickens in the journey made by Nicholas Nickleby and the boy Smike down the Portsmouth road. The stone survives, having been moved to a churchyard in Thursley.

But what of the invisible consequences? The sailor was unknown but he was not without relatives. He may possibly have been one Edward Hardman, who had recently bade farewell to his family in Lambeth and set out down that same road for a ship in Portsmouth, only to disappear off the face of the earth.[30] Families who saw their men come and go, who knew the exhilaration of an unheralded return in 'the true Sailor way', would feel again pangs at departure, and then in many cases never hear from them again. Hardman's family were far from being alone in never knowing the fate of a loved one.

———

Jack was the worst kind of family man. While most commoner households of Georgian society were necessarily close-knit units, a seaman's wife was an object of pity – a woman no sooner united with her wandering man than abandoned once more to cope with his brood on the dregs of his pay. Upwards of one in five families received poor relief, which by 1786 was costing their local parishes an astronomical £2 million per annum, and a fair number of these were sailors' dependants. Thomas Trotter, a sympathetic naval surgeon, saw Jack's fickleness as a natural consequence of having 'no settled home to fix domestic attachments'.[31] But the author Daniel Defoe inveighed against the kind of men who 'grow clamorous and noisy, mutinous and saucy, and in the meantime disperse, run away, and leave their families upon the parishes'.[32]

Rarely is this family side of the seafaring community seen or heard, and there is a vast gap in our knowledge of those who stayed at home, to wait, hope and endure. Unlike Jack, who would celebrate his moment of pomp after Trafalgar with a spate of memoirs, no wife sat down to relate her struggles with raising children while living on the edge of poverty. Every now and again though, we get a glimpse of a domestic hinterland.

William and Ann Greenhalgh had a farm near Bury in Lancashire where, a few times a year, letters would arrive from their eldest son, Ordinary seaman

Richard Greenhalgh. Addressed to 'Loving Parents' or sometimes 'Honoured Parents', these were in the main written not by Greenhalgh himself but by a variety of messmates and were intended principally to reassure his family that he was still alive. The forty letters, spanning almost ten years, provided little detail of life on board the 74-gun ships on which Greenhalgh served. Most were written from British ports shortly before he sailed, and as ships' companies were usually kept in the dark whither they were bound until the last moment, the family was left none the wiser about where he was likely to be engaged or when he might return. Months – in one case almost a year – would then pass before another folded single sheet of paper reached the farm:

> Permit me to acoast you with a few serious words tho at the same time they don't come from my lips but Dear Parents they come from my hearty good wishes to you and from the Bottam of my heart.[33]

Usually Greenhalgh was content simply to set at rest the minds of those at home. On sailing away to conflict, he wrote:

> I am thanks to my Creator well and hearty according to my station in life. I means if possible to out brave my Enemies in the best manner.[34]

These letters served to reassure not only Richard's family but neighbouring farmers in their part of Lancashire, the Cass family, whose son Stephen had been his friend since childhood and was now a messmate. The two had gone to sea together, followed one another from ship to ship, and served on the *Powerful* at the Battle of Camperdown:

> Thanks be to god for it I am very happy to inform you that I got through this action with out any damage which will be of great satisfaction to you. We gave them a great drubing and took 8 sail from them and sent them in with a sorrowful story. I have no more to tell you at present only that I am safe and sound and so is my messmate Stephen Cass.[35]

One revealing aspect of the correspondence is how it shows the interdependence of this particular seaman and his farming family. After a poor harvest one year, Greenhalgh wrote that his mother should go to the Excise Office in Bury 'and receive half my wages monthly as an order from me', and whenever in funds he would send the family amounts of between five and eight guineas.[36] Seemingly as profligate as he was generous, however, Greenhalgh was occasionally obliged to request help from them – once for the stupendous sum of £20.

A windfall of the kind that every Jack dreamt of seemed to be in the offing once: Greenhalgh was on the *Ganges* when she captured 'a Spanish galloon leadin [laden] with Dollars Gold and Jewels which is thought to be the richest prize ever took'. In the end, two years passed before the rewards reached the lower deck, and although one farming family in Lancashire doubtless enjoyed the eight guineas that accompanied their son's fond wishes 'that you may have a good Christmas', this was no bonanza on the Anson scale.

Greenhalgh's scribe on the *Powerful* was another messmate, an Irishman named Thomas Crown who thus became almost part of the family circle. ('He thanks my mother for her love and kindness to him in many of your letters to me.') When Thomas was drafted onto another ship, Greenhalgh found others to write on his behalf, or in extremis resorted to his own, tortured, script: 'Excuse my bad writing I have not practised it much lately.'

Although they tell a warm domestic story, the over-arching narrative of Greenhalgh's letters is melancholy. His early service was marked by enthusiasm for a seafaring life and the companionship which, with other hands from his own region, gave it a domestic familiarity: 'We have plenty of Lancashire on board from Bury and Bolton and all Round which makes it like home.' But as the years passed, and the Revolutionary War with France dragged on without leave or sight of home, his tone became jaundiced:

I am a long time tasting the Beer which was Brewd for my reception these two winters back and unless our statesmen take shorter methods to the definishing of this tedious war I fear it's double 2 before I am partaker of [it].[37]

A year later still no end was in sight. Greenhalgh's yearning, expressed through one of his more lucid scribes, had become palpable. 'I have not forgot the names of my brothers, nor yet the croft, nor the meadow, neither do I forget where the plumb tree stands.'[38] Soon afterwards he suffered a severe blow with separation from his boyhood friend Stephen Cass and, on being sent into the *Racoon* sloop, started to contemplate desertion. 'My intentions was to see home this summer if possably I could and you may depend I will if an oppertunity serves.' His chance came finally when the *Racoon* was in the Mediterranean.

Nine months later William and Ann received a letter from Newfoundland. Their son and four men had run from the *Racoon* in Naples and found a ship bound for Boston. It was a long way round to get home, but he expected to sail for Lisbon and thence to Scotland within a few weeks. 'I am in as much hurry to see you as you are to see mee,' he wrote. It was not stated, but the message was clear: he might just be back in time for Christmas.

There the story ends. His parents received no more of Greenhalgh's letters and what became of him is not known. It seems likely that he reached home, to be reunited with the family and to see once more the meadow and the plum tree. But if we may like to think that no misfortune befell him, causing him to disappear like the Unknown Sailor, nothing was ever certain at sea.

———————

Another loving mother was elated to learn in a newspaper that the *St George* had returned from Biscay to anchor in Plymouth. Sarah Hubbard's son Thomas had departed their home in London more than a year earlier and the fact that his ship had returned to port brought the initial reassurance that all families craved. She wrote to him directly:

> My dear child it makes me very happy to hear that you are save arrived but o what happiness it wood be for me to see you once more . . .[39]

Sarah's anxiety was not without a financial aspect. She had other sons too and they were all dependent on Thomas's earnings for, as she put it, 'if it was not for what you alow me out of your pay we must all starve'. There was no question of her travelling the 200 miles from London to see him in Plymouth, however, and being aware that he might not be granted leave she could only send 'kind love from your ant and couzens and all friends'.

Thomas meanwhile, far from anticipating leave ashore, was on trial for his life.

The 90-gun *St George* had spent many months off the French port of Brest, a service detested by all mariners – combining as it did the grinding monotony of blockade duty with the buffeting delivered by the Bay of Biscay. Thomas Hubbard, aged twenty-five and rated Ordinary, was not the only hand to have eased his misery with grog. Heavy drinking continued when the ship put in at Torbay for fresh provisions on 10 November. That night 'a great moving' was observed in a hammock and when a lantern was brought to bear it revealed the half-naked bodies of Hubbard and George Hynes.

On a bitter December day at Spithead they were taken across to the *Gladiator* and, a week later, brought up for trial. Thomas Hubbard was identified to the court as 'the young man', his co-accused George Hynes as 'the black man'. The key testimony came from a master of arms who said that when Hubbard was pulled from the hammock, Hynes was under him, naked and on his belly: 'I saw Thomas Hubbard's yard come from between the backside of George Hynes.' Or, as a marine put it, 'His tool came out of his fundament.'

Lost for words in front of his bleak-faced judges, Hubbard could only stammer that he had been 'very much in liquor', then threw himself on their mercy. Hynes said nothing.

Captain Sampson Edwards confirmed that both men had frequently been drunk and said nothing of Hynes; but he gave Hubbard a good character: 'a very quiet lad'. As further testimony, the letter from his mother Sarah was produced, showing that he was the financial support of his family, and concluding:

> Your ant and couzens and all friends desires their kind love to you and wishes you save home again to me . . . I have no more for to say now but my prays to God to protect you.
>
> From your loving mother till death. Sarah Hubbard

Whether the presiding officers read it or not made no difference. Both men were convicted of sodomy and sentenced to hang.[40]

Even then their fate was not sealed. The sentence was sent for review to the Channel commander, but Earl St Vincent was a flinty zealot to whom mercy, especially for homosexuals, was a weakness. Three days before Christmas, an entry was made in the log of the *St George*:

> At 8 the Admiral made the signal for punishment. Performed Divine Service.
> At 10 Thos Hubbard & George Hynes (seamen) were hanged, one at each
> Fore Yard Arm. Sent the deceased to the hospital. Received fresh beef.[41]

How Sarah Hubbard learnt of her son's fate is unknown. One of Thomas's messmates, William Edwards, who agreed he was 'a good lad', may have passed on the news. Generally it was a captain's duty on a man's death to inform his family – provided their whereabouts were known. In a great many cases there was no such finality.

Another family cast away by the whimsical tide of a seaman's life were the dependants of William Jones. The trial of his wife Mary became a cause célèbre, with a resonance that still echoed during the Great Mutinies more than twenty years later. Mary Jones was among the many wives to lose their wage-earners to a press gang; William, a merchant seaman, was taken by the Navy in London in 1770. Mary, with two children including a newborn baby, was first forced to beg and then driven from her lodgings off the Strand.[42]

Mary entered a draper's in Ludgate Street on 7 August 1771, with the baby and her friend, Ann Styles, asking to see children's frocks. The baby was set on the counter while the women inspected linen. None was found satisfactory and they had reached the door to leave when they were stopped. Beneath Mary's cloak was found muslin valued at £5.

The two women spent a month at Newgate before being brought to trial at the Old Bailey. Mary did not deny theft but said: 'I have been a very honest woman. I have two children. I work very hard to maintain my two children since my husband was pressed.'[43]

Ann was acquitted. Mary was found guilty and sentenced to death. According to newspaper reports, perhaps fanciful, she was still suckling the baby as she mounted the gallows at Tyburn on 16 October.

Among those who kept the tragedy of Mary Jones alive were the campaigning journalist William Cobbett and the Whig politician Sir William Meredith, whose ringing denunciation spread the blame between the law and impressment:

> The State bereaved the woman of her husband and the children of a father.
> The law deprived the woman of her life and the children of their remaining
> parent. Take all the circumstances, I do not believe a fouler murder was ever
> committed against law than the murder of this woman by law.[44]

Which was well enough said. But of what became of the children of William and Mary Jones, nothing can be added.

Once at sea, most Jacks became naturally oblivious of domestic matters. Admiralty policy, on the other hand, touched them all – and the changes being introduced by their lordships at around this time would affect seamen in fundamental ways. Few were for the better. It has been observed that when Britain's ruling class drew a lesson from the American Revolution it was not that the empire 'had been too strictly governed or that policy had been too selfish or inflexible, but rather that it had been too permissive, conciliatory and ineffective'.[45]

These attitudes influenced naval policies too. The court-martial records seen here indicate that punishments had started to stiffen. Any offence that smacked of a dangerous libertarianism attracted particular wrath. It took some time for change to filter down from the Admiralty to the quarterdeck. A bold and robust soul like Daniel Stewart could still escape with a relatively mild fifty lashes for mutiny after telling the officers of the *Scipio* that given half a chance he would send them to Hell and Damnation: Stewart had objected to the clapping in irons of a shipmate, then demanded to be put in irons as well before launching into his diatribe, by way of remarking that he could write as well as any of those damned officers. Stewart was acknowledged to have borne 'a very good character', which helped.[46]

But already the relatively paternalistic old ways were giving way to hard-nosed expediency. When the need for good hands had been high, a practice known as turning-over came into being. Instead of being given leave at the end of a commission, men would be sent straight from one ship to another, parting from officers with whose ways they were familiar – even if they were not esteemed – and starting all over with another set. One young officer, Horatio Nelson, fulminated at what he called this 'infernal plan' in 1783, observing, 'Men cannot be attached to their officers, or the officers care two-pence about them.'[47]

Admiralty dogma gave rise, as we shall see, to a sense of injustice – much of it stemming from their lordships' refusal to increase rates of pay which had remained the same for almost 150 years. The coming of peace that year of 1783 may, paradoxically, have only stoked up grievance. Now more than ever, seafaring was big business and many Jacks were departing the Navy for the merchant service.

Those two old hands John Nicol and Jacob Nagle were among a growing cohort to find that the rewards of private enterprise much exceeded those of the king's service. As an Ordinary seaman on a coastal transport, Samuel Kelly's wage had just been set at 40s a month, compared with the Navy's 19s, while his Able shipmates were getting 60s.[48] The upshot was when the day came that Jack had perforce to join a navy ship again, he would show a greater willingness than ever to challenge the established order.

10

FRUITS OF PEACE
1783-92

A DECADE of peace might not be thought the best preparation for twenty years of war. There is, indeed, no empirical evidence that it was. At the time, loss of the American colonies was actually seen as having cost Britain its place as a world power.[1] Yet a surge in seafaring from 1783 tells its own story. British seamen – or more accurately seamen on her ships – simply went further and in greater numbers than those of their traditional foes. Mainly they sailed in pursuit of trade; but because they encountered more frequent challenges their skills were constantly being sharpened. They gained more than just experience. They learnt teamwork and confidence. It could be argued that the dominance which appeared to come so naturally to the Navy when war with France resumed was forged in a time of peace.

For once the Navy did not sign off all hands. On the contrary, it engaged in an arms race with France and Spain. The number of ships of the line – the great cathedrals of seventy-four guns and more – grew, from 137 to 145, while the peacetime establishment of men was increased from 10,000 to 18,000, and then again to 20,000.[2] Meanwhile the stricture that only those 'who use the sea' could be impressed gave way without fanfare to a new regime when in 1787 London's mayor agreed to an Admiralty request to send out his constables 'to apprehend all persons who have no visible means of obtaining a livelihood' and establish whether they were fit to serve as sailors.[3] A precedent for pressing landsmen had been set.*

Trade by sea exploded. The East India Company, the principal agent of mercantile traffic, developed into a maritime power all of its own. To meet the demand for new vessels, Indiamen started coming off the blocks not only at Blackwall but in Bombay. In the decade up to the peace, the Company's ships had made 129 voyages to and from the Eastern Seas. In the decade after it, the number more than doubled to 272 voyages.[4] Booming trade gave a consequent impetus to the coastal traffic of smaller vessels – brigs, snows and hoys.

It was a period of fresh imperial expansion too. The Pacific was turned from an ocean of exploration and discovery into a region of settlement. As a result of Cook's voyages, two fleets transported convicts to colonize the territory he called New South Wales – somewhat bizarrely, for a small, green, wet protrusion of the British isles could scarcely have been more dissimilar to the continent that became Australia. Another consequence was the despatch of a small vessel to collect a plant from Tahiti that Sir Joseph Banks believed could feed the West Indies plantations; William Bligh's mission in the *Bounty* would resonate in seafaring history. And all the while, more and more British ships were rounding the capes – the Horn of South America and the Good Hope of Africa – in a growing challenge to what has been called 'the tyranny of distance'.

Peace meanwhile broadened the diversity, ethnic and national, that had become a feature of the lower deck. Gazing around him, one Jack observed 'complexions of every hue and features of every cast, from the flat nose, thick lips and frizzled hair of the African, to the slender frame and milder features of the Asiatic'. Here were to be seen lascars, the Muslim sailors of Bengal. Over there were 'the sun-burnt Portuguese, the kilted Highlander, the sons of Holland, the shirtless sons of the British prison-house, the haughty Spaniard'.[5]

There too were Jacob Nagle, the American, and John Nicol, the Scot.

---

* Restrictions on impressment appear to have been eroded during the 1770s when the American War of Independence and the war with France led to early violations. In 1776 a lamp-lighter named Tony Tearney was seized in London, leaving the mother of his two children destitute; eighteen months later a lace-maker with a wife and two children living near the Strand suffered the same fate. Rogers, *The Press Gang*, pp. 2–3.

The era found Nagle entering his thirties yet as ready for adventure as ever. Among the hands to sail with the First Fleet to Australia, he was shipwrecked in the Pacific, seized by a press gang on his return to England, and was just about to join the renewed war with France when he decided instead to desert, joined an Indiaman and sailed for Bengal.

For his part, Nicol returned home in time to join the Second Fleet. Of his voyage in the *Lady Juliana*, transporting women convicts, he would reflect: 'I did not by any means like her cargo – yet to see the country I was resolved to submit to a great deal.' In the event, it set him on the quest of his life.

———

Being a prime hand, Nagle was among those retained by the Navy. But without a war to fight, the 74-gun *Ganges* remained at her Spithead anchor for months while Nagle chaffed at a combination of inactivity and the regime of a tartar named Lieutenant Edward Riou, whom he thought 'a villen and a terror to seamen'.[6] Relief came in the form of the frigate *Sirius*, recruiting for an extraordinary voyage. 'She was bound to Botnay [sic] Bay with a fleet of 11 sail of transports, full of men and wimen convicts,' Nagle wrote. He was among the hands picked out in person for the flagship by Captain Arthur Phillip, governor-designate of the penal colony of New South Wales.

The First Fleet made seafaring history. This was not the first time Britain had emptied prison hulks of misbegotten souls and sent them to an alien and distant exile. Never, though, had a fleet been used to transport so large a group of civilian convicts to a destination so far off that it was almost unthinkable they would ever return. Indiamen carried between twenty and thirty passengers at a time on voyages of four to six months. Estimates were that the First Fleet would be eight months in taking 736 men and women prisoners almost 16,000 miles across the world in eleven transports.

This 'Noah's Ark of small-time criminality', as it has been called, sailed in May 1787, and to start with the convicts were noted to be 'humble and submissive', probably as much thanks to seasickness as anything else. However, the enormity of their fate, 'the fearful prospect of a distant and barbarous country', and the realization that they would never return, gave rise first to misery, then turbulence. The four female transports turned into varieties of bedlam: 'The desire of the women to be with the men was so uncontrollable,' wrote the *Charlotte*'s surgeon, 'that neither shame nor the fear of punishment could deter them from making their way through the bulkheads to the seamen'.[7] On the *Lady Penrhyn* liaisons with convict women made fathers of three Jacks, including Joshua Bentley, whose child was christened at Botany Bay and has been counted the first white Australian.[8]

The novel pleasures of sex at sea and a constant female presence threatened to destabilize normal order. A lieutenant on the *Sirius*, alarmed by what he saw as a threat to discipline, started to hand out random floggings, which only added to the turmoil below. Finally, officers across the fleet were summoned by Phillip and told that anyone striking a sailor would be broken. As Nagle put it, the governor had said:

> Those men are all we have to depend upon and if we abuse those men, the convicts will rise and massecree us all. Those men are our support . . . We cannot expect to return in less than five years. If they are ill treated by their own officers, what support can you expect of them?[9]

Nagle was well informed about the officers' circle, being a member of Phillip's barge crew with a position of trust and permitted therefore a degree of forthrightness. He spoke and behaved towards officers in a manner that was respectful, but that defined him as worthy of respect himself. While at Rio he was allowed ashore, overdid the roistering, and got left behind by the barge. Coming back on board, he expected to be thrown in irons; instead, Phillip 'said he was glad to hear we ware alive and desired we should be sent to our hammocks to get a sleep, as we would be wanted in the barge at nine o'clock'. Nagle was that asset all good captains recognized, a prime hand.

As predicted, the voyage took eight months. On every ship, on every day, a record was kept of longitude and latitude, of weather and sea conditions. We can still scan these daily records – meticulous in details of wind direction, parsimonious as to human conduct – for signs of the lives going on in the background of daily routines, decks being scrubbed, meals served. We can see the sea passing through its various manifestations, from an immense calm of almost oily flatness, to white caps whipped by the breeze and to high, rolling blue mountains. We can imagine the frustration as the fleet had continually to shorten sail, enabling two slow dogs – which happened to be those dens of vice, the *Lady Penrhyn* and the *Charlotte* – to close up. Once monotony had subdued the convicts there was little real drama apart from a failed uprising on the *Alexander*, for which the ringleaders were brought across to the *Sirius* and flogged.

Nagle had meantime survived an accident of a kind fatal to many topmen. They had rounded the Cape of Good Hope and were sweeping due east on latitudes between 30° and 40° S when:

> We ware struck with a sudent [sudden] white squall which laid us down on our beam ends. Taking in sail, she rightined. The main topmast staysail being hall'd down, I run up to pass a gasket round the sail. I gumped on it to ride it down. The wind blew so powerful it blew me off like a feather, but ketching one of the leastings of the foresail that blew out, it brought me upright, and I fell with my backside on the bit head without being hurt. The officers seeing me fall came runing forward, expecting I was kill'd, but recovering myself I run up the lee rigging and furled the sail.[10]

The last of the laggards came in at Botany Bay on 21 January. Given their cramped quarters, infestations of various vermin and the risks of scurvy, the convicts had come through in reasonable shape. In all, forty-five had died, about 6 per cent, including five children and a woman, Jane Bonner, transported for stealing a coat, who suffered another familiar shipboard hazard, being killed by a falling longboat while on deck.[11]

A few days later Nagle was among a party that set out in three longboats, rowing up the coast beside sandstone cliffs until they reached the twin heads of a spot that Cook had named Port Jackson. Entering what is known today as Sydney Cove, Phillips exulted at finding 'the finest harbour in the world'.

Sydney Cove. The settlements of New South Wales and Van Diemen's Land had a darker aspect than most other Pacific destinations.

Jack was intimately engaged in the saga of Australia's founding.[12] What makes Nagle's observations particularly noteworthy is how they reflect troubled dealings with the Aboriginal population from the outset. 'The natives came down to us and apeared as though they did not aprove of our viset,' he wrote. The fact was, of course, this was no visit but an armed occupation. Barely had they landed than 'the convicts ware employed in cutting down timber and clearing to build log houses and the wimen employed in carreing the stones away'. The intruders had come to stay.

Phillip used his best endeavours to reassure the Aboriginals. 'He gave them clothes and trinkets, though he run many risks of his life . . . [and] would not allow us arms to defend ourselves for fear we would kill them.'[13] Firearms were used instead to demonstrate how unwise resistance would be; when the Aboriginals became 'mischievous' a pistol was fired to blast a hole in a bark shield. Hostility persisted. Nagle had formed a close friendship with a messmate, Terence Burne, and the two of them would fish at night, make a fire on the beach, then

. . . cook our supper, and take our grog, lay down in the sand and go to sleep till morning, though we would be often disturbed by the natives heaving there spears at us at a distance.[14]

Jack's usual avenues for congress – trade and sex – did not apply in New South Wales. Male Aboriginals had nothing to sell and the women were thought undesirable thanks to 'the stinking fish-oil and soot with which they besmear their bodies'.[15] The easy-going if rough fraternizing with Pacific islanders never found a place here. On one excursion Phillip was speared in the breast by a warrior and as Nagle and his crew rowed him back to the *Sirius* at top speed the governor 'made his will, not expecting to live'. Survive he did, and by persisting with his non-confrontational policy ensured the natives suffered no retribution.

————

The new colony's birth was painful, and not just for the natives and convicts. When the first plantings failed, exposing the newcomers to a threat of mass starvation, the *Sirius* was despatched to the Cape of Good Hope for provisions. This was a voyage that epitomized 'the tyranny of distance', for to reach Africa in the shortest time Captain John Hunter gambled on the prevailing westerlies to take the far longer passage via the Horn – in effect sailing right round the world to obtain food for the settlers. Though the weather was not contrary, all the men suffered from scurvy as well as the brutal cold. Nagle had to be carried below three times in one night but recalled with pride, 'I done my duty the next day.'

Another little trial, revealing of both his own self-respect and the esteem in which good men were held by their officers, occurred after they reached the Cape. Nagle and the boat crew were rowing ashore when a midshipman started laying into them with a rattan:

[He] being a striplin not more than 15 years of age, I told him we would not be treated in such a way by a boy. When we got on shore, five of us left the boat, not intending to return.

On hearing of their desertion, Captain Hunter sent Nagle's good friend Burne ashore with a master's mate to ask him to return. So, having run, Nagle went back; and when he explained himself to Hunter, it was the abusive midshipman who was confined for three weeks.[16]

But the mission had turned into a test of endurance. Returning to New South Wales, they ran into a tempest off what Nagle referred to in his phonetic style as 'Vandemons Land'. Demons, indeed, seemed to dance atop the waves as furies drove the *Sirius* through an inky haze out of which they glimpsed, every now and again, 'surf beating over rocks higher than our mast heads . . . I don't suppose their was a living soul on bd that expected to see daylight'. Small wonder that their arrival at Sydney Cove with food brought rejoicing – especially ashore, where the convicts were by now facing famine. Still, the passage around the entire southern latitudes of the globe had taken seven months.

Next *Sirius* was despatched with a brig to take a third of the convicts to Norfolk Island, which lay 1,000 miles to the east of the mainland but, because of its soil, had better potential to sustain them. Barely had the island been sighted than *Sirius* was swept onto a reef.

What followed had distinctly Crusoe-esque echoes. Although they all came safely ashore, crew and convicts were turned into castaways, and while the brig sailed for Sydney to raise the alarm, Nagle and a few other hands went out to salvage provisions from the wreck – he being among that small number of Jacks who could not only stay afloat but were powerful swimmers. (Mostly, Jack took the logical view that in the event of a shipwreck, the swimmer was only prolonging his own agony and that it made far more sense to break into the liquor store for one last carouse.) Nagle it was who churned his way to and fro through the surf with ropes and messages over the next two weeks, so that by the time the *Sirius* went to pieces, casks had been hauled ashore and copper salvaged to fashion cooking vessels. Coming ashore for the last time, Nagle may have been aggrieved to find his shipmates had built 'huts near the beach, which was call'd Irish Town, and most of them had wimin to live with them'.[17]

Another five months passed before help arrived. They survived thanks largely to the presence during the most critical spell of migrant mutton birds, *Pterodroma melanopus*, which had not previously seen humankind and in their nesting tunnels were the easiest of game, as well as 'very fine eating, very fat and firm'. The creatures did not long survive on Norfolk Island but while they did were known as Birds of Providence.[18] Even so, Nagle noted, it was remarkable that for all the castaways' hardships there had been just one death and she an elderly woman.

When the Siriuses embarked again for Sydney almost a year had passed since the wreck and, Nagle noted, 'a great many of the seamen would rather have staid on the island than come away'. In the event, it was fortunate that they did not: with a population of around 950, mainly convicts but with soldier-guards, Norfolk Island became arguably the worst place in the English-speaking world. Tyranny, brutality and murder were marks of a colony that, before it was abandoned in 1814, echoed conditions on the worst naval hells afloat.

Whatever its drawbacks, the land that became Australia always had potential and here too many Jacks wanted to settle. When the governor invited hands on the *Sirius* to come forward if they were interested in becoming farmers, all but a handful did so. Nagle was not among them. His was the true seaman's temperament – unflappable, living in the moment, aware that his fortune might change for better or worse in an instant, and, above all, restless.

Instead, he and his old messmate Terence Burne, with the remaining Siriuses, were put in a snow, the *Waaksamheyd*, bought at Batavia to carry them home. That took another year, as their listless vessel crawled back across two oceans, putting in at St Helena – a pinprick of an island in the south Atlantic which in these times was the principal refuelling station for British ships en route to the Indian and Pacific oceans – before reaching Spithead in April 1792. Five years had passed and Nagle was among just 37 of the 160 officers and men who sailed in the *Sirius* to have returned. Terence Burne had not, dying on the final leg home. He and Nagle had spent nine years together in two ships and, as was common when messmates were close friends and neither had family, each had made a will naming the other as beneficiary.[19] When Nagle was paid off he received Burne's wages too.[20]

It was spring and he and a few shipmates set off 'to go amayin, as is custamery, to gather flowers and drink punch . . . [and] we fel in with two hansome young ladies'. Nagle was happy to escort one of them home, and even happier to spend the night with her – but had to make himself scarce on discovering that her husband was an officer in a 74 at anchor.[21] That survival instinct had guided him through scrapes before. Plenty more lay ahead.

In the meantime colonization had moved on. Two years after the First Fleet, another batch of petty criminals was rounded up and loaded aboard transports for New South Wales. Among the Second Fleet was the *Lady Juliana*, carrying 226 women – and John Nicol.

Nicol may have said that he did not like her cargo and only signed on to see a distant part of the Pacific, but he could just as easily have joined the *Guardian*, a frigate carrying supplies to relieve the hard-pressed convict settlers. With her freight of strumpets, sharpers and shoplifters, the *Lady Juliana* was always likely to have a volatile passage, as the female transports in the First Fleet had demonstrated.

Nicol remained a caring soul. He witnessed the procession of women brought to Dartford as 'the jails in England were emptied to clear our cargo' and was moved by their plight. Skilled as a cooper, he was employed in striking off their irons as they came on board, and was haunted by the memory of how one Scottish girl retreated below in despair, where she died even before they sailed. 'I have never yet got her out of my mind . . . young and beautiful even in the convict dress, but pale as death, and her eyes red with weeping.'[22]

Most of the others were hardier types and some even saw their fate as a chance. 'We are not ill-treated or at the mercy of every drunken ruffian as we were before,' one woman told Nicol. But it was a Lincolnshire lass named Sarah Whitlam who caught his eye:

From the moment I knocked the rivet out of her irons upon my anvil . . . I fixed my fancy on her . . . and resolved to bring her back to England when her time was out, my lawful wedded wife.[23]

The *Lady Juliana* was one of four transports privately contracted from a company that usually transported slaves and the only one to escape the horrors that marked the Second Fleet – which had an overall mortality rate among the convicts of 21 per cent. Yet there was no shortage of misery on any ship starting for Australia in those days, and the yearning verse of one prisoner setting off into the unknown spoke for all:

> The distant shore of England strikes from sight
> And all shores seem dark that once was pure and bright,
> But now a convict dooms me for a time
> To suffer hardships in a forein clime
> Farewell a long farewell to my own my native land
> O would to God that I was free upon thy strugling strand.[24]

Whatever the crimes of the *Lady Juliana*'s women – and Nicol thought most to be harmless, 'victims of the basest seduction' – they did not lack shrewdness. One, Nelly Kirwin, had an intimate knowledge of Jack and his ways, having run a bawdy house in Gosport before her horizons broadened into forging seamen's wills. Hard-eyed pay clerks were used to sizing up women who presented themselves to claim wages due to a deceased husband and Nelly was fortunate to be pregnant because it saved her from the gallows.[25]

Mary Rose, a petty thief, had a talent for beguiling men. To Nicol she appeared 'a timid modest girl', a victim of various villains and tricksters, but her true history was rather more complex and Nicol was far from the only one to be taken in. He was equally trusting of Mary's friend and fellow thief. Sarah Whitlam was not only the object of his passion but 'as kind and true a creature as ever lived' – like Mary an innocent who had done no more than borrow a cloak from a friend. In reality, Sarah had stolen enough clothing to stock a small shop. It would have made no difference to Nicol who, had there been a clergyman on board, would have married her on the spot.

What the women experienced upon sailing was a sensation known to Jack on first going to sea – recognition that here was an alternative state, a separation not only from the land but a new dimension in which nothing was familiar. To these worldly creatures, suddenly vulnerable on this strange and terrifying element, the men who had their destinies in hand were bulwark and saviour. As for Jack, surrounded by femininity, he felt a rare sense of command. It was not therefore surprising that such ships, like those of the First Fleet, became so many floating bordellos.

The women were supposed to be battened down in their own quarters at night to prevent 'a promiscuous intercourse taking place', but the officer in charge of them, Lieutenant Thomas Edgar, was a hard-drinking pragmatist who could see a line between discipline and common sense, and evidently allowed free movement around the ship. By Nicol's own account, they were barely out to sea before 'every man on board took a wife from among the convicts – they nothing loath'.[26] Thus they proceeded, to Tenerife and across to Rio. By that time Sarah and Nicol were not only lovers; she had fallen pregnant.

Details are scant. The ship's log was lost and Nicol's is the sole surviving account of this fascinating passage which enclosed more than 200 women and some 40 men on a vessel less than 100 feet in length for a year. Yet given the volatility of the company and the crude closeness of their quarters, which required men and women to share the heads – the platform extending over the sea through which they pissed and defecated – along with all the other routines revolving around cleaning and taking meals, it seems to have been remarkably trouble-free. It was certainly a frolic by comparison with the nightmarish voyages of three other Second Fleet transports.*

---

* The *Lady Juliana* departed with the frigate *Guardian*, some months ahead of the *Neptune*, the *Surprise* and the *Scarborough*, on which the convicts suffered appallingly thanks to profiteering by the contractors. Out of 1,006 transportees, 267 died at sea and 150 more soon after arriving.

The only real emergency on the *Lady Juliana* was a fire on board while at the Cape of Good Hope, which caused a shrieking stampede before it was doused.

It helped that the female roost was ruled by a strong personality: Lizzie Barnsley, 'a noted sharper and shoplifter', came from a family of highwaymen, retained a flashy wardrobe and her own money, and could have run a gin palace in her sleep. At Tenerife and again at Rio she led excursions ashore to shop and take wine, and, having installed herself as a queen who dispensed gifts and favours among her fellow convicts, was probably in charge of negotiations when sailors from two American slavers came aboard midway across the Atlantic for some female company.[27] Mrs Barnsley also had experience as a midwife, which proved handy towards the end of the voyage.

It also helped that there was a preponderance of women, and that along with the younger, street-wise prostitutes and thieves, were some older, maternal figures; those who paired off with seamen appear to have formed stable partnerships, at least for the voyage.

Among them were Sarah Dorset and Edward Powell. Sarah was young and pretty, a true innocent driven into prostitution, whose harrowing parting from her parents had been observed by Nicol. Taken to his hammock by Powell, rated Able, she was among at least nine women to give birth on the *Lady Juliana* before they reached the Cape.[28] (How many more children were born between Africa and Australia is not recorded.) Both Sarah Dorset and Edward Powell married on reaching Sydney – but to different partners.[29]

For Nicol, however, there was only ever Sarah Whitlam, especially after she bore his son. His unworldliness is painfully apparent in the one great love affair of his life.

Sarah had fallen pregnant early in the voyage and after giving birth to John – under a tarpaulin set up on deck by the women, to escape the broiling heat below – was helped with washing and other chores by her friend Mary Rose, who was now also seen by Nicol as being 'under my protection'. Their little circle was the closest he had come to domesticity and having so long searched for love, he was happy. It was 'almost to our sorrow', as he saw it, that they reached their destination, anchoring in Sydney Cove on 3 June 1790, a day short of a year since sailing. Now 'the days flew on eagles' wings, for we dreaded the hour of separation which at length arrived'.

Desperate to stay with his new family, Nicol went to the captain, offering to sacrifice his wages if he could be released. No, came the answer, they were short-handed as it was. Most other Jacks – a Nagle for one – would not have hesitated before deserting. Nicol, however, retained even now some of the rectitude of his youth:

> I thus was forced to leave Sarah, but we exchanged faith. She promised to remain true, and I promised to return when her time expired and bring her back to England.[30]

He would fail, though not for want of effort. The *Lady Juliana* sailed on to China and home, where he made immediate enquiries about further expeditions to New South Wales. None being scheduled he signed on the *Amelia*, a south-sea whaler with the intention of using her to find another way to Sydney. While hunting south of the Horn, and after making a record haul of ambergris, she fell in with another vessel, the *Venus*. As was the way, men from the *Venus* came aboard the *Amelia* and in the exchange of accounts it emerged that they had recently been in New South Wales – that moreover one of their number was an escaped convict. With a mixture of excitement and apprehension, Nicol began to question him: 'I feared, yet wished, to hear of Sarah':

> How shall I express my grief when informed she had left the colony for Bombay. Thus were my worst fears realised. Unconstant woman! Why doubt my faith?

Grief was mixed with confusion. At the time of their parting, Sarah had three years of her term to serve and these had still not expired. How then could she have gone to India? His informant was unable to say. Nor did he know what had become of Nicol's son; most children were taken from unwed convict mothers and put into institutions, but there was some suggestion that the boy John had accompanied Sarah.

Once the initial shock had passed Nicol tried to reassure himself. It was right and proper for her to have left Sydney Cove. She had done it to escape 'bad company'. His romantic instinct thus revived, he determined to resume his quest, following her to Bombay. Finding a passage on an Indiaman would at least be easier than a ship for Australia.

First, though, he had to get back to England. When the *Amelia* came to off Rio he was taken on a Portuguese vessel bound for Lisbon – a passage he soon came to regret in the company of these 'execrable, superstitious sailors'. The great days of Portuguese seafaring were past and when a blow came on, Nicol and three other British hands watched dumbfounded as their fellows threw themselves at the feet of a priest dispensing holy water, 'while we were left to steer the vessel and hand the sails'. Finally, picking up a brig in Lisbon, he started on the last leg home 'with a joyful heart, to look out for an Indiaman that I might get to Bombay to inquire for Sarah'.

But the world had moved on. During his homeward passage, Nicol was told by a Spaniard that the king of France had been decapitated by his subjects. 'I understood what he meant but did not believe the information.'[31] Still less comprehension did he have of what it heralded. The land to which he was returning was at war, the Navy was preparing itself for what would turn into more than twenty years of conflict, and press gangs were once more hunting the streets for Jack.

Nicol never did get to India. He would not forget Sarah though, and – disguised as a civilian, in a cocked hat, a wig and a cane purchased for a guinea from a customs officer – set out for her home town of Lincoln, a journey of almost 200 miles, in the hope that 'she had reached her father's house and there was pining at my absence'. On arriving, it was to find that her parents had heard nothing from her either – which he thought 'very neglectful'. Perhaps it was at this stage that he started to think he had been too trusting. However, destined as he was to rejoin the Navy and be swept up in the great events ahead, Nicol was spared full knowledge of Sarah's infidelity.

When they parted on 25 July 1790 he left his Bible with her, their names inscribed together inside, certain that they would be reunited. The very next day, on 26 July, Sarah married John Walsh, a convict of the First Fleet. Seven weeks had passed since her arrival at Sydney Cove and though the circumstances of how or when she met Walsh are not known, it is plain she had only been waiting for Nicol's departure to move on. She and Walsh, their terms served, sailed with two children for India. Walsh would return to Australia alone in 1801. What became of Sarah, and her son by John Nicol, is a mystery.[32]

11

'A TERROR TO SEAMEN'
1788-92

SO MUCH of that era can be traced back to Cook – from the settlement of New South Wales to the discovery of the Pacific's resources and the opening of the whole region to enterprise, missionary activity and colonization. Cook's companion Sir Joseph Banks had been as much taken with the Pacific's potential as the great navigator himself, and it was Banks's notion of shipping an abundant and nutritious Tahitian plant known as breadfruit to feed slaves in the West Indies that gave rise to the most notorious voyage in the age of sail.

Contrary to legend, the *Bounty* mutiny was no classic rebellion by the lower deck against a brutal commander. Her company of forty-six included just thirteen able seamen and none was involved in the constant quarterdeck spats between Lieutenant William Bligh and Fletcher Christian, the master's mate, which concluded with Bligh and a few loyalists being dropped over the side into a boat somewhere south of Tonga in April 1789. It was a curious business altogether. Apart from Christian, the main target of Bligh's appalling temper had been John Fryer, the master, and he too had ended up being cast off with the captain.[1]

What gave the seamen common cause with Christian was that old lure of the Pacific – sex. Prior to the mutiny they had spent five months at Tahiti – a handful of unkempt, snaggle-toothed and bowlegged men who found themselves surrounded by uninhibited and beautiful women versed (as Bligh noted with horror) in the practice of fellatio.[2] Departure from what they called 'the happy island', with hundreds of breadfruit plants, was accompanied by much heart-searching and three attempted desertions, so clearly the prospect of returning to it had appeal. Even so, only one able seaman, Thomas Burkett, joined the core of mutineers led by Christian who entered Bligh's cabin at daylight on 28 April 1789. Three others, Thomas Ellison, Alexander Smith and Matthew Quintal, stood guard. The rest were passive while one, Michael Byrn, openly declared his loyalty to the commander, and was kept aboard the *Bounty* against his will while the cry went up, 'Huzzah for Otaheiti!'

Fresh divisions soon appeared among the mutineers, who split into two main groups. Some were left on Tahiti, only to be hunted down by a naval expedition. The fate of the rest was not discovered for almost twenty years and only came to light when an American sealer called at a remote and uncharted island called Pitcairn to find a bronzed and half-naked man in the tattered remnants of his trowsers, surrounded by an extended family of Anglo-Polynesian youngsters. John Adams was the last survivor. Despite the idyllic appearance of thatch huts among palm trees along the beach, it was clear that the mutineers' colony had been a wretched place, scarred by sexual slavery, insanity, massacres and suicides. Christian himself was long dead, although whether by murder, disease or his own hand was unclear. What did become plain as seafaring lore accumulated around the *Bounty* was a shift in perception of the South Seas: utopia had become dystopia.

Another legacy was the tarring of Bligh with the reputation of a monster; but though hot-tempered, he was far from the sadistic brute of popular history, and few seamen of any stamp could have successfully navigated a 23-foot launch 3,618 miles to safety with his eighteen fellow castaways.

From a wider perspective, we may note that Bligh was among a trio of Cook's protégés who led ventures to the Pacific after sharing in his voyages, each of whom offers an insight into the tense dynamic between a commander and his subordinates – or what the seaman Samuel Leech somewhat blithely called the 'set of human machinery in which every man is a wheel, a band or a crank, all moving with wonderful regularity and precision to the will of its machinist – the all-powerful captain'.[3] The truth is, when things went wrong it took a special officer to get the machinery working at all, let alone with precision.

There is no shortage of observations by Jack's superiors on what made a good hand. Jack, for his part, while he had plenty to say on impressment and discipline, was more sparing about what made a good commander. A hard-bitten cynic William Robinson, the self-styled Jack Nastyface, was quick to identify the bad ones, recalling 'a self-important demagogue' and 'a great bashaw . . . imperious, unfeeling and, of course, detested'. He had a pithy maxim too for zealots: 'The greater the tyrant, the greater the coward.'[4]

One thing is clear, and that is the modern notion of popularity had no place on the quarterdeck. A captain might be revered, even loved: Robert Hay served under two of the Navy's greatest commanders, Cuthbert Collingwood and Edward Pellew, and said both had 'the confidence, love and esteem of seamen'; a mere look of displeasure from Collingwood 'was as bad as a dozen at the gangway from another man'.[5] But the idea that a captain might be liked by his men would have been thought bizarre. The *sine qua non* of a capable officer was that he should be respected; better still, he should have respect for his men.

Jacob Nagle, a useful barometer in such matters, defined the key to a happy ship as being what he called the 'excelent yousage' of men practised by Captain Francis Bond of the sloop *Netley*. It sounds simple enough: Bond, he said, 'took a delight in making his ships company comfortable and when in harbour [granted] as much liberty as could be expected'. Like Collingwood, he detested the cat and would shame offenders rather than flog them. Malefactors might have a wooden collar padlocked around the neck while for lesser crimes they had to wear a scarlet cap like those of French revolutionaries, and when strangers came on board anyone stigmatized in this way 'would sneak below for shame'.[6]

Candid in his admiration for Captain Bond, Nagle was equally forthright about another officer; but whereas he would have followed Bond to the ends of the earth, he had done precisely the same to get away from Edward Riou, his lieutenant in the *Ganges*. Tyrants came in a variety of forms ranging from stupid bullies to ill-tempered martinets, and there was no shortage of either. Calculating sadists were rare, although the corrupting effect authority can have on human decency was fed by the isolation of a ship; Nagle's experience of being thrashed with a rattan by a teenage midshipman once the boy found himself freed from an officer's presence is one such example. It is also the case that a certain kind of officer revelled in being considered a tartar. Lieutenant Riou certainly did. As Nagle put it, Riou 'gloried in having the name of a villen and a terror to seamen'.[7]

Commanding a ship was never a straightforward matter, however, and Riou became the unlikely hero of a true seafaring epic in which far from being a terror, he proved a saviour to his men. In this respect his case has remarkable resonance with Bligh's; and both were disciples of Cook.

Nagle had of course been on the 74-gun *Ganges* prior to joining the First Fleet, and it was at her gangway that he felt the bite of the first lieutenant's displeasure. Riou, he declared, 'made it his study to punish every man he could get holt of and for the most frivolous fault':

> He would make them scrape the anchors in the coldest day in winter. He would tie them up in the riging and gag them with a pump bolt till it frose in their mouths. If he saw the least speck of dirt on your shirt in mustering you was brought to the gangway and floged. The severer the weather, the more he would have all the lower deck ports up, that the wind should fly through the vessel to keep you in motion. There was scarcely a man in that ship but what was punished by him.[8]

Riou's obsession – for most tartars had a particular mania – was cleanliness. This probably arose from having sailed in the *Discovery* on Cook's third voyage, and because it concerned the health of a ship as a whole it was at least grounded in common sense. Some idea of Riou's fixation, however, can be gathered from an extended note he made in a memorandum on the subject which concluded grimly: 'Whilst one half of the company are washing and scraping in one place, the other half are making dirt in another place.'[9]

Nagle escaped from Riou by joining the *Sirius* and sailing for New South Wales. Soon afterwards his old *bête noire* was given command of the 44-gun *Guardian*. Remarkably, Riou would be with the Second Fleet following in Nagle's wake. The *Guardian*, bearing two years' of supplies for the starving settlement and another twenty-five convicts, who were to do duty as seamen, departed England late in 1789 soon after the female convict ship *Lady Juliana*, with which she was intended to fall in.

What Lieutenant Riou would have made of that slow-sailing and sinful ark we cannot know for the rendezvous never did take place. Curiously, however, the *Lady Juliana*'s commander was another pupil of Cook's third voyage; yet while both Riou and Bligh were strict disciplinarians in their own respective ways, Lieutenant Thomas Edgar was, as we have seen, an easy-going pragmatist – 'a kind, humane man' according to John Nicol.

The *Guardian* fairly whistled down the Atlantic to the Cape of Good Hope, from where Riou was happy to write home that all those on board, including the convict sailors, were 'in as good health as if they had never been at sea'. The botanical collection compiled by Banks for the colony was in a less robust state – the artichokes and camomile looked to be dying – and Riou felt obliged to reassure Sir Joseph of special measures to protect the trees and plants from what he called 'my rabbits', which he had taken on at the Cape. (As the first man to contemplate introducing these pests to Australia, Riou thought them 'an animal too useful to be disregarded'.) The rabbits were not alone below; on sailing again the *Guardian*'s hold resembled a large farmyard, with two bulls and sixteen cows, two stallions and five mares, two rams and twenty ewes, and four boars and twelve sows.[10]

Thirteen days out of the Cape, on Christmas Eve, they had run far south to pick up the easterly trades and met with brutal cold – like Newfoundland in winter, Riou noted – when at Lat 43° 1' S they sighted an iceberg. Floating ice was not unusual in these latitudes but this was the size of a mountain – 'as high again as our main topgallant mast'. Soon the *Guardian* was surrounded by more drifting leviathans of ice, so that from the quarterdeck it appeared they were 'shut up in a thick mist and scarcely able to see the ship's length before us'. When she struck, an icy spike ripped a hole in her hull and the force was enough to spin her round on her stern and hurl her backwards into the embrace of another iceberg.

Ice was the seafarer's worst fear, according to John Nicol. Even in a storm on a lee shore, 'there is exertion to keep the mind up'; but 'locked up in ice, all exertion is useless'.[11] On the *Guardian*, the horror was apparent in the 'dreadful expressions of despair' Riou noted around him, and it served as a warning 'to collect myself and show as much as was within my power an example of forti- tude'. His first task was to manoeuvre the ship from the iceberg, then to divide the two watches into teams manning the pumps with such energy as to prevent the water gaining on them.

At dawn on Christmas Day the *Guardian* was a wreck – her rudder and tiller broken, beams fractured, sails in shreds and seven feet of water in the hold. Livestock and cannon had long gone over the side, with the exception of two stallions and a cow which resisted all efforts to shift them. Still, the pumps were working effectively and a sail had been fothered underneath the ship with dung, oakum and tar in an effort to seal the gaping hole in her hull. Critically, as the master Thomas Clements recorded, Riou's energy and his calm had 'prevailed on the people to overcome the first panic' and they bent to their duty in 'the hopes of safety of themselves and the ship'.[12]

Although the *Guardian*'s state was the primary cause for concern, the weather added to their peril – down in the icy misery of 44°S latitude, blowing a gale with rain and hail, the sea running high and breaking over the sides in explosions of spray. The men were battered themselves and by mid-afternoon had been struggling for twenty hours to keep her afloat, pausing only to take biscuits, cheese and weak grog. Clements noted how some 'became almost unable to perform any duty, their limbs being benumbed by the frequent tran- sition from the heat of labour and resting in wet cloaths'. A few desperate souls concealed themselves and had to be threatened that if they did not rejoin the common endeavour they would be cast overboard by angry shipmates.[13]

Late on Christmas night, this state of suspension ended when the winch on the starboard pump broke. Water in the hold started to rise. At 6 a.m. it was back to seven feet deep and although most of the hands were unaware of this, once the carpenter came up to say it had reached the orlop, concealment was no longer possible. And now 'many of the people desponded and gave themselves up to perish'.

Riou had led as he ought, encouraging, cajoling and by personal activity, even after his fingers were crushed as he joined in shifting a cask. Order had been maintained and the men allowed just enough grog to refresh them. But, as he noted, they now 'began to require a great deal of calling to the pumps', and he believed the ship would go down within twenty-four hours. Utterly exhausted himself, he tried to keep their spirits up while admitting:

I could no longer propose plans that promised success ... [and] was reduced to the common expression of 'Huzza! Heave round! etc.'[14]

At daylight, two days into the ordeal, he was approached by a group of hands who 'seeing no possibility of saving the ship, demanded the boats'. Here lay a further threat – that in a rush for safety, order might be lost. To preserve it for the time being, Riou promised to have the boats prepared while urging the men back to the pumps. Then he took aside Clements, the officer he thought best able to navigate a cutter to the Cape, and told him to make ready. On being urged to join, Riou replied that he was staying with the ship – and the majority who would have to remain on her:

I consider it in the first place my duty to look to the safety of my people, then comes my own. I will do my endeavours to effect them both, although I fear the impossibility. My opinion is fixed.[15]

It was almost certainly his decision to stay, commanding to the bitter end, that made the separation relatively orderly. Out of a company of 124, about forty

Seafaring disasters such as the wreck of the *Guardian* provided dramatic fare for the popular prints of the day.

men managed to scramble aboard the five boats hoisted over the side into a surging sea. One of these, a jolly boat, was immediately dashed to pieces against the ship. Another jolly boat, a cutter and a launch got clear, but without any provisions for the occupants. Only a longboat carrying Clements and fourteen other men had the supplies and the sails that might enable them to weather a passage back to the African coast, some 1,300 miles to the north-west.

Also in Clements' possession was a note hastily scrawled by Riou as the boats were about to put off. Addressed to the Admiralty, it was a generous and not entirely true attempt to absolve the survivors from any suggestion of guilt for abandoning the ship:

> If any part of the Officers or Crew of the *Guardian* should ever survive to get home I have only to say their conduct after the fatal stroke against an Island of Ice was admirable & wonderful in every thing that related to their duties either as private men or on his Majesty's Service.[16]

At dawn on the longboat nine days later, a gunner awoke and wiped his eyes in disbelief. A little way off, under bare poles, lay a ship. Bellowing and waving in frantic excitement, the castaways came up with what turned out to be a French merchantman whose company welcomed them aboard 'with unbounded friendship and attention'.

But for this fantastic stroke of fortune Clements believed they must all have died. As it was, there was no doubt in his mind on coming ashore at the Cape again two weeks later that no hope could be entertained for the other boats, nor for the *Guardian*.

When the boats put off, those remaining on the ship had little doubt either. They were dead men. As for Riou himself, all that now kept him going was a sense of responsibility. When a sea of faces turned to him, wanting to know what was to be done, he realized that his previous authority and a threat of force would not be enough. As he addressed them, the one-time tartar had come to a point few commanders at the time would have comprehended – that he needed to compromise with his men as well as to inspire them, even though he had no belief in survival himself:

> You have seen my conduct. You are now convinced, I believe, that I should be the last man out of the ship . . . But since you are wishing to know what you shall do, I will tell you if you still feel able to carry it into execution. You have worked well but we may still do more though the boats are gone. There are still hopes if your strength is equal to continuing at the pumps. Go to them. *You* never forsake them, you keep them going at all events. *I* will try another sail and fother the ship.[17]

Keeping the ship afloat was the first step to survival. Second was bringing her back into some kind of sailing condition. Though Riou, as he put it, 'entertained not the least prospect of success', activity was still preferable to the despair he saw threatening order. Now for the first time it became plain some men had got into the spirit room and were drunk. 'It was hardly a time to be a disciplinarian when only a few more hours of life presented themselves,' he noted, 'but this behaviour greatly hurt me.'

He could not bear to watch another collapse of order when one of the boats returned and the occupants asked for a sail. None could be spared and without provisions it was fairly clear that they were doomed. Yet that did not stop another twenty men reacting instinctively by jumping into the sea and attempting to board her. Riou turned away in despair.

A glimmer of hope appeared meanwhile in the form of a group of hands among whom two in particular were to the fore. Richard James and John Quinton, as might be expected, were senior men, aged forty-two and thirty-four, a Cornishman and a Scot, and widely respected. When they stood up and declared that 'the ship was not so bad, that she was still lively and that if we succeeded [in getting up a foresail]' she might be saved, their fellows took courage. Riou was hugely relieved. Though he still saw no prospect of survival, 'I rejoiced at such spirit and hoped to see it diffused'.

Another light came from a more unexpected source. Since being brought aboard from various jails and hulks, the convicts doing duty as seamen had learnt the ropes and were now more active than all but the ablest hands. Despite their miserable fate – half had been given life terms and would never be allowed to return home – they appeared more determined to fight on than the sailors. Or perhaps, being less aware of how hopeless their situation was, they were more willing to follow orders that might prolong life. It was certainly the case that their desperate efforts at the pumps had kept the *Guardian* afloat.

Riou's priority – gaining control over the water level below – was achieved by a combination of pumping and baling until more canvas could be fothered over the hull. Although the precise location of the damage was always unclear because of the sheer quantity of water still swirling around within the ship, the fothering was fairly successful once strips of blanket and bedding were sewn to a tattered foresail and the entire shroud brought beneath to plug the puncture.

Next, Riou set to manufacturing 'a steering machine' to replace the fractured rudder so the ship might be moved in a controlled way. Days were spent in cutting two 6-foot lengths of timber from the gangway, bolting them to a spare jib boom and lowering the entire contraption into the sea from a rear cabin window. Quinton and James were again to the fore with other prime hands, and a few convicts.

All the while, order as well as survival hung in the balance. Riou found his cabin had been ransacked, his watch, silver buckles and sword stolen. Mutterings could be heard among a demoralized cabal led by a troublesome hand, Thomas Humphries, who got drunk and taunted Riou to the effect that there would be 'no more flogging now'.[18] Some men wanted to build a raft. Others insisted their best hope lay in making for the Prince Edward Islands to the south, when Riou knew the only sensible course was north, where, even if they failed to reach Africa, there was a chance they might fall in with another ship, possibly the *Lady Juliana* following in their wake. Rather than confront the dissenters, Riou confided to another respected hand, Henry Johnson, that the islands were uncharted, uninhabited and surrounded by icebergs. This intelligence, casually passed down via a conduit, reached the whole company and had the necessary effect. Talk of the islands ceased.

Still a spirit of revolt persisted. On the first day of 1790, Riou was told that some men meant to take command because 'I was not in my senses, I wanted to die and the ship was going the wrong way.' An Irish hand, Edward Dwyer, was heard to say: 'Then let's heave him overboard.'[19] What exchanges took place between the malcontents and the loyal hands on whom Riou had come to depend is not known, but something prevented insubordination turning into mutiny.

Very slowly, the *Guardian* started to labour north-west. The means by which this desperately crippled vessel was first kept afloat and then set on a staggering course towards Africa could provide a specialist study in sailing mechanics and technique.[20] More generally apparent from the log kept by Riou is that after weeks in which one emergency was followed by another and the ship did little more than drift with the current, a southerly breeze came up and a few sails were raised. Stalwart physical efforts by the best men, allied to Riou's seamanship, had kept hope alive and on 21 January he was able to write: 'This day's run was beyond expression encouraging.'

One tower of strength was the Cornishman Richard James, who, in his commander's words, 'performed wonders' when the ship was heavily down by the stern. James went into the spirit room where timber from shattered casks was 'floating to and fro with great violence as the ship rolled very heavily', and despite his forty-two years, and although 'dashed by the sea and very cold', he withstood the bruising, swirling debris and brought up enough of it so that lesser mortals could go down and start baling.[21]

A gradual dawning of hope brought with it a return to some kind of normality – and a restoration of Riou's authority. He struck a surly hand for failing to carry out an order, and harangued a group for doing their duty only when they were in danger, slacking off as soon as it passed. The leading agitator, Thomas Humphries, first lost his influence then became an outcast, shunned by his fellows who would no longer speak or eat with him. Finally, Humphries was heard admitting to Riou: 'Had it not been for you, we should have all been at the bottom long ago.'

By the end of January, five weeks after the calamity, Riou was able to consider whether they should make for Africa or Madagascar. While he evidently had the experience of the *Grosvenor* castaways in mind when reflecting that the natives might prove hostile if the *Guardian* was driven onto the African coast, it would at least be closer the Cape. Over the next three weeks a ruined ship held to a more or less steady north-east course, covering some 1,200 miles – or roughly 40 miles a day.

When land was sighted on 21 February, Riou was in his cabin. Aptly, the news was brought by James, the burly Cornishman, and coming up on deck, they experienced a moment of exultation:

I saw it directly and, thank God, it was the only land I knew on the coast.
It was the Cape of Good Hope!

The wreck and salvation of the *Guardian* is among the lesser-known seafaring epics, yet it offers compelling insights into the nature of command on a sailing ship. All those who stayed after she was impaled on the ice – sixty-one souls – were saved. Of the sixty-three who took to the boats, only fifteen survived. Jacob Nagle might have described Edward Riou as 'a villen and a terror to seamen', yet he would have seen him in a different light had they been together in a crisis. A gulf of tension would always – indeed, had to – divide officers and men, quarterdeck and lower deck. As Riou himself later reflected: 'Broomstick had more effect than Cicero.'

Riou's occasional severity as a commander was balanced by real human warmth, as is evident in letters to his mother and sister from the Cape – 'My dearests . . . God has been merciful.' It is also to be seen in a plea he made to the Admiralty for pardons on behalf of the twenty-one surviving convicts:

> Not one of them, so far as [it] depended on myself, should ever be convicts. And I may with undeniable truth say that had it not been for their assistance and support the *Guardian* would never have arrived to where she is.[22]

Royal pardons were duly forthcoming. Meanwhile Riou also singled out fourteen of the ship's company in another letter to the Admiralty, for 'having merited the highest approbation I can bestow on their conduct in the many melancholy scenes that were exhibited in the *Guardian*'. They included John Quinton but not, however, the hero of the lower deck, Richard James. Why this figure so central in saving the ship was omitted is not clear; but James had a weakness for drink, which may have revived the tartar in his commander.*

---

* Readers of Patrick O'Brian may have noted echoes of the *Guardian* epic with the novel *Desolation Island*, in which Jack Aubrey is seen in the role of Riou. The *Guardian* story should also be viewed in the light of events on the 74-gun *Centaur* a few years earlier. She suffered severe damage in a mid-Atlantic gale and after a week struggling to keep her afloat 'the men quitted bailing . . . and the love of life began to level all distinctions'. Captain John Inglefield was candid enough to admit that faced with a choice 'to remain and perish with the ship's company, whom I could not be any longer of use to, or seize the opportunity of escaping', it was the love of life that prevailed. He was among twelve men who scrambled into a pinnace and, with a few quarts of liquids, a piece of pork, a small ham and a bag of bread, navigated eastwards for the next two weeks to reach the Azores. The ship and some 600 men were never seen again. Inglefield's decision to quit the *Centaur* once her fate became inevitable was deemed perfectly acceptable and a court-martial hearing found that he had done everything possible to save her (see *Captain Inglefield's Narrative of the Loss of the Centaur in 1782*, London, 1813, available online).

They were still at the Cape when a floating bordello came in. Seldom can two vessels at anchor have so vividly illustrated the contrasting extremes of Jack's existence: death and desperation on the *Guardian*; hedonism and dissipation on the *Lady Juliana*. What opportunity the two companies had for sharing their experiences is not clear, although there must have been some fraternizing when the *Guardian*'s remaining supplies for New South Wales were taken across to the *Lady Juliana*. John Nicol, at this stage still happily set up with his Sarah, gave a garbled, second-hand account of what had occurred on the *Guardian* while, with seamanlike insouciance, failing to reflect that he had nearly signed on her himself.

We come back to a simple if awkward truth. Jack might respond best to the command of supremely gifted and perceptive officers like Collingwood, Nelson and Pellew – men capable of inspiring love. But such individuals were always rare and the Navy, especially in moments of crisis, depended on the strict and sometimes crude discipline exercised by lesser mortals. And, at bottom, Jack was often able to see that the methods of a supposed tartar like Edward Riou were not quite as straightforward as they presented.

Jacob Nagle, having recalled that Riou 'gloried in having the name of a terror to seamen', went on to relate a touching and entirely paradoxical anecdote of his former lieutenant – of how Riou, wrapped in a cloak one night in Portsmouth, had hired a waterman to take him out to the *Ganges*. The fellow was reluctant because, he declared, there was on board an officer named Riou, 'the biggest villen that ever God let live upon earth'. Still the cloaked figure insisted on being taken alongside. He then disappeared up the side. Some time later the boatman came on board to claim his fare – and was horrified to be brought before a uniformed lieutenant:

'Did you no tell me I was the biggest villain in the world?' enquired Riou.

'Sir, I beg a thousand pardons. I did not know it was you.'

'Very well, here is a shilling for you, and go to my steward and get a bottle of rum. Then you may go ashore.'[23]

As Nagle said, it was the reputation that mattered. An officer who bore the reputation of a tartar did not necessarily have to behave like one.

In the last peaceful summer of 1792, Nagle found himself back on familiar ground in Wapping – insofar as he found any landscape familiar – among the inns and lodgings that ran east from Tower Hill down the Ratcliffe Highway. He took a room at Mr Goodall's boarding house which, in the St Katharine's area, counted as positively luxurious. Nagle was flush, having received not just his own wages from five years in Australia and the Pacific but those of his deceased shipmate Terence Burne – and he liked spending.

Nagle's accounts of his capers ashore are as illuminating as those of life at sea. Told with an unaffected candour, they show a man rambunctious among his fellows and quick with his fists, yet, when it came to women, thoughtful and fond of those who crossed his path. He was also wise enough to acknowledge his mistakes but often blithely unaware, or at least unheedful, of the unpredictable currents carrying him this way and that. Nagle was back in London at a turning point in history. He was also at a crossroads in his life.

His appreciation for the finer things could extend beyond taverns and women, and with another old Sirius, William Hunter, who lived near St George's-in-the-East, he went off to 'amuse myself in plays and opparas'. Yet even with money in his pocket he would never be respectable. One night he accompanied Mr Goodall and his guests – an East India Company army officer, a navy purser and their wives – to the playhouse at Drury Lane, where Goodall had bought box tickets at 3 shillings each, but which barred them because Nagle had on a jacket rather than a long coat, so they had to move to the one-shilling gallery.[24] A few nights later he was back at an inn among friends, picking up news of sailings, playing cards, and frolicking with a light-fingered hussy named Liddy.

For some time Nagle had been thinking of home. More than ten years had passed since his last sight of America and, having been paid off, nothing now stood in his way of returning. So one morning he wandered down to the Pool, the hub of British merchant shipping on the Thames west of Tower Hill, and found a vessel for Philadelphia – only to storm off when the captain demanded that he pay ten guineas on top of working his passage. The consequence was that another ten years would pass before he reached home.

Later, at the Red Lion, two lads told him they were heading to Ostend because an American ship there was recruiting hands. He and a friend, Bill Beard, resolved that before setting off they should have 'a last cruise', and a riotous outing ended in a final romp with Liddy – she 'full of glee and good youmer'.

Early next morning, down at Billingsgate to pick up a sloop for Dover, he discovered that his belt with 35 guineas sewn inside was missing. 'Well, thinks I, Liddy had done me':

> When I came up the stairs she asked what was the matter. I said nothing but went to the bed, which had not been made up, hove the covering and sheet back, and there laid my belt [which] had got loose from me in the night. She asked me if I had mistrusted hur. I said could not tell till I return'd to see. She cried. I pittied hur. I gave hur two guineas. She refused and I made hur take it, bid hur good by, and started back to my shipmates.[25]

He duly reached Ostend and signed on a ship for Philadelphia – whereupon the captain received orders to proceed to France. Nagle saw no alternative but to return to London, the poorer by various fares and a month's lodging laid out on behalf of an ailing companion. The brig across the Channel ran into a gale and but for the intervention of Nagle and his skills might have run aground. After an altercation with the captain, he walked back to Wapping.

Liddy, at least, was pleased. She 'apeared rejoic'd to see me, and we had supper'.

A few weeks later, still looking for a ship to America, Nagle was seized by a press gang. The onset of more than twenty years of war with France had opened a new era in maritime history and in the lives of those who wrote it.

INTERLUDE: THE DEEP

The sea has never been friendly to man. At most it has been the accomplice of human restlessness.

Joseph Conrad

THE greatest mystery for anyone who lived at sea was the element itself. That inescapably immense surface is the closest our planet comes to another world, and in Jack's experience it was everywhere and everything. Just as it could be benevolent and soothing, the space in which seamen felt their concerns drift away as they left the shore, it was awesome and terrifying, and all the more because it was totally unpredictable. Like all things sublime, it defied description or comprehension.

Sensibly, seafarers in general made no attempt to do so. The sea can be reduced to shades – ranges of blue and grey, running to white and black – sometimes to a dazzling, luminous phosphorescence. It can be defined in dimensions – in surface area, in depth, in the distance between two land masses, or even in its entire volume, which is estimated at 320 million cubic miles. Ships' daily logs passed over it in banal terms – 'Calm' or 'Heavy Swell' – because it was easier to cite the weather above which would define what transpired below. We can reach out hopelessly for it in words, with adjectives like those employed here. Even so eloquent a writer as Herman Melville struggled in *Moby Dick* to summon the firmaments of sea and sky, 'hardly separable in that all-pervading azure; only, the pensive air was transparently pure and soft, with a woman's look, and the robust and man-like sea heaved with long, strong, lingering swells, as Samson's chest in his sleep'.

Aaron Thomas, a young fellow from Herefordshire, had a more lyrical bent than most of his fellows and grappled valiantly with the challenge:

> The briny Ocean dashed in furious combat against the potent winds, both seeming momentarily to lay aside their dispute and combine in terrible junction to strike a vehement revenge, a mortal or destructive blow to the Mariner for thus presuming to traverse the unfathomable, watery empire.[1]

Precisely because of its immanence, the sea often escaped note in Jack's daily life until it became fearsome. Yet the experience of living within the sea in all its unknowable majesty – its moodiness, mystery and fury – left a mark on the most prosaic soul. With a few notable exceptions, these men had no great appetite for conventional religion. A chaplain lamented: 'The most reprobate among them would not treat me very badly; but I did not see the smallest likelihood of effecting any material change in their morals . . . To convert a man-of-war's crew into Christians would be a task to which the courage of Loyola, the philanthropy of Howard and the eloquence of St Paul would prove inadequate.'[2]

Joshua Marsden, whose experience of being shipwrecked in the frigate *Amethyst* turned him into a missionary zealot, had this to say of the common sailor:

> He rarely thinks, seldom reads, and never prays . . . Speak to him about the call of God, he tells you he hears enough of the boatswain's call . . . If you talk of Heaven, he hopes he shall get a good berth aloft: is hell mentioned? He jokes about being put under the hatchway.[3]

Yet, then as now, Christianity and spirituality were not synonymous. One of a new generation of hands, Daniel Goodall, ventured into the spiritual aspect. Goodall believed that solitude and danger engendered a simple faith beneath the veneer of 'recklessness and dash so generally characteristic of Jack ashore':

Vice and dissipation I have witnessed in large measure and in revolting forms . . . but I never met an infidel among seamen – certainly not among those who had been afloat for any length of time.[4]

Goodall alighted on something profound. Left alone with the elements, humankind has ever felt touched by the divine or the mystical. Superstition, myth, legend – these loomed large for Jack in moments of crisis. At the bottom of it all lay the elements. Wind and sky, water and sea. To those ashore, these were manifestations of God. To those at sea, they were God.

Among our small band of literate hands, Charles Pemberton perhaps came closest to capturing the stately spectacle to be found all around them:

When the sea was up, how terribly grand it appeared to be, as the green hills rose higher, hills chasing hills and bounding after each other in magnificent delight. The whole sea was alive – as one vast spirit . . . tossing its mighty arms aloft and sweeping its hands across the verge of the horizon as if to crush the feeble intruder.[5]

An uncommon seaman in every respect – he went on to a modestly successful career as an actor – Pemberton also brought insight to the heart-stopping exhilaration enjoyed by men in presuming to challenge the elements: topmen going aloft to save their ship, standing a hundred feet or so above a plunging deck, braced against the yards, feet planted on ropes slung below and swaying with a mast that might be moving through sixty degrees:

The leaping hills of water yield; the ship is mistress of their strength as she rides a moment of their arched backs, and laughs as she scatters the foam from their crests, then swings herself round into the deep gorge, and with the impetus remounts and laughs again . . . So it was now; so with my feelings I learnt to look saucily on the sea. A sort of braggart spirit rose in me as the ship lifted me with her in her overtopping sovereignty.[6]

Insouciance could turn in a moment to terror. Disease, it is estimated, carried off roughly four times as many hands as were lost to accident or shipwreck.[7] But it was storms and disasters at sea that loomed large in the dramatic narrative.

The great majority of wrecks occurred in home waters, close to shore. The Channel was the grave of innumerable vessels which, typically, would have found themselves beating against the wind and driven ever closer the land before being caught in the situation dreaded by every mariner – embayed and on a lee shore: in other words, trapped between headlands by a wind forcing them towards the rocks. Just such a fate befell the 90-gun *Ramillies* on the Devon coast in 1760, when more than 700 men died. Only twenty-seven escaped.

The wreck of the *Halsewell* Indiaman off Dorset in 1786 created a sensation because the 170 souls lost with her were not just seamen but passengers and civilians, including the two daughters of Captain Richard Peirce, who opted to die with them rather than save himself. Among numerous images of the disaster, J. M. W. Turner painted a harrowing picture of the ship in her dying moments while Thomas Stothard created an affecting scene of doomed souls in a darkened cabin and Peirce comforting his girls towards the end.

But when it came to the stories that gripped listeners at the Three Daws or the Mucky Duck, it was of storms in alien waters that old hands would tell – of rounding the Horn in a maelstrom, or of a storm in the Eastern Seas, with waves higher than the foremast, the ship on her beam ends, canvas shredded, a black and purple sky dashed by lightning, and a screaming from demons in the rigging. Few subjects so stimulated the flow of ale as the fury known – from a Caribbean word meaning 'evil spirit and big wind' – as a hurricane.

It took a great deal to sink a ship in open seas. Thanks to her natural buoyancy a wooden vessel might spend hours on her beam ends – down on her side – and remain afloat, provided she did not go right over, fill up and get dragged down. She might actually go right over and still spring back. She might lose every mast, and all means of control, yet somehow bear up. All these states were experienced by ships struck by the firestorm of hurricanes in the Indian Ocean over three successive monsoon seasons from 1807. The toll was unprecedented. In the first year, two men-of-war went down with all hands off Madagascar. The following season, three Indiamen were swept into oblivion. The last year was the worst – four more Indiamen lost and nine others and three navy ships taken to the very edge. Almost 250 passengers had died. So had more than 2,000 seamen.[8]

Among the hands to survive the final, most furious of these hurricanes, Robert Hay of the *Culloden* noted how some hands were gripped by visions. Awe at the sight of unbridled natural forces was never far from superstition:

> Some of our men gravely affirmed that shortly after the commencement of the gale they had seen the Flying Dutchman cross our bows under a very heavy press of sail . . . Consternation and dismay were depicted on every countenance and many had bidden their mess mates a last farewell.

The mythical Flying Dutchman was a ghostly ship with a deranged captain at the helm, destined to sail the seas endlessly. Another dark legend concerned Davy Jones, a monster whose locker, or chest, was the resting place of those lost. As a former naval surgeon, Tobias Smollett was well placed to provide the first definition of this creature in his novel, *The Adventures of Peregrine Pickle*:

> This same Davy Jones, according to the mythology of sailors, is the fiend that presides over all the evil spirits of the deep, and is often seen in various shapes, perching among the rigging on the eve of hurricanes, shipwrecks, and other disasters to which seafaring life is exposed, warning the devoted wretch of death and woe . . . I know him by his saucer eyes, his three rows of teeth and tail, and the blue smoke that came out of his nostrils.

Mythical monsters came in feminine form too. Mermaids belong more to classical legend and the romantic imagination than to our seafarers, whose tales were fired rather by the likes of Mother Carey, a witchlike counterpart to Davy Jones. *The Seaman's Manual*, published in 1790, defined 'Mother Carey's children' (synonymous with her chickens) as the sailors' term for 'birds which they suppose are the forerunners of a storm'. In more scientific terms, Mother Carey's chickens are *Hydrobatus pelagicus*, or storm petrels.

Most seamen had stories of gales they had not expected to survive, John Nicol and Jacob Nagle among them. The danger was aggravated, as Nagle observed after numerous encounters with Mother Carey, by Jack's instinctive response to the seemingly inevitable, which was to drink himself into oblivion. More than once Nagle was ordered 'to open the after hatchway and stave all the liquor to prevent the seamen from getting drunk'.[9] Interestingly, even he could be touched by a sense of the spiritual. After one miraculous escape in the Tasman Sea, this phlegmatic character, who never expressed faith of any kind, wrote: 'Through Gods assistance we ware saved, where we had no hopes but in him.'[10]

Usually men simply gave up to await the end, as Samuel Leech did. 'Some of us went below and turned in with the full expectation that our ship would founder before morning; and thinking it would be as well to go down in our hammocks as on deck':

> Some manifested great alarm about eternity. They prayed aloud in deep distress. Others only cursed and said, as if in bravado, 'We are all going to hell together.' For my own part I kept repeating the Lord's prayer, and renewing those promises so often made in the moment of apparent destruction.[11]

A similar blend of defiance, resignation and prayer was recorded by a survivor of the tempest that did for the 74-gun *Centaur* off Newfoundland. Dismasted and with seven feet of water in the hold, she was preserved for days by men bailing with canvas buckets until, hit by a renewed blast, she started to founder. At the last, many of the doomed men were seen to be 'putting on their best and cleanest clothes'.[12] More than 400 died. They would have borne no resentment for the captain and ten others who escaped in a pinnace and survived two weeks adrift in the Atlantic to reach the Azores.

We have seen enough of castaways to know that shipwreck did not necessarily end at sea. From John Duck of the *Wager*, washed up and enslaved by nomads in Patagonia, to Joshua Glover of the *Grosvenor*, whose landfall in Africa carried him into the arms of another tribe, hands lived their own versions of the Robinson Crusoe narrative. Of the 280 souls on the *Winterton*, another Indiaman, wrecked on Madagascar in 1792, fewer than twenty drowned; yet only a handful ever reached home.[13]

Storms and coastlines do not tell the full shipwreck story. Ice was a constant peril in extreme latitudes. John Nicol found being trapped in an icy waste off northern Scotland 'far worse than any storm I was ever in':

> In a storm upon a lee shore, even in all its horrors, there is exertion to keep the mind up and a hope to weather it. Locked up in ice, all exertion is useless. The power you have to contend with is far too tremendous and unyielding. It, like a powerful magician, binds you in its icy circle, and there you must behold, in all its horrors, your approaching fate [amid] the crashing of the ice and the less loud but more alarming cracking of the vessel.[14]

Then there were those wrecks so freakish, so unaccountable, they stimulated fresh episodes of tribal mythology and superstition. The *Essex* was whaling in the Pacific when one of her intended prey, an 80-foot sperm whale, rammed her repeatedly with a fury and force that sent her to the bottom, forcing the crew of twenty to take to the boats and starting another survival epic, of men adrift for more than three months. The *Essex* inspired Melville to write the most famous maritime novel. It also added to the rich seam of fantastic, chilling yarns shared by seafarers, which concluded in this instance with the cannibalization of seven men in open boats, in order that their fellows might survive.[15]

Superstition was fuelled by the mariner's whimsical fate. A man could be pressed into a ship which, his messmates later heard with a shaking of heads, then vanished in a storm. Another might desert on impulse and thereby avoid the same misadventure. The effect was observed by the naval surgeon

Thomas Trotter: 'The appearance of the sky, the flight of a bird, sailing on certain days of the week – these with other incidents fill their heads with omens and disasters.'[16]

Sam Leech recalled how once a story told by a shipmate made 'a melancholy impression on my boyish mind' and convinced him 'that [we] would never return home again'. Soon afterwards an Atlantic storm descended, battering the ship to a floating wreck; and as the hands became sure they were about to die, blame was placed on an old man 'who had been cast away several times' and was deemed a Jonah, cursed by ill-fortune:

> But not being so resolute as the mariners of Tarshish [sic] they did not cast him into the sea . . . and after several days of pleasant weather we found ourselves safely anchored near New York.[17]

And so it went on. For as long as men were at sea under sail, their state would veer between hope and dread, relief and resignation. The same might be said of the human condition in general. Yet the highways of the oceans added a further aspect to the unknown and the unknowable. For this was the very font of existence – 'a vast theatre of life, the element in which all living things originated, and the stage on which they have acted out the greater part of the evolutionary drama'.[18] Of all men, Jack lived closest to the mystery of creation, and to visions of extinction.

The sea would always be there. But a time of enlightening discovery and exploration was about to give way to an era of unrelenting warfare.

PART TWO
ATOP

'THESE VALUABLE BUT HELPLESS PEOPLE'
1792-97

THE great wars between 1793 and 1815 were essentially between French land power and British sea power, and it follows that without victory at sea there could have been no success on land. If Jack did not exactly win the wars that redefined British history, he played the pivotal role in turning the tide, for forces could never have been launched against Napoleon in Europe without naval supremacy.[1] But soldiers also served nobly, and Pitt the Elder's dictum – 'when we endeavour to exert our strength by sea we become the dread of the world; when by land the contempt of it' – no longer held after the Peninsular War, let alone Waterloo. It could even be argued that France's Navy, previously an aristocratic preserve, was so damaged and demoralized by the Revolution that Jack's triumphs paled beside the harder-won victories of Wellington's troops. For the first time, sailor and soldier stood shoulder to shoulder.

Insofar as terms of service were concerned, it may be fair to conclude that the Army was dealt the better hand. When a soldier enlisted during wartime it was for a set number of years. He had time to say farewells and order his affairs. He might never leave his native shore and would have opportunities for family contact. His pay was better too. An infantryman received a shilling a day, roughly 30 shillings a month, minus deductions. His two or three meals a day were usually of fresh produce and certainly of a higher standard than those dished up at sea.

Meanwhile, an Able seaman was still being paid 24 shillings per month of twenty-eight days, an Ordinary hand 19 shillings, with deductions for Greenwich Hospital and other benefits of 1s 6d. Such wages might attract men and boys from rural areas, but they had been unchanged for more than a century and discontent was on the rise: a London labourer expected two shillings a day and a craftsman three shillings. The problem was that the Admiralty stood under a constant budgetary lash. Precise figures for this period are hard to come by, but at times of war the Navy is estimated to have accounted for a quarter of government spending.[2]

When it came to battle, one of Wellington's army officers offered this pertinent if rather blithe note after seeing an English brig blast a French corvette to smithereens in Biscay:

> We came to the conclusion that sea-fighting was more agreeable than land-fighting as the crews of the vessels engaged without previous heavy marching, and with loose light clothing, there was no manoeuvring or standing for hours on the defensive, the wounded were immediately taken below and attended to, and the whole affair was over in a pleasingly brief period.[3]

Captain Rees Gronow had a point. Brevity was indeed typical of sea actions, based as they were on obtaining an advantageous position then discharging as much ordnance as possible from a shifting deck before the wind or current moved both sides on. And for harsh service it is hard to argue that even the sailor who spent month after winter month in the squalid misery of a 74 blockading Brest, constantly tacking close inshore against easterly winds and blasted by the storms of Biscay, had it tougher than the soldier to be seen tramping through savage Iberian wastes, sweating blood under blazing skies or freezing in snow on the sierras, and snatching a few hours' sleep wherever his captain called a halt.[4]

But comparisons between terms of service invariably come back to one difference. A soldier enlisted. He went to war voluntarily. Although local militia were raised by ballot, men could buy their way out. They might be persuaded to join a regular regiment, but there was no legal coercion.[5] Military conscription did not come into being for another century.

Impressment, on the other hand, was entrenched by custom and practice; and at the start of a new war, nobody – especially at the Admiralty – was willing to grasp alternative methods of mass mobilization. Naval conscription by another name intensified. So did the arbitrary and sometimes pitiless methods by which it was applied. Images of the press gang remain among the most enduring of the age – typically a band of thugs, cudgels in hand, tearing a forlorn figure from the bosom of a family cowering in the background. The caricatures of James Gillray and Thomas Rowlandson are not, self-evidently, historical records but cultural snapshots of an age when satire was at its savage zenith. Yet awareness of impressment reached all levels of society after 1793, partly because of a growth in libertarian values, but also because it was a practice that became increasingly visible.

Alternatives had been proposed. As far back as 1777, in response to the torn loyalties of the American Revolution, a Bill was introduced to Parliament based on a plan for manning authored by Lieutenant Robert Tomlinson, whose first-hand experience had left him with an abhorrence of impressment and who proposed a limited service for volunteers of between three and five years. The Bill was defeated but the campaign continued for a decade.[6]

The next, similarly doomed, parliamentary motion by William Pulteney in 1786 was notable for an electrifying pamphlet from the pen of another naval officer. Lieutenant John Mackenzie pulled no punches in his passionate denunciation of 'this abominable custom', quoting directly from Magna Carta as evidence that the law was being violated and accusing those who cited 'the force of custom' as justification of sophistry and feudalism. They were also, he added, blind to an inherent nobility in the common seaman's character:

> The multitude of these men are wholly illiterate, their ideas wild, confused and indeterminate as the elements they have to combat with; their dispositions naturally generous, though turbulent; fearless, or rather thoughtless

The Liberty of the Subject by Gillray passed a caustic comment on impressment as early as 1779 but the practice was to become more prevalent still.

of consequences (from being inured to hardship and danger) they will run every risk to satisfy the caprice of the moment . . . Yet [they are] possessed of the strongest notion of personal freedom and their own independence; for out of the King's service they are in general citizens of the world, they have a home in every climate.[7]

This instinct for freedom, Mackenzie argued, made impressment counter-productive, as was evident from the high desertion rate. Indeed, the 'forcible attempt to rob them of every social happiness [which] they were, after many dangers and fatigues, returning to enjoy', served only to excuse the actions of 'these valuable but helpless people'.

Lieutenant Mackenzie spoke from experience. He cited conditions in Jamaica where, due to the prevailing winds, ships sailed in the early morning, often before men could even remove personal effects from their berths after being pressed, let alone claim outstanding pay. Being then homeward bound, they had no prospect of recovering either. Losses, as he pointed out, extended to families in the event of a seaman's death. There was an instance of men pressed out of returning Indiamen and sent on a ship to the West Indies, which went down with all hands. Because their details had not yet been logged, the families received neither the year's wages due from the India House nor anything from the Admiralty.

Mackenzie's fervour and his humanity did him credit, especially as this diatribe from a junior officer would have gone down at the Admiralty like a 42-pound ball over the side. His belief, he declared, was that almost every naval officer shared his disquiet, and he intended to write 'an Essay towards a plan for manning the Royal Navy without expense to government, injury to trade, or oppression upon individuals'. The essay failed to appear.

A resumption of war in February 1793 against a French state consumed by revolution silenced the reform debate. No one had any expectation that a conflict 'between all the order and all the anarchy in the world' would continue into the next century; but tensions between the Navy with its need for seamen, and ship-owners and merchants with their demand for its protection, could only grow. Never was the essential truth of British maritime endeavour – that Jack was a resource on which his country depended – more clearly demonstrated than over the next two decades.

Jacob Nagle related the outbreak of war and his own impressment in a single sentence, as if they were interconnected – which of course they were. On being picked up in Portsmouth, he was sent on the 74-gun *Hector*. No hint of resentment shows over his thwarted plan to go home to America. Within a matter of days he was involved in a similar exercise himself when the *Hector* fell in with a homeward-bound Indiaman, the *Ganges*, in the Channel and took every man Jack out of her. Nagle was one of the topmen assigned to take the now-crewless Indiaman to the nearest port.

The port happened to be Falmouth on the Cornish coast, where Nagle and his fellows had to await a warship to escort the *Ganges* and other Indiamen to the Downs. A frigate, the *Nymphe*, duly came in under the command of one described by Nagle as 'Capt'n Purlew'.[8]

Edward Pellew was that rare thing in the Navy – a common seaman who had risen to command. He came from a family of Cornish sailors and was raised in Penzance, where the sea opens on the Atlantic like a gateway to the world. Boys like Ned grew up looking not inwards to the hinterland, but out and into a space that shifted as rapidly as it did mysteriously. The sea offered allure as well as occupation to Britain's coastal dwellers. It was, as Joseph Conrad observed, 'the accomplice of human restlessness'. For Ned Pellew it was also a form of escape from a family fallen on hard times. Unhappy and rebellious at school, he was barely ten when he would run down to Penzance harbour to mix with the fishermen and sailors, then 'spring into the first boat he found afloat, cast off and away to sea'.

It was Pellew's fortune at the age of thirteen to come to the attention of Captain John Stott. Stott was Cornish himself, had just been given command of a frigate, and found himself with a severe shortage of hands. So he set off on a recruiting drive to his native county, taking on dozens of men and three local lads, including Ned Pellew. The boy took to the tops like a circus artist. A natural athlete, nimble yet strong, he revelled in the thrill and challenge of working at height. Before long he was performing gymnastic feats, including handstands out on the yards, that had older hands shaking their heads in bemused wonderment. 'He was like a squirrel,' one recalled.[9]

By the time he was fifteen, Ned had been rated Able and during the American war served with such flair and gallantry that he won promotion to lieutenant aged twenty-one. Disastrously, his captain and mentor was killed in battle soon afterwards, and for a young man of common origins – without 'interest' it was said – that signified, especially after the peace of 1782. While young officers with influence retained their commands, Pellew was sent ashore and spent most of the next decade back in Cornwall. He married and fathered a large brood but could not settle. His attempt at farming proved hopelessly inept even by a seaman's standards; he once sold a neighbour's cow in the belief that it was his own. The misery of failure was compounded by the farm's setting on high ground looking out to sea. He remained desperate for a ship, as only one who had recognized his destiny could be.

Though painful, those years of peace taught Pellew lessons in patronage and, because he had already made a mark of sorts, he won the support of a local aristocrat who obtained him a command. In January 1793, three weeks before the outbreak of war, he was given the *Nymphe*, a frigate entirely without hands.[10] Even after resorting to impressment just to get her to sea, Pellew wrote to the Admiralty: 'Nymphe is under every embarrassment with so weak a ship's company.' It was at this point that he arrived in Falmouth to convoy the Indiamen, and Nagle came to his attention.

The convergence of their courses was brief. Nagle described it thus:

> We ware sent on board the Nymph to assist in fitting hur out for see till there was an opportunity to send us round to Spithead. Capt'n Purlew made applycation to the Admaralaty to keep us, as we ware all call'd prime seamen and his ship was poorly maned, but he could not have his wish.[11]

It is tempting to speculate what might have come from an association that would have forged an ideal blend of captain and seaman. Pellew rose higher than any other common seaman of his time, from being the Navy's most successful frigate captain to admiral and viscount. It was a stormy voyage, marked by battles with his better-born peers and beset with lee shores thanks to his poor social navigation. Throughout, he retained an affinity with the lower deck, taking with him others of humble origins whose careers he nurtured and guided. Pellew, like Nagle, was a seaman first and foremost. Had Nagle joined the *Nymphe* he may well have been given a chance of promotion, and he would certainly have been assured of action and prize money of a kind that rarely if ever came Jack's way.

As it was, Nagle departed the *Nymphe*. From a prospect of challenge and adventure in a frigate, he was transferred to the *Brunswick*, another 74, for what turned into a prolonged and miserably tedious spell in the Channel Fleet under Lord Howe. Boredom may have resolved him to desert anyway – but when an Indiaman captain offered him a handsome bounty, along with pay at least twice the naval rate, he barely hesitated.

Had he been caught, he would probably have escaped hanging but might well have been flogged round the fleet. Had he stayed, he would have been at the first major fleet battle of the war, the so-called 'Glorious First of June'.

Instead he went off in the *Rose* to Calcutta, where he met a pair of convict girls he had known in New South Wales and who had managed their own kind of desertion, escaping the penal colony and making their way to India where they were doing very nicely as courtesans in nabob society. 'A grand situation they ware in, sedans and chairs,' Nagle observed wryly, 'with two Negroes to carry them wherever they wished to go and a boy a long side to fan them'.[12] Told that they kept no company besides officers and gentlemen, Nagle rejoiced to discover that in India even he counted as a gentleman.

John Nicol managed to elude the press a little longer. He too was back in home waters after his fruitless pursuit of Sarah Whitlam and hoping to sign on another Indiaman. His romantic nature always inclined him for travel rather than battle and when the brig bringing him from Lisbon reached Gravesend and a man-of-war came alongside, Nicol stowed himself away below among the cargo. This time he was lucky. He donned his best shore outfit and thus disguised made his way 'to Wapping where I took up my old lodgings'.[13]

Presumably he retained a landsman's appearance while living in this seafaring enclave, where press gangs were most active, for he managed to find his Indiaman, the *Nottingham*, bound for China. Although he still intended to resume the quest for Sarah, it was no longer with quite the same passion and he had by now to admit that her departure from India without waiting for him, 'showed she cared less about me than I cared for her'.[14]

The fact is he no longer felt the same wanderlust either. He was almost forty and even the prospect of China did not stir his imagination as it once had. The *Nottingham*'s log shows the voyage to have been full of frustration – a fast, new

Indiamen of 1,200 tons held back by a fleet of seventy-seven sail – until they rounded the Cape, hit some hard gales and shed the slow dogs. As so often, a long spell at sea helped put matters in perspective. When *Nottingham* came to at Whampoa, five months after leaving the Lizard, Nicol had cast Sarah from his thoughts and was resolved. He would return to Scotland and settle. 'I had some cash and had seen all I could see.'

The *Nottingham*'s log picks up the story as they sighted the Downs in the summer of 1795:

> July 23: An armed Boat from the Venerable of 74 guns with an officer came to press the People . . . At 4pm the Venerable's boats finished taking the People, their chests, etc.[15]

Virtually the entire crew, seventy-seven men, had been pressed. After a year off in the Eastern Seas, and with no more than a glimpse of England, they found themselves in the dark bosom of a 74. Some would have been dreaming of home, some yearning for nothing more than a Wapping cruise. All were about to be swept off to war without so much as a word or touch with family.

Nicol, shrewd old hand that he was, had anticipated it – growing a beard and cultivating an especially unkempt appearance in an attempt to show that here was one Jack no self-respecting captain would want. When the press gang departed he did a little jig. But the next day one of the pressed men was returned with a leg injury, and this time Nicol's camouflage had no effect. He was taken:

> Thus were all my schemes blown into the air . . . I found myself in bondage . . . and no hopes of relief until the end of the war.[16]

Here again is seen the press at its most indefensible, snatching a man away when he was not only in sight of home, but as he was about to be paid for a year's work – for it often happened that ship-owners, who were as vociferous as any in condemning Admiralty policy, made no great effort to ensure that men pressed at the end of a voyage received their wages. Yet Nicol, like many of his fellows, had become almost inured to loss of freedom: 'I made up my mind to it and was as happy as a man in blasted prospects can be.'

Sent on board the *Edgar*, a 74, Nicol was soon subjected to further deprivation when she came to anchor in Leith roads near his Edinburgh home, and was refused shore leave by a lieutenant who said 'it was not safe to allow a pressed man to go on shore at his native place'.[17] By now we may discern symptoms that in Nicol's case amounted less to resignation than a loss of spirit. He had been at sea for almost twenty years and the regime defined by a captain's orders and a bosun's pipe could ultimately have the effect of eroding precisely the same boldness on which its success depended.

The most prolonged strain on maritime manpower in history pushed the Navy to desperate measures. From a low of 16,613 in the final year of peace, the number of mustered hands rose fourfold in a matter of months to 69,868. By 1797, during the Navy's greatest crisis – essentially over wages – it had reached 118,788 and two years later 128,930.[18] These numbers were obtained in the face of a daily withering by death from disease, accident and action. Ultimately, after the short-lived Treaty of Amiens (1802–3), it reached a peak of 147,047.*

So, how were these men found?

The number of Impress Service rendezvous centres around the country grew from twenty-three to thirty-four. They flew flags, dispensed ale and displayed patriotic appeals to:

Englishmen willing to defend their country against all Republicans and Levellers, and against the designs of our natural enemies who intend this

---

* Despite the manpower conflict, the figures for merchant seafarers held up remarkably over the same period. When naval manning was at its highest recorded level, in 1813, the mercantile sector stood at 115,380. (David Starkey, 'Britain's Seafaring Workforce 1650–1815', in Fury, ed., *The Social History of English Seamen*)

year to invade Old England, to murder our gracious King as they have done their own; to make whores of our wives and daughters; to rob us of our property, and teach us nothing but the damned art of murdering one another.[19]

Volunteers were paid the standard bounty of £5 for an Able man, £2 10s for Ordinary hands and £1 10s for Landsmen. And, naturally, many seamen – when confronted by a press gang – took the money and were entered as volunteers.

But the impressment centre, or 'rondy', had a darker aspect too. The regulation that only men who used the sea could be impressed was abandoned. Now, in a 'hot press', gangs really did seize men with no experience of the sea – men like Michael Quick, whose fate may have been decided by living with his family in the Seven Dials, a slum notorious for London outcasts, 'knife-grinders and street-singers, bird-dealers and shoe-makers, hawkers of prints and sellers of herring'.[20] It was also a stalking ground for the oldest rondy in the city, St Katharine's Stairs in Wapping, with its press room – in reality a dungeon where men were held pending transfer to a tender. Admiralty records are not short of petitions from women like Mary Quick, declaring her husband – a coach spring-maker – to be:

> . . . no seaman, nor seafaring man, nor ever worked upon the water nor any business relating thereto. He now lies onboard a Tender in the River. Your petitioner with 2 small children and pregnant has no other support, which must soon bring her and them to ruin unless he is speedily released.[21]

This petition, written in a neat hand on Mary's behalf by a member of the parish and certified by Quick's employer, H. Wildey, a coach spring-maker of Soho, was referred to the captain of the tender holding Quick. Whether he was released is unknown.

The abuse of 'protections' became routine. Those supposedly exempted from the press included not only those already in service but certain categories of men who used the sea – fishermen, ferrymen and colliers among others.

Although it had been established practice that protections might be ignored in times of war when the Admiralty authorized a 'hot press', the extent of violations touched new levels after 1793.

The damage to families grew. The case of Mary Jones – executed twenty years earlier for stealing £5 worth of muslin after the impressment of her merchant-seaman husband – was revived as a *cause célèbre*, a rallying cry for campaigners. But it was not only the wives and children of pressed hands who suffered. When men of the labouring class volunteered for the Navy and left home for years on end, their dependants were made vulnerable, especially those without family networks to call on. Severe hardship gave rise to the Navy Act of 1795, which was designed to improve the system by which seamen could allocate a portion of their wages to wives or other dependants. The money was distributed every twenty-eight days at payment centres in London, Portsmouth, Plymouth and Chatham; otherwise it could be collected at the nearest tax or customs office. That still meant travel of some distance for many wives as the money had to be collected in person, unless the recipient could produce a certificate of infirmity from a clergyman or surgeon. Impersonation was a felony punishable by death. And if the seaman died in service, payment ceased directly.[22]

Still there were not enough Jacks. A year after the onset of war, figures show a rough equivalence between the number of hands in navy and merchant ships – 83,891 and 81,534 respectively.[23] As more sailors were plundered, the Admiralty came under fire from the mercantile sector for damaging trade. Homeward-bound merchant captains entering the Channel would break away from convoys to evade the navy ships awaiting them, only then to fall prey to other predators, French privateers. At bottom, the needs of the two sectors were irreconcilable because the demands of waging war did not diminish the need for raising the economic means to sustain it.

Another method of keeping ships at sea was scarcely less reviled and, as one admiral said, 'became vexatious by growing into a practice, instead of being used only occasionally, as an emergency':

THESE VALUABLE BUT HELPLESS PEOPLE

I mean the plan of turning the men over to newly commissioned ships on their return from foreign service, and perhaps again sending them abroad or what was worse, keeping them at home without the opportunity of leave.[24]

William Richardson was one to suffer the double blow. He was in an Indiaman in Calcutta when war started and was promptly pressed into the frigate *Minerve*. On reaching home in 1794 – after two years away – he was among thirty-seven hands turned over directly into the *Prompte*, 'without a moment's liberty on shore after being so long abroad in unhealthy climates'. As he put it: 'Here was encouragement for seamen to fight for their king and country! A coolie in India was better off!'[25]

The next recruitment drive was embodied in legislation known as the Quota Acts, passed in 1795 and 1796, requiring local authorities to raise a certain number of volunteers for naval service or pay a fine in lieu. The influence of the Acts is disputed. Criminals and vagrants were supposedly barred, but one respected historian has claimed that it introduced to the Navy a corps of troublemakers: 'Counties tended to select their "bad boys", their vagrants, tramps and idlers . . . towns sent beggars, minor thieves and pickpockets.'[26] A more recent study states that quotas produced only about 30,000 hands during the entire war, and they no criminals but respectable men in need of work.[27] Whatever else, the inclusion of convicted smugglers did at least add craft as well as experience to the mix.

But the great majority of those selected as 'volunteers' were not the ablest nor fittest members of their communities. Nor were they seamen; and it follows that quota men attracted resentment and suspicion from real hands, partly because of their backgrounds but also because they were paid an absurdly high bounty for signing on – up to £70 in some cases, compared with £5 for a volunteering Able hand. One officer thought the quota bounty 'the most ill-advised and fatal measure ever adopted by the government for manning the fleet', adding how:

. . . one of these objects, coming on board with £70 bounty was seized by a boatswain's mate who, holding him up with one hand by the waistband of his trousers, humorously exclaimed 'Here's a fellow that cost a guinea a pound!'[28]

Fringe industries flourished. Crimps in various guises, from tavern keepers to prostitutes, came up with profitable methods of procuring hands. A related enterprise was directed at seamen's pay: Eleanor Mahoney presented herself at Deptford to claim almost £50 due to her son Timothy, an Irish hand late of the *Medway*. Her efforts to reproduce an Irish accent alerted clerks to the fact that she was not Mrs Mahoney at all but a Poll working with a publican and a Drury Lane milkman.[29]

All the while the Marine Society continued to recruit boys, providing 'a nursery of seamen for the public service', and they at least went relatively willingly. Along with an outfit of jacket, waistcoat, trowsers, shirts, shoes, knife, pillow, blanket and one of Hanway's religious tracts, some 22,973 Marine Society protégés entered the Navy between 1793 and 1815.[30]

Underlying all manning figures for the Revolutionary and Napoleonic Wars lies a mystery. Just what proportion of navy hands were pressed? The question has stimulated an intense academic debate.

Until relatively recently it was accepted that in the early years of the Revolutionary War about 50 per cent of naval hands were pressed. This ratio, it was argued, increased in the later years to 75 per cent; but the case was also made that the data is so conflicting that no accurate estimate is possible.[31]

These figures have been challenged by a recent study based on the musters of eighty-one ships in service between 1793 and 1801. The claim is made that entries for the 27,174 men whose details are recorded show that 42 per cent arrived as new volunteers, 41 per cent had been turned over from other ships, and some 5 per cent were 'quota men'. Only 10 per cent were newly pressed. Allowing for the fact that some of those turned over had already been pressed, and that impressment intensified towards the end of the war, the study concludes that perhaps 16 per cent of all Jacks had been taken.[32] (It does not pursue this case into the Napoleonic War when press-gang excesses undoubtedly became more blatant.)

An accurate figure will remain elusive. Ships' musters, though a valuable resource for research, are not absolute records. Many of those entered as volunteers were pressed men who, when facing the inevitable, took the bounty. No figure is offered here to contest the specialist studies cited above, but while 50 per cent could be too high, 16 per cent appears too low. For anecdotal evidence it may be added that virtually every Jack given a voice in this narrative was pressed at one time or another, some repeatedly – a fact proved by the musters. And whatever the proportion was during the Revolutionary War, it certainly rose in the Napoleonic War, when – as we shall see – a mass demobilization at the Treaty of Amiens gave way to a frantic and at times criminal scramble to reman the Navy a year later.

One case from court-martial records points up the paradoxes during such demanding times. A body of enemy prisoners – including French, Dutch and Spaniards – were noted to have volunteered for the Navy in 1801 when they seized the *Charlotte* tender en route to the Nore, casting the master, a mate and two men down the hatchway. Eleven escaped in a cutter but seventeen were recaptured and tried. The master, in his testimony, admitted uncertainty over the identity of those active in the 'mutiny'. Six men were found guilty and sentenced to fifty lashes, followed by internment as prisoners of war. That the eleven acquitted were then offered a chance to re-enlist is some indication of the Navy's desperate need for hands.[33]

Seamen voted against impressment with their feet in unprecedented numbers. No less an authority than Horatio Nelson believed 42,000 men deserted between 1793 and 1802, and that figure may have been too low.[34] Meanwhile, public hostility reached new levels – as did resistance. In the first year of the war, press gangs were confronted by angry mobs on at least twenty-seven occasions.[35]

Nagle sighted England again from the tops of the *Rose*, back from Calcutta, as she ghosted up the Channel. He knew what to expect. Fortunately, so did the captain of the *Rose*, who saved his best men by sending them to hide down among the cargo. Yet by the time a lieutenant from the *Diamond* had taken his pick of rest, and another from the *Garland* followed suit the next day, thirty out of fifty-four hands had been pressed.[36]

Behind these spare facts lies a drama of coincidence. When Nagle and his shipmates looked out across the anchorage where dozens of sail lay below Dover Castle, they would have sighted the *Nottingham* where, that same day, 23 July, John Nicol was trying vainly to conceal himself from another press gang. The Indiamen returning in the summer of 1795, it is plain, offered rich pickings. Nagle and Nicol had again passed in one another's wake.

Nagle thanked his stars that he was not immediately taken. Aware of his peril since deserting from the Navy, he had concealed his identity by serving in the *Rose* under an alias – Jacob Lincoln.[37] But one narrow shave was just the start. These Indiamen hands had returned to a country in turmoil, gripped by rumours of invasion. Captain Alexander Gray, who had him flogged when he tried to desert in Bengal, now made an astonishing gesture – lending Nagle and the remaining hands pistols and swords with which to defend themselves on the road to London. Formidable force appeared to be everywhere across a Kent countryside swarming with fired-up soldiers. On reaching Wapping they had to pass through no fewer than four press gangs. They did this by hiring coaches and advancing through Poplar with men standing atop, flourishing pikes and pistols until they reached Leadenhall Street and reported to East India House. Here they received their wages and handed over the Company's weaponry.

Nagle was still in dangerous waters. He took shelter at the White Swan while sending word to his old boarding house keeper. Mr Goodall escorted him to Tower Hill but pointed out that he could not stay in hiding indefinitely; so a meeting was set with the captain of the local 'rondy', who offered a compromise: Nagle agreed to sign on with the Navy again; in return he received the standard £5 bounty and a 'protection' notionally exempting him from impressment; and, as the 44-gun *Gorgon* was not ready for sea, he was given a clear two months before he had to join her. With a full purse, the old Nagle would have gone off on a Wapping cruise. Instead, he took a quite different tack.

Nagle had made acquaintances among local families, including a boat builder named Pitman who had a daughter named Elizabeth. Out of the blue, the impulsive Nagle 'took a liking to [her], a lively hansome girl in my eye, and maried hur'.[38]

Of Elizabeth Pitman, or Mrs Jacob Nagle, little is known other than her respectable if simple origins. They were married at St Botolph's Aldgate in August 1795, an occasion that goes undescribed in his journal, where she is referred to only as 'my wife'. Although they had at least two children, they too are unnamed. Nagle was not so restrained in describing tarts like Liddy, and it appears that grief still clouded memories of his family when he was writing. Only one incident of their life together is recorded. Almost inevitably, it involved a press gang.

They were walking in the ghostly wilds of St Katharines when the gang came. Nagle said he belonged to the *Gorgon* and had a protection in his room, at which one of the gang:

> . . . begin to make free with my wife and I nock'd him down, and a nother coming up, I made him stager. I told a midshipman of the gang I would go where he pleased but not to allow his vagabons to insult my wife. He said they should not. Then I walked on with them, and my wife with me.[39]

With his protection, Nagle negotiated a passage to the *Gorgon* and was given a liberty ticket to spend a month with his wife. One final temptation came his way, an offer from his last ship *Rose* of a passage back to India at a wage of £10 a month – five times the naval rate – if he would desert again. But, as he put it, 'I [k]new death would be my portion if caught again, therefore I would not attempt it.'

Nagle's parting from his wife might recall one of those daubs, so popular in its day, of *The Sailor's Farewell*, with a few lines which were no less resonant for being doggerel:

> *The topsails shiver in the wind, The ship she's bound to sea;*
> *But yet my heart, my soul, my mind, Are, Mary, moored with thee.*

After the *Gorgon* sailed for the Mediterranean, Mrs Nagle accompanied her parents to Portsmouth. Unlike many seamen's wives left without resources and forced to seek parish relief, she was reasonably placed to await her husband's return. When he did, two years had passed and Nagle was father to a child he had never seen before.

FAMILY AND FRIENDS
1793-98

FORCE was not the only way to recruit hands. Captain Edward Pellew of the
Nymphe, whose desperate need for men had been noted by Jacob Nagle,
resorted to means that smacked more of the old world than the new. Pellew
sent an appeal through his family into their Cornish hinterland. What came
back was perhaps the most bizarre collection of men ever to come up the side
of a British man-of-war. One observer thought they resembled:

> . . . an irruption of barbarians . . . dressed in the mud-stained smock-frocks and
> trowsers in which they worked underground, all armed with large clubs and
> speaking an uncouth jargon which none but themselves could understand.[1]

No seamen or fishermen these. They were in fact the product of another
Cornish industry – tin mining; and they were volunteers. Pellew's tinners
formed the basis of the *Nymphe*'s company and though they may have appeared
improbable Jacks, their robust physiques and the strong regional identity they
shared with their commander were to be the making of a fearsome crew.

Frigates usually produced the most effective companies. Smaller ships could
also turn into seaborne nightmares, but more often they offered opportunity

and the kind of kinship in which men like Nagle thrived. Another hand, Robert Hay, who later served with Pellew, pointed out a simple wisdom in observing that 'the crew of small vessels, like other small communities [are] much better known to each other and much more knit together than the crews of large vessels'.[2]

Pellew tended to the kinship aspect with special care. Reflecting on his own sparse education, he employed teachers to ensure that boys on his ships learnt to read and write, as well as how to tie a knot. Experience on the lower deck gave him insight into how to nourish the less tangible elements of a happy ship. He would join his men in dancing and sports. He was attentive to their needs. One summed up his method as 'a kindness which allowed every safe indulgence'. And, partly out of pride, partly to remind them of his own lowly origins, he remained active in the tops, demonstrating his physical prowess in a way that commanded a kind of awe. An officer who served under him recalled:

> Whenever there was exertion required aloft, to preserve sail or a mast, the captain was foremost at the work, apparently as a mere matter of amusement; and there was not a man in the ship who could equal him in personal activity . . . I have often heard the most active seamen say, 'Well, he never orders us to do what he won't do himself.'[3]

Pellew had his flaws. He was avid for wealth and guilty of nepotism on a scale conspicuous even among an officer class to whom these were standard practice. In seamanship and managing men he had few peers, being of that select group Jack counted himself blessed to serve. Hay said he had 'the confidence, love and esteem of seamen'.[4]

His first command of the war brought immediate prominence. Three months into hostilities, the *Nymphe* fell in with the *Cleopatre* and in twenty minutes these two closely matched frigates exchanged a dozen broadsides. It was sharp and bloody. The *Nymphe* had twenty-three men killed, the *Cleopatre* more than thirty. Overall casualties were between 25 and 30 per cent – exceptionally high for naval actions. But when a boarding party from the *Nymphe* surged over the bows to receive a French surrender, Pellew had claimed the first victory of the war.

The Nymphes savoured their moment. Anchoring in Falmouth and heading ashore, former tin miners like Theophilus Coad and Ephraim Noy discovered that along with status, carrying home a captured enemy meant prize money. The *Cleopatre* was assessed at £7,798 17s 1d, of which two-eighths was distributed among the 112 surviving Jacks – about £17 9s a man, or almost a year's pay.[5]

They were in for plenty more as they followed Pellew from ship to ship, from the *Nymphe* to his second frigate, *Arethusa*, which took a larger French frigate and a corvette, along with numerous smaller vessels. This time the prize money of the Arethusas – or the 'Harrythusers' as they became known in the popular prints – produced a celebration that entered folklore and inspired a George Cruikshank cartoon. After anchoring in Plymouth, five hands hired a

The antics ashore of the 'Harrythusers' after their prize-money windfall under Edward Pellew brought them to the attention of a shocked public.

coach, loaded it with musicians and women and charged around the country-side for days until their money ran out.

Pellew's exploits at the start of war established a benchmark. The king was overjoyed, press and public united in acclaim, and a knighthood set the seal on Ned's triumphs. A romanticized folk tale – the ship's boy who rises to glory – had become reality. Praise also came from the Commander of the Channel fleet, Lord Howe, who told Pellew he had 'set an example for the war'. That accolade would prove remarkably prescient.

Tom Allen was another man taken to sea by family ties. He came from farming stock and was raised in poverty after the deaths of his father, an agricultural labourer, then his mother, when he was a boy. In his youth he ploughed the flatlands of north Norfolk, which normally would have destined him for a lifetime following the same furrows as his father. The sea, it is true, was just a few miles away, up muddy creeks seeping across a landscape that yielded barley to be transported up and down the east coast of England, so it was always possible that he might quit the soil. But it was because of being taken into the service of a local family, the Nelsons, that in February 1793, Tom Allen became a seaman.[6]

In the early days of the war, officers still used personal networks to recruit men. While Pellew turned to Cornish relatives for the tin miners who became his crew, Cuthbert Collingwood, from Newcastle, centre of the coal trade – which C. S. Forester called the most instructive and exacting school of seamanship – asked friends 'to use their influence with the seamen, which they did so effectually that nearly fifty men entered'.[7] Both officers had local standing and reputations for the kind of 'good usage' that attracted followers and which they did well, for pragmatic reasons as well as honour's sake, to uphold.

Horatio Nelson, a captain of no great seniority or distinction, had spent five years kicking his heels on half pay at his father's rectory in Burnham Thorpe, so the declaration of war and appointment to a ship was an opportunity to be seized with fervour; but the 64-gun *Agamemnon* needed almost 500 men, and she had none. Nelson sent officers to local ports. His name meant little and few hands were to be had. So, being of the opinion that 'a Norfolk man [is] as good as two others', Nelson started looking to those in his neighbourhood. Tom Allen, a rough fellow already employed by a branch of the family as a ploughman, came to his attention. Thus began a lifelong and – given their difference in station – astonishingly familiar bond. 'Next to Lady Hamilton,' wrote an officer who observed them at close quarters, 'Tom Allen possessed the greatest influence with his heroic master.'[8]

Fame of any sort could not have been more remote on a mid-winter's day in 1793 when Allen turned his back on the village of Sculthorpe, making his way the eight miles to Wells where the *Nancy* tender was taking men to Chatham. Tenders were pits of grimness, usually packed with pressed men, and the need to confine reluctant recruits gave these ill-named vessels the aspect of a lower-deck prison. Looking down through a grating, one newcomer observed 'a crowded mass of disgusting and fearful heads':

> . . . with eyes all glaring up from that terrible den; and heaps of filthy limbs, trunks and heads, bundled and scattered, scrambling, laughing, cursing, screaming and fighting at one moment.[9]

Allen would have been an uncommon fellow had he not regretted departing from a landscape, 'shaped as if by a kindly hand for thinking, dreaming, dying on'.[10] At last, brought to Chatham dockyard, he mounted a ship's side for the first time on 28 February. Four weeks had passed since France's declaration of war.

Captain Nelson's recruiting drive had not been a success. Tom Allen came on *Agamemnon* with just eleven other Norfolk men. She was still more than 300 short of a full complement. Allen's details were recorded in the ship's muster – aged twenty, a volunteer, and, despite being without experience, rated Ordinary, which was seemingly a sign of favour from the captain owing to his connection with the Nelson family.[11] He thus became due not only a higher wage but a bounty of £2 10s, when as a volunteer Landsman he would have received only £1 10s. He was issued with two hammocks, to be used in rotation between washing, and went below to huddle with his new messmates against the cold and savour a repast of stale provisions that would have gone down ill with any farmhand.

The next day Tom Allen began to learn how an unmasted hulk, laid up at Chatham for years, was refitted. The weather was foul – rainy and blowing gales – as they swayed up the mizzen top and rigged the main, and there was some grumbling among the Landsmen, until the bosun told them sharply to pipe down, they would have more than this breeze to deal with in Biscay. Taking on fresh beef and coal did little to appease the croakers. Within days, nine men ran from *Agamemnon*. In all likelihood they had only signed on for the bounty.[12]

More men entered in batches – twenty-three from the Marine Society, by now a source of vagrant males as well as ships' boys, along with volunteers from London, Essex, Lincolnshire and Kent. But as weeks passed and the ship neared readiness for sea it was to be noted that the new arrivals were no longer volunteers but pressed men. The *Agamemnon* remained short-handed at the end of April when Captain Nelson gave the order to weigh and make sail, and she slipped down the Medway, tacking occasionally.

He was a slight, almost boyish figure, this captain, yet with a bearing that combined command with an easy familiarity towards the men. Like all fresh companies, they watched him keenly, noting a quickness and activity to his movements, the long hours he spent on the quarterdeck and his distinctive Norfolk drawl: the name Edward, for example, he pronounced Ed'ard. As he had yet to acquire any sort of reputation they would have been unaware that in his last command, the frigate *Boreas* in the West Indies, he had been thought quite a tartar, having ordered sixty-six floggings in eighteen months. On the *Agamemnon*, however, he exercised a light hand. Months would go by without a beating.

Of Allen's early dealings with Nelson there is no record. Tom's movements are invisible as the *Agamemnon* anchored at Spithead where she finally filled her 500-man complement and orders came that she was to accompany Admiral

1. *Heaving a Lead* is a rare contemporary portrayal of hands at their daily labours by John Augustus Atkinson, noted for his sharp observations. Artists of the time were not known for going aloft to record seamen's work in the rigging.

2. *A Married Sailor's Adieu*, by Julius Caesar Ibbetson. Seamen's partings from their families, and their reunions after years apart, were a theme of popular art.

3. The vast majority of shipwrecks occurred in home waters. Coastal dwellers were often observers and Joshua Cristall's watercolour of 1808 shows Sussex fishermen pushing off a boat to rescue hands from a ship in distress.

4. Tom Allen was a Greenwich pensioner when John Burnet painted this portrait of the devoted hand who enjoyed an endearingly informal relationship with his master Horatio Nelson but sailed too close to the wind once too often.

5. *The Shipwreck*. Stories of disaster at sea, a feature of the Romantic age, were never more powerfully portrayed than in J. M. W. Turner's vision of the element in all its terrifying majesty.

6. The wreck of the *Grosvenor* off south-east Africa in 1782 created a sensation thanks to the mystery of what occurred after seamen and their wealthy passengers alike were cast away among those regarded as savages.

7. At a time when seamen were social outcasts, their dress and appearance attracted the interest of John Augustus Atkinson, a roaming artist whose subjects included coastal and rustic life.

8. William Hodges' alluring landscape of Tahiti in 1776 with Polynesian women bathing naked conjured up an image of the South Seas as an erotic arcadia.

9. Hodges accompanied James Cook's second voyage to the Pacific and also hinted at the tension of an encounter between alien cultures in *Landing at Tanna*, an island in the archipelago now known as Vanuatu.

10–11. Gabriel Bray, a second lieutenant on the 44-gun *Pallas*, was gifted with pen and brush and a collection of his watercolours from a voyage to Africa in 1775, including a seaman bringing up his hammock and another resting on a forecastle gun, are unique records of life at sea.

12. *The Point of Honour* by George Cruikshank is more than a simple caricature of naval discipline, representing the bond between sailors – a hand coming forward to confess to the offence for which an innocent shipmate has been tied up for flogging.

13. Portsmouth Point was a bridge between land and sea, where sailors came ashore for a frolic in a warren of taverns and brothels, or departed for the naval anchorage of Spithead.

14. The first of the great mutinies of 1797, at Spithead, for improved pay was remarkable for its orderliness. But once protest spread the mutineers were widely perceived as stooges being manipulated by radicals sympathetic to the French Revolution, here concealed under the table.

15. A death mask of Richard Parker, leader of the second mutiny at the Nore, where events did have insurgent elements which swept Parker away.

16. Victory at Camperdown brought redemption. In this canvas of Admiral Duncan receiving the Dutch admiral's surrender on the *Venerable*, a plain hand named John Crawford is seen descending. He had gone aloft to nail Duncan's flag to the mast after it was brought down by enemy fire.

17. Sailors and marines boarding an enemy man of war by John Augustus Atkinson. The spirit and confidence of British seamen reached new heights during twenty years of war with France.

18. Amid the smoke-infused chaos of broadside-to-broadside fire, John Christian Schetky's grand canvas of Trafalgar shows the detail of men at their stations in battle – aloft handling the sails and reaching out of ports to service the guns.

19. Trafalgar had been Jack Tar's finest moment. George Harlow's drawing of sailors on the *Royal William* dates from 1806 and reflects a growing general respect for those once seen as turbulent troublemakers.

20. The most demanding duties were those of the topmen, as shown in this detail from a painting of 1783 of the *Ramillies* with her sails close-reefed as a storm descends. After a three-day struggle for survival, she had to be abandoned.

21. *A Sailor's Return in Peace*. Thomas Stothard's canvas dates from 1798 but is a timeless record of the moment recalled by one seaman: 'She, being surprised, could hardly speak, for she knew not whether I was dead or alive. I laid down my pack, and had my relations come about me with joy.'

22. The *Guardian* departing for Botany Bay in 1789 – the serene prelude to a seafaring epic after she was impaled on ice south of the Cape of Good Hope. The watercolour is said to be by Benjamin Toddy, a Greenwich pensioner who executed a number of such works despite the loss of both hands.

23. Billy Waters lost his leg in a fall from the *Ganymede's* yards. He became a familiar figure with his fiddle busking on the streets of London to support his family.

24–25. In preparing a grand canvas for the Duke of Wellington to celebrate seamen's deeds, John Burnet spent time at Greenwich in 1832 and painted nine portraits, the only faithful portrayals of common seamen such as Joseph Miller and a man known only as Handyson.

26. In *The Fighting Temeraire*, voted Britain's favourite painting, J. M. W. Turner captured once and for all the passing of the heroic age.

27. Last hurrah. John Burnet's oil painting of naval heroes celebrating Trafalgar Day at Greenwich in 1832 still hangs with Wellington's collection at Apsley House. This watercolour copy is by Stephen Poyntz Denning.

Hood's fleet to the Mediterranean. Allen's progress as a seaman is also unclear, though he went on to fight an upper-deck gun, was young and brawny, and, from all the evidence, as brave as a lion; he would never have found favour with his captain had his sole virtue been a Norfolk twang. The *Agamemnon* was a fast, sweet sailer – Nelson's favourite ship, some say – and there were opportunities aplenty as she entered the sea of his destiny: in August they were off Naples, where the captain first met Sir William Hamilton, the British diplomat, and his common yet extravagantly alluring wife, Emma; in September it was Leghorn; in October off Corsica the Agamemnons had a taste of action, engaging four French frigates and suffering severely in the masts and rigging before having to break off and run; Nelson's first battle was not exactly a debacle, but it was the only one not to be mentioned in the *London Gazette*.[13]

Tom Allen's real role in his captain's story began two years later. The people had settled into a happy and able company who referred to the *Agamemnon* affectionately as the Eggs and Bacon. (Jack had his own vernacular for these mythological Greek swabs: the *Bellerophon* was known as the Billy Ruffian, the *Polyphemus* as the Polly Infamous.) And they had triumphed in a second action with a French squadron, boarding the 80-gun *Ça Ira*.

A problem had arisen, however, with the captain's servant, Frank Lepee, who was more often drunk than sober. Lepee, too, was from Nelson's home county and upon his discharge another son of Norfolk took his place. The appointment raised some eyebrows, because although Allen had distinguished himself in boarding the *Ça Ira*, he was seen as little more than a slow-witted oaf. George Parsons, a midshipman, wrote:

> Clumsy, ill-formed, illiterate and vulgar, his very appearance created laughter at the situation he held.[14]

Yet, as Parsons added, there was a Nelsonian element to this, for Allen's 'affectionate, bold heart made up for all his deficiencies'. Curious but true, if one word defined the relationship between Britannia's god of battle and his warriors, it was affection.

War with France drenched Jack in salt-water glory. Centuries of prowess and mythology were distilled in a series of epic battles and personified by that slight, golden figure who went in a decade from obscurity to greater renown than any living Englishman. Nelson inspired his men to fight like demons partly by demonstrating his fondness for them, but also by his frank admiration for their character: 'Aft the more honour; for'ard the better man,' he used to say.[15] Not the least of his legacies was how he transformed seamen in the public eye, from being suspect outsiders to his fellows as national heroes. Trafalgar was also Jack's finest hour.

To say it was a storm-tossed voyage that carried him there would, however, be verging on the droll. Never had British sailors so shocked their commanders and frightened their countrymen as they did in the years preceding Trafalgar. Shocking does not begin to describe the events of 1797 when they seemingly turned into insurrectionist Jacobins. Trust in the common man had withered since the onset of revolution in France and Jack's own rebellion, in demanding fair play, was described by one of their lordships at the Admiralty as '[t]he most awful crisis that these kingdoms ever saw'.[16] The bloody spectre of France, engulfed by the Terror, appeared at hand.

Those who made the voyage include some old faces. Jacob Nagle was one, winning plaudits from Nelson himself and remaining in the king's service – so long as it suited him – before finding more gainful employment in merchantmen; Nagle knew nothing else but the sea and would remain a wanderer, through shipwreck, illness and the one great tragedy of his life, into his fiftieth year. John Nicol, though already ageing, still had enough zeal to fight at two of Nelson's great battles – Cape St Vincent and the Nile.

But the expansion of naval enterprise also introduced a more diverse and complex range of individuals to Jack's story. There, along with Tom Allen, was William Robinson, also known as Jack Nastyface, a hard-nosed cynic who fought at Trafalgar and saw his next duty as writing a tract to exalt his fellows at the expense of their gold-braided superiors. Robert Hay, a bright but troubled boy, ran away from home to become one of the most articulate of these improbable chroniclers, one known laconically by his fellows as 'the Gentleman'.

Other fresh voices included John Wetherell, a born seaman of the old colliery school who was pressed into serving a bungling captain and was shipwrecked off France where he spent eleven years as a prisoner. Daniel Goodall enjoyed particularly strong bonds with his shipmates yet went over to the enemy, so to speak, by joining the marines and becoming a 'lobster'. George Watson went to sea aged ten and never looked back until being wounded in battle and ending his days 'safe moor'd in Greenwich tier'.

We have seen enough of these men to guard against stereotypes. As George Watson said: 'A man-of-war may be justly styled an epitome of the world, in which there is a sample of every character – burglars, pickpockets, debauchees, gamesters, ruffians, poets . . .'[17] For each dreamy John Nicol there was a rakish Jacob Nagle; along with a self-educated philosophizer like William Spavens came a pragmatic opportunist like Joshua Davis. A few were volunteers who really did go to sea in search of adventure – Robinson, Goodall and Hay among them.

To take random individuals as examples of diversity, John Chilton was a highway robber transported to Botany Bay in 1791 who escaped to India and signed on with the Navy, going on to serve in battle on the frigate *Diana*. 'I never saw a man behave better in my life,' said one of his officers. The upshot was that when Chilton was recognized at a tavern back in England and convicted of returning from transportation, his death sentence was commuted. He may even have gone back to sea.[18]

Aaron Thomas, on the other hand, was a romantic whose presence in the 32-gun *Boston* with a convoy to Newfoundland in 1794 is a mystery. The son of a tenant farmer in Shropshire, he kept a journal addressed to an unnamed muse which opened: 'How much I lament the separation from you I shall not here declare, but suffice by saying that Pleasure has an end, and so has Sorrow.' What particularly distinguishes Thomas is the intimacy of his tone and, possibly, his sexuality:

Do you know that as I am writing these Sheets and my Pen is forming these letters I fancy I am telling a Tale? I think I am relating the Chit Chat of the day to you! I seting on one side of the Table, and you on the other – but what is my mortification, on raising my head, that I do not behold you! . . . But still while my mind is plunged in deep thoughts I always fancy I am in your society.[19]

In another confidential passage, Thomas relates a passionate friendship in Ludlow 'where it was remarked that there did not exist two such intimate souls as we were', and recalls an evening when 'I am not ashamed to confess that in the Society we were then in something occr'd which may be termed vice'.[20] Quite possibly, Thomas was the first homosexual memoirist of the lower deck.

Jacks recognized certain types among themselves. 'Croakers', for one, were found on every ship – 'unhappy mortals who are but too well disposed to meet misery half way,' Daniel Goodall called them. Two seamen from the age of Nelson were outstanding croakers. William Robinson spent his fury in a diatribe against the naval system. Charles Pemberton, who went on to minor renown on the stage, made much of the grimness of his six years as a seaman in what reads as a moody drama straight from the Romantic age.

But somehow, when all these elements came together in that crucial unit of lower-deck life, the sailors' mess, they transcended their individual parts. Goodall thought one of his messmates, an Irishman named James Fitzgerald, a croaker, 'though there were times when his native humour and good sense got the better of his cynicism'.[21] And their mess was a contented one. When Goodall joined them he was mired in misery after having all his possessions stolen. Their table between the guns shaped his faith in their world. 'They had come as a healing to my spirit in the darkest hour; and I am quite sure they gave me a bias for good that made my after-life happier,' Goodall recalled. 'They encouraged me to keep up my heart and to do my duty manfully, trusting to obtain fair play in the long run.'[22]

Aaron Thomas, despite reflecting on his Shropshire idyll, with 'plenty of Corn, orchards of Apples, good society and everywhere the most luxuriant fields', could conclude: 'But amongst these blessings I remember that I was not a whit happyer than I am at this moment, cooped up in so narrow a compass with near 300 of his Majesty's best subjects.'[23]

Fellowship was the seaman's greatest bond. When combined with a sense of self-worth, it made him a handful even when fighting ashore. An infantry officer who witnessed a party of seamen attacking Fort Royal in Martinique wrote:

> You may fancy you know these fellows, but to see them in action exceeds any idea that can be formed. A hundred or two of them, with ropes and pullies, will do more than all your dray horses in London . . . They will draw you a cannon or mortar on its proper carriage up to any height . . . On they go, huzzaing and hulooing, sometimes up hill, sometimes down hill; now sticking fast in the brakes, presently floundering in the mud and mire; swearing, blasting, damning, sinking and as careless of everything but the matter committed to their charge as if danger or death had nothing to do with them. We had a thousand of these brave fellows sent to us by the Admiral, and the service they did us, both on shore and in the water, is incredible.[24]

What is striking about this observation is not so much the enthusiasm of the seamen as their bravado ashore – their noisy, chest-thumping swagger in the Army's presence. One of the marks that distinguished Jack from soldiers and other plain folk who laboured for weekly wages was his lack of humility. He might make the ritual signal of deference to authority, tip a hand to his forehead on addressing an officer, yet he blurred the usual confines of class. The nature of his service had something to do with this. Although the Navy was never quite as egalitarian as some would have us believe, it was impossible to maintain all the usual social barriers within a space that never exceeded 200 feet in length and 50 feet in breadth.

Again we should guard against simplification. Charles Pemberton, for one, perceived class at work on the quarterdeck, believing that even 'in a jolly boat with a pair of mizentopmen on the wide waste of the Atlantic' an English officer's thoughts would be on 'discipline, decorum and distance'.[25] But Pemberton's romantic nature and artistic aspirations made him an outsider among both types. Aaron Thomas was closer to the mark when he admitted: 'It is a little irksome to the seaman to see a train of seventeen or twenty dishes borne in state to the Great Cabin – full of savoury meats and vegitables [sic], with jellys and blomonges, when they themselves have din'd off a gob of fatt pork or pease and water.'[26]

The mere fact, however, that a plain seaman could feel irked at the treats enjoyed by his officers hints at the intimacy of their world. They did not fraternize, plainly, but nor could they ignore one another.

Jack's comparative familiarity with his social betters had other aspects. Seamen and officers alike appreciated that no ship could function without a level of teamwork. Robert Wilson, a topman, once tried to explain to lubbers at home the various roles of his fellow seamen, only to throw up his hands and conclude:

It is impossible to elucidate all the employments at once allotted to each class as the ship's duty is such that all the classes are in a manner blended together.[27]

All of which casts some light on the familiarity that developed between an illiterate Norfolk ploughman and his admiral.

———

Tom Allen was rated Able three years after signing on. He had recently been appointed Nelson's servant and was aged twenty-four. Nelson was thirty-seven, so considerably Allen's senior in age as well as his superior in rank, standing, education and intellect. Nelson was slight, Allen sturdy. Having the duty of caring for an officer's personal needs would of course have involved intimacy and, in the circumstances of Nelson's liaison with Emma Hamilton, confidentiality. In addition, Allen had known Nelson before he became famous, and had the further connection of their shared hinterland; he had been to the great man's home, was acquainted with his family. They were together for the period that saw Nelson's transition from obscurity to national hero, from captain to vice-admiral, fond husband to infatuated lover. As well as fighting at Nelson's side and being severely wounded, Allen protected and occasionally supervised him. When they came under fire, Allen was known to 'interpose his bulky form between [the guns] and his little master'; and at dinners in the great cabin would caution him against taking too much wine, then usher him away from the table.[28]

Their first major battle together was at Cape St Vincent. This was a defining moment. Nelson established himself as a leader of unique qualities, leaving the British line in the 74-gun *Captain* to engage the *Santissima Trinidad*, a 120-gun Spanish behemoth, then the *San José* of 112 guns. When he joined the boarding party on another Spanish ship, the *San Nicolas*, Tom Allen was at his shoulder. At some point Allen was badly wounded – 'in his Privates'. This was not serious enough to stop him later becoming a father, but it appears to have affected one leg so that the seaman's usual side-to-side gait became in his case 'like a heavily laden ship rolling before the wind'.[29]

In the disastrous landing at Santa Cruz, Allen was again at his master's side and when he in turn was wounded – in the right arm by a musket ball – helped him back to the ship. Tom then held the arm while it was being amputated and as Nelson said, 'nursed me tenderly'. Whether he was already acquainted with Fanny Nelson is unclear but in the months Nelson spent at Bath recuperating Allen became part of their domestic milieu. He may indeed have been responsible for the chaotic packing and dispersal of their trunks when some items belonging to Fanny went back to sea with her husband, while some of Nelson's possessions, including a watch, were lost altogether.[30]

During the Battle of the Nile that year Allen was in action at the guns again, and now with an anxious eye to Nelson's disdain for danger. By one account, he sewed a pad into the tricorn hat which helped to absorb a missile that wounded Nelson in the head, saving him from serious, possibly fatal, injury.[31] Allen, said Midshipman Parsons, came to see himself as Nelson's custodian: 'He watched his lordship with unceasing attention, and many times have I seen him persuade the admiral to retire from a wet deck or a stormy sea to his bed.'[32]

He also had a unique insight into the passion that gripped Nelson after the Nile victory and his return to Naples. When Emma Hamilton came on board the *Foudroyant* she entered the seamen's world as few ladies did. 'An overweight, blowzy seductress . . . full of animal magnetism and an armoury of attention-seeking skills', as a Nelson biographer described her, Emma enchanted the lower deck.[33] Tom Allen would have years to observe the admiral's new love at close quarters. From the little evidence that exists, Emma regarded him with indulgent amusement, laughing at his social ineptitude. Nelson would send Tom to call on her, bearing his love letters, enquiring after her health and returning with her replies.[34]

It was perhaps because of this familiarity that the Norfolk rustic started to enter stormy waters. One who knew him said that 'no man is a hero to his valet de chambre' – or, as Tom styled himself, Nelson's 'wallet de sham'.[35] Whether because of his 'infantile simplicity', or because of basking in the celebrity of his new status, Allen began to test his master's temper. In one incident, he declined to kiss the hand of the king of Naples as he came on *Foudroyant* where the admiral and a line of glittering navy officers awaited him. Instead Allen gave the proffered royal hand 'a truly Norfolk shake, likely to effect a dislocation', and in a coarse growl asked: 'I hope you are well, Muster King. How do you do Muster King?' This:

. . . created astonishment in the King and courtiers, anger in Lord Nelson, and great mirth in Lady Hamilton and her fair coterie who, approaching honest Tom, tried to persuade him to kneel and ask permission to kiss his Majesty's hand; but Tom gruffly declared he never bent his knee but in prayer, and he feared that was too seldom.[36]

He crossed another line during a grand dinner on the anniversary of the Battle of St Vincent. Food had been served and the officers were setting to when Allen's stentorian bass was heard across the table, enquiring of a visiting captain after the health of his foretopman. When the captain's eyes popped in astonishment at this impertinence, Allen repeated the question. A furious Nelson ordered 'Quit the cabin, Thomas Allen!', then apologized to his guests: 'I really must get rid of that impudent lubber. I have often threatened, but somehow he contrives to defeat my firm intentions.'

Later, after the decanter had circulated repeatedly, Allen re-entered the great cabin and warily approached the admiral:

'Yow will be ill if yow takes any more wine.'

'You are perfectly right, Tom, and I thank you for the hint . . . Gentlemen, excuse me for retiring, for my battered old hulk is very crazy – indeed, not seaworthy.'

And the greatest naval hero of the day was led from his own table by his faithful and attached servant, after drinking five glasses of wine.[37]

But sailing close to the wind had become second nature to Tom and it would carry him onto the rocks. His place in Nelson's story is disputed: one authority believes him to have been 'vastly overhallowed';[38] after Nelson's death Allen certainly played up his own prominence – desperate as he then was to make ends meet. Be that as it may, he epitomized the bond between Nelson and Jack.

Already, however, the need for men was wringing changes which challenged that union. The Admiralty's priority was for vessels to be constantly manned, so when a ship was laid up for refitting, her hands – instead of being given shore leave – were 'turned over' directly into another. The changes went deeper. Recruitment passed almost entirely to the Impress Service. And as the Admiralty wanted to be in control, even when it was no longer in touch, officers were discouraged or forbidden from raising hands through personal contacts.[39] Even an influential commander like Pellew was prevented from taking his Cornish tribe with him from ship to ship. Overall the loyalty of settled companies was lost, discontent grew and desertions surged.

Which was at least partly why the nation that would acclaim seamen as saviours had first to see their fearsome aspect in another light – as a threat to its very survival.

A RISING TIDE
1794-97

TWO years after the Revolution across the Channel, a tract was published in London acclaiming the overthrow of the French monarchy and setting a landmark in the battle for civil rights in Britain. The author was a former seaman. Not surprisingly, the book created a monumental outcry, picking up as it did on his earlier campaign for American independence and extolling war against despotism of any kind. *Rights of Man* was a publishing sensation, selling some 50,000 copies from its appearance in 1791 and being read aloud in coffee shops and inns.

Among those Tom Paine had in mind when writing *Rights of Man* were old shipmates. Born the son of a Quaker corset-maker in Thetford, Norfolk, Paine's own sailor life – in a privateer, possibly as a sailmaker – was short (though he seems to have profited quite handsomely in prize money from a six-month cruise in the *King of Prussia*) and ended more than twenty years before he took up his campaigning pen. The experience nevertheless informed his belief that:

> Never did so great an opportunity offer itself to England . . . as is produced by the two Revolutions of America and France . . . The oppressed soldier will become a freeman; and the tortured sailor, no longer dragged along the streets like a felon, will pursue his mercantile voyage in safety.[1]

These words would have touched a chord with many a hand (had they been read), yet Paine was too radical a spirit for all but the most fervent of his countrymen, especially once Britons united in the face of war with France. So long as Britain avoided invasion, and a foreign yoke, her people could proclaim their freedom. But the values of a simpler, more rustic world had not just been challenged; they had passed. America, which nourished Paine's early activism, was seen by many as the land of true liberty, and it was far more accessible to seamen than to other would-be migrants. Thousands of sailors deserted in order to cross the Atlantic. At bottom, the Navy's aversion to reform sat ill with an age when Enlightenment thought had touched even the common man.

C. S. Forester believed there was an enduring superstition, surviving from the Middle Ages, that flogging had some intrinsic reformative effect on the victim.[2] That certainly chimes with the chillingly bald tone of entries in ships' logs – punishment of feudal severity reduced to numbers, from a standard twelve strokes of the cat for minor infringements like drunkenness, through a commonplace twenty-four lashes for, say, neglect of duty, to forty-eight for more serious or repeat offences, and on to the extremes – from 300 to 500 lashes for desertion or mutinous behaviour; and the ultimate case of Martin Billin and James Brian, who suffered the atrocity of 1,000 lashes for sodomy in 1762.

Flogging was arguably necessary to maintain order because of the strains that life at sea imposed on the human condition. Even John Nicol, mildest of fellows, was lashed more than once – and for fighting, no less. Jacob Nagle certainly took his share of beatings and on one occasion, as a senior hand, was ordered to flog a shipmate for theft; on meeting him again, Nagle was reminded, 'You gave me a thrashing I never shall forget.'[3] Men accepted it, and generally preferred quick-fire pain to long-term loss, whether of pay through disrating or denial of their comforting grog. But what were the effects of being tied up and thrashed with a whip composed of nine lengths of rope, each about two feet long and knotted in three places at the end?

Samuel Leech thought human flesh treated by the cat resembled 'roasted meat burnt nearly black before a scorching fire' – and that was after just twenty-four lashes.[4] A man flogged through the fleet would take hundreds. No discrimination was exercised as to the individual's physical or mental fortitude: one man might faint even before being strung to the grating; another could take two dozen without a groan. Nicol recalled seeing a shipmate, 'his back swelled like a pillow, black and blue', and how vinegar was applied to prevent infection, which roused the fellow from insensibility so 'his shrieks rent the air'.[5] A chaplain, Edward Mangin, observed a victim bound upright to spars in a boat, then rowed off attended by a drummer beating the Rogue's March, with other small craft following in their wake:

> The procession thus went from ship to ship and at each the boatswain's mates were ready at the gangway to descend; and the sufferer being stripped he received the allotted number of blows . . . He was very faint and bloody and must have endured what to me appeared worse than death.[6]

As Mangin went on to point out, however, naval discipline was often less severe than the criminal code of the day. For the same offence of wounding with a knife, the man he saw taking 150 lashes would probably have died on the gallows. Seamen could be shocked by what they saw of the civilian justice system. Jacob Nagle certainly was: his distress at the hanging of a woman convict, Ann Davis, in Sydney for stealing clothes is palpable:

> When brought to the gallos by two wimen, she was so much intocsicated in liquor that she could not stand without [others] holding her up. It was dreadful to see hur going to aternity out of this world in such a senceless, shocking manner.[7]

Discipline per se – or 'the lash' – was not therefore the reason for a rising sense of grievance that became visible during the Revolutionary War. The Navy had requisitioned men in unprecedented numbers from a diversity of sources, so the social cohesion essential to maritime life was being eroded. Society itself was in a state of flux. Belief that events in America and France provided a spark for reforms overdue in England had visible support – from intellectuals, radical clerics and schoolmasters among others. Thirteen political activists were tried for treason and acquitted in the summer of 1794, hardening respectable men in the opinion that their Scepter'd Isle was on the verge of cataclysm. Libertarians in society, like Charles James Fox, could get away with dangerous views, but suspicion that these might spread to the lower orders had taken the form of countryside witch-hunts.[8] In the Navy, there was a trend among a new generation of officers to regard Jack with suspicion or contempt.

Samuel Leech cited the case of 'reckless, honest-hearted Irishman' Bob Hammond. On receiving four dozen for drunkenness – another instance of medieval brutality for a mundane crime – Hammond went straight back to the bottle, then compounded his offence by addressing the captain, Lord William Fitzroy, thus: 'Halloo, Billy my boy, is that you?' He was promptly strung up again, for five dozen more:

> Most heroically was it borne. No sound escaped him; the most profound silence was observed by all, broken only by the dead sound of the whip as it fell every few moments on the wounded back. The scene was sickening in the extreme . . . It is questionable which of the two appears to the best advantage; poor, drunken Bob, suffering degrading torture with heroic firmness, or my Lord Fitzroy, gloating on the scene with the appetite of a vulture.[9]

An assumption of obedience was combined, in the naval establishment, with complacency. Jack's conditions of service had remained unchanged for more than 150 years, during which he had become an invaluable asset to the nation. Signs of a new defiance emerged in a mutiny that created the biggest stir of its kind since the *Bounty*.

Ships were cruelly cold places in winter and the gale howling through and around the *Culloden* was reason enough for the men to be huddled below on a vile night at Spithead in December 1794. Lieutenant Anselm Griffiths was hunched on the quarterdeck at about 10 p.m. when 'a great noise', a clamour of voices, came from the focsle and he went forward to investigate. Descending a ladder to the lower deck, he found himself in the dark and realized that the outcry was a chant – 'A new ship! A new ship!' Then, from out of the gloom, came the sound of cannonballs rolling across the deck towards him.*

The mutiny on *Culloden* by about 250 men, armed and barricaded below, lasted five days. A procession of admirals and captains came out to negotiate, watched by the entire Channel Fleet lying at anchor. Finally, the Cullodens surrendered their muskets and swords and came peacefully up on deck. And then the trouble really started.

Any survey of mutiny is based on incomplete evidence because naval records are subjective and selective. What one captain saw as gross insubordination might be overlooked by another as waywardness. When order really was at risk a gifted officer might restore it by diplomacy, just as another could destroy it altogether by mismanagement. A sensible captain, having nipped an incident in the bud, would make no further mention of it. Another might conceal it for fear of drawing unwelcome attention to his ship. But patterns in the treatment of mutineers are still clear.

During the Seven Years War from 1756, just one classic case of mutiny is mentioned in Admiralty digests: a rising on the sloop *Stork* against a tyrannical officer, for which four men were hanged.[10] Of the other twenty-seven cases brought to trial, two-thirds involved a single seaman abusing or assaulting a superior; and as most of the targets were midshipmen – some coming it a bit high with a senior man – the threat to authority was hardly serious. All these mutineers escaped with a flogging. In five other cases men attacked officers with knives. One was acquitted on being found insane, one was flogged and three were hanged.

---

* ADM 51/1130, log of the *Culloden*. ADM 1/5331, *Culloden* court martial. Although his experience in this notorious mutiny might have made a tyrant of him, Anselm Griffiths went on to prove himself a true seaman's friend as a frigate captain and after the war he campaigned for the abolition of impressment.

In the thirteen years of peace that followed, six mutinies came to trial, all of a lesser order. Thomas Sherlock certainly went up in his fellows' esteem by going aloft on the *Portland* and bellowing from the tops: 'God damn the captain, lieutenants and all the officers in the ship for bloody red-flag'd buggers.'[11]

During the next war, also over a seven-year period, nineteen cases were noted. A few were minor, notably that of William Brennon of the *Ajax* who, on being ordered to sweep the deck, 'took his broom and began to exercise it, as a soldier would a musket'. Challenged by the bosun over this sassy tilt at authority, Brennon rested on the broom, grinned in his face and said: 'Bejasus, I'll be hung for you.' His 'mutiny' earned him a savage 500 lashes.[12]

But if there were fewer cases, they included some of a far more serious nature. The American Revolution sparked an attempt on the *Narcissus* to go over to the rebels. Insurrections on the *Jackal* and the *Sylph* were still more shocking as the mutineers had it in mind to take their ships to France. All those convicted in these cases were hanged. Small beer by comparison was the letter written by John Mitchell of the *Chaser*, charging his captain with 'inhumanity, cruelty and barbarity' and stating that the people would 'submit no longer to such insufferable usage'. Mitchell was still hanged.[13] Eleven of the nineteen mutinies between 1776 and 1783 ended on the yardarm.

Peace naturally brought a reduction of incidents and, except for the *Bounty* trials, an easing of punishment. Among the lighter sentences was that of fifty lashes dealt out to Daniel Stewart of the *Scipio*, who championed a messmate placed in irons by demanding to be chained as well, saying that his friend was being ill-used by officers 'deserving of Hell and Damnation'. It helped that Stewart was described as among the best men in the ship.[14]

What set the *Culloden* mutiny apart from anything that preceded it was the degree of organization, the secrecy of the ringleaders' identities, and its disastrous legacy.

As a mass revolt it was serious enough for Lord Bridport, second in command of the Channel Fleet, to come on board in person the next day with two other admirals, Cornwallis and Colpoys, to 'endeavour to perswade the men to return to their duty'.[15] He did so by praising their 'valour in so Glorious a Victory' – a reference to the Battle of the First of June earlier that year – a ploy that in most instances would have done the necessary.*

Instead, the response was a letter passed up the hatchway 'from the point of a stick'. It too contained some requisite *politesse*, but stated that the company believed *Culloden*:

> Is not fit for His Majesty's Service without being either overhauled or more properly examined and is surprised that any Ship Wright should report a Ship sound after so many and Violent Strokes.[16]

Two weeks earlier, on 19 November, she had gone aground off Spithead and the company spent a week pumping out water and clearing tons of ballast to lighten and bring her back on an even keel. *Culloden* was an elderly 74 and in being holed in several places had suffered quite serious damage; but repairs had sealed the leaks.[17]

If concern over the ship's condition was the ostensible cause, a second complaint hinted at discontent with her regime. This was 'the indifferent usage of our first lieutenant Mr Whitter', who had 'represented us as a set of Cowardly Rascalls'. Tristram Whitter had been promoted to first lieutenant a week earlier. That same day James Calaway, an Able hand, was given two dozen lashes for 'mutiny and contempt to his superior officer'.[18] What were called 'murmurings among the people' began.

The causes remained obscure, but the course dictated by the mutineers was clear. They demanded a new ship or to be dispersed into other vessels. But everything was conditional on 'your Lordships word and honour not to punish

---

* This Atlantic battle in which seven French ships of the line were taken was the first major victory of the war.

any man concerned in the present business or to mention or remember it there after'. This blunt declaration was underscored by a term that brought the admirals up with a start. It was signed 'A Delegate'. At that point alarm bells rang. The word 'delegate' had become synonymous with the French Revolution.

Over the five days they spent barricaded below, only one mutineer could be identified with certainty. The voice of James Johnstone, twenty-three, rated Ordinary and from Surrey, was heard in negotiations. He was also the scribe who had penned the letter of protest: in a thoughtless moment he added his name to it; and he it was who passed it up at the point of a stick.

There may have been no certainty over the instigators, but Thomas Troubridge was not a captain who entertained doubts. The *Culloden* had a high proportion of Irish hands, and though that was not rare – after Englishmen, the Irish now made up the largest number, followed by Scots and Welsh – they tended to divide opinion between commanders who appreciated their combative fire and those who thought them as likely to give battle to a friend as a foe: 'The finest peasantry in the world,' said one; 'I have an exceeding bad opinion of the Lower Class of people of that Nation,' wrote another.[19] Troubridge tended to the latter view.

Another factor was starting to colour perceptions. The Society of United Irishmen, founded in 1791, reflected the new age of radicalism in its goal for an independent Irish state and had in Wolfe Tone a polemicist whose tracts matched those of Paine. It was also riven with sectarianism and as turbulent as that country's subsequent history was to prove.

The Irish Cullodens were an unusual mix. They included about twenty experienced hands of various backgrounds. Then there was a group with a distinctive profile: young men – aged between twenty and twenty-three – from the west – Cork and Limerick – and almost all Landsmen. No fewer than eighty-five fell into this category.[20] Among them was Cornelius Sullivan, aged twenty-two, from Bandon, who was glimpsed pointing a musket up from the hatchway. As those to the fore in any crisis tended to be senior men, this was unusual. Troubridge's conclusion was that out of the 250 men below, the core group numbered 'about 50 or 60 and [were] mostly of the lower order of the Irish'. They had 'over-awed' and were terrorizing the rest.[21]

Whether or not he was right about the numbers, coercion was indeed the ringleaders' method. Anyone of suspect loyalty was cornered and forced to swear an oath on the Bible. The wording was never revealed because witnesses at the subsequent trial were, as in everything else, forgetful or vague; but it came down to a pledge 'not to desert until it was all over and not to divulge any secret' – essentially, the names of those who had borne arms.[22]

Strains were showing below. Days into confinement in their dark, filthy, stinking space, men were shitting and pissing out of the ports. Less sturdy spirits openly wished themselves anywhere else. There were still enough diehards to hold sway – men like Jeremiah Collins, who went around swearing: 'By the Holy St Jesus, before we go up without honourable terms, I'll blow them to the bounds of buggery.'[23] Collins was from Cork, rated Able, and, aged forty, among the most senior men.

The Admiralty resolved on action. Preparations were in hand to lay two First Rates alongside when three captains were sent on board. Among them was Thomas Pakenham who had two attributes: he was popular with seamen, and he was Irish. At this point demands were lowered, but still conditionally: there would be no surrender without an amnesty.[24]

On day five, Captain Pakenham returned and this time he was allowed below. What passed there became a matter of significant dispute. Pakenham's main recollection was that 'the people behaved very civil and attentive to me'. Soon afterwards men started to come up the ladders, where he was waiting for them. Out of relief he called Francis Watts, who had been wielding a sword for the past five days, 'a good fellow'.[25]

Ten days before Christmas, ten of the alleged ringleaders were brought to trial:

The Cullodens' court martial was pure theatre. The causes, whether the ship's condition or the first lieutenant's disdainful manner, were not addressed. So far

as the Admiralty was concerned, this was a show trial. The accused were repre-
sentatives of 'the people' who had conspired in a coordinated rebellion: part of
the ritual was that some should die while some would be spared in a show of
magnanimity; some might even be acquitted.

The ten accused were a cross section – five Irish, five English. A few were in
deep: Francis Watts, seen with a sword, and Cornelius Sullivan, with a musket.
Jeremiah Collins had threatened to blow everything 'to buggery'. The scribe
James Johnstone was another likely to receive a death sentence, despite making
a persuasive plea that he had been acting under threat. Nobody else had a
legible hand and he seemingly came to the fore only because a clerk was
required. Said to be a 'quiet man who did his duty in the Waist', the twenty-
three-year-old from Godalming had a most untypical profile for a ringleader.

All of which posed the question: who were those unseen figures in the
shadows? Witness after witness was summoned to provide an answer, only to
depart leaving the adjudicating officers in purple frustration. Asked who had
administered the oath, the typical reply came: 'Really, I cannot tell. There were
many of them.'[26] One witness was so evasive the court sent him to prison.
Another was threatened with it. The prosecution's key card, Solomon Bostock,
whose testimony condemned most of the accused, professed ignorance when it
came to the organizers' names. He would, after all, be going back to join them.

Another question at the trial was crucial to later events: did the mutineers
surrender in the belief that they had been granted an amnesty? Watts, for one,
seemed taken aback to find himself on trial, having been greeted as 'a good
fellow' by Captain Pakenham when he came up on deck. Of the negotiations
that led to surrender, the court asked Pakenham:

Were there any conditions proposed by the people below?
    A: Yes, they desired me to give my word and honour for Pardon for
them but this I declined.[27]

Whatever passed was known only to the participants. Yet a conviction became
entrenched among seamen across the Navy that the Cullodens had been

promised an amnesty. In the words of one historian: 'An essential bond of trust had been severed.'[28]

Eight of the ten accused were sentenced to hang – Watts, Sullivan, Collins and Johnstone, along with Joseph Curtain, twenty-two, David Hyman, twenty-two, Samuel Triggs, forty-six, and John Morrish, twenty-four. The last three were recommended to mercy 'in consideration of the excellent characters given by their officers'. Two more were acquitted. The ritual was almost complete.

With Christmas just around the corner, some sensitivity was in order, especially as the mood on *Culloden* remained volatile; three men were flogged for riotous behaviour and insolence. On Christmas Eve, Troubridge had thirty-one hands he suspected of being activists dispersed into other ships. Only on 13 January, three weeks after sentencing, did the log record the final rites:

> At 10 fired a gun, hoisted a yellow flag forward, read the Articles of War. Boats of the fleet attending alongside manned and armed. Marines under arms. Hung at the fore yard Francis Watts, James Johnstone, Cornelius Sullivan, Joseph Curtain, Jeremiah Collins.

Mystery endured over what had occurred on *Culloden*. The Admiralty tended to dismiss complex events as senseless and unpredictable – an outcome of men being long and closely confined. A rebellion on the *Defiance* a year later elicited the comment: 'As is usual, the mutiny did not appear to have any solid foundation or any rational purpose.'[29] It is true a ship's temper was a curious thing and seemingly trivial issues could spark unrest. In the *Defiance* case, for which five men were hanged, the trigger was diluted grog.

The *Culloden* was different – distinguished by the degree of organization and political agenda. A radical term, 'delegate', had been used by mutineers for the first time – though by no means the last. And Irish hands with a distinctive profile had played a critical role. It seems fair to conclude that the real leaders had concealed themselves to the end. Some of those executed had, in effect, been scapegoats.

These events were forgotten soon enough – at least by those in charge of the war. For those fighting it, though, *Culloden*'s rebellion endured, as a symbol. Discontent was rising on the lower deck and in three years would precipitate the biggest explosion in naval history.

———

Jacob Nagle makes no mention of the *Culloden*, but then he had his own mutiny to reflect upon. Fortunately it had a better outcome, thanks to the intervention of an officer wiser than Troubridge.

We last saw Nagle as he prepared to join the frigate *Gorgon*. Here he came close to a court martial himself, his lieutenant being one of those overweening types whom Jack Nastyface thought should 'think a little more of *national honor* and a little less of *self-importance*'.[30] Nagle's wife Elizabeth came out in a boat at Spithead for a final farewell and was then refused permission to board – at which Nagle hurled a rattan cane overboard in rage. The lieutenant threatened him with trial for disrespect and it was only because of support from the bosun, a fellow American, that Nagle escaped with an order from the captain to apologize.[31]

Still the lieutenant's usage rankled and when *Gorgon* reached Corsica, Nagle applied for a transfer to the frigate *Blanche*. He went from a dissatisfied ship to an unhappy one. Her sole virtue was to be joining Commodore Nelson's squadron in the Western Mediterranean. A letter from the Blanches tells part of the story. Addressed to the Admiralty and written in a phonetic style typical of Nagle, it is a 'Hombel petition on a count of ill yousage':

> We are imployed from Morning to two or three o clock in the afternoon washing and scrubing the Dicks and every day ower Chest and Bags is Ordered on Dick and not down till night nor our selves neither . . . If we gate wett and hang or spread our Cloes to drip our Captain throes them overboard by which we big the favour of an other commander or an other ship. We still remain your most worthy subjects.[32]

Obsessive tidiness was not Captain Charles Sawyer's only vice. He had, Nagle noted, 'a fondness for young men and boys', who would be summoned late to his cabin and engaged in conversation until he took hold of them 'around the privates'.[33] Those forced to submit included two mids, a coxswain and a seaman. Disgust at the captain's habits had undermined discipline across the ship.

Action provided a diversion. Nelson's squadron, responding to Bonaparte's sweep through northern Italy, was blockading Leghorn when *Blanche* came under fire from shore batteries, starting a blaze near the magazine that nearly blew her to pieces. For Nagle there was an even narrower escape when a ball came through the side, close enough to singe the hair on his neck. Had he not just responded to an order to lie flat, 'the shot would of beheaded me completely'.

Soon afterwards Captain Sawyer's conduct exploded in a court martial that brought his dismissal for 'odious misconduct'. Since command of the Mediterranean had just fallen to Admiral John Jervis, whose zeal for hanging was matched by his loathing of homosexuality, Sawyer was lucky to escape with mere dismissal and disgrace.

Some normality returned under a temporary captain. With Commodore Nelson in *Minerve*, they sailed for Elba to evacuate the British garrison and took a Spanish coaster carrying silk. With that gift of endearing himself to hands, Nelson, according to Nagle, 'ordered 7 bails of silk hoisted out of hur for a drink for the sailors' – in effect, bypassing the prolonged prize-money system to treat the men and boost morale.[34]

Directly, they fell in with two Spanish frigates. The *Minerve* took the heavier *Santa Sabina* while *Blanche* engaged the *Ceres*. Nagle recalled:

> We ware not idel. We run as close along side as we could without runing on board of hur and gave hur a broadside fore and aft. We played so hot upon them, they run from there quarters . . . Rounding under her lee, we gave hur another broadside. Hur colours came down by the run.

Two prizes meant a good deal more reward money was in the offing – until they ran into a Spanish 74 and two more frigates, and had to make haste to get away. Yet even loss could be softened by a thoughtful commander. When the *Blanche* reached Elba:

> Nelson came on board . . . and shook hands with us as he went along and telling us he was rejoice'd to find that we had escaped.

The final act in this masterly display of man-management followed the appointment of Henry Hotham as *Blanche*'s new captain. Hotham was a reputed tartar and, in Nagle's words, 'our ship mutinised'. As Hotham came on board to have his commission read on 7 January 1797, the Blanches set up a roar: 'No! No! No!' And a petty officer went onto the focsle, turning two carronades towards the quarterdeck.

Hotham hastened across to Nelson's ship, returning with a lieutenant who summoned the hands aft. 'Now, my lads,' he called out, 'if you resist taking Captain Hotham, every third man shall be hung.' In response the men returned to the focsle, 'with match in hand, likewise crowbars, handspikes, and all kinds of weapons they could get holt of'. Mutiny on the *Blanche* had suddenly the potential to turn even uglier than the *Culloden*.

Nelson came on board himself. Once more the Blanches were called to the quarterdeck to state their objections. Nagle described Nelson's response:

> 'Lads,' said he, 'you have the greatest caracter of any frigates crew in the navy. You have taken two frigates supperiour to the frigate you are in, and now to rebel . . . If Capt Hotham ill treats you, give me a letter and I will support you.'
>
> Amediately there were three chears given and Capt Hotham shed tears, and Nelson went on bd his ship. All being ready . . . we sailed for Giberalter.[35]

So ended a second mutiny of the utmost gravity without a hanging or a drop of blood, thanks to the helmsmanship of an officer who had showed his luminous qualities for the first time.[36] The *Blanche* crisis was quietly overlooked by everyone present – it does not appear in the log, and Nagle's is the sole account – while Hotham duly took command. The Blanches never liked him but there was no further unrest.[37]

The Cullodens, meanwhile, were about to redeem themselves.

Strategically, the Mediterranean had become a sea of disaster. With French troops in control of territory that had supplied his fleet, Jervis could no longer operate effectively in these, his designated waters. While Nelson's frigates were away evacuating the Elba garrison, Jervis had remained at Gibraltar awaiting a chance to strike at the Spaniards. With exquisite timing, Nelson returned to rejoin him on 12 February 1797. Two days later, off Cape St Vincent, they intercepted a Spanish fleet bound to join Bonaparte's planned invasion of Britain.

The Battle of Cape St Vincent was one of the defining actions of the war – fifteen British ships of the line against twenty-three Spanish. Leading the way was Troubridge in *Culloden*. Bringing up the rear was Nelson, now in the *Captain*, another 74. The speed with which the British hands manoeuvred their ships for battle caught the Spaniards off guard, leaving a fatal gap in their line. Through it went *Culloden*, cheered on by Jervis as she engaged the main body of Spanish ships: 'Look at Troubridge there! He tacks to battle as if the eyes of England were upon him, and would to God they were!'[38]

The Spanish admiral José de Córdoba recovered promptly enough to bring the second part of his fleet round, threatening to cut the line of British ships in *Culloden*'s wake. But now Nelson in the *Captain* turned out of the line followed by the *Excellent* and went straight for the mountainous four-deck 120-gun *Santísima Trinidad*. Again the odds appeared overwhelmingly stacked. What counted at close quarters, however, was gunnery, and over three hours Jack proved by his training, accuracy and stamina that a 74 could humble the largest ship in the world. To round off an epic display, Nelson led sailors and marines in boarding two other battered Spaniards. Tom Allen was at his side, until suffering what was subsequently described as 'the wound in his Privates'.

It was a triumph of teamwork over an enemy fleet with almost twice the firepower. Four Spanish ships of the line were taken, and more than 1,000 Spaniards killed. By way of comparison, the *Captain* had twenty dead, the *Culloden* thirteen. Nelson had won immediate fame, Troubridge the love of his mentor Jervis, who was created Lord St Vincent. Both Nelson and Troubridge were great sea officers, yet with utterly contrasting methods. Nelson inspired love. Troubridge instilled fear. He may not have been a brute, but he was a tartar.

Victory brought little visible celebration on *Culloden*. Over the weeks she underwent repairs, beatings took place regularly: insolence and disobedience were common.[39] The punishment rates are not especially high: three or four floggings a month was fairly standard for a 74; and on occasion Troubridge showed a human side: James Holt was sentenced for desertion by a court martial to receive 200 lashes while being beaten round the fleet; after seventy-seven 'he was brought on board, not being able to bear his punishment'.[40]

But *Culloden*'s spirit – assertiveness combined with a capacity for organiza-tion – was symptomatic of a rising tide. There had always been individuals willing to stand their ground in the face of abuses, and a great many more hands had come to the opinion that they were subject to a treatment as bad as tyranny – neglect. Within weeks they would turn their fellowship, the bond of service to the king, to mass rebellion.

15

REVOLUTION AT SPITHEAD
1797

THAT it was the greatest rebellion in maritime history is not in doubt. The events at Spithead in 1797 could, however, be seen in a wider context, as a turning point in the rise of the common man. The coordinated revolt by thousands of seamen that spring, challenging a state that had come to take their service for granted, not only demonstrated to men of power that these poor, simple folk were capable of organization and resistance, but it also served as a reminder that they held the nation's destiny in their calloused hands. A state that failed to recognize these truths did so at its peril.

What many saw as revolution began with a petition. Moderate and sober, it came from eleven leading ships of the Channel Fleet and respectfully drew attention to a single grievance – the fact that seamen's pay had not been increased for almost 150 years. What had once been a 'comfortable support' had become a hardship. Moreover – and this was a further and quite galling aspect – soldiers had enjoyed a pay increase two years previously. No mention was made of other blights on the lower deck, notably poor rations and tyrannical officers. In the same emollient spirit, the appeal was sent to Lord Howe, recent commander of the fleet, known as 'the Sailor's Friend', requesting that his lordship help to obtain 'speedy redress' over wages, not only for seamen but for their families labouring ashore under the rising costs of 'every necessary of life'.

As the petition's preparation as well as its substance was crucial to what followed, it bears examination. The first draft was drawn up on the *Queen Charlotte*, the flagship at Spithead, in February 1797. How the content was agreed upon and who was responsible for the startlingly elevated tone – 'Your petitioners humbly presume their loyalty to their sovereign is as conspicuous and their courage as unquestionable as any other description of men in His Majesty's service' – is not evident. However, it arose from musterings of hands from the largest ships then at anchor who had formed a circle of activists by rowing across to one another and acting as spokesmen for their fellows in discussing grievances. The number involved at this stage is not clear either, nor is the structure of any core leadership, but among the most prominent were Valentine Joyce of the *Royal George*, aged twenty-six, from Jersey, who had been afloat since he was eleven; and Patrick Glynn, a thirty-five-year-old Irishman of the *Queen Charlotte*, rated Able. The others were either Able hands, like Glynn,

Portsmouth and the anchorage of Spithead were the centre of naval operations, and scene of the great Channel Fleet mutiny in 1797.

or seamen risen to petty officer rank, like Joyce, who had been recently promoted to quartermaster's mate. Once the petition had been agreed, copies were sent to ten other ships of the line for endorsement by their companies.

The original – anonymous but stating that it came from *Queen Charlotte* – found Lord Howe taking the waters at Bath where he had retired with the gout. It was followed by the other ten, exact replicas, as Howe noted, 'decently expressed but without any signature'. While declaring sympathy for men wanting 'to make better provision for their families', he shrugged off any responsibility as 'I could not reply to applications which were anonymous'. It was true the petitions were unsigned, but coming from eleven of the largest ships in the fleet, including two 100-gun behemoths, they could not be so readily dismissed – as the admiral came belatedly to recognize. Seeking to escape blame for the earthquake that ensued, he went on: 'The petitions though differing a little in the handwriting, were obviously dated by the same person and I had therein further reason to think they were fabricated by some malicious individual who meant to insinuate the presence of a general discontent.'[1]

Howe also declined to send the petitions to Lord Bridport, the senior officer at Spithead, because the two admirals were at war with each other. Instead, almost a month later, he passed them to a third admiral, Hugh Seymour, asking whether they had any substance. Seymour agreed that they were 'the work of some incendiary', before forwarding them to the Admiralty board, who simply ignored them.[2]

Thus was the tone set for a systemic failure by the Navy's command to accept that there was, and had been for some considerable time, a rising discontent among seamen – or to face the real injustices that had become Jack's lot.

Social change had touched the entire nation since the onset of war, but no other body of men (and a strategic resource at that) had been affected to the same extent. The declining purchasing power of Jack's wages was real, with inflation rising ashore and aboard where the cost of 'slops', or clothing, deducted directly from his wages by the purser, had gone up by 30 per cent. But that was just one grievance. The fact that hands could go unpaid for a year was more – it was a gross injustice, and it was not uncommon. With the state labouring under unprecedented financial pressure and a constant intake of new hands, corners were being cut. To many it appeared that pay was being deliberately withheld. Families suffered more than their menfolk, who were at least assured of shelter and food; but therein lay another wrong because corruption on top of cost-cutting meant that rations were often short and of poor quality.

The fact was that the ruling class had become complacent about Britain's sailors. Two years earlier naval officers had enjoyed a pay increase. So had all ranks of the Army. Jack was overlooked. Meanwhile, changes in naval service – the princely bonus paid to quota men, the hasty introduction of the new generation of Landsmen, including parish outcasts and jailbirds – was a source of resentment to old hands.

On top of money, discipline was a growing bone of contention. Since the *Culloden* mutiny, complaints about despotic or disdainful officers had become routine, taking the form of petitions such as that from the Shannons in June 1796, about ill-treatment by their

> . . . tiriant of a captain . . . which is more than the spirits and harts of true English Man can cleaverly bear, for we are born free but now we are slaves . . . We hope your Lordships will be so kind to us and grant us a new commander or a new ship for the Captin is one of the most barbarous and unhuman officers.[3]

One reform may inadvertently have encouraged the new assertiveness. In 1795 the government passed an Act allowing seamen to send and receive letters for a single penny, cutting the cost from the absurd amount of two shillings and making it feasible for men to stay in touch with family and loved ones. Samuel Leech was among the hands to celebrate the mailbag's arrival and how it awakened 'conjugal, fraternal and filial affection':

> The men crowd around as the letters are distributed, and he was pronounced a happy fellow whose name was read off by the distributor; while those who

had none, to hide their disappointment, would jocularly offer to buy those of their more fortunate messmates.[4]

During the upheavals of 1797, however, the cheap postal service came under suspicion from senior officers who believed it was used by quota men and agitators, 'ruined politicians and corresponding society men', to instigate unrest.[5]

———

As the two admirals involved at Spithead, both Howe and Bridport were subsequently blamed by a conscientious officer, Captain Cuthbert Collingwood, for what he called 'this great national calamity'.[6] But the First Lord at the Admiralty, Lord Spencer, also ignored loud-ringing alarm bells. Spencer had, in fact, been warned the previous December of rising bitterness over pay by Captain Thomas Pakenham, negotiator during the *Culloden* mutiny and an officer well connected with hands across the fleet.[7] Pakenham was not the only captain to sympathize with them, or to tell Spencer of their disgruntlement. At the time, Spencer, unwilling to challenge a parliament beset with financial stress, responded that there was simply no more money – or, as he put it: 'In the present state of the country, it is not possible to enormously increase disbursements.'[8]

All this needs to be set within the context of a country in crisis. Bonaparte, dominant in Europe, had mustered an army across the Channel at Brest, poised to launch an invasion of the British Isles. The Navy's supposedly impassable Wooden Walls stood in the way, reassuring citizens that their island bastion remained secure – until a French fleet appeared off south-west Ireland in January and, a month later, 1,500 French troops managed to land near Fishguard in Wales. Although that inept foray was swiftly dealt with, it precipitated a run on the banks and the Bank of England was forced to suspend cash payments.

Through March part of the Channel Fleet was off Brest, bottling up the French invasion force. It was only in April, on Bridport's return to Spithead, that he, as the new commander, received the original eleven petitions forwarded by the Admiralty, along with three new ones. Not that he was animated to do anything about them. It is fair to add that exploring the origins of each petition would not have been simple: the Channel Fleet was a complex organism, with ships variously dispersed between those blockading Brest, those at Spithead, and others anchored at Plymouth and Torbay. But even the newspapers sensed trouble in the air. The *Morning Post* reported that when the fleet returned on 30 March, 'a gloomy discontent pervaded every crew'; this had become the topic of conversation 'in every public house in Portsmouth . . . and the most fatal predictions have been made'.[9] Bridport remained blithely oblivious of the mood on his ships. In the lead-up to mutiny, it seemed the Channel Fleet did not have a commander-in-chief at all.[10]

All the more remarkable therefore was the collective strategy being coordinated by sailors dispersed around Portsmouth's waters and beyond. Of the original eleven ships to sign the petition, just four were back at Spithead during the critical first week of April; the others remained at sea or were refitting. But hands on at least thirteen more ships of the line, including the 100-gun *Royal Sovereign*, continued to use boats to meet and exchange letters; and because Bridport and his senior officers had gone ashore, the men were able to hold their parleys quite openly. From the original informal leadership a process of electing spokesmen emerged – two for each of the seventeen largest ships at Spithead. They chose to be known as delegates.

Delegates: that highly charged term was reflected in a new and extended agenda of grievances they were about to present. It started of course with the indisputable issue of pay, unchanged since Charles II's reign:

> . . . a time when the necessaries of life and slops of every denomination was at least 30 per cent cheaper than the present time which enabled seamen and marines to provide better for their Families than we can now do.[11]

Other complaints included shore leave and the treatment of wounded or disabled men as well as food. All were legitimate. Two ounces in every pound of provisions were retained by pursers to allow for waste; this not only deprived men of their stipulated rations but was a source of corruption. Hands were not allowed ashore on returning to port until they had been paid off; that process was frequently delayed, frustrating well-earned recreation and family reunions. And men wounded in action received no pay, while those deemed no longer fit for service were simply discharged – discarded into the world without care or support.[12]

It took weeks for signals to be recognized, that the principal ships at Spithead were so many powder kegs. On 14 April, Good Friday, the port admiral Sir Peter Parker delivered a thunderbolt, informing the Admiralty that he had 'received a private intimation that the crews of some of His Majesty's ships at Spithead, particularly the *Queen Charlotte* and *Royal Sovereign* . . . intend to refuse doing their duty till their wages is increased'. Belatedly, Parker indicated that he was surprised Bridport had done nothing to address signs of 'disagreeable combinations'.[13]

Two days later, on Easter Sunday, Bridport issued orders for these two largest ships to set sail. Neither raised anchor. Instead three cheers went up from *Queen Charlotte* and a boatload of men put out from her side, proceeding from ship to ship around Spithead to address their companies. That evening, two delegates elected by each of seventeen ships of the line gathered on the *Queen Charlotte*. The first mutiny by an entire fleet had begun.*

An image of the moment appears as vivid today as it did then. The great cabin of the admiral's flagship – and there, gathered at a table spread across her stern,

---

* The Cullodens, the first company to use the term 'delegates' in a protest, remained in foreign waters during the mutinies at Spithead and the Nore. On 21 July, 150 of them were involved in a shore raid on Santa Cruz, Tenerife, that went disastrously wrong. Thirty-eight were killed, three times as many as at Cape St Vincent, twenty-seven of them former mutineers. The ship still had 239 seamen from that time, including some of the turbulent young fellows from the west of Ireland. A few were never reconciled. James Shanley and John Poor, from Waterford and Dublin, were among the landing party who took sanctuary in a convent on Santa Cruz and who opted to stay with the Spaniards: 'Deserted to the enemy', records the muster (ADM 36/12170).

not a single golden epaulette, no wigs nor tricorns, but a cohort of roughly dressed Jacks, serious, solemn even, with their responsibility. The agenda they produced after hours of debate was a simple, dignified demand for fair treatment that stands the test of time. But it was the symbolism of the insurgency, an incursion by the lower orders, that rankled with those fearful of all-out revolution mirroring France and that continued to infect understanding of these events.

The nature of leadership during the mutinies of 1797 has been a subject of contention ever since. This is not surprising as even some of the delegates' identities remain unclear. So a notion gained hold that behind a facade of useful idiots and malcontents, the strings were being pulled by an invisible leadership. Various cabals have been invoked – Irish revolutionaries, dissident quota men, even egalitarian evangelists. The prevailing conspiracy theory of the time, subscribed to by Pitt's administration and parts of the press, concerned traitorous Jacobins. Until relatively recently historians accepted variations on the claim that 'some of the mutinies were assisted, if not actually fomented, by French agents'.[14]

The picture that emerges from a more dispassionate examination is that the leading figures represented a cross section of their tribe – and were, therefore, a compendium of all sorts – but that in most cases (and certainly at Spithead) they were elected because they were the best, most respected hands; that a genuine sense of grievance produced a unified spirit at Spithead, determined in its pursuit of fairness and successful in obtaining it; and that subsequently, on spreading to other anchorages, the revolt splintered into fragments of personal ideology, individual power-seeking and plain human fallibility.

Valentine Joyce was the leading figure at Spithead, in what may be called the south coast mutinies. Little of his early life is known, though he was one of eleven children of a soldier father in the Jersey militia.[15] Joyce went to sea as a boy and his fifteen years of solid experience may partly explain why he – a quartermaster's mate on *Royal George* – was appointed spokesman when the prime movers up to this point had been from the leading ship, *Queen Charlotte*. Aged twenty-six, Joyce was also among the younger delegates; but what emerges clearly from his handling of talks with lords, admirals and others of superior rank and standing is his intelligence, determination and dignity. That Joyce managed to hold his thirty-three fellow delegates on a steady course through weeks of storms speaks for his authority as well.*

There is no suggestion, however, that the leadership constituted a straight-forward hierarchy. In one seaman's words, each delegate possessed on his own ship, 'a strong influence over all hands, fore and aft'.[16] There are, unfortunately, no accounts of their debates; yet it is evident that the Spithead delegates spoke for their own ships while still preserving resolve and unity as a negotiating body representing many thousands of hands. Others identified as key figures were Joyce's shipmate from *Royal George*, John Morrice, a Scot, aged thirty-three and Able. The *Queen Charlotte*'s delegates were the Irishman Patrick Glynn, an early activist, and John Huddlestone, yeoman of the sheets. The *Royal Sovereign*, another 100-gun colossus, was represented by two Englishmen still in their twenties and rated Able, John Richardson and Joseph Green. The oldest delegate was George Salkeld, aged thirty-nine from Norfolk, yeoman of the powder room on the *Terrible*.[17]

That night, in *Queen Charlotte*'s state cabin, they drew up rules to govern the fleet now effectively in their hands. In essence these were that every seaman and marine was to take 'a Oath of Fiddelity not onely to themselves but the Fleet in General', that watches were to be diligently maintained as usual and 'the greatest attention be paid to the Orders of the Officers' (other than to make sail), that no liquor should be brought into any ship, and that 'every man swear by his maker that the Cause we have Undertaken we Persevere in until Accomplished'. Any infringement, it was warned, 'shall be severely punished'.[18]

Faced with this resolve, Bridport threw up his hands. He was not among the Navy's more impressive figures: 'Scarcely worth drowning, a more contemptible or more miserable animal does not exist', in the opinion of one of his captains, Edward Pellew.[19] That night Bridport wrote to the Admiralty:

---

* Of the thirty-four Spithead delegates, thirteen were rated Able, sixteen were petty officers and five were midshipmen (Manwaring and Dobree, Appendix I).

'Using vigorous and effectual measures for getting the better of the crews . . . is impossible to be done. I therefore see no method of checking the progress of this business but by complying in some measure with the prayer of the petitions.'[20]

Their lordships, having failed utterly to address the petitions or to recognize Jack's determination, were shocked into action. Yet as Spencer and three other board members set out by coach for Portsmouth on 17 April, it appears they still had no notion of what they were dealing with: the mutineers, incapable as they must be of organization and coherent debate, would surely surrender once isolated from their trouble-making leaders and offered token concessions. Spencer declined to meet the delegates, sending three admirals to the *Queen Charlotte* to hear their wishes. Back came the demand: pay increases for Able seamen from 22s 6d a month to 28s and Ordinary hands from 19s to 23s 6d, a raising of pensions from £7 to £10 a year, and improved rations.[21]

The delegates were equally clear about conditions. Until their claims were met, and a pardon from the king was granted to every man, no anchor would be raised on any ship – unless the French set out from Brest, in which case they would sail to give battle directly.

By a recent estimate, more than eighty ships manned by more than 30,000 men were at Spithead at this point, a quarter of the Navy's manpower.[22]

Over the next few days a ploy by Spencer to divide the leading ships from the rest of the fleet was attempted and failed. Minor concessions were offered and rejected. Meanwhile a group of officers regarded as harsh or despotic were sent ashore, yet without violence. Delegates maintained order and enforced discipline. One man who brought liquor on the *Pompee* was flogged – but just the dozen stipulated by naval regulation.[23] On 19 April, for a state visit by the Duke of Wurttemberg, salutes were fired and yards manned as normal.

Their lordships surrendered. Pay increases were agreed. (Spencer actually went on to acknowledge that wages had been 'undoubtedly too low in proportion to the times'.)[24] A pound of provisions would in future mean just that – not 14 ounces. And wounded men would receive full pay while they recovered.

Other claims, over pensions and shore leave, were left open. Satisfied that this would end it all, the admirals came aboard *Queen Charlotte* on 21 April to order a return to duty.

At this point Joyce demonstrated his mettle as a leader. He insisted there would be no agreement without an indemnity for all mutineers, signed by the king and with the royal seal; and he did so with a warning that reminded his fellow delegates of a notorious betrayal, urging: 'Remember the *Culloden.*' Promises of pardon were not to be trusted without proof. At this impudence, one of three admirals, Sir Alan Gardner, erupted; the delegates deserved to be hanged – 'skulking fellows, knowing the French were ready for sea, and they afraid of meeting them'.[25] In the closest the Spithead mutineers came to disrespect, Gardner was manhandled and hustled off *Queen Charlotte.*

Spencer left for London that night, arrived at 5 a.m. and went on with Pitt to Windsor where a proclamation of pardon was set before the king. He signed it. A hundred copies were printed, despatched to Portsmouth and on 23 April were being read out by captains across the fleet. The original draft was sent to *Royal George* and shown to Joyce and the company, who gave three cheers and pulled down the yard ropes as a sign of their acceptance. The Queen Charlottes remained sceptical until the original was boated across to them, when they also gave three cheers.[26] At that point, it appeared, the mutiny was over. Only it didn't end there.

Pitt moved as swiftly as possible to get Parliament's approval for the pay increase. There was never any doubt that it would be forthcoming: the mutineers had the ship of state in their grasp. But two weeks would pass before the Commons voted in favour of the £372,000 required, while the shock of these cataclysmic events resonated across the land.

To the modern eye the delegates' demands seem perfectly reasonable. They may have exploited their power at a time of crisis, but they had been too long ignored and were still demonstrating a readiness to do their duty: any French advance would be dealt with. To a nation fearful of invasion, however, the

Spithead mutiny represented a contagious anarchy among the lower orders. *The Times* declared that seamen were being 'spurred on by traitors who have nothing in view but the destruction of their country'.[27] Members of Pitt's cabinet said much the same thing in Parliament, while a prominent voice at the Admiralty lamented 'the most awful crisis that these kingdoms ever saw'.[28] The reformist politician, Edmund Burke, initially supportive of the Revolution in France but appalled by the course it had taken, wrote to the secretary for war, William Windham, that the war was lost, 'and as to our Navy, that has already perished with its discipline forever'.[29]

These denunciations filtered back to Spithead. Newspapers were being read around the fleet, kindling mistrust of the authorities. There were also signs of civilian elements trying to inflame matters: handbills printed in London claimed that the government would refuse to ratify the pact. As fear of betrayal began to rise, letters were passed between ships again, the following from *Pompee* to *Royal George* being an example:

> Our opinion is that there [is] not the least reliance to be placed in their promises . . . Now, brothers, your steady friends the Pompees beg of you to give them a final answer and whatever may be your proposals we one and all will never deviate from being determined to sink or swim.[30]

Another came from the *Ramillies*:

> They mean to lull us into a supposed state of security . . . by granting us a temporary increase in provisions etc. . . . with no other view than to keep us in the dark as to their intentions respecting the main point in view. If they once divide us and get us upon different stations, be assured they think they can then make their own terms.[31]

Suspicion, and failed expectations that the pay rise would be forthcoming immediately, precipitated what is sometimes called the second Spithead mutiny. On 7 May cheers went up from ship to ship, the yard ropes that had symbolized the original protest were hung up again, and once more delegates put out in their boats. By noon the fleet was back under the seamen's control. Their officers offered no resistance.

The violence started when the delegates decided to hold a new convention on the *London*, flagship of Vice-Admiral Sir John Colpoys. In an attempt to keep them from coming on board, Colpoys sent all hands below, had the ports closed and stationed marines on deck. When the Londons tried to come up, guns were fired – on both sides – and three seamen fell fatally wounded. Then, at what amounted to a turning point, the marines joined the mutineers. For once, blue and red jackets stood together against the quarterdeck.

Amid the turmoil, hands shouted for blood. Lieutenant Peter Bover was dragged to the focsle and a noose thrown around his neck. Crucially, one of *London*'s delegates, John Fleming, intervened. As Bover wrote later, Fleming 'was principally instrumental in saving my life'. For a while, though, Colpoys himself and Captain Edward Griffith remained in peril and – again according to Bover – it was only Fleming's 'manly eloquence [that] procured a pardon for the admiral and captain when everyone conceived it impossible that they could be saved'.[32] The three officers were nevertheless taken below and confined in their cabins.

Another critical intervention was made by Valentine Joyce, who came on board and, according to one witness, 'called the delicates [sic] aft into the cabin and begged them to suppress their passions':

> Shipmates, said he, this has gone too far; what can we promise ourselves by the destruction of an old man? What advantage shall we obtain by it? Believe me it will be a mark of disgrace upon a blue jacket. No, let us rather send 'em ashore and wash our hands of blood.[33]

Joyce's peacemaking was bolstered by news that Parliament had voted unanimously in favour of the pay increase. Admiral Colpoys, Captain Griffith and Lieutenant Bover were allowed ashore. It was perhaps fortunate that press reports of the Commons debate took another day to reach Portsmouth, for the mutineers were angered again by the contribution of Richard Sheridan, the playwright and an opposition MP of usually radical opinion, who sided with those seeing agents provocateurs at work, declaring that there had been 'a foul interference' with the mutiny and that while the grievances might be legitimate, the methods were 'inconsistent with the brave, generous and open character of British seamen'.[34]

Other unpopular officers were sent ashore – ten captains and 103 junior officers in all – drenched with humiliation yet still without violence. At the same time, Captain John Talbot of the *Eurydice*, who was already ashore, received a letter from his men declaring:

> We join in our earnest wishes and desires that you will once more join the flock of which you are the tender shepherd. We wish by this to show you, Sir, that we are men that loves the present cause as men ought to, yet we are not eleavated [sic] to that degree to neglect our duty to our country or our obedience to you.[35]

Nothing like it in English history had occurred before. Empowerment of the lower orders was visible and inescapable: The nation's fate lay with Jack. While men of rank gaped and the Hampshire countryside bloomed with spring on the slopes behind Portsmouth, a carnival was in progress below where seamen savoured their liberty. 'Some took their ease on the beach at Southsea, others in the public houses of Portsmouth and Gosport,' it was observed. 'No one on shore had orders to oppose their landing; the inhabitants were friendly; and the sailors came and went unmolested.'[36]

Finally, the Admiralty turned to 'the Sailor's Friend'. Lord Howe was one of only two individuals deemed capable of dealing with the mutineers, and as the king was never going to be a negotiator, the task fell to the gouty admiral whose negligent attitude towards petitions had set the train in motion in the first place. On 11 May, three months on, Howe's coach pulled in to Portsmouth. But if he was late, the assurances of their former commander-in-chief were crucial in restoring the men's trust. When he went on board *Royal George* and

Queen Charlotte that day and told them the government intended to meet their demands as promised, he was believed. When he produced a fresh proclamation of the royal pardon, a settlement was in sight.

Even now, though, delegates insisted that the banished officers could not return. Ultimately, individual cases became subject to negotiation. Perhaps half were allowed back. (In a gesture of reconciliation, the delegates asked that no officer be subjected to a court martial based on their allegations.) As a precedent and a symbol of Jack's authority – the fate of officers being decided by their subordinates – it set the seal on the Spithead mutinies. Recent studies have suggested that these events amounted to strikes, and it is fair to liken the delegates' organization to an early form of trade union activism. But at the time such forceful challenges from the lower deck could only be called mutinies. Edmund Burke, whose dismay at 'this rebellion' has already been noted, continued to fume:

> The Mutineers now choose their own Officers . . . All officers who go to sea . . . must in future comport themselves, not as Naval commanders; but as Candidates at an election.[37]

On 13 May, Howe was able to pronounce loftily that he was 'fit to acquiesce in what [is] now the mutual desire of both officers and seamen in the fleet'.[38] In celebration, delegates carried him off on their shoulders – gout sometimes rendered him too infirm to walk – and shared the table at a banquet with his lordship and Lady Howe.[39] The admiral was quite won over by the supposed Jacobins, finding one delegate 'of a temper, character & degree of intelligence that I think I could have employed to good purpose if I had continued in service'. This appears to have been John Fleming, whose intercession prevented bloodshed on the *London*. As for the chief revolutionary, Howe had this to say: 'Joyce, much as he has been spoken to his disadvantage, prejudiced me by his conduct equally in his favour.'[40]

Respect was not confined to the delegates. A lieutenant on the *Monarch* wrote of the Spithead mutineers as a whole:

They have demanded nothing but what to every unprejudiced person must appear moderate and just, and they have conducted themselves with a degree of prudence and decency which I thought them incapable of . . . I had always great respect for an English seaman; I like the character now better than ever.[41]

Horatio Nelson, having demonstrated his skills in handling an earlier uprising, was of much the same opinion: 'For a mutiny . . . it has been the most manly that I ever heard of, and does the British sailors infinite honour.'[42]

But while one mutiny was ending, another was beginning. Valentine Joyce and his fellows were still celebrating when four men were brought to them – four sailors, and they delegates too, who had just arrived from another anchorage, the Nore at the mouth of the Thames. As they related, shipmates had sent them to Portsmouth to find out what was going on and to report that their ships were willing to join the rebellion.

Since their departure, in fact, the Nore had erupted.

THE MACHINATIONS OF EVIL INCENDIARIES
1797

A CAPTAIN named William Bligh knew something about mutiny but he too missed what was in the wind whispering up the Thames estuary that last week in April. Nine years had passed, almost to the day, since his expulsion from the *Bounty*, but Captain Bligh's logbook in his new ship, the 64-gun *Director*, recorded merely that weather at the Nore had turned decidedly wet. The flogging of two men for insolence on 2 May may have been a sign of incipient trouble, but nine days then passed before a stark entry pointed the way ahead:

> The first appearance of mutiny. The ship's company ordered that Lts Ireland
> and Church and Mr Birch the Master be dismissed [for] ill-usage to them
> as they alledged.[1]

At 9 a.m. the next day Bligh observed turmoil on the 90-gun *Sandwich* anchored nearby: 'The people assembled on the Focsle in a great body.'[2] They then raised a red flag. This was a prearranged signal to Bligh's ship, as the horrified captain wrote: 'Instantly our men rushed aft on the poop and seized the arms.' Both ships were now 'in a complete state of mutiny'.[3]

What may be called the east coast mutinies started at the Nore, a sheltered anchorage at the Thames mouth, and initially matched events at Spithead.

Once more a flagship – in this case *Sandwich* – was the focus of activity, as if seamen, like their officers, took their cue from the command vessel even when in rebellion. Once more men had been rowing back and forth, exchanging views and plans of action. At that point, as we have seen, four men were nominated to travel to Spithead – to express support and report back. Seamen clubbed together to fund the journey by Charles McCarthy and Thomas Atkinson of the *Sandwich*, Matthew Hollister of the *Director*, and Edward Hines of the *Clyde*.

There similarities end. Events at Spithead and what followed on the east coast differed in order and nature. Facile though comparisons may be, the mutinies were almost defined by the two men identified as their leaders: Valentine Joyce – steady, authoritative and in command; and Richard Parker – troubled, vacillating and swept away by elements he could not control. And whereas the Spithead leaders' identities and objectives were clear, some key figures at the Nore did have other agendas and remained unknown to the end.

The Nore was the anchorage of the North Sea Fleet, but for operational reasons most of the ships were based at Great Yarmouth. At the time, vessels at the Nore numbered twelve, of which only three were ships of the line. Dispersed as it was, the North Sea Fleet lacked the unity seen at Spithead. Moreover, *Sandwich* was a sickly vessel in more ways than one, her timbers rotting with age, her company a miserable blend of old hands and transient supernumeraries – mainly new-signed Landsmen awaiting a ship – all packed into a space utterly insufficient for their number of between 1,100 and 1,300 and susceptible to an alarmingly contagious fever. These conditions had bred seething discontent.[4]

But two other ships were to play an even more bellicose and incendiary role as events unfolded. They were a pair of 64s, Captain Bligh's *Director* and the aptly named *Inflexible*.

Initially, this second revolt, on 12 May, did not cause undue alarm at the Admiralty. That same day news of the Spithead pact was being celebrated and the Nore outbreak was seen as a gesture of solidarity. It followed that normality would return once the agreed terms were read to the ships there. Seamen at the Nore numbered only 3,500 compared with 30,000 at Spithead.

How events then took the turn they did will never be absolutely clear. The final judicial process was grotesquely flawed and evidence by the few men to testify is often contradictory, tainted as it was by an instinct for self-preservation. What follows, an interpretation of that evidence, is necessarily subjective but is offered as an addition to previous studies.[5]

———————

Of the four hands sent as observers to Spithead, only two returned to the Nore. Thomas Atkinson drank himself penniless in Portsmouth's taverns while Edward Hines very wisely seized the moment to desert. That left Charles McCarthy and Matthew Hollister to report back to their shipmates. They returned on 19 May, expecting the pact secured at Spithead to be embraced. Instead, according to McCarthy, they found the situation at the Nore much changed. A previously unknown individual was now notionally in overall charge. But real authority rested with a hard core of troublemakers who had no interest in accepting the Spithead terms and were resorting to bullying and intimidation.[6]

The *Sandwich*'s most active leader had been William Gregory, often seen at the head of meetings and 'in boats haranguing other crews'.[7] Other identified hardliners were a core of Irish hands on the *Inflexible* led by John Blake and John Patmore. Another intractable cabal was to be found on Bligh's *Director*, though its leadership remains mysteriously obscure even now. All these men were still vociferously vocal and on a ruling committee made up of two delegates from each ship. But McCarthy returned to find that ships had in turn elected their own committees, each with a 'captain'. The new figurehead of this clumsy and unruly mechanism, the 'president', was one Richard Parker of the *Sandwich*.

Parker was a curious choice to lead a mass mutiny. He had not been to sea for years, was virtually unknown on the ship he had joined just two weeks earlier, and claimed to have been a reluctant candidate, presenting himself only after observing 'a most fatal spirit creeping into the breast of the seamen'.[8] But then Parker could be wilfully disingenuous. It was widely noted that he posed

Educated and eloquent, Richard Parker had a commanding appearance but was
manipulated by less visible militants at the Nore.

a striking – even theatrical – figure, with vanity to match, and was seen
'parading about on shore with a vast number of people and a red flag'.[9] He had
been made 'president' on 17 May, just two days before the delegates' return
from Spithead.[10]

According to McCarthy, the committee's reaction to his report was initially
favourable. Quickly, however, objections were raised by two ships, *Inflexible*
and *Director*. At the next committee meeting, McCarthy claimed, Parker
turned hostile, accusing him of never having gone to Spithead and saying he
'had forged Lord Howe's name' on the documents he produced.[11] McCarthy
perhaps exaggerated when he testified that Parker had wanted to hang him for
advocating a settlement, but another witness agreed there had been an angry
exchange with the committee that ended with McCarthy being placed in
irons.[12] A few days later he was turned out of the ship. Parker announced from

the focsle that McCarthy had 'been enflaming the minds of the people against the committee'.[13]

The upshot was that papers explaining the Spithead pact were, in McCarthy's words, 'concealed from the crew' – and from the other ships' companies as well.

He was not alone among the Nore activists alarmed at the direction affairs were taking. William Thomas Jones, a *Sandwich* delegate, declared it 'contrary to everything right' to make demands beyond those granted at Spithead. Jones could have been speaking for many other hands when he fulminated:

> There are a set of damned rascals in this place against the good of their King and country and they are converting everything to the use of their own private resentments.[14]

One he had in mind was William Gregory, who, though notionally junior to Parker, still played the dominant role at the committee table. Gregory, a thirty-one-year-old Scot from Montrose, one of the carpenter's crew, cherished visions of America as a land of the free and Ireland as a potential source of further revolution against the Crown, which he detested. Gregory it was who ordered the show of hands in votes, testing and challenging Parker's authority. His speeches were more belligerent, bordering on the treasonous. He once told the *Sandwich*'s company: 'You are as fit to be our sovereign as George Rex. He has power and we have the force of gun powder.'[15]

What then of Richard Parker and his role as leader?

Parker had some common history with Valentine Joyce, his Spithead counterpart. Born in Devon, he went to sea at fifteen and served on naval and merchant ships, voyaging to India. There similarities ended. Parker's service had been interrupted by ill health and bouts of what he termed 'misfortune', which translated as mental illness. He was once earmarked for promotion to officer rank before disobedience saw him court martialled, so he became a schoolmaster. His domestic life had been unsettled too, notable for debt and illegitimate children, and he only went back to sea to avoid debtors' gaol:

Parker was a quota man, one of those fellows – usually disdained by their shipmates – recruited by local authorities; he had signed on for a bounty of 20 guineas to avoid his creditors, but having some experience was rated Able on joining *Sandwich*.[16]

The key question, however, is why, as a complete unknown, Parker was made president, particularly as he was in the midst of another personal crisis. The day after arriving he wrote to an officer in hope of a discharge: 'I am at present a most unhappy young man.'[17] For a cohort of leading mutineers, however, keen to conceal their own identities and present a spokesman and negotiator, he was ideal for the part – confident in manner and with an education matched by few sailors: 'In handwriting and grammar as accomplished as some admirals.'[18] It was when things became challenging that he went to pieces.

Later, in giving his own version, Parker avoided blaming individuals such as Gregory, if only because it went against the grain for seamen to accuse a shipmate. But Parker did lament the influence of the *Inflexible* and *Director*. The *Inflexible*'s committee was particularly militant, the dominant force of the mutiny.[19] 'There is not a man in custody,' Parker said later, 'who does not attribute to the conduct of the *Inflexible* the melancholy consequences that have happened.'[20] It is reasonable to conclude that this vain and tormented man had seized what he saw as his moment – only to discover that he was the tool of those he saw as 'the lower classes', with their 'ignorance and duplicity'.[21]

The Nore mutiny was a week old before it became clear that this was no copycat protest. Officers were sent ashore, most notably Captain Bligh whose entry in the *Director*'s logbook on 19 May reads: 'I left the ship per order of the delegates.'[22]

The following day Vice-Admiral Charles Buckner, commander-in-chief at the Nore, went onto *Sandwich* with a copy of the king's pardon in the hope of resolving matters. He was met by Parker who, in a brazen gesture of disrespect to an admiral on his flagship, declined to doff his hat. Parker then presented

Buckner with a letter demanding 'every indulgence granted to the Fleet at Portsmouth' – plus seven further concessions.

The issue of shore leave was revived: 'Every man, upon a ship coming into harbour shall have liberty (a certain number at a time, so as not to injure the ship's duty) to go and see their friends and family.' This was an entirely reasonable claim, as it was to insist that pay arrears be cleared before a ship put to sea. But to demand that prize money be more equally distributed was perhaps pushing the boat out. Three further demands were an invitation to battle. These were: that the Articles of War – the Ten Commandments of life at sea – be redefined, with some unspecified articles being moderated and several others 'expunged'; that officers turned out of a ship could not return without the crew's consent; and that all deserters be indemnified, in effect, pardoned.[23]

Whatever the rights and wrongs, at this point the Admiralty drew a line.

A week later Captain Bligh was in a coach bound for Norfolk with a secret despatch for Admiral Adam Duncan, commander-in-chief of the North Sea Fleet, with the main body of ships anchored at Great Yarmouth. In the convoluted prose of the day, their Lordships were asking Duncan a simple question: Could the ships' companies of his fleet be depended upon if necessary in 'reducing the crews in the Nore to a state of submission'?[24] Two regiments had been moved to the garrison at Sheerness and the mutineers forbidden to land. Now it was a matter of how to get them to surrender and bring them to book. When it came to it, would British seamen obey Admiralty orders to fire on their fellows?

The answer came smartly enough. The North Sea Fleet had suffered gross neglect in respect of two real grievances – overdue pay and shore leave. When Duncan gave the order for his thirteen ships of the line, two frigates and two sloops, to sail, only two ships and a frigate obeyed. The rest came under the command of delegate committees and sailed for the Nore, 90 miles to the south. They arrived just in time to save that mutiny from collapsing.

What passed for a flagship had been reduced to a hellish state. While bravado ruled in *Sandwich*'s great cabin where Parker and Gregory held sway, pure misery prevailed in the foul air below. Demoralized hands besieged the surgeon, John Snipe, desperate to leave and not just because of sickness. 'Many good men in the ship had applied to me and been sent [ashore] to sick quarters for the purpose of getting out of the way,' he recalled.[25]

Two voices among those present reflect the contrasting perspectives. George Gainer, just twenty-one but a senior mutineer, wrote full of braggadocio to 'Dear Jenny', a fellow seaman's wife he had set his eye upon, of how he had gone from ship to ship 'to give them their orders' and being piped up the side with 'as much respect as if I was the Admiral':

> We are all determined not to return to our duty until all our Greavances are redrest, the articles are too tedious to mention at present, but one of them are that all prize money are to be equally sheared between every Man.[26]

Thomas Hewson, on the other hand, was among those mightily fearful about where it would all end. Divisions were emerging and Hewson had been appalled to see a boat of Inflexibles come alongside *Sandwich*, threatening to fire on her if any mark of respect was paid to Admiral Buckner. At this point one of his messmates remarked gloomily how 'English sailors were once the ornament of their country but he was afraid they were about to do something which would clap a stamp on their character which would never be recovered'.[27]

The question is who was driving the mutiny? Who were the Inflexibles and Directors?

The 'captain' of the *Inflexible*'s committee was John Blake, a twenty-four-year-old Irishman from County Clare. Here was another instance of a young firebrand taking the lead, but what makes Blake's captaincy notable is that, unlike most of those elected by their fellows, he was not an experienced man, being rated Ordinary. At least five other of the most prominent Inflexibles were Irish, all young, aged between twenty and twenty-eight. Overall, fifty-two of the crew were Irish.

Of the *Director*'s ringleaders even less is known, thanks to an intervention that, as we shall see, preserved them from identification or retribution. The senior delegate, Matthew Hollister, was a most improbable agitator – a fifty-six-year-old yeoman from Bristol who had been on the mission to Spithead. Once again, though, the ship had a significant proportion of Irish hands, including their 'captain', Joseph Mitchell.

Radicalism, the spread of egalitarian thought, clearly had an influence. Thomas Paine's *Rights of Man* had been published six years earlier and some of the Nore activists appear to have drunk of his cup. William Gregory, the Scot with a loathing of the monarchy, was one. Thomas Jephson, an Irishman also of the *Sandwich*, was of the same mind. He refused to fiddle during 'God Save the King', adding: 'I care nothing for kings and queens. Bad luck to the whole of them.' Jephson thought the mutiny 'glorious' and said 'he would be damned if it ended till the head was off King George and Billy Pitt'.[28]

Small wonder then that notions of plots involving incendiaries arose. An authoritative early study of the crisis claimed: 'Many of the Irishmen whose sedition had filled the prisons of their country to overflowing enlisted with more subtle motives than the desire for a bounty or for the comparative freedom of the navy.'[29] Whether or not they were real revolutionaries, inspired by the United Irishmen preparing an uprising, is not possible to say, though the trend in recent works to dismiss the idea as mere conspiracy theory should be questioned. The prominence of young Irishmen in the *Culloden* mutiny and at the Nore suggests nationalist sentiment was indeed at work. It seems unlikely, however, that these were cabals who came aboard with an agenda for insurgency and it may be relevant that *Inflexible* had been a profoundly unhappy ship for months. While she was at Chatham between January and April men had deserted almost daily – fifty-nine in all.[30] On balance it may be concluded that Blake, Jephson and others were tough, patriotic fellows who found themselves caught up in a moment of nationalist possibility.*

That manipulation was going on is evident – and in some cases for political reasons. More often, though, activity at the Nore appears to have been driven by the exhilaration of men discovering their power. As time went by desperation crept in. Dangerous situations evolved not because of any clear revolutionary objective, but because those notionally in charge began to see how far they had overstepped the mark and, knowing there was no way out, were driven deeper.

There was, of course, danger for any seaman who accepted a role in challenging power. When it was asked how delegates in the east coast mutinies had been elected, it would be said that 'the hands agreed he was a proper person for it and they asked him'. The truth was, anyone who spoke up stuck his neck out and few wanted the responsibility. William Welch of the *Standard* was far from alone. 'I told [the crew] I would rather not,' he testified. 'Some were surprised and some angry with me.'[31] John Taylor of the *Grampus* avowed he had only become a delegate 'by force of the ship's company'.[32]

Officers too observed the pressures at work. In the opinion of Captain John Knight of *Montagu*, 'the greatest promoters [of mutiny] were generally the least conspicuous'.[33]

Another captain, Thomas Parr, asked to describe those who had seized his ship, the *Standard*, replied: 'All very good men. They were the best of the ship's company.'[34]

---

* Overt conspiracy did emerge the following year, during the uprising by United Irishmen, when concerted plans for mutiny were hatched by Irish hands on four ships of the Channel Fleet: *Glory, Caesar, Defiance* and *Captain*. (Both *Glory* and *Defiance* had been at Spithead.) The details vary, but in each case the mutineers' intention was to seize their ship, kill anyone who opposed them and sail to France or Ireland. The plots were discovered before they could be carried out, having been reported by other seamen – mainly Irish hands who had declined to join. Evidence against seventy would-be mutineers was that they had taken oaths of allegiance to the United Irishmen. Twenty men from the *Defiance* were hanged, eight from *Glory*, six from *Caesar* and two from *Captain*.

If one thing is evident it is that there was no clear pattern, no single chain of command, defining the increasingly chaotic developments at the Nore.

Time was running out and so was food. The mutineers were no longer free to land at Sheerness and march through the streets with a brass band. The ships at anchor were isolated. Troops held the town and provisions had been cut off. That was enough to sway some who had been reluctant participants from the start.

On the evening of 31 May the frigates *Clyde* and *San Fiorenzo* slipped their cables to drift down the estuary. For this act of desertion they came under fire from *Inflexible* and another militant vessel, the 16-gun sloop *Swan*. Here brother was at war with brother, for Abraham Renshaw was on the *Swan*, his sibling John on *San Fiorenzo*. Days later John wrote to Abraham from Spithead, reporting that despite severe damage to the rigging they had escaped without any casualties:

> I have heard talk of father against son, brother against brother, but I have now experienced it, I little thought when I left you that ever that would happen, but I forgive even you, supposing you was the foremost of the whole . . . Pray write and answer directly and I remain your loving brother until death, John Renshaw.[35]

It was at this point, just as the mutiny was fragmenting, that eleven ships of the line, a frigate and two sloops from the North Sea Fleet, arrived to revive it. They included the 64-gun two-deckers *Belliqueux*, *Lion*, *Repulse*, *Nassau*, *Standard* and *Agamemnon*, captained until recently by Nelson, and they were to show varying degrees of commitment. The real diehards were always the three original leaders, *Sandwich*, *Inflexible* and *Director*.

Briefly revitalized, the ruling committee ordered a blockade of the Thames. By stopping all shipping bound upriver to London, so the plan went, they would establish a stranglehold on the capital. But while Parker was once more seen 'with a red flag and a band, rowing from ship to ship and speaking to the crews', the mood remained sombre.[36] Letters to relatives, intercepted by the authorities, sound a uniformly subdued tone. Robert Dobson wrote to his wife from the *Nassau*:

> What the consequences will be I cannot tell. We have all Yard Ropes riv'd for hanging any Man that refuses the proposals they've sworn to . . . if it is not a Peace there will be very bad Work.[37]

Joseph Devonish of the *Belliqueux* was full of regret as he wrote to his wife Jane in Clerkenwell:

> I long to see you and to be free'd from such an unhappy piece of business. And yet my dearest Life I would not wish you to come to me, when I have not anything to nourish or comfort you . . . I wish that every method may be try'd to bring about this long wished for Peace, that I may once more hug you to my longing breast, and if it was possible never to part any more I would most certainly come to you.[38]

John Cox, also writing to his spouse, was plainly and simply fearful:

> I should be more hapear to be at [h]ome than to be hear with 1000 Pound in my Pockit for whe are under the Men of Wars Juri[s]diction to do as they please . . . whe are afraid of our Lives.[39]

Ashore, attitudes had shifted as well. Nelson, a supporter of the Spithead petitions, saw the east coast uprisings in an entirely different light: 'For the Nore scoundrels, I should be quite happy to command a ship against them.'[40] In the nation as a whole there had been sympathy with the seamen's complaints – if not their actions – until the restraint of Spithead gave way to the Nore chaos. Disquiet was being felt even by the mutineers' families.

Joseph Pritchett, a delegate on *Serapis*, was informed severely by his brother Samuel that he was involved in 'the machinations of evil incendiaries'. The mutiny 'bears so different a complexion [to Spithead]' that it was universally condemned:

> Shocked indeed we are for the dreadful consequences which this ever lamentable disaster may bring upon you and our Country. You say in your letter of the 26th Ulto that you and another man was forced to be Delegates, we shall say nothing on that detestable subject until we are more informed how irresistibly you came to be enforced . . .
>
> In the name of all goodness pray do let us beg you will take the first oppertunity to extricate yourself . . . Consider your Country weeping, remember her Songs in praise of the Sons of the Waves which you have often delighted in; think of the exultation of her inveterate enemies; feel for your relations and friends and for God's sake, begin to feel for yourself.[41]

An equally impassioned note was struck by John Cudlip writing from Deptford to his brother Peter on *Belliqueux*:

> Let me beg of you, if you respect a Brother who is anxious for your welfare, to be true and loyal to your King and Country . . . Every brave and true Briton ought to come forward as one man to resist every attempt of the enemy. If my advice is not taken never expect for me to countenance you any more as a Brother.[42]

Pitt's government sensed the time for decisive action. On 5 June, the day Cudlip wrote his exhortation, Parliament passed a law making it a capital felony to be on a ship in mutiny, or to communicate with one. The mutineers had been reduced to common criminals.

Parker appeared oblivious of the approaching fire and brimstone. A lieutenant with whom he spent an evening and who gave him drink, 'knowing his propensity that way', wrote how a drunken Parker was roused 'to display his powers of oratory':

Whenever the subject [of mutiny] was broached his brain took fire; he seemed intoxicated with a sense of his own consequence and uttered nothing but incoherent nonsense.[43]

Vanity notwithstanding, Parker's gift with prose is indicated by two statements. The first was intended to revive public sympathy. It purported to come from the ruling committee but if a single hand can be discerned it is surely that of the former schoolmaster. Addressed to 'Countrymen' and with references to despotism and Tom Paine, it mixed radical polemic with a thinly veiled threat:

Shall we who have endured the toils of a long and disgraceful war bear the tyranny and oppression which vile pampered knaves wallowing in the lap of luxury choose to load us with? Shall we who in the midst of tempests undaunted climb the unsteady bondage and totter on the topmasts in dreadful nights suffer ourselves to be treated worse than the filthiest dregs of London streets? . . .

No – the Age of Reason is at length arrived, we have been endeavouring to find ourselves men. We now find ourselves so. We will be treated as such . . .

The British seaman has justly been compared to the Lion, gentle, generous and humane. No one would certainly wish to provoke such an animal . . .[44]

A second appeal, almost simultaneous, was to 'the King's Most Excellent Majesty' from his 'faithful and loyal subjects', and while adopting a mantle of humility it bordered on *lèse-majesté*. Seamen's grievances, it stated, had 'never [been] properly stated to you' and:

. . . we are sorry to have reason to remark the Conduct of your present ministers seems to be directed to the ruin & overthrow of your Kingdom.[45]

It went on to deliver an ultimatum, setting 9 June as a deadline 'to know your Majesty's final answer' to the demands made two weeks earlier. The answer was a flat rejection.

Parker was desperate. With the gallows looming, talk among the delegates turned to escape – to America, the Caribbean, even the enemy, France. On 8 June he and the committee toured the fleet, with the aim of persuading all ships to leave England. At the last, oratory failed him. On the *Ardent*, he was jeered as 'a precious admiral'.[46]

The real test came the following day, on 9 June, when *Sandwich* gave the signal to sail. It was ignored. Not a single vessel responded.

Within days each ship became a battleground. On the *Leopard*, which since arriving had seemed to associate with the hardline *Inflexible* and *Sandwich*, factions took up arms against one another. A newspaper reported, 'a very severe conflict ensued . . . at length the loyal party got the better and twenty-five of the most violent mutineers were laid in irons'.[47]

The *Leopard* was first to quit, lowering the red flag and raising a blue. As she made for Sheerness to surrender, *Repulse* also slipped her cables and followed. Now the disarray of the mutineers' regime was exposed. Militants on *Standard* took it upon themselves to fire on *Leopard*. Command had collapsed. Men used to carrying out orders from others, dependent on a structured hierarchy, were adrift without them.

Parker was as lost as any. He went on *Director*, and seeing guns being brought to bear on *Repulse* shouted 'how dreadful it was for one brother to be firing on another'. He was ignored. As firing began, he changed his mind and 'ordered the broadside to be brought to bear'.[48] On crossing to *Monmouth*, he adopted a positively warlike persona. As one sailor related, he became frenzied and gave orders to fire on *Repulse* 'and send her to hell where she belongs and show her no quarter':

He then said he would go on [another] ship and despatch her after the Leopard to send [her] to hell likewise.[49]

In the event, *Repulse* escaped without injury, probably because the guns were deliberately fired wide; even fervent mutineers were reluctant to aim at their fellows. Parker returned to *Sandwich* knowing all was lost.

That night the *Ardent* followed *Repulse*. Over the next two days storms blew up on the remaining twenty ships at anchor, but the wind was all in one direction. From dawn on 12 June they started to surrender – *Agamemnon*, *Nassau*, *Vestal*, followed the next day by thirteen more, including *Sandwich*. When the *Standard* slipped her cable, delegate William Wallace raised a pistol and fired it into his head.

Others took a different form of avoidance. Hundreds of supposed leading activists were rounded up but, amid the ensuing pandemonium ashore, dozens of others managed to slip away. Among them were the 'captain' of *Montagu*, a stout-bodied Able hand, Michael Harrison from Liverpool, and his two enforcers, James Brock from Bristol and Dennis Corbett from Limerick. They were not seen again.[50]

The most spectacular escape was staged by the group who in all likelihood were the most accountable, and best placed to explain the whole disaster – the Irish hands of the *Inflexible*. Captain Ferris, who had kept his head down throughout, came up to take command on 14 June to find that the twelve leading Inflexibles, including their 'captain', John Blake, had left in boats.[51] Descriptions of Blake – 'dark complexion, long brown hair tied up, blue eyes, small mouth' – and the likes of Thomas Ryley of Dublin – 'ruddy, carroty hair, freckles' – were circulated but, unsurprisingly, produced no return. They had already escaped down the estuary, seized a sloop in the fishing village of Faversham, and crossed to France.[52]

The execution of justice was prolonged, confused and utterly arbitrary. The Admiralty's priority was a show trial to make an example of figureheads while an investigation was set in train. It did not help that some key activists had escaped, but that does not account for the whimsical nature of punishment.

An initial wave of executions gave way to comparative restraint and a resort to pardons. This is not to impute compassion to the authorities: the instinct for vengeance that marked uprisings was partly tempered by an Admiralty grappling with its need for manpower; but there were other factors too, and the flaws were grotesque.

A magistrate, Aaron Graham, was sent to investigate connections between delegates and 'any private person or society on shore', a clear reference to the London Corresponding Society. He started with zeal, confident of ferreting out 'incendiaries' at Spithead, but after interrogating Valentine Joyce and his family concluded that Joyce had actually maintained 'good order'.*

As for the Nore, the magistrate found that although 'wicked designing men' had been active, no link with Jacobin groups could be established.[53] That, he concluded, was down to the escape of the Inflexibles, because 'if any proceedings of a Political nature were introduced into the fleet, they originated on board that ship'.[54]

Richard Parker was the first to be tried, a week after the surrender, and his fate was never in doubt. He did not help himself. Presented with evidence that he had ordered *Director* to open fire on *Leopard*, he said: 'I was obliged to give way to the general storm and pretend to sanction a thing I utterly abominated.'[55] After the formality of a guilty verdict, the court urged that Parker be 'hung in chains in some conspicuous place as an example'. The king thoroughly approved of the idea but the Admiralty decided it would be unduly provocative.

Two days before his execution Parker wrote to an unnamed friend, taking comfort 'that I am to die a Martyr in the cause of Humanity'. Yet he was still full of contradictions, having belatedly realized that he had been a useful fool:

> Remember never to make yourself the busy body of the lower classes, for
> they are cowardly, selfish and ungrateful; the least trifle will intimidate

---

* Joyce resumed his life as a seafarer, won promotion to midshipman, and appeared set to become an officer when his sloop, the *Brazen*, was wrecked off Newhaven in 1800. All but one of the crew were lost, Joyce among them.

them, and him whom they have exalted one moment as their Demagogue, the next they will not scruple to exalt upon the gallows . . . Now my dear Friend, I take my leave of you and may Providence return every kindness that I have received from your hands. Oh pray for me, that in the last scene I may act my part like a man.[56]

That, by all accounts, he did. Brought up onto *Sandwich*'s quarterdeck on 30 June, Parker acknowledged the justice of his sentence and asked for a moment to collect himself, then said: 'I am ready.'

Among those observing these events from a boat was a woman. Parker's wife, Ann, had done everything in her power to save the man to whom, for all his faults, she was plainly devoted. Ten days earlier she testified to magistrates in Edinburgh that Parker had been 'in a state of insanity' at times during their marriage, and that his navy discharge in 1794 was specifically due to being 'deranged in his intellect'.[57] She then hastened to London and had a scribe draw up a petition for mercy which she delivered to the Queen's residence. There she called daily without receiving a reply. On the morning of the execution she was rowed out to *Sandwich* but despite pleas that she be permitted to see her husband for the last time, the boat was turned away. It was still off to one side as the death gun boomed and some of those lately under Parker's command hauled his body up to the yardarm.*

Another twenty-three *Sandwich* mutineers were tried next. The flagship had been the focus of attention and it followed that salutary punishment should be directed here first. All but six of the accused were sentenced to death, including William Gregory, the would-be revolutionary, and Charles McCarthy, who had opposed him and spoken up for the Spithead terms.

---

* Parker's body was interred in the naval graveyard at Sheerness, but Ann – determined that he should be buried 'like a gentleman as he had been bred' – had the coffin dug up and transported to a Tower Hill tavern where crowds gathered to inspect it. Fearing that Parker might be turned into a martyr, magistrates ordered the coffin to be laid in a Whitechapel church vault. Ann Parker was soon overtaken by the poverty known to many seamen's widows but received charitable donations from – it was said – William IV, the last Hanoverian King.

Crucially, however, they were not consigned straight to the yardarm. Belatedly, the Admiralty was considering the lessons of those weeks – eight terrifying and transformative weeks – in the spring of 1797. How decisions were taken that defined the fate of particular ships and individuals is not entirely apparent. But two strands emerge: their Lordships' desire to be seen as merciful; and the role of certain captains in saving their men from the yardarm.

Of 414 men ordered for trial, only eighty-four were brought to courts martial. They came from six ships – *Sandwich, Leopard, Monmouth, Grampus, Montagu* and *Standard*. Fourteen were jailed or flogged, eleven acquitted. Of the fifty-nine sentenced to death, thirty were spared and jailed or transported to New South Wales. The bodies of the twenty-nine men hanged were left for an hour, placed in coffins with 32-pound shot at their feet, taken out to sea and dropped over the side.[58] McCarthy may have been considered unlucky to be among them.

Contemporary reports emphasize the contrition of those on the brink of oblivion. Richard Brown of the *Monmouth* shared a glass of wine with his captain – who, at his request, 'forgave him from the bottom of his heart' – before turning to urge his shipmates 'to beware of very bad and designing men if they had any regard for their own character, or love for their wives and families'. Such accounts may be dismissed as flummery, the validation of a return to order, but it is feasible that remorse on the scaffold was heartfelt. These were men diminished by separation from their known world, lost like solitary vessels in a storm.

The lucky ones included John Blake and his fellow Inflexibles who, having escaped across the Channel, were embraced by the enemy and went on to serve in French privateers. They were far from alone in evading justice. Some 330 of the men detained in the initial roundup of those identified as suspects were pardoned and released. Among them were forty-one more Inflexibles and thirty-one Monmouths – another group identified as activists. Thomas Jephson of the *Sandwich*, who had been all for beheading the king and Pitt, received 100 lashes.[59]

More fortunate still were the men of no fewer than fourteen ships who were not brought to trial at all and received blanket pardons. Some companies had indeed been reluctant rebels. It would still be interesting to know how such a conclusion was applied to the sloop *Swan*, which fired on *San Fiorenzo*, or *Nassau*, where nooses were set up to threaten dissidents, or *Lion*, which had forty-six suspects taken ashore in the initial round-up.

Most curious of all, not a single man from *Director* was tried, though her company bore a responsibility matched only by the *Inflexible*. As to why, it may be noted that Captain Bligh, his reputation tainted once by mutiny, was desperate to avoid further stigma. On returning to his ship he assured the crew 'there would be a pardon'. He then informed an admiral that he was 'apprehensive the confinement of a further number would cause very serious dissatisfaction in the crew'.[60] Whether or not as a direct upshot, all twelve of *Director*'s leading mutineers were pardoned without trial. A note in the muster stating 'wages forfeited for Mutiny & Rebellion' is scratched out, so they appear to have been paid as well.[61]

On 10 July the *Director* was at anchor. Beside her lay the *Leopard*. All hands were on deck of both ships when, at 9.40 a.m., six men were brought up on *Leopard* into brilliant sunshine. By 9.55 the bodies of Dennis Sullivan, Alexander Lawson, William Welch, Joseph Fearon, George Shove and Thomas Starling had ceased their writhing.

An hour later Captain Bligh performed divine service for his grateful penitents.[62] Still subject to whimsical fortune, from shipwreck to battle, impressment to captivity, they had endured. Small wonder theirs was a superstitious tribe.

17

HELLFIRE AND REDEMPTION
1797–1801

UNREST did not end at the Nore. Events that year unsettled elements of the officer class. 'The weaker captains lost their nerve,' one historian has written, 'the tougher ones reacted with severity to the slightest sign of trouble.'[1] So-called 'mutinous language' was seized upon. Colin Brown was three sheets to the wind when, a few days after the last mutineers surrendered, he solemnly informed his shipmates of the *Phoenix* that the royal pardon was not to be trusted because 'the Old Bugger of a King was asleep and a'fucking of the Queen when he made that speech'. Brown was challenged by a gunner who insisted: 'He is a very good King. We never heard or read of such a good king.' Alas, Brown had also been overheard by a lieutenant, was tried for using treasonable language, and sentenced to hang.[*]

The bloodiest mutiny in naval history broke out just months after the Nore, and it may be suggested that Captain Hugh Pigot was among those officers whose notions of discipline were contaminated by those events. The truth is Pigot had already given ample proof of his brutality. He had risen with the

---

[*] ADM 1/5340. Brown also said: 'Damn the dog that would not rather wear a French cockade than be here.' However, his officers acknowledged him to be 'a thorough seaman' and further testimony in his favour was given that although captured by a French privateer earlier in the war, he had escaped back to England.

absurd ease that betokened interest – an admiral father – and was given his first frigate aged twenty-five. Indulged as well as privileged, he was insecure, whimsical and subject to irrational rages, yet came under the protection of the West Indies commander-in-chief, Vice-Admiral Hyde Parker.

The log of Pigot's first ship, the *Success*, shows that over thirty-eight weeks he ordered eighty-five floggings: in total, 1,392 lashes, roughly thirty-six a week, were imposed on a crew of 160. Actually, Pigot had his particular favourites, so eight men absorbed the majority of those blows. Two, John Charles and Jeremiah Walsh, died as a consequence.[2]

The punishment details on Pigot's next ship, the frigate *Hermione*, can only be imagined because they were lost in the nightmare that started to unfold on 20 September 1797, as she cruised off Puerto Rico. During a squall the captain bawled that the topmen aloft were not being active enough and the last one down from the mizzen would be flogged. In their haste to avoid a beating, three men fell to the deck and were killed, including a black lad of sixteen, Peter Bascomb, from Barbados. Pigot's response to the trio of bodies splayed before him was an order: 'Throw the lubbers overboard.'

The next day he had the other twelve topmen flogged anyway.

That night the door to his cabin was smashed in by several men wielding cutlasses and axes. Pigot, in his nightshirt, was hacked and slashed before being left, draped over a canon. Those leading this phase of the mutiny included David Forester, aged just nineteen from Sheerness, Joe Montell, an Italian, and Hadrian Poulson, a Dane – all maintopmen. Significantly, however, petty officers were also active, two of them bosun's mates.

With the ship in their hands, the mutineers were joined by a number of other senior hands. They turned on a detested lieutenant, hacking him to death and throwing his body overboard. Next they went back to the cabin where Pigot, bleeding profusely but still alive, pleaded for mercy. 'You've shown no mercy,' shouted Montell. Pigot was carried to a stern window and pushed out. His cries were heard as he disappeared, trailing in *Hermione*'s wake. A shout went up: 'Hughy is overboard! The ship is ours.'[3]

Any notion that a more humane regime might replace him was quickly dispelled. More hands joined in, calling for reprisals against the officers. 'Cut the buggers! . . . Heave the buggers overboard!' A second lieutenant and a midshipman were slashed and thrown over the side. A bacchanalia of dancing, drinking and singing commenced.

Eighteen men had emerged as ringleaders, twelve Able hands and six petty officers. Another forty or so had taken a less active part. Half of the company had tried to stay out of the way altogether.

A new figure asserted himself. Lawrence Cronin, an Irishman, addressed the company, declaring himself a follower of France's revolutionaries and insisting that every officer had to die. In the subsequent uproar a group broke into the gunroom. Amid shouts of 'hand the buggers up', the last of the three lieutenants, the surgeon, the purser, a marines officer and the bosun were hacked with hatchets and cast overboard. So too was the hapless figure of the captain's clerk. Among those to the fore in these events, baying for blood, was the surgeon's fourteen-year-old servant, James Hayes.[4]

The *Hermione* had become no less a hell afloat in their hands than under Pigot.

A measure of order was restored when William Turner, the master's mate, accepted command. While the most violent faction continued to press for more killings and lives hung in the balance for days, a guard was formed around the remaining men of rank – the master, another midshipman (who was spared because he had been openly humiliated by Pigot), the carpenter and the gunner. They survived.

A course was set for Spanish territory, La Guaira in Venezuela, where the mutineers handed the ship over to the enemy. From there, most of the Hermiones went back to sea. Adopting aliases, they signed on French, Spanish and American ships.

The first arrests were made a few months later with the capture of a French privateer found to have five Hermiones on board, including the Italian Joe Montell. Executions followed directly, the dead being hung in chains upon gibbets.

The Admiralty's zeal in pursuing Hermiones did not flag. By 1802 thirty-three men had been captured. Twenty-four were hanged. The last was a leading mutineer. David Forester had served four years on another navy ship before he was spotted, by uncanny coincidence, on a Portsmouth street by Pigot's steward. An identical fate befell the unfortunate William Bower, who had taken no active part but was seen 'dancing, singing and drinking with the rest'. He too was sighted in Portsmouth four years later, and hanged.

The case of John Williams offers a rare instance of light. A Liverpool man with sixteen years at sea – and a wife and three children at home – he took no part in the mutiny and was palpably horrified by the whole affair. After coming ashore, he made his way home via a merchantman to surrender himself and at his trial produced a statement signed by the masters of six previous ships that he was 'a peaceable quiet character and a very good seaman'.[5] Williams was among the eight Hermiones to be acquitted.

That left more than 100 unaccounted for, including most of the ringleaders. Despite the rewards for information, none was ever heard of again. The revolutionary Cronin appears to have done quite nicely, though, settling in La Guaira and marrying.[6]

The shadow of that mutinous year notwithstanding, the war had entered a phase when battle and national survival took due precedence. A continuing threat of invasion, the emergence of fresh theatres of action – these curtailed the time when wounds might have festered. Battle cauterized them soon enough. And for all the petty tyrants of the quarterdeck – and the odd genuine monster – naval leadership attained the heights for which it became legendary. As the war at sea moved towards its decisive phase, a generation of great commanders reached out to their men with humanity and understanding. The combination was irresistible.

Among those commanders was a forgotten figure, Admiral Adam Duncan. After the Nore mutiny, he had cruised off Texel with the pathetic remains of his North Sea fleet and, by brilliant seamanship and signalling ruses, convinced the Dutch that a large squadron was just over the horizon. Thus he averted the threat of the Dutch sailing to join the French and proceeding to Ireland to precipitate a nationalist rebellion. Adverse winds also helped to contain the Dutch, and with them the Irish leader Wolfe Tone, who spent summer on the flagship *Vryheid* fuming about the weather and playing flute duets with Admiral Jan de Winter.[7] Britain's foes somehow remained ignorant of the '97 mutinies until they were over.[8]

Duncan was back at Yarmouth for revictualling when intelligence came on 6 October that the Dutch had left Texel. He signalled for an immediate departure and within hours those recently deemed 'evil incendiaries' were aloft once more, a cooling breeze at their backs, racing eastwards the 120 miles or so across the North Sea towards an enemy fleet.

Most of the ships going into battle had been in rebellion, including several of the main belligerents – *Director*, *Monmouth*, *Montagu* and *Ardent*. And among their crews were a significant number of Irish hands who would probably have taken up arms with Tone's United Irishmen had they been ashore.*

The *Montagu* is a case in point. Seven of her leading mutineers were Irish and the Duke of Portland, the Home Secretary, who deployed spies and repressive legislation to counter domestic radicalism, had identified her as a hotbed of subversion. Months after the mutiny ended, five more men, three from Cork, were listed as 'Discharged on the orders of the Duke of Portland'.[9] Yet the *Montagu* still retained a substantial proportion of Irish hands when the fleet caught up with the enemy at dawn on 11 October.

The Battle of Camperdown is often overlooked among acclaimed naval actions, perhaps because it was not led by Nelson and did not feature the French. But it set a tactical benchmark and was achieved against an enemy with a great maritime tradition – one, moreover, unafflicted by revolution. The fleets were roughly equivalent, each with sixteen ships of the line: the Dutch

---

* Tone returned to France and continued to lobby for support in pursuit of a revolution against the Crown, but Bonaparte was never really committed to invading Ireland and the rebellion of 1798 by the United Irishmen saw only 1,000 French troops landed. Within six months the rebellion had been brutally suppressed.

were better designed for the shallow waters where they met; the British had the edge in weight of armaments, notably the short guns of large calibre known as carronades, or 'smashers'.

Duncan proved as bold in battle as he was canny in blockading, sailing in two divisions to break the Dutch line – despite the perilous shoals – and so cutting them off from Texel and escape. Questioned by his pilot whether the flagship *Venerable* might not be about to go aground, Duncan replied: 'I'll fight the ships on land if I cannot by sea.'[10] At about forty minutes after noon the first of the wooden fortresses came up on one another and, as fire commenced, decks began to shake.

Roaring guns released not only metal projectiles weighing anything from 24 to 60 pounds but the spray of sharp wooden fragments that they created in their passage. When ship was ranged alongside ship few balls went astray, so the most effective death and destruction was dealt by the rate of fire. At Camperdown, it has been calculated, British guns fired three shots for every two by the Dutch.[11] It is testimony to the courage and resilience of the enemy that they endured as they did. In some cases, bodies simply disintegrated. On the flagship *Vryheid*, Admiral de Winter was the only man left standing on his own quarterdeck.

The two British ships to suffer the heaviest casualties, *Ardent* and *Belliqueux*, had also been among the troublemakers at the Nore. The *Ardent* lost 41 killed and 107 wounded, among them a sailor's wife who served at the guns, refusing to go below until, an officer reported, 'a shot carried away one of her legs'.[12]

The *Ardent*'s surgeon recalled:

Melancholy cries for assistance were addressed to me from every side by wounded and dying, and piteous moans and bewailing from pain and despair . . . Many of the worst wounded were stoical beyond belief; they were determined not to flinch and, when news of the shattering victory was brought down to them, they raised a cheer and declared they regretted not the loss of their limbs.[13]

Belliqueux suffered 106 casualties. Also in the thick of things were the recent mutineers of *Montagu* and *Monmouth*, the Irish as active in battle as anyone.[14] Captain Bligh took *Director* within 20 yards of *Vryheid*'s larboard quarter, 'firing tremendously at the Dutch Admiral and across his bows, almost touching. We carried away his fore mast . . . and left him nothing standing.'[15] Fortunately for the Directors, *Vryheid* had already been brutally mauled and they suffered just seven wounded. William Bligh, the flint of maritime legend, raised his arms in thanksgiving: 'Of such good fortune I had no idea, for it passed belief.'[16]

No seamen's accounts of Camperdown survive. That indefatigable correspondent Richard Greenhalgh was there in *Powerful*, but his letter home was

John Crawford of Duncan's flagship *Venerable* was hailed as a hero for nailing the admiral's standard to the mast after it had been shot away.

simply to reassure his parents that 'I got through this action with out any damage which will be of great satisfaction to you'. He rightly assumed that 'the peticulars of it you will hear before you receive this'.[17] It was also the case, however, that Camperdown did not receive the accolades of, say, the Nile, and, as the literary critic John Bayley has said: 'Warriors in heroic times only knew what they had been through when they heard about it from the bard in the mead-hall.'[18]

A triumph it was nonetheless – an emphatic victory close to home against a foe set on invasion. Nine Dutch ships of the line and two frigates had been taken, along with three admirals including De Winter. Any prospect of a convergence with the French fleet and Bonaparte's army at Brest was laid to rest.

An elated nation's faith in its sailors revived. The king went down to the Nore, so recently the site of naval shame, to welcome and thank 'those brave fellows ... for defending me, protecting my people and preserving my country'.[19] Duncan presented him with a petition to pardon some 180 mutineers still in prison. It was granted, and both the king and Duncan attended a magnificent service of Thanksgiving at St Paul's in December.

Relief at the victory may account for the first instance of a common seaman being cast in the mould of a popular hero. John Crawford of the *Venerable* had gone aloft when the admiral's colours were brought down from the maintop and nailed them back in place, being wounded in the process. Crawford was introduced to the king, named in the press and celebrated in art. On returning to his native Sunderland he was presented with a silver medal 'for gallant service' and became the subject of a statue that still stands in a local park. Even after being invited to join a procession at Nelson's funeral years later, 'Jack' Crawford appeared bewildered by his status and questioned about his heroics would reply: 'Never mind – that's nowt.'

For ordinary citizens it was simply reassuring to know they could again trust those who defended them – men of a kind whom Dr Johnson identified as 'a peasantry of heroes':

They who complain, in peace, of the insolence of the population, must remember that their insolence in peace is bravery in war.[20]

Britain remained on the back foot against France, but with the war at a critical point Jack was set on a voyage to redemption.

———

John Nicol declined to see himself as a hero. He had no time for chest-thumping bravado and counted himself blessed to have been out of the way during the great mutinies, which recalled to him his part in an earlier uprising: Nicol, with others in the *Edgar*'s gun crew, had faced the grim duty of bringing the mutinous *Defiance* to order. 'She was manned principally by fishermen, stout resolute dogs,' he wrote. 'When bearing down upon her my heart felt so sad and heavy, not that I feared death or wounds, but to fight my brother . . . We were saved this dreadful alternative by their returning to duty."*

Nicol had been at sea for twenty years – for him a time of wonder and discovery; but his ill-starred pursuit of Sarah Whitlam had exhausted some of that romantic spirit and, now in his forties, he was nearing the point when he would no longer be fit for service. He was in a new ship, *Goliath*, under sufferance – a pressed man fighting, literally, for his liberty. 'We wished to be free to return to our homes and follow our own pursuits,' he recalled. 'We knew there was no other way than by defeating the enemy. "The hotter the war the sooner peace" was a saying with us.'[21] As it happened, this quiet wanderer was to end his seafaring days in the bloody blaze of battle.

He had been at the Battle of Cape St Vincent, which ignited in him some of his younger shipmates' passion:

> When everything was cleared, the ports open and guns run out, we gave them three such cheers as are only to be heard in a British man-of-war. This intimidates the enemy more than a broadside, as they have often declared to me. It shows them men in the true spirit, baying to be at them.[22]

———

* Nicol, p. 174. Mutiny on the *Defiance*, triggered by the watering down of grog, led to five men being hanged (see Chapter 14). The same ship went on to play a significant, orderly, part in the Spithead rebellion.

But the defining action of Nicol's service, and the Revolutionary War, came in the summer of 1798. There was never any telling where Bonaparte's ambition would turn next and when he launched a colossal armada with an army of 55,000 men from Toulon into the Mediterranean their objective was unknown. Uncertainty only set pulses racing all the faster in Whitehall.

The *Goliath* was in a fleet under Nelson sent to find them.

Nicol has little to say about the golden admiral. The subsequent tendency of naval types to bask in that reflected glory was not for an old hand who, in relating his own story, confined himself to personal observation; Nicol never saw Nelson in person and is honestly sparing about his own part in what was arguably the admiral's greatest victory. In the weeks they trawled the Mediterranean in search of the French, bewildered crews were unaware of Nelson's belief that Bonaparte planned to land troops in Egypt and proceed to India. As Nicol recorded, they had sailed from Sicily to Egypt and back before capturing a French brig which provided key intelligence: Bonaparte's army had landed. A few days later the French fleet was sighted in Aboukir Bay. Though it was late afternoon on 1 August, Nelson went straight into action.

With the *Goliath* leading the way, Captain Thomas Foley took the initiative of crossing the head of the French line and coming down on the land side, having perceived that the enemy's port guns would be unprepared for action. Nicol observed:

> The sun was just setting as we went into the bay, and a red and fiery sun it was. I would, if I had had my choice, been on the deck. There I would have seen what was passing . . . but every man does his duty with spirit, whether his station be in the slaughterhouse or the magazine. [The slaughterhouse was the area on the upper deck, between the main and mizzen masts, where enemy fire was concentrated.]

Jack had little awareness of Nelson's tactical boldness at the Nile, and Nicol, for one, stationed below in the powder magazine, 'saw as little of this action as I did of the one off Cape St Vincent'. Stripped to the waist, pouring with sweat, he filled and passed sacks of gunpowder to the boys and women acting as powder monkeys; and they returned through the smoke with reports on the state of battle.

Women were only allowed on a ship at her captain's discretion and in this respect Foley appears to have been a most liberal spirit as *Goliath* had an extraordinarily large body of women on board. Four were named in the muster as widows of men killed in the battle and who were therefore entitled to their victuals. They were Sarah Bates, Ann Taylor, Elizabeth Moore and Mary French.[23] As a proportion of widows to the number of men killed, it has been pointed out that this suggests *Goliath* had about 100 women aboard.[24]

In serving gamely, women were also among the casualties, as Nicol recorded:

Any information we got was from the boys and women who carried the powder. The women behaved as well as the men, and got a present for their bravery . . . I was much indebted to the gunner's wife who gave her husband and me a drink of wine every now and then. Some of the women [were] wounded, and one belonging to Leith died of her wounds and was buried on a small island in the bay. One woman bore a son in the heat of the action. She belonged to Edinburgh.[25]

The Battle of the Nile was as defining in its way as Trafalgar and quite as dramatic, with a key moment frequently reflected in grand maritime canvasses. At around half-past nine the 120-gun French flagship *Orient* blew up with a flash that ignited the night sky and a force that shook the timbers of every surrounding ship. Nicol, still below, was convinced his own had suffered an explosion 'until the boys told us what it was'.

An Ordinary seaman on the *Orion*, John Jupp, tried to explain it to his parents as sensitively as possible:

She blue up with the Admiral and the Governer of Malta in her . . . the Explotion made the whole element shake and was a most Glorious Scean to us altho [it] would have been teriable to people which had never seen the like.[26]

Back on *Goliath*, Nicol served out powder through the night while the boys and women 'brought us the cheering news of another French ship having struck, and we answered the cheers on deck with heartfelt joy'. In the morning just two French ships of the line and two frigates were in a state to escape. The rest, thirteen ships in all, had been taken or sunk.

Nicol came up on deck to 'an awful sight':

The whole bay was covered in dead bodies, mangled, wounded and scorched, not a bit of clothes on them except their trousers.

There too, floundering in the sea beneath *Goliath*'s bows, were survivors from the *Orient*. 'Poor fellows, they were brought on board and Captain Foley ordered them down to the steward's room to get provisions and clothing.' John Jupp wrote that on *Orion*, hands threw down ropes 'and took them in and Stript their own Cloths and gave them to cover their Nakedness and went without themselves'.[27]

Nicol's account makes a point in passing yet revealing of the state of morale at this turning point of the war. French prisoners would once have kept their spirits up, saying with a defiant shrug, '*Fortune de guerre*'. Now they were 'thankful for our kindness but . . . sullen and as downcast as if each had lost a ship of his own'.[28] As Nicol said, it was no longer a case of 'You take me today, I take you tomorrow.' The French had fought gallantly at the Nile, and a harrowing defeat further eroded their confidence as a maritime power.

The British toll from this crucial victory was remarkably low at 218 dead (202 of them seamen) and 678 wounded. The heaviest losses were on the *Bellerophon* – forty-nine dead from her broadside-to-broadside duel with the 120-gun *Orient* – and *Majestic* with fifty dead. A modern estimate has put the number of French dead at 2,012.[29]

Victory was the key ingredient in rebuilding the bond between officers and men. Nelson himself was a catalyst, with his care and instinct for sailors' well-being. Legend has it that on being wounded over the right eye at the Nile and taken down to the surgeon, he insisted that serious cases be tended to first: 'I will take my turn with my brave fellows.'[30] Whether such tales were true matters less than the fact that they were believed, and because they entered maritime folklore were part of the human paradox to which Jack was subject.

Brutes like Pigot notwithstanding, it bears repeating that the sadists common to maritime fiction were rare. And in an age acutely conscious of status, when men were defined by whether they came from the upper or lower orders, the best commanders – from Nelson to Collingwood, Pellew to Pakenham – transcended class. The new generation of officers had its brittle, violent components. More often, though, it produced thoughtful, humane individuals like Captain Anselm Griffiths, a lieutenant on *Culloden* in 1794 who had drawn the right lessons from that mutiny. Noting how some anxious captains tried to interfere with the traditional right of men to choose mess-mates – their companions at meals and leisure – Griffiths insisted it was 'their Magna Carta, and I attach much benefit to it'. In deploring 'a too constant interference with them', he also spelled out a personal respect:

Seamen are nowadays a thinking set of people and a large proportion of them possess no inconsiderable share of common sense, the most useful sense after all.[31]

Among the new generation of hands, Robert Hay was one who witnessed empathy between officers and men. Hay named Edward Pellew as an officer who had 'the confidence, love and esteem of seamen'.[32] Yet in Hay's experience no commander won the lower deck quite like Nelson's friend Cuthbert Collingwood: 'A man who could not be happy under him could have been happy nowhere . . . He and his dog Bounce were well known to every member of the crew.'[33] Hay told the story of a lieutenant who, 'fearful of too much familiarity with seamen, never addressed a man by name but always by the contemptuous expression, "You Sir" '. Noting this, Collingwood made a point of asking the name of a topman, then calling up to him from a trumpet 'Dan Swain' and eliciting a smart reply: 'Sir':

> 'The after end of that last ratline is too high; let it down a handbreath.'
>
> 'Aye, aye, Sir.'
>
> The lieutenant knew right well for whom this was intended and forthwith expunged You-Sir from his vocabulary.[34]

Hay, then a boy of fourteen, experienced at first hand Collingwood's consideration for youngsters:

> Blow high or blow low he had us arranged on the poop every morning, and he himself inspected us to see that we were all clean, and our habiliments in good trim . . . No swearing, no threatening or bullying, no starting were to be heard or seen. Boatswain's mates dared not to be seen with a rattan or rope's end in hand; nor do I recollect of a single instance of a man being flogged aboard. Was discipline neglected then? By no means. There was not a better disciplined crew in the fleet.[35]

Nelson and Jack shared a self-belief that fed off aggression towards the enemy and affection for each other. Nelson used to say that his Agamemnons were 'what British seamen ought to be – almost invincible. They really mind shot no more than peas.'[36]

A frigate captain, Graham Moore, wrote simply: 'I have a set of famous fellows in this little bum boat. If the admiral takes any of them from me he will break my heart.' Moore's insight into the paradoxes of his men's character is likewise eloquent: 'If they were totally free from the vices and follies which so often lead them into scrapes, some of their peculiar excellences would quit them at the same time.'[37]

Moore did not eschew the cat. The log of the *Melampus* shows that over four months off Jamaica sixteen men were flogged, or one a week. But he was scrupulous in limiting the lashes to twelve, all for drink-related offences.[38] And he had a strategy for preventing desertion:

> Tomorrow our men will receive about fourteen months pay; I intend to let one third of them go on shore to have their swing, and on their return to let another third and so on until they have all had a surfeit of the shore.[39]

Skills and pride helped to bind a ship and could foster a healthy rivalry. Robert Wilson of the frigate *Unite* crowed: 'We were counted the smartest ship in the [Mediterranean] . . . Other ships that had been in company with us would tell us they hated the sight of our ship because we always surpassed them.'[40]

Another communal force was music – 'always welcome in a man of war', according to Samuel Leech. Harmonies from the focsle at this time ranged from a one-eyed pockmarked Billy Cumber with a voice 'as melodious as a raven', to the lyrical tenor of Charles Incledon, who went from Ordinary seaman to Covent Garden's favourite opera singer.[41] Leech had a shipmate on *Macedonian* nicknamed Bloody Dick who deserted but was welcomed back by officers because of his talents. 'Seated on a gun, surrounded by scores of men, he sung a variety of favourite songs amid plaudits and encores.'[42]

Dancing also brought them together. 'Every moonlight night the sailors dance,' wrote Collingwood, 'and there seems as much mirth and festivity as if we were in Wapping itself.'[43] Some captains, like Pellew, even joined in. 'He was a great promoter of dancing and other sports,' one follower recalled, 'such as running aloft and heaving the lead, in which he was a great proficient.'[44]

Jacob Nagle would have thrived under a Pellew or Moore. As it was, life on the *Blanche* took a turn for the better with Captain Sawyer's dismissal for paedophilia; but she was not especially active. Then, in the summer of 1798, Nagle was assigned to the sloop *Netley*, and finally found his perfect match – a new, fast-sailing vessel made to the latest specifications. To top it all, the *Netley*'s commander, Francis Bond, saw the affinity directly and made Nagle his quartermaster – in effect the ship's leading seaman, with duties for navigation and steering. Nagle, for his part, esteemed Bond the most of his many captains:

Capt Bond took a delight in making his ships company comfortable, and when in harbour [granted] as much liberty as could be expected. He could not bare to punish men at the gangway . . . Having such excelent yousage . . . we could at any time get as many seamen out of the merchant ships as he wanted and would not except of them unless they ware good seamen.[45]

With her liberal commander and a tight company of just sixty, the *Netley* was Nagle's ship for the next three years in what was seemingly the most rewarding service of his life.[46]

A sloop's speed and manoeuvrability made her ably suited for landings on enemy shores and the *Netley* was initially based off Le Havre, monitoring French ship movements while engaging in espionage. 'We had some French men going backwards and forwards as spies,' Nagle noted. In these Maturin-like operations, royalist agents were landed at night and sent up fire signals when they were ready to be taken off.*

One operation went badly wrong when the boat landing an agent was met by waiting French militia: 'The spy they hung on the first tree, the crew ware made prisoners.'[47]

From an enemy coast the *Netley* was sent to cruising off Portugal, with friendly ports in Lisbon and Oporto. It was an unusual commission, protecting British mercantile interests (and ensuring that the war cabinet was fortified with port wine, of which Pitt and his deputy Henry Dundas were heroic consumers) while sweeping offshore for French and Spanish privateers. *Netley*'s sixteen guns included 24-pound carronades which, combined with pace, gave her a formidable capacity for taking prizes in seas swarming with

---

* This network was seemingly the child of Sir Sidney Smith. A brilliant, egocentric naval officer, Smith had been captured and spent two years in Paris, where he had contact with French royalists who helped him to escape. Smith came on the *Netley* at Portsmouth in September 1798, a few months later. See *The Nagle Journal*, pp. 214–15.

smaller vessels; Nagle records eleven captures in a single day. He was given charge of taking the larger prizes into Oporto and became a regular presence ashore.

One foggy morning off Cape Finisterre in August 1800 they sighted a large three-master which, on being challenged, ran up Spanish colours. Though she carried twenty-four guns, a volley from *Netley*'s carronades was enough to bring her to, and on boarding Nagle's eyes popped. She was not exactly a treasure ship but the *Reyna Luisa*, homeward bound from South America, carried 'a good quantity of King's money . . . dollars, half joes, doubleelons, 7lb bars and 14lb bars of gold'.[48]

Still celebrating his fortune, Nagle was on the waterfront at Lisbon when two men seized him from behind, held a dagger to his chest and made off with his gold watch and forty-five gold dollars. Nagle's anger was nonetheless appeased by the prize money he received from the *Reyna Luisa* – some £200, or roughly six years' pay. He was a rich man. (This freakish windfall may be compared with the legendary pay-out of £300 to the few survivors of Anson's treasure hunt.)

A few months later he was back in Portsmouth and reunited with his wife. Now aged forty-one, Nagle found himself a father of two children, and was considering a change of course; taking his family back to America was one possibility. That prospect became clearer when it was announced that a new government under Henry Addington had made peace with France. The war was over, or so it seemed.

———

Those who came home for the last time after the Peace of Amiens included John Nicol. He had been at sea since he was nineteen and although now forty-seven was still in decent health. That was a blessing, as the naval physician Sir Gilbert Blane observed many sailors of that age looked more like sixty.[49] Nicol, moreover, had plenty of pay and prize money on his discharge, and just enough residual ache for Sarah to want to purge his mind of her once and for all. A final visit to Lincoln established that her family had still not heard from her and he accepted that he was 'too old for any more love pilgrimages'. So, after twenty-five years, Nicol returned to Edinburgh.[50]

The city was transformed. He knew no one and 'wandered in elegant streets where I had left corn growing'. Yet he found the strangeness somehow reassuring, for after a lifetime of seeking curiosities across the world he could at last recognize the charms of his native soil. Twice he had circled the globe, touching six continents and observing distinctions of culture and landscape from the South Seas to Newfoundland, from China to the West Indies. He had been a whaler and an explorer, had transported convicts and fought in battle. It was time to discover home.

Some months later he was reunited with a childhood friend, a cousin Margaret: They were married, after she extracted a promise that he would never go back to sea, and bought a house on Castlehill, the historic centre of Edinburgh, from which he plied his original trade, as a cooper. Yet visions of the press gang haunted him, and they moved to a village, Cousland, ten miles away. Business was never so profitable again and in time the press extended even to rural Scotland, forcing Nicol 'to skulk like a thief'. By his own account, the marriage was companionable rather than loving. He and Margaret had seventeen years together, in which time she 'never gave me a bad word or made any strife'. But, as he added, 'all have their faults'. Hers was to spend more than he could earn, and at times he was tempted to return to sea. When she died childless in 1818 her debts and funeral costs reduced him to poverty.[51]

Four years later Nicol was spotted collecting fragments of coal in Edinburgh by a bookbinder and scribe named John Howell. Nicol had recently returned from his final voyage, down the coast to London on an expedition to claim a naval pension. That it failed is testimony to the whimsical nature of the system to which navy hands contributed from their wages and the arbitrary way it was awarded or denied: Nicol had spent fourteen years in the king's ships – in addition to Indiamen, convict vessels and whalers – winning his captains' respect and serving at the battles of St Vincent and the Nile. At Somerset House, he duly received verifying certificates. But when Nicol presented

John Nicol towards the end of his life, a portrait engraved by the Edinburgh
artist William Home Lizars to illustrate Nicol's memoir.

himself at the Admiralty an officious clerk informed him that he had left it too
long before applying for a pension; and none of his former captains could be
located for a testimonial to challenge the ruling. Despite this crushing disappointment, Nicol could recall the journey for an old pleasure. 'My spirits were
up. I was at sea again. I had a crowd round me listening to my accounts of the
voyages I had made. I was very happy.'[52]

Now on an Edinburgh street, Howell stopped to question the hobbling
scavenger and fell upon a trove. The product of this encounter, *The Life and
Adventures of John Nicol, Mariner*, first published in 1822, did not transform
the fortunes of either, though it was evidently a spur for Howell, who went on
to write more books, including a life of the castaway Alexander Selkirk. So far
as the Nicol narrative is concerned, however, a literary comparison with
Howell's style indicates that it contains far more of the seaman's work than his
scribe's.[53] Nicol's is a distinctive voice. He loved a good story and told it with
relish as well as a concern for truth.

The conclusion is manifestly his own. At the time of writing, he said, he was surviving on potatoes with a single luxury – his pipe and tobacco. He dreaded having to enter a poorhouse. But 'to beg I never will submit':

> I have been a wanderer and the child of chance all my days, and now only look for the time when I shall enter my last ship and be anchored with a green turf upon my breast, and I care not how soon the command is given.[54]

John Nicol was found dead at home in his bed, aged seventy, in 1825.

18

TOM BOWLING
1801-03

SEAMEN came home in October 1801 to the strains of a ballad that signalled their renewed status and touched the nation's heart. The composer Charles Dibdin, grieving after the death of his seafaring brother, had concluded that popular culture did not adequately represent 'the character of the British tar, plain, manly, honest and patriotic'. His answer, 'an opportunity through public duty of expressing private affection', was a song that redefined the sailor's persona:[1]

> *Here, a sheer hulk, lies Tom Bowling, The darling of our crew;*
> *No more he'll hear the tempest howling, For Death hath broached him to.*
> *His form was of the manliest beauty, His Heart was kind and soft.*
> *Faithful below, Tom did his duty, And now he's gone aloft, and now he's gone aloft.*

Dibdin had seized a moment and his elegy to Jack set itself into folklore. A decade later Edward Mangin, a writer and clergyman with friends among Bath's intelligentsia, spent some months as chaplain of the 74-gun *Gloucester* and recorded the death of a hand named Thomas Flynn in terms that echo 'Tom Bowling' with almost transparent intent. Flynn's 'gentleness of manner and high spirit,' he wrote, 'attached everybody to him':

Five days before his end I had seen him active and busy as he always was; a model for the painter and the statuary, from the fine style of his features, and the majesty of his figures: now he lay in a cot . . . mad, pale as ashes, and convulsed with dying spasms. Four or five of his messmates stood about him, holding lanthorns to his face, dropping silent tears on him, or in the most heart-rending accents calling him 'Poor Tom' and 'honest messmate!'

When stripped, I observed that he had on the upper part of one arm a drawing, not very rudely executed, of a female and a seaman parting and a motto, 'Thomas come home to Ann'.[2]

An idealized Tom Bowling aside, homecomings were of course an earthy business and the peace of 1801 was accompanied by scenes at ports around the land unprecedented in scale. What was seemingly the largest mass demobilization in naval history followed a common pattern: though ships came to anchor, hands remained on board for weeks awaiting paymasters with what amounted to years of outstanding wages. In the meantime, the appetites boiling below on dozens of men-of-war were dealt with by another formidable tribe. An admiral of the time shuddered to recall the advancing invasion of boats bearing hundreds of women and the spectacle of heaving hammocks in an orgy of mass gratification 'where [they] must be witness of one another's actions':

Let those who have never seen a ship of war picture to themselves a very large low room (hardly capable of holding the men) with 500 men and probably 300 or 400 women of the vilest description shut up in it, and giving way to every excess of debauchery that the grossest passions of human nature can lead them to; and they see the deck of a 74-gun ship the night of her arrival in port.[3]

Daniel Goodall was witness to scenes on *Temeraire* 'that no time effaced'. An unworldly sixteen-year-old, Goodall had entered as a 'Boy Third Class' just months earlier.[4] On coming home she was boarded by 'the Delilahs of

Plymouth . . . the harpies that prey upon poor Jack, and how keen was their scent when plunder was in prospect':

> They displayed such a reckless disregard of decency and morality as Jack, even at his worst, could never hope to equal . . . The brawling and uproar never ceased.
>
> There were, too, some few – alas, how very few! – really virtuous females amongst them, wives of seamen on board, whose modesty and worth was unsullied amid all the vice and pollution by which they were surrounded, and whose virtues shone the purer.[5]

Finally, on each returning ship, a commissioner of the Navy Board came aboard with pay clerks and chests of coins and notes. As each man's name was read from the muster, in the order of having joined the ship, he would come forward to receive his pay, minus deductions for slops or tobacco. Some had also asked for portions of their wages to be paid to wives or other dependants; but they were a minority and in a typical case an Able hand back after four years at sea would be taking away more than £60, an Ordinary man more than £50.

We have had previous accounts of Jack's profligacy. (Goodall noted with awe his shipmates' indulgences. Spending on drink and women apart, they ate like lords, 'legs of mutton, geese, turkeys, hams, sausages, red herrings, soft bread, butter, eggs, tea, sugar, coffee and tobacco'.)[6] What made this habit particularly costly in the peace of 1801 was that in most cases it came with unemployment.

The First Lord at the Admiralty was Earl St Vincent. A severe, bigoted commander before becoming minister in charge of the Navy, he went to war against what he perceived as budgetary wantonness with frenzied zeal. His term in office, generally seen as having been a disaster, included a cancellation of shipbuilding contracts, the closure of some institutions supporting seamen, including hospitals, and a mass discharge.

Within months the number of navy hands had been cut from some 126,000 to fewer than 50,000.[7] Little attention is generally given to this demobilization because the peace was short-lived – and was followed by a recruitment process of unprecedented ruthlessness. At the time, however, the social impact was severe.

For all the costs of war, the mercantile world had boomed. In crushing France's overseas commerce, Britain secured a growth in its own trade of 90 per cent between 1793 and 1801.[8] India was the principal source but China and other destinations in the Eastern Seas followed as East India Company profits rose on monopolies over tea, cotton, silk, opium and saltpetre. In theory, this surge in merchant shipping offered opportunities to discharged naval seamen, with the prospect of a significant increase in wages – by at least a third, and in individual cases a good deal more.

But mass discharges created a surplus. William Richardson, a merchant sailor himself, observed a 'great influx of men lately paid off. Hundreds of them, poor fellows, were starving and begging through the streets for employment, some without a shoe to their feet.'[9] Even those who found a berth were squeezed:

> The owners of ships, though floating in wealth, were very hard on poor sailors, not shipping them till the last minute, and then giving them low wages.

In home waters, a man who had received £9 for a voyage shipping coal during the war saw that reduced to £4.[10] The Company seized its chance to maximize profits from the thirty to forty Indiamen outward bound each year with similar cuts. Of course, once war resumed wages would be driven up again – at least for a man who managed to evade the press. Then again there was a good chance he would be pressed on reaching India where disease continued to take a frightful toll on the naval squadron based at Madras.*

---

* By now most homeward-bound Indiamen were substantially manned by lascars and other foreigners. William Hickey recorded his ship in 1808 having 'a strange motley crew, consisting of natives of almost every nation of Europe, besides nine Americans and eighteen Chinese. Certainly we had not more than ten English seamen.'

A great many discharged men could not find a ship at all. Riots such as those recorded at North Shields a year later, though aimed at the ship-owners who were cutting wages, also saw seamen being dragged off vessels by others who remained unemployed.[11]

* * *

Jacob Nagle returned to England 'flush of money' from the *Netley*'s prizes and spent a month in luxury – a furnished room at Deptford with his wife Elizabeth and two children. He was in his forties and although still a match for the ablest of his shipmates was contemplating a new start in America with his young family. The Nagles sailed to Portugal where, awaiting a ship, Jacob rented a house in Oporto with two small rooms and a kitchen.

There, as he wrote in the starkest sentence ever to come from his pen:

> My wife and children took the fever and in the space of six weeks I was left alone.[12]

Nagle's family had been among the victims of a yellow fever epidemic that afflicted ports in Portugal that year. Of grief there is scarce a hint. That was not his way. But, as the editor of his journal has noted, a certain loss of purpose in Nagle's life is discernible from the tragedy of 1802. His journal continues to tell a seafarer's story. On his inner world he fell silent.

Arriving back in America that summer, Nagle discovered other losses. His parents had died and the rest of the family, having heard nothing during his twenty-four-year absence, had presumed him dead too. One sister failed to recognize him and only an elderly uncle gave any sign of pleasure on seeing him. Within weeks Nagle was employed in the Philadelphia coastal trade. In time he would cross the Atlantic to sign on an Indiaman again. Thus he got on, married to the sea to the end of his days.

Tom Allen had no immediate concerns. He too came home with pockets full of prize money and the assurance of domestic employment with Nelson. Tom married a Norfolk lass, Jane Dextern, and on his master's return with

Emma Hamilton, they joined the Nelson household at Merton in Surrey – Tom as butler, Jane as dairymaid. Tom may have played up the association in later years, but there is still evidence that he could influence Nelson where others failed. On the eve of the Battle of Copenhagen, an army colonel in the great cabin had noted how Tom, 'who assumed much command on these occasions', found Nelson exhausted after hours drafting orders and 'insisted that he should go to his cot'.[13] At the Nile, Tom claimed to have stopped Nelson going on deck in full uniform, thereby camouflaging him from the French musketry that killed him at Trafalgar.

Allen's services were not indispensable, however. He and Jane left Merton to return to Norfolk in 1802 and although their first son was named Horatio Nelson Allen, a rift had appeared. Tom's carelessness in losing a trunk and money had exasperated Nelson once too often. 'He will one day ruin me by his ignorance, obstinacy and lies,' the admiral fumed.[14]

Not all naval hands were discharged. While manning in home waters was slashed, thirty-two ships of the line and 217 smaller ships were still in commission and squadrons in the Mediterranean and the West Indies remained on a wartime footing. This ambiguity gave rise to tragedy on a ship that became part of naval legend.

Seamen took ships with them to the grave, for, like all homes, a ship had a place in the memory – of a mess table, a storm survived, a view of landfall from the focsle. With those visions came a reminder of her character, for a personality she undoubtedly was, one not to be forgotten. 'She has her rights as though she could breathe and speak,' wrote the author Joseph Conrad, himself a seaman of the nineteenth century. 'Indeed, there are ships that, for the right man, will do anything but speak, as the saying goes.'[15] No ship speaks to Britain's maritime memory with quite the same power as the *Temeraire*.

By 1801, the 98-gun three-decker had completed three years of the most intensive blockade duty off Brest – a relentless process of manoeuvring against a deadly coastline, with none of the morale-boosting release of battle. Her company were as battered as her timbers, and when news of the peace reached them in Plymouth it produced, in the words of the prim young Daniel Goodall, 'a delirium of joy amongst the whole of the men'. Soon afterwards, as the flagship of Rear-Admiral George Campbell, she led a squadron of fourteen sail to Bantry Bay on the west coast of Ireland, but there was no dismay, 'as it was generally believed that we were to remain there until the definitive treaty of peace was signed'.[16] The mood was buoyant, money remained plentiful for the time being and because there was no longer concern that men might desert, they were allowed ashore where, for lack of much else, some took to the unlikely pastime of horse-riding.

Goodall viewed the events that followed with a boyish admiration for these older hands. An Edinburgh lad, he had volunteered at sixteen on a whimsical notion of adventure and, like others before him, had been both intimidated by the grim reality of life on the lower deck and grateful to the men who took him under a collective wing and preserved him from harm.*

The Temeraires were, by general agreement, a first-rate body. Most of the 480-strong company had been with her for four years and their shared hardships in the Channel bound them to these wooden walls in a way that transcended suffering. Again, Conrad is illuminating: 'There are ships which bear a bad name,' he wrote, 'but I have yet to meet one whose crew for the time being failed to stand up angrily for her against every criticism.'[17] Unity made them resolute. The Temeraires were still off Ireland when 'rumour whispered' that, far from being discharged, they were bound for the West Indies, 'a most unhealthy and consequently unpopular station'.

It was intrinsic to the lower-deck code that when mutterings of dissent arose and gathered momentum, spinning towards the wave that turned into mutiny, boys like Goodall were kept in the dark, being thought 'too young to

---

* Daniel Goodall's memoir was not entirely his own work, having been subjected, in the publisher's words, to 'revision by a hand more practised in the art of composition'; and it has clear echoes of other lower-deck books then enjoying a vogue, in particular *The History of Pel Verjuice* by Charles Reece Pemberton. But there can be no doubt of Goodall's presence on the *Temeraire* during the events he describes, as shown by the muster; and his publisher insisted that these incidents 'stand exactly as put down by Goodall' before his death in 1857.

be trusted in so dangerous an affair'. Two of Daniel's messmates were, however, among the ringleaders, and proximity gives his account a rare insight into how these enterprises evolved towards inevitable doom.

It began, as ever, with low voices at mess tables and proceeded to a noisy gathering on deck of leading men – a 'disturbance', as it was termed. Admiral Campbell, addressing them from the quarterdeck, said they could state their grievance without fear of reprisal. One hand spoke up. It was very hard, he said, that they should have to go to a dangerous station when the war was over. Campbell's reply was that, like him, they had no option. Wherever they were ordered, they must go.[18] That evening, 1 December, they carried out duties and watches as normal.

Five days later the leaders ordered gunports to be lowered, then came up and told the admiral they would not sail anywhere but England. A letter stated their case:

> We have most of us served our King and Country with the greatest Alacrity
> from Seven to Nine Years. It has pleased God to bless our Country with a
> Peace. We therefore expect the Indulgence of free born Britons of enjoying
> the Blessings arising from the same.
>   The Temeraires[19]

Daniel Goodall was among the majority of Temeraires who watched events unfold more or less passively. But he had close insight, being acquainted with the four leaders, including the key figure, James Fitzgerald – captain of the foretop, Irish, and universally admired. 'One of the best seamen on board,' Goodall wrote, 'a man of quick intelligence and great decision of character.' His flaw 'was a deep discontent with everything'; but 'when his native humour and good sense got the better of his cynicism, then it was a treat to hear Fitzgerald talk':

> [He] belonged to a class of men very rare in the navy at that time, being
> a violent politician and, which certainly would be deemed far worse in

the eyes of authority, a still more violent radical. When in a worse mood than usual he would often declare that so soon as he was released from his bondage he would be off to America and enrol himself as a citizen.[20]

Also among the leaders were two of Goodall's messmates: John Allan, a fellow of 'superior education, and by no means of a discontented nature'; and William Cooke, 'good-hearted but with little will of his own, and very apt to be led into a scrape through sheer thoughtlessness and love of grog'. Both were stationed in the maintop, so fine sailors. His fourth acquaintance was William Hillier, 'a foretopman, and a favourable specimen of the rough, honest seaman, knowing next to nothing of anything unconnected with ships and seamanship'.[21]

What grieved Goodall, in hindsight, was 'the mystery of infatuation'. How could these old hands, for all their foibles, have failed to see they must be defeated in a confrontation? 'It is strange, but not more strange than melancholy,' he mused, 'how often men are blinded to the consequences of a rash course upon which some so heedlessly enter':

But it is the same sad story, as old as the world itself, of passion obscuring every gleam of reason.[22]

The confrontation came when a marine who had expressed support for the seamen got drunk and was thrown in irons. About 100 protesters took up positions on the focsle. On the admiral's appearance they were held there, isolated by a hawser strung across the ship by marines who fixed bayonets and levelled their muskets. The rest of the company was mustered while officers went among the protesters and picked out fourteen supposed ringleaders.

Their trial was especially sombre. A sense prevailed that something flawed in naval justice had been revealed. These were not agitators but some of the Navy's best hands, with years of service and battle experience to their credit. Their officers gave them uniformly favourable characters. William Hillier was able to produce an admiral no less, Charles Pole, who described him as 'a very good man', adding: 'I sent him on dangerous services and he performed them well.'[23] Twelve men were still sentenced to hang, two to 200 lashes each.

Edward Brenton, a lieutenant who witnessed the trial, deplored 'one of the most fatal blots on our naval annals':

> They were the noblest fellows, with the most undaunted and prepossessing mien I ever beheld – the beau ideal of British sailors; tall and athletic, well-dressed, in blue jackets, red waistcoats, and trowsers white as driven snow. Their hair, like the tail of the lion, hung in cue down their back.[24]

Four were brought back to *Temeraire* for hanging, including Hillier and Fitzgerald. The boy Goodall, attending his first execution, saw them meet their end 'with a firmness and resolution greater than many of the onlookers'. Fitzgerald in particular showed calmness and dignity, 'kindly endeavouring to cheer his mates, whom he bitterly regretted having led into danger'.[25] Reflecting in later years, Goodall still found the memory painful:

> I have witnessed the extinction of human life in various ways, all more or less revolting, but never did death assume a more ghastly form than when the smoke of the guns cleared and disclosed my late shipmates hanging from the yards in which they had so lately and creditably served.[26]

The *Temeraire* duly sailed for the West Indies. Her mood remained dark, despite the efforts of Admiral Campbell and his officers who 'seemed desirous of doing their utmost to efface the painful impressions and were sedulous to show the men that they were as much trusted as if nothing had occurred'.[27] A few months later peace was ratified by the Treaty of Amiens and she returned home again to be paid off in October 1802. The last great mutiny of the wars, and the most lamentable, had been a wasteful human sacrifice.

Daniel Goodall's scars ran deep. He left *Temeraire* aged seventeen, having been promoted to Boy Second Class.[28] When he signed on again two years later it was not as a seaman, subject to discipline's vagaries, but as a marine, its soldier of enforcement.

———

The martyrdom of the *Temeraires* did, however, remind the nation of its debt. Their trial received widespread press coverage, and it was a callous reader who could not sympathize with these Tom Bowlings whose sole desire had been a return to hearth and home. Civic society started to pay attention to the seamen once more in its midst. Reform was in the air.

A campaign mounted by *The Times* mixed the usual condescension with genuine concern. Sailors had long been prey to the species known as crimps – agents lurking in seafaring haunts who recruited hands for the merchant trade, usually by underhand methods. By now they had found new ways to defraud what *The Times* called 'these careless though useful members of the State'. As fleets came to anchor, crimps would go on board and offer shelter, making exorbitant charges for bringing men ashore with their chests. 'By entertaining them and furnishing lodging, liquor and cloaths, and in many instances bringing women to them, the seamen get suddenly in debt.' Interest charges were applied, and instances had been recorded of men paid off with £40 owing £15 within a fortnight. In the view of *The Times*:

> The known improvidence of the run of seamen [requires protection] against these gross abuses to which their total ignorance of the means of protecting themselves, their habits of life and their thoughtless dispositions, peculiarly expose them.[29]

Ashore, the paper's tone indicates, Jack still resembled a fish out of water and a wary society kept him at arm's length. Yet other campaigns and reforms were in the air. Early in 1801 a group of private citizens, mindful that this 'Nation of Humanity' had made 'no provision for the Orphans of our brave Seamen', started the Naval Asylum for children's maintenance and education.[30] Three years later it was established as a royal foundation, opening at Greenwich with facilities for 1,000 orphans.

Another charity was directed at families. Since 1733, the state had provided a form of support for the wives of men killed in action – a fund created by setting aside the wages of two 'Widow's Men' for every hundred men borne on a ship's muster. The great battles from 1793 spurred John Julius Angerstein, the marine insurance broker and art collector, to go further – setting up public subscriptions for the families of the disabled as well as the dead. The First of

Jack's reputation for profligacy endured long after any prospect of prize-money riches gave way to the all-too-visible reality of poverty.

June raised £21,280, Copenhagen £15,580, and the Nile as much as the two together. By the peace of 1801, the Lloyd's Patriotic Fund had raised a total of £193,330.[31]

Ringing the changes at the Admiralty was another matter. True, some significant improvements to naval service had been won – in wages, in victuals, in family care and in health. Their lordships had also abolished charging men 15 shillings for treating venereal disease (on the entirely pragmatic ground that sailors were concealing it until they became unfit for service).[32] Other reforms were under discussion. 'Starting', the beating of men to their posts, excessive flogging and running the gauntlet, were increasingly frowned upon. Wages, it was often said, were still too low. But it would take yet more years of war, yet more reminders of Jack's role as the guardian of national security, to bring about change in these areas. Small wonder that a hardened old hand like the mutineer James Fitzgerald had been a cynic. Flattered though he might be in song and print, Tom Bowling was still treated as a natural resource rather than a respected citizen.

Peace with Bonaparte was never going to last and the Navy began preparing for a resumption of conflict well in advance. From March 1803, two months before Britain declared war, official proclamations went out recalling seamen and prohibiting their service in the ships of foreign states. Rewards were offered 'for discovering such seamen as shall conceal themselves'.[33] In short, press gangs were back at work.

Bounty from the hunt was celebrated in newspapers with hand-rubbing glee:

The impress service has proved uncommonly productive in the number of excellent seamen. The return on Tuesday amounted to one thousand and eighty of whom no less than two thirds are considered prime hands. At Portsmouth every merchant ship was stripped of its hands.[34]

The crisis was admittedly unprecedented. Thanks to St Vincent's mass discharge the previous year, the Navy was down to less than 40 per cent of its wartime strength. Moreover, the best men had found new berths in merchantmen and, being better paid, they were not going to come quietly. Desperate times produced desperate measures.

Resistance to impressment reached a new pitch that year. By one study, seventy-five brawls involving press gangs were reported between March and December, twice as many as in any previous year.[35] A gang in Chester seized farm servants, tradesmen and apprentices, as well as a forty-six-year-old former seaman, Daniel Jackson, who had opted to join the Army. His fellows wreaked havoc on the rondy before breaking into the jail where Jackson was held and liberating him. In another notorious case, a press gang landed near Weymouth in Dorset to be met by 300 local quarrymen who drove them off. Reinforcements came in and opened fire, killing two quarrymen and a blacksmith and wounding a woman; the officers were tried for murder and acquitted.[36]

The naked man-hunting practised from 1803 arguably defined the modern image of the press gang. An Admiralty survey over the next two years shows that 48 per cent of the 11,600 men raised at thirty-two ports had been pressed.[37] William Wilberforce's simultaneous campaign to abolish the slave trade cast a grim perspective on impressment when the seizure of four black men from a slaveship intercepted off Gravesend in November brought an outraged protest from the owners: 'They are our property & Natives of Africa . . . and were on board for attending the Slaves.' In reply, the Admiralty agreed to release the black men, on condition that 'you find four able seamen to serve in their stead'.[38]

Cornwall was a rich source at the start of the Napoleonic War. William Lovett recalled his boyhood in Newlyn where 'the cry that "the press gang is coming" was sufficient to cause all the young and eligible men to flock up to the hills and away to the country'. Then troops would descend and 'great numbers were taken away, and many never more heard of'.[39]

But perhaps the press's most profitable source of plunder at this point was the east coast, with its traffic of collier brigs, fishing vessels and North Sea traders.

———

John Wetherell of Whitby offers a snapshot of the innumerable lives turned upside down that year. He was twenty-one and from a seafaring family in the classic mould – his father a whaling captain, he a product of that exacting school of seamanship, the Newcastle coal trade. Early in March, Wetherell bade farewell to his sweetheart and family before sailing south for London. His prospects were bright with the offer of a post as mate in the Atlantic trade and he was armed with a protection.

Hours after leaving Whitby his vessel was intercepted by a frigate, *Hussar*, and he was taken. His protection was summarily dismissed. In the next week, Wetherell saw dozens of others dragged in his wake. *Hussar*'s logbook tells the story in prosaic terms: 'March 9. Sent 2 boats on the impress service and obtained 15 men.' And: 'March 19. Sent the boats. Impressed 5 men.' In four raids, at least thirty men were seized.[40]

Wetherell's account is more personal. In 'the horrid outrage in Harwich', he saw virtually every able-bodied male rounded up, 'from the parish priest to the farmer in his frock and wooden shoes . . . Even the blacksmith, cobler, taylor, barber, baker, fisherman and doctor were drag'd from their homes.' Overnight they were held in the market house where wives gathered in the morning, demanding their release, and were assured that only 'men who gain their living by salt water' would be kept. This still came with a warning that the marines would fire on anyone who tried to flee. So it proved as they were marched down to the boats, leaving the shore 'crowded with hart broken wives and parents' when one man:

. . . sprang from the boat and ran with the swiftness of a deer pursued by marines firing at him furiously but all in vain. He gained the other bank where he stood and wav'd his hat in defiance.[41]

The fact was that in isolated or remote coastal regions, the press was able to plunder without restraint. A midshipman wrote how, in the Scottish isles, 'we carried off every able-bodied male we could lay our hands on. I think the number we captured in Shetland alone amounted to 70 fine young fellows.'[42]

Bitterness at a custom that changed lives in a moment was natural and it coloured many a memory of the Napoleonic War. Wetherell himself was never reconciled to the Navy, finding it 'a golden rule to be sober, silent and submissive, and above all to curb your tongue and temper'.[43] He had been unlucky in his ship; Captain Philip Wilkinson was a beetle-browed fault-finder, inept to boot; and Wetherell loathed him. In January 1804, *Hussar* was wrecked in the Bay of Biscay.

Almost all the company came safely off, but they had landed on enemy shore. John Wetherell was to spend the next eleven years a prisoner in France.

———

As impressment reached men and places previously exempt, so desertions increased. Nelson believed that over almost ten years of the Revolutionary War 42,000 men had run. During the first two years of the Napoleonic War, another admiral calculated, 12,301 men deserted. Of these, 5,662 were rated Able – those whose skills were most in demand by a resurgent yet man-starved mercantile service.[44]

Thanks to the wages obtainable elsewhere, naval pay went up again in 1806, taking an Able man's rate from 28s to 33s 6d a month, Ordinary from 23s 6d to 25s 6d, and Landsmen to 22s 6d. After 150 years on the same pay, sailors had won two increases within a decade. Even then it did little to stem the desertion rate.

The government tried another recruitment tactic. Ballads had extolled Jack's virtues for well over half a century and 'Tom Bowling' was almost as popular as 'Rule, Britannia!' and 'Heart of Oak'. In an appeal to loyalty, the Admiralty commissioned Charles Dibdin to compose a patriotic song every month. The idea was not without risks. Dibdin had frequent run-ins with authority and his lyrics included at least one joust against the ruling class,

SONS OF THE WAVES

making a disdainful comparison between 'You Lords with such fine baby faces, that strut in a garter and star' and 'the kind honest heart of a tar'.[45]

From the declaration of war in May, Dibdin produced eight *British War Songs*. It was said they were worth 10,000 men. None, though, has endured like his most heartfelt ballad:

> Yet shall poor Tom find pleasant weather, When He who all commands,
>> Shall give, to call life's crew together, The word to pipe all hands;
> Thus death who Kings and tars dispatches, In vain Tom's life has doff'd,
> For though his body's under hatches, His soul has gone aloft, his soul has gone aloft.

– 310 –

19

APOTHEOSIS
1805

TWO years into the renewal of war, the tide of history turned. Britain's most comprehensive and far-reaching sea victory set to rest immediate fears of invasion and effectively destroyed France's capacity to launch such an operation. It established naval supremacy into the next century and beyond. It cloaked the officer class in glory. Tales of Trafalgar are legion. Few, however, represent Jack in what was also his finest hour.

One who ran against this effusive tide, and stated his perverse credentials by calling himself Jack Nastyface, was a plain seaman who took a derisory scoff at 'the quarterdeck and epaulette authors [who] splice together the miracles [they] have seen to show noble friends'. He too had been at Trafalgar, he wrote, and in 'unfurling a foremast man's log' would speak truth on behalf of 'my brother seamen and old shipmates'.[1] The broadside was well aimed. The only pity is that it came from one who had been a hopeless failure at sea.

His real name was William Robinson and his story has some familiar echoes. He was born in rural Surrey to a shoemaker who put him to the trade 'which my roving mind would not suffer me to pursue'. On making his way to London and the rondy at Tower Hill, he volunteered in anticipation of a life 'which fancy had moulded into a variety of shapes, gilded by hope, with fortune, honour and happiness'. His first and only ship was the 74-gun *Revenge*, and he came on board with another young Landsman, John Powell. It would be interesting to know what they made of each other. Both were aged about twenty, both were unusually literate and wrote of their experiences. They shared quarters and were acquainted. But the hard-nosed malcontent and the evangelical Christian had nothing else in common when *Revenge* sailed to join Nelson's fleet in May 1805.

Stories of Trafalgar are familiar. Less well charted are the months of sea chase and travail that preceded it. They still help to explain the love the admiral inspired in his men.

Nelson had established a base in the Mediterranean with the objective of intercepting any fleet of the combined navies of France and its new ally Spain launched by Napoleon to carry his forces abroad. Feeding a fleet in hostile seas, let alone making it fit for battle, would have overwhelmed many commanders. As it was, Nelson's tactical brilliance and human skills were matched by logistical flair. Fresh food was brought from Portugal, North Africa and even the Middle East, including, crucially, citrus fruit, now recognized as a tonic as well as an antiscorbutic. 'The great thing in all military service is health,' Nelson wrote to a doctor, 'and you will agree with me that it is easier for an officer to keep men healthy than for a physician to cure them.'[2] Although thousands of miles from home, his sailors as a whole were fitter than ever.

They were also in a state of constant activity. Early in 1805 a French fleet escaped from Toulon and Nelson went searching for them. Where they were bound was anyone's guess: Napoleon, it was known, had an army of 140,000 at Boulogne poised for a cross-Channel invasion, but conflicting sightings and intelligence suggested he had other objectives. Over nine months, Nelson's *Victory* led a hunt down the Mediterranean, then right across the Atlantic to the West Indies and back.

The chase was itself revealing of morale. Admiral Pierre de Villeneuve had more ships at his disposal yet did everything he could to avoid battle; and while that may be partly ascribed to preserving resources for an invasion, Napoleon's disdain and ignorance of naval matters had demoralized his commanders. 'All one can expect from a career in the French navy today is shame and confusion,' Villeneuve fumed.[3]

Meanwhile on *Revenge*, men had been finding their feet. Naval ways came as a shock to two Landsmen. In close confinement William Robinson soon regretted his contempt for the shoemaking trade. The devout John Powell was appalled that he could not read the Bible without being interrupted, 'for this is the place where Blasphemy reigns triumphant', and had to comfort himself with *Aesop's Fables*.[4]

But men settled to their wooden world. A week later, after being assigned to the mizzen top, Powell wrote to his mother: 'I have the most agreeable ship-mates that can be.' Literacy earned respect and he was asked to write letters on their behalf. 'I don't think I have one enemy, they either love or fear me.'[5]

From July, the *Revenge* spent weeks off Ushant with a fleet under Collingwood before sailing for Cadiz to await Nelson in *Victory*. After their transatlantic dance, the enemy was known to be back in European waters and a whiff of battle was in the air. An exhilarated Powell wrote home: 'I grow every day more attached to this way of life.'[6]

His shipmate Robinson was a more awkward character, opinionated, intel-ligent and, to start with, condescending towards the simpler members of their fraternity. It seems unlikely that 'Jack Nastyface' ever really joined the tribe he later celebrated; and while his dislike for the officer class was pronounced, he was too prudent to show it, resolving 'to be obedient, however irksome to my feelings'.[7] In that, at least, he was successful. His name is invisible among those listed as being flogged.

His account of the approach to Trafalgar is pithy and accurate:

We were ordered to proceed on the Spanish coast to look after the combined fleets. Having heard that Sir Robert Calder had fallen in with them a few days previous, we pursued our course, looking in at Ferrol and other ports, until we arrived off Cadiz, where we found they had got safe in.*

---

* Robinson, p. 12. Calder intercepted the enemy fleet on 22 July and took two Spanish ships but was denounced as a failure after an inconclusive action by a nation that had come to expect nothing less than emphatic victory.

Here Collingwood's fleet established a blockade in August to await Nelson.

Nelson had been at sea for more than two years when he came home that month, to be mobbed and hailed as Britain's saviour. What would happen next was an open question but the prevailing wisdom had one thing as certain: if the enemy came out, Nelson and Jack would destroy him.

The *Victory* left Portsmouth on 14 September. A signal absentee was Tom Allen. By some accounts Nelson was to have been joined by his former servant who only missed the sailing because a hasty departure left him insufficient time to get from Merton to Portsmouth; Tom himself later informed any listener that had he been there he would have insisted that his master wear a modest uniform, as he had at Copenhagen, rather than the outfit that made him conspicuous at Trafalgar. According to a more recent study, however, Nelson had tired of Tom's sloppiness and haphazard timekeeping and sent him packing once and for all.[8]

Nelson's return to the fleet on 28 September was greeted with 'a sort of general joy'. If confidence was never lacking, their talisman still gave his men assurance. Ten days was enough to bring the turning point. In Robinson's words:

> To decoy the enemy out, stratagem was resorted to, and five sail were sent to Gibraltar to victual and water, whilst Lord Nelson, with his five sail, kept out of sight of the enemy, and thus they thought we were only twenty-two sail of the line whilst their fleet consisted of thirty-three sail. With this superior force they put to sea, with the intention, as we afterwards learned, of taking our fleet; and if they had succeeded they were to occupy the Channel and assist in the invasion of England.[9]

The combined fleet of thirty-three ships was heading for the Straits of Gibraltar when twenty-seven ships of the Royal Navy came up with them on 21 October.

We may bring these floating fortresses to mind again. On the upper level a rising structure of masts streaked about with ropes, drenched in canvas, and there in a golden light – for seasonal change came slow in the western

Mediterranean – lightly clad men, feet bare, streaming to their posts, rising aloft, hauling, chanting. And on the lower deck, a darker, altogether tighter space where they took their rest in rotation and ate shoulder to shoulder at tables, each mess of eight hands located between two guns.

How many men were sharing those spaces that day came down to the size of their ship. The 100-gun *Victory* had 606 mustered hands spread across three decks, the 74-gun *Revenge* 380 hands over two decks.[10] They represented the most assorted and cosmopolitan crews yet mustered by the Navy. Along with those born to the sea, they included weavers, farmers and – as in the case of Robinson – shoemakers. They were blacksmiths, masons and miners, tailors, butchers and ironmongers.[11] Or ranging, as Robert Hay put it vividly:

> From the brawny ploughman to the delicate fop; the decayed author and bankrupt merchant who had eluded their creditors; the apprentice who had eloped from servitude; the improvident father who had abandoned his family, and the smuggler and the swindler who had escaped by flight.[12]

Most were English, followed by Irish, Scots and Welsh. But around 10 per cent of Britain's seamen at Trafalgar were foreigners. Americans made up the largest group with 373, followed by 136 from Italy and 83 from Sweden. No fewer than 57 Frenchmen had gone over to the old enemy.[13] Others came from the West Indies, Holland, Prussia and Bengal.

Robinson's fellow Revenges were a fairly typical cross section: 249 English, 58 Irish, 51 Scots, 8 Welsh, 4 Americans, 4 Portuguese, 3 Germans, 2 Caribbeans, 2 Danes and a solitary Frenchman. They included a high proportion of men rated Able. The great majority were listed as volunteers, seventy-two as pressed.[14]

Boys were numerous. Strains on traditional industries, agriculture and weaving, had brought an influx of youth, and there were thirty-five lads on *Revenge* alone. (While both Robinson and Robert Hay claimed they had gone to sea for adventure, it may be noted that their respective family trades, shoe-making and weaving, were in a depressed state.)

However disparate their backgrounds, ethnicity or age, they shared one characteristic – absolute confidence in victory. The accounts of those present are unanimous. From sailing skills to gunnery, British seamen had proved their superiority time and again, and they knew it. In preparing for the ultimate battle they had two further spurs – the conviction that came from defending their homeland, and faith in a commander who had never been defeated.

In a letter home, John Brown on *Victory* described the approach to action:

> On Monday the 21st at day light the french and Spanish Fleets Was like a great wood on our lee bow which cheered the hearts of every british tar in the Victory like lions Anxious to be at it.[15]

A lieutenant on *Belleisle* wrote that Jack's roars of delight on sighting the enemy 'exceeded those when our native cliffs are descried after a long, distant service'.[16] Even Robinson, who had a mocking eye for chauvinism, was unequivocal:

> If I may be indulged the observation I will say that could England have seen her sons about to attack the enemy on his own coast . . . from the zeal that animated every man in the fleet, the bosom of every inhabitant of England would have glowed with an indescribable patriotic pride.[17]

As Robinson observed, they had almost six hours to prepare for battle 'while we glided down under the influence of a gentle breeze'. Ships' bands struck up the usual fare, from 'Rule, Britannia!' to 'Heart of Oak'. Hornpipes were danced. Practical measures involved the taking down of bulkheads to reduce casualties from flying splinters and laying down sails for the wounded to be placed on and carried for surgery. Robinson saw messmates agreeing to 'a sort of mutual verbal will', saying:

> 'If one of Johnny Crapaud's shots knocks my head off, you will take all my effects; and if you're killed and I'm not, why, I'll have yours.'[18]

On the *Victory* they were piped to a dinner of pork and a half pint of wine. John Brown recalled the genesis of a famous signal:

> Lord Nelson went round the decks and said My noble lads this will be a glorious day for england who ever lives to see it I Shant be Satisfied with 12 Ships this day as I took at the Nile . . . the signal was made to Prepare for battle and that england expected every man would do his duty.[19]

From the frequency that Nelson's exhortation is mentioned in seamen's letters and other contemporary accounts, it clearly made an immediate impact. Robinson quoted it accurately, as 'England expects each man will do his duty.' On *Bellerophon* a cry went up, 'No fear of that!'[20] On the *Ajax* an officer heard a muttering: 'Do our duty? Of course we'll do our duty! Let us come alongside of 'em and we'll soon show whether we'll do our duty.'[21]

They advanced in two columns, led by Nelson in *Victory* and Collingwood in *Royal Sovereign*. The latter was first into action. *Revenge*'s log records the start of battle as 12.25, when *Royal Sovereign* opened fire.

Robinson relates that the company had been briefed on Nelson's tactic of breaking the line. The two columns advanced into enemy broadsides, absorbing severe punishment while men at the guns 'became impatient to return the compliment' and had to be restrained 'so all our shots might tell'. Once they broke the French and Spanish lines, passing under the stern or across the bow of an enemy, they would be able to unleash their own broadsides to run her entire length and disperse carnage.

The *Revenge*, almost a mile astern of *Royal Sovereign*, broke the line as 'it fell to our lot to cut off the five stern-most ships,' wrote Robinson. After that all was mayhem as they were beset by a French 74 to starboard and a Spanish three-decker that ran her bowsprit over their poop. 'We could not see for the smoke, whether we were firing at a foe or a friend, and as to hearing, the noise of the guns had so completely made us deaf that we were obliged to look only to the motions that we made.'[22]

Heading the second column, *Victory* was running towards the French flagship *Bucentaure* and the 120-gun *Santísima Trinidad*, the largest ship in the world. At the guns, 'some were stripped to the waist, some had bared their necks and arms, others had tied a handkerchief round their heads'.[23] John Brown wrote to his parents:

Got our guns double shotted to give them a doce and all ready for Action when the four-decker fired a broadside into us before We could get a gun to bear on them.[24]

Twenty men were killed and thirty wounded on *Victory* before she fired a shot.[25] But, as ever, it was the quality of gunnery that counted. So close did *Victory* pass by *Bucentaure*'s stern that when 68-pound carronade balls atomized the French cabin windows, shards of glass and wood showered around Nelson on his quarterdeck. As each gun ran by, further devastation was released the length of the French flagship. Half her crew were wounded or killed.

On *Royal Sovereign*, Collingwood joined his company on the quarterdeck, 'looking along the guns to see they were properly pointed, and commending the sailors, particularly a black man, who was afterwards killed, but who, while he stood beside him, fired ten times directly into the portholes of the *Santa Anna*'.[26]

Accounts are full of casualties of the 'head-off' variety. One man related turning to the fellow beside him just as 'a shot cut his head right in two, leaving the tip of each ear remaining on the lower part of the cheek'.[27] Mostly the reality was far messier. At first though, virtually nothing could be seen as smoke clouded the between-decks:

Every man was so isolated from his neighbour that he was not put in mind of his danger by seeing his messmates go down all round.[28]

The casualties became apparent as men started to slip on blood and viscera underfoot; and once the smoke had cleared on *Royal Sovereign* one mid

The ferocious gunnery of British ships, from the rate of fire to accuracy,
was the crucial factor in victory after victory.

was stunned to see 'many brave seamen mangled so, some with their heads
half shot away, others with their entrails mashed, lying panting on the
deck'.[29]

In the thick of it was *Temeraire*. She had followed hard astern of *Victory* and
when the flagship started to absorb punishment, *Temeraire* advanced to
confront the unmistakable four-deck *Santísima Trinidad*, pouring fire into the

Spanish mountain with her ninety-eight guns. She then moved up to *Victory* as she was rammed by *Redoutable*, most gallant of the French ships. They remained locked in a deadly embrace for more than half an hour, exchanging fire at point-blank range.

More than 200 Temeraires were killed or wounded. Mutiny four years earlier had been redeemed in the bloodiest way. Among those on *Victory* to raise his arms in gratitude was John Brown: the French, he wrote home, 'would have Sunk us only for the Timmera. [She] took the firy edge off us.'[30]

British broadsides came much faster; and as the French and Spanish crews were withered, so their capacity to return fire diminished. When prisoners came on *Victory* afterwards, Benjamin Thompson wrote to his sister, 'they sayed that the Devel loded the guns for it was impossible for men to load and fire as quick as we did'.[31]

Chivalry was occasionally glimpsed through the smoke. On the *Billy Ruffian* an old hand, Christopher Beatty, seeing the ensign shot away and determined that the foe should not think they had struck, took a new flag on his shoulder and clambered up the mizzen rigging while musket balls from *L'Aigle* flew around him. When the French marksmen realized that his only purpose was to raise the flag, they ceased firing. Casualties on both these ships were particularly high.

Surgery took place in the 'butcher's shambles' – the cockpit – where the wounded were laid out on mess tables. A surgeon recalled having to discriminate between those 'bad indeed and painful, but slight in comparison to the dreadful condition of others' while trying to keep up morale and 'throw momentary gleams of cheerfulness amidst so many horrors'. On the *Victory* that day, nine legs and two arms were sawn from men being dosed with brandy as the ship shook with the impact of shot.

Robinson saw a shipmate with both calves blasted away. After one leg was cut off the fellow 'very coolly observed that he should like to have one leg left to wear his shoes out'. When the other had to be amputated as well, he exclaimed: 'Now to the devil with all shoe-makers, I have done with them!' Despite his fortitude, he died quickly.[32]

Casualties on *Revenge* were comparatively light, but among the sixteen dead was a detested midshipman. The gruesome death of Edward Brooke, aged fourteen, from Wakefield, was described by Robinson with unseemly relish:

He was killed on the quarterdeck by grapeshot, his body greatly mutilated, his entrails being driven and scattered against the larboard side . . . The general exclamation was 'Thank God we are rid of the young tyrant!'[33]

A key moment came at 14.05 when the French flagship, *Bucentaure*, surrendered. The Spanish giant *Santísima Trinidad* followed at 14.30, by which point twelve ships of the combined fleet had lowered their flags. Among the British, *Royal Sovereign* was a shattered forest, all three masts downed; *Temeraire* was another shambles. But none had surrendered. When the guns fell silent at 17.50 after five hours, eighteen enemy ships of the line had been taken while one, *l'Achille*, had blown up.

Victory was complete; but already word of another momentous event had started to spread around the fleet. On *Royal Sovereign* a hand named Sam wrote to his father:

Our dear Admiral Nelson is killed! So we have paid pretty sharply for licking em. I never sat eyes on him, for which I am both sorry and glad. For to be sure I should like to have seen him but then all the men in our ship who have seen him are such soft toads they have done nothing but blast their eyes and cry ever since.[34]

Not for the first time, it may be noted how easily these warriors wept – and were ready to admit it. Another sailor's memoir speaks of men grieving for Nelson, 'with all the tenderness of women'.[35] Even Jack Nastyface mourned the loss: 'He was adored and in fighting under him every man thought himself sure of success.'[36]

In terms of resolution, efficiency and fortitude, British sailors set a mark that day which placed them among the invincibles of fighting history. Almost as telling, yet quite anonymous, were the feats of seamanship in the furious storms that followed. A French captain wrote:

> [What] astonished me most was when the action was over. It came on to blow a gale and the English immediately set to work to shorten sail and reef in topsails with as much regularity and order as if their ships had not been fighting a dreadful battle. We were all amazement, wondering what the English sailor could be made of. All our seamen were drunk or disabled.[37]

The gale of 22 October would have tested ships in fine fettle. On hulks already battered by human forces, nature wrought devastation. Toppled masts and shredded sails were replaced with makeshift jury masts, men went to the pumps and another battle for survival began. The storm lasted for two ferocious days, abated, then returned in even greater force. One captain even described it as a hurricane.

Again, the enemy bore the brunt of the suffering. Driven ashore, the *Fougueux* was lost with most of those on board, including thirty Temeraires sent to man her. On *Redoutable*, Jack and Jean were at the pumps together before she too went down; boats from *Swiftsure* went across in swirling black seas and picked up as many as could be found afloat. The *Bucentaure* ran ashore. The biggest prize of all, *Santísima Trinidad*, was sent to the bottom on Collingwood's orders after he decided she could not be saved. First, though, *Prince* took off the wounded, 'the poor mangled wretches [tied] round their waists and lowered into a tumbling boat, some without arms, others no legs, and lacerated all over'.

The *Revenge* also came to the rescue. Robinson, who could in one moment rejoice in the death of a midshipman, described 'a very distressing and affecting scene'. A Spaniard had reached the boat, which was about to put off when his son came down the side of the sinking ship and reached out. The boat was full, the sea high and the crew refused to take him on, but as they started away, he leapt into the sea. When the father made to join him, the crew threw caution to the wind, deciding to 'save both father and son, or die in the attempt . . . Both were brought safe on board of our ship.'[38]

So was a Frenchwoman – widowed during the battle – who emerged 'in a state of complete nakedness'. Jeanette was given needle, thread and sheets to sew herself a dress and on landing at Gibraltar left *Revenge* praising '*les bons Anglais*'.

A virtual wreck, *Victory* was towed to Gibraltar. The day after she anchored, on 28 October, six men received thirty-six lashes each for 'contempt and disobedience'.[39]

It may be true, as John Bayley wrote, that warriors in heroic times only knew what they had done when they heard about it from the bard in the mead-hall.[40] Trafalgar was different. The scale of victory partly defined it. While British casualties numbered 449 dead and 1,241 wounded, some 4,000 French and Spaniards had been killed. And the death and transfiguration of Horatio Nelson gave Britain's hour of salvation an almost biblical resonance. Trafalgar was grist to the mill of a publishing phenomenon as admirals and lieutenants, captains and midshipmen set down their versions of what had passed that day.

Accounts from the lower deck are scant. Robinson, aka Jack Nastyface, only weighed in with his memoir more than thirty years later. Otherwise, seamen's voices are heard in the letters they sent home on reaching port. Jacob Richards of the *Euryalus* was among those who testified to the power of Nelson's signal:

[It] was such as Ought to Light in the Brast of Every Partiot . . . [He] fell in the heart of the Action by a Musquit Ball the World does not Possess a more brave Man, Or History a Better fought Battle . . .

The ships Company would Not Part With him he was Opened & his Entrails taken Out & hove Overboard in a Ledden case and his Body put in a Butt of Rum . . . the last words he Spoke was that he had Lived to see that Victorious Day and Now I Die Happy.[41]

From the *Victory*, Benjamin Thompson gave a brief account of the battle to his sister but felt overwhelmed and, in holding back on details 'too Crual for your feelings', prayed for peace:

Dear Sister, I canot express the Pleasure I would have of seeing you all A gain. I trust to god that he will turn thing into A better understanding between the two Nations and let us have A Pece for it is time fore me to have A little pleasure in my life for this is A miserable one at present.[42]

On the other hand, John Powell, the once-timid evangelical of the *Revenge*, had taken a liking to war. 'French hunting,' he wrote to his mother, 'is glorious sport.'[43] Robert Hope on the *Temeraire* was similarly triumphant in writing to his brother: 'What do you think of us Lads of the Sea now? I think they wont send their fleet Out Again in a hurry.'[44]

Home connections between hands meant that survivors sometimes had grim news to impart. James West of the *Britannia* wrote to his parents, relating the death of a family friend:

I am sorry to inform you I am wounded in the left shoulder and that William Hillman was killed at the same time. The shot that killed him and 3 more, wounded me and 5 more . . . I hope you will inform his poor friends of it. He went to his Gun like a man and a true Briton.[45]

Pride in their own ship's deeds could bring scorn for others who had escaped lightly. Brown of the *Victory* grumbled at the 98-gun *Prince* which 'scultk away' with 'nobody Killed or Wounded'. Edward Harrison of the *Temeraire* thought the *Neptune* 'might as well been laying in Cawsand Bay' (which was unfair as she had been closely engaged).

But rejoicing ashore was universal. Collingwood's despatch, published in *The Times* on 7 November, proclaimed 'the invincible spirit of British seamen when engaging the enemies of their country'. Returning crews landing in Portsmouth 'were loudly cheered and welcomed home by an immense number of persons'.

Old John Nicol, by now long ashore, was overjoyed. Since retiring to the country he had not known much respect from lubberly farm labourers and often fumed at their Scottish gloom. 'When they talked of heavy taxes I talked of China. When they complained of hard times I told them of West Indian slaves.' Then they would taunt him about press gangs:

> One would ask what I thought of British freedom; another if I could defend
> a government which did such things? I was at no loss for my answer. I told
> them, 'Necessity has no law.' Could the government make perfect seamen
> as easily as they could soldiers there would be no such thing as pressing, and
> that I was happy to be of more value than them all put together.[46]

Then came tidings of Trafalgar. 'None but an old tar can feel the joy I felt,' he crowed. For days he walked around with 'the greatest desire to hurra aloud, and many an hurra my heart gave that my mouth uttered not'.

Trafalgar, according to one historian, contributed to 'a general humanisation of the Navy after about 1805', though it could be argued that process was already under way.[47] It certainly guaranteed Britain's economic prosperity and security, both as a trading power and a bastion against Napoleon's ambitions.[48] At the start of 1805, the British, French and Spanish navies possessed about 330,000 tons of shipping each. By the end Britain had 570,000 tons compared with the 336,000 tons of France, Spain and the Netherlands combined.[49] While Napoleon drove his armies across Europe, and his economy towards ruin, Britain would benefit from global trade without competition from her European rivals.

Officers who served and survived the battle were awarded a silver metal. As a tribute to seamen and marines, the manufacturer Matthew Boulton struck 15,000 medals in white metal inscribed 'To the Heroes of Trafalgar'. However, as Jack discovered that they had no intrinsic value and could not be bartered, many were simply discarded.

The Revenges were given a six-day liberty ticket to savour the delights of Portsmouth before returning to European waters as blockaders – or 'Channel gropers' as Robinson called them. He was in *Revenge* another six years, but had little to say of them. While puncturing in print her next captain, Charles Paget – 'pompous, proud, imperious, unfeeling and, of course, detested' – he drew a discreet veil over his own later service.

It may have been thanks to his literacy that Robinson was appointed purser's steward, a well-paid position but one unlikely to have endeared him to his shipmates, pursers being regarded as corrupt profiteers who benefited at Jack's expense. Whether or not, as has been suggested, Robinson was reduced to Landsman again because of fraud, demotion to the lowest rank for a seaman marked the end for him, and may have been the makings of his jaundiced outlook.[50] In Portsmouth in 1811, 'I quitted and took my leave of the naval service.'

The truth is, he deserted.[51]

In one respect 'Nastyface' stuck to his guns. Twenty-five years later, married and a family man, he published the volume of memoirs in which he inveighed against the naval service, the 'stains of wanton and torturing punishment', and an officer class represented by the likes of Paget, a 'self-important nautical demagogue . . . ever ready with his Nero heart and famed for his support of these diabolical systems'.[52]

Robinson's memoir was, in its day, a campaigning tract – and a healthy corrective to the standard portrayal of Jack's dutifully sentimental side. In part, at least, he retained the dreams that had first taken him to sea:

To the youth possessing anything of a roving disposition it is attractive, nay, it is seducing; for it has its allurements, and when steadily pursued and with success, it ennobles the mind, and the seaman feels himself a man. There is, indeed, no profession that can vie with it; and a British seaman has a right to be proud, for he is incomparable alongside those of any other nation.[53]

20

WINNING WAYS
1806-09

TO SAY that Nelson and Trafalgar reinforced a bond between men and officers cannot be proved. This narrative has seen enough evidence of the unpredictability in seamen's lives to guard against simple maxims, and the saturnine example of Captain Robert Corbet, a frigate captain who worshipped Nelson yet could not distinguish between zeal and mania, is a reminder that monsters remained afloat.[1] We may nevertheless note a tendency in Jack's writings at this time to cast an appreciative eye to the quarterdeck.

George Watson's passage from Newcastle boy to old hand followed a well-run course. He was ten when his mariner father took him on board a collier and he coasted to London and back for years before sailing the Atlantic. What makes him exceptional is that he never had to be pressed. Coming ashore at Gibraltar from his merchantman in the spring of 1807, he met an old friend from Newcastle, William McKenzie, now in the Navy. Together the two twenty-year-old hands went on his ship, the *Fame*.[2]

> I spent the evening with him very pleasantly, and the sailors of his mess procured us plenty of wine, and everything that could be got to make a stranger comfortable. When morning came, I felt reluctant to part with my friend and instead I volunteered to serve his Majesty.[3]

Watson's years in *Fame* saw no great feats of battle. With the enemy unwilling to engage, commanders had to find other ways of keeping their ships active and entertained, and from Watson's testimony Captain Richard Bennet found the right balance as the 74 sailed for the Mediterranean:

> He wished to make every man in the ship a sailor, and for that end divided the whole of the crew . . . All sorts in our ship took their turn in the tops and in short time could reef or furl a sail, send up or down topgallant yards with any of us . . . These things gave us many advantages over our compeers so there was not a ship in the fleet could exceed us for reefing, making sail, &c &c.[4]

Plays were staged regularly, the captain paying for costumes and scenery to be brought aboard at Valletta or Palermo. Local women joined them and Watson recalled that, unlike the Polls of Portsmouth – 'where a modest woman is as hard to find as a Mermaid' – Palermo's Catholic hussies were a devout lot who went ashore in the morning to confess to a priest:

> What a delightful task he must have, to hear all their amorous relations, and to be able, after such a night's work, to speak peace to the minds of so many guilty Magdalenes![5]

Back on board, they were 'at it again at night, as fresh as ever, believing that one stroke from the magic wand of a confessor, grey in iniquity himself, can remove all their guilt'.

Captain Bennet, the men observed, liked women too; a succession of mistresses occupied his cabin, notably one 'with large black eyes' and a tendency to coquette with the hands rowing her ashore.[6] But the captain's most admirable quality was seen in the time he lost his temper and slapped a negligent sailor:

> After retiring to his cabin, he sent for the man, gave him a guinea and apologised for an act unbecoming a King's officer.[7]

Watson's decision to quit his merchantman for a king's ship would bring him great pain – a crippling wound in action which set him on another voyage, to the Royal Naval Hospital at Greenwich. But of regret, he had not a word to say.

———

The most perceptive account of how a thoughtful officer went about culti- vating an awkward squad comes from one of the enigmas of the lower deck. He bequeathed to history a journal rare in its complex portrayal of seafaring society and the realm opened by Britain's new dominance in the Mediterranean. Of the man himself almost nothing is known.[8]

Six months after Trafalgar, the frigate *Unite* lay at anchor off Constantinople where a clear day opened up a vista from the Golden Horn to the Topkapi palace, stippled with the domes and minarets of Ottoman grandeur. Diplomacy was in the air and Jacks in their best white duck had been turned up to man the yards in a display of naval smartness. 'Several Turkish grandees visited our ship,' wrote one of the topmen, Robert Wilson, 'and seemed highly pleased with the fine order she was kept in.'[9] The next day, *Unite* hosted a ball for consuls of the neutral powers where her band kept the diplomats busy in the arms of Armenian ladies brought aboard for the occasion.

Robert Wilson appears as another of those individuals entirely lacking in grievance. He recorded without rancour his impressment as a merchant seaman on returning from Jamaica, passed over with sangfroid the vile conditions of a tender. Within days he was drafted on *Unite*, 'a fine ship lately put in perfect repair', where he was recognized as a skilled hand and placed in the maintop to mentor less experienced fellows. Once a lieutenant saw the extent of Wilson's gifts he was made signalman, which conferred the weighty responsibility of receiving as well as transmitting messages to ships in company, and sighting and identifying strange sail. Robert Wilson was then aged all of twenty years.

(Youth and seamanship have been noted before, but the association bears repeating. Jacob Nagle, John Nicol and John Wetherell were all about twenty- one when they were rated Able, George Watson was twenty and William

Spavens twenty-three. Valentine Joyce was twenty-six when he led the Spithead revolt but had been a topman for years, and many other prominent mutineers were between twenty and twenty-four. Those termed old hands were hardly ancients.)

The eastern Mediterranean was close to a sailor's delight – almost invariably blue, brilliantly lit, often dazzlingly so, warm too, and rich in fresh provisions of a most palatable variety. And *Unite* was the pride of her crew – taut, smart and efficient, fleet enough to escape tight corners or superior antagonists, yet with the 40-gun firepower that could blow an enemy frigate out of the water. (She had been the *Impérieuse*, French-built and therefore among the finest of her class, until being taken in '93.)

But not all was sunny. Captain Charles Ogle and his first lieutenant shared a passion for minutiae and though neither could be called severe, tautness had antagonized a mess where a turbulent Irishman held sway. John Kelly drank as heavily as any of his compatriots and he was not alone. For all her talents, *Unite* had a drinking problem.

Soon after Kelly joined, Wilson was appalled to note, 'some evil-minded person or persons cut nine gun-tackle falls'.[10] These were the ropes holding guns in place, and whoever cut them had freed tons of iron to rumble across the deck with potentially catastrophic results for the ship and anyone who happened to be in the way. Outraged men came forward to name Kelly and two others, Robert Leaky and William Fairbottom, for 'drinking together and expressing contempt of the ship and the service'. Few lamented when Kelly received seventy-two lashes and his accomplices twenty-four each.[11]

Weeks later Wilson related in five sentences a drama that might have come from a story by Patrick O'Brian:

Jan 18th, 1806: William Fairbottom in the frenzy of his mind threw himself overboard and sunk to rise no more. We got a boat out to try to save him, but to no purpose. He had been observed to be very low spirited ever since the affair of the gun-tackle falls. He left a mother and sister to deplore his fatal end. He was certainly a fine young man, had been impressed on his return to England from an absence of three years, two of which he had remained on a desolate island in the South Seas, killing seals for his ship.[12]

An auction of Fairbottom's effects, along with the pay from his service in the South Seas, raised the remarkable sum of £36 11s 6d, to be sent to his mother.[13]

Ogle kept the company on their toes, 'reefing, furling, making and shortening sail, and all nautical manoeuvres insomuch that we were often exhausted, but were made so smart that we were counted the smartest ship in the sea'.[14] A change in command added humanity to *Unite*'s flair. Captain Patrick Campbell announced himself by banning the practice of starting and easing a code of cap-touching servility. Exercising aloft was cut from daily to twice weekly. They remained as smart as ever, but 'did their duty more cheerful'.

The benefits were seen during a taxing commission. From 1806, *Unite* cruised the Adriatic, from Trieste in the north to Corfu, with occasional exits via the Ionian Sea to Malta. These were unfamiliar waters for British vessels and uncertainty was compounded by a delicate point in the war. Since Austria's defeat at Austerlitz in December 1805 and the collapse of the Holy Roman Empire in August 1806, alliances had been shifting. Trieste was a neutral port yet subject to French occupation. Venice was in enemy hands. The Russians too were a maritime presence and from a peace with France in mid-1807 their intentions were unclear. The Adriatic was a narrow sea, filled with innumerable sail, mainly trading *trabaccolos* but also numerous enemy – French, Venetian and Danish – and neutrals – Russian and American.

While their captain's orders were secret, Wilson and his fellows knew that intercepting strange sail might provide valuable intelligence, especially after reports that Russia was likely to declare war and activate a twenty-five-strong fleet near Trieste. 'Scarcely a vessel could pass us without our examining them, which made our favour courted and our sway dreaded':[15]

So ready was every individual at his station, and so confident was the First Lieutenant of every one's abilities and exertion that instead of saying hoist away this, that and the other sail, he had only to say two words – 'Make

Sail' – and in a few minutes the ship, from appearance as a naked tree would be as a cloud.[16]

In a salute to Jack's skills, Wilson composed a few lines (adding with due modesty, 'such as they are') that echo William Mowett, master of doggerel in the Jack Aubrey novels:

> *In stormy winds and rude boisterous gales*
> *Lofty ships are forced to carry low sails.*
> *But when the weather is mild and serene*
> *Then under all canvas they may be seen*
> *To do which, the Topmen act the chief part*
> *And boldly show the skilful seaman's art,*
> *While others, less competent to their charge*
> *On deck do haul upon the ropes at large.*[17]

But while *Unite*'s bronzed topmen revelled in their exertions under an Adriatic sun, an all-too-familiar vice was seen on the focsle where the older, less agile men worked the ropes. Campbell's biggest challenge was dealing with his ship's craving for alcohol.

Twice he addressed the company after floggings. It troubled him, he said, to have men beaten for weakness. 'You are now on an enemy's coast and who knows how soon our utmost exertions may be required to defend ourselves.' When next three men were found sprawled below, the company was again summoned and told: 'I shall punish the innocent with the guilty and make you all have 4-water grog.'

Reform came in part through action around Venice. *Unite* took three French brigs, along with numerous privateers, gunboats and *trabaccolos*. The crew were also active ashore, capturing an island fortress held by sixty French troops – which 'our party jocundly called going a-maying'.

By this point Campbell's methods had started to work. He praised the company and took eleven men off a black list of twenty-one regular drunks 'for their good conduct'. He cultivated the harder cases, like John Kelly – still a quarrelsome and disobedient fellow – with other measures of respect. When two fellow captains proposed that their three vessels share all prize money, he put it to a vote of the company. He sent money ashore from his own pocket to feed four hands captured in a prize, and because he did so without telling anyone, when the men came aboard again his standing grew all the greater.[18]

All the while, Robert Wilson noted these events in his diary, a form of extended log that he kept partly for himself, partly for a civilian couple, Mr and Mrs Thomas Tomkison, to whom he felt a deep obligation. The nature of this relationship is not known but Tomkison was a man of some influence and may indeed have been the Soho piano-maker of that name whose instruments were starting to find a place in fashionable London homes. Nothing at all is known of Wilson's background. He never spoke of his own family and was perhaps an orphan who had been schooled thanks to Tomkison. Among even the most educated hands, he stands out.

As for accuracy, his journal closely mirrors the ship's log while filling in the human spaces and adding details of individual fortunes – the suicide of William Fairbottom being just one. John Russell had his testicles ruptured in being struck by a midshipman, who was properly punished in return. Three men suffered terrible burns when a gun was accidentally discharged 'and lived about 15 minutes entreating with prayers and curses to be killed and put out of their misery'. Four more were seemingly lost while navigating a prize caught in a gale, but turned up months later, having been captured, escaped and 'travelled barefooted' from Naples to reach a neutral port.[19]

There was William Skill, who fell overboard and was drowned. Because Skill was a hopeless drunk, his fate was not unexpected. Yet, as Wilson noted, Skill had been among the unfortunates to have been pressed from an Indiaman in sight of home after three years away; and while he had sold all his possessions for grog, the gifts he had bought for his mother and sister in the East were found intact.[20]

There was William Thompson, reduced to a skeleton before dying of 'the venereal':

I am sorry to say I heard him exclaim 'Well, I'll get well soon, at any rate by the time we go again to Malta, and then I'll have another rattle at a b[itch] of a w[hore].'[21]

And there was John Kelly – the alcoholic nemesis of a messmate. A year after Fairbottom's suicide, and yet another flogging for intoxication, Kelly was entrusted with handling a prize. He and a fellow hand, espying an enemy *trabaccolo*, came up on her and brandished their muskets, intimidating eleven men into surrendering a vessel laden with food and guns.[22] As Wilson saw it, the captain's methods helped even wild creatures like Kelly find their way.

Valletta was *Unite*'s home port but visits were rare enough to give rise to riotous romps. At one Christmas feast, extra liquor was allowed on board and 'there was mirth, glee, there was dancing, singing, quarrelling, fighting and such an uproar fore and aft that if your life depended on it you could not make out a sentence that was said'.[23] Men were allowed ashore for twenty-four hours – in groups to discourage desertion – and received advances on prize money the day before sailing, for the same reason. They dined at inns and drank their full:

We lost one poor fellow by his falling from a high rampart and meeting instant death. For all our mad capers no other person was hurt, excepting [a] few who were wounded by Venus.[24]

Just how deeply Wilson immersed himself in these excesses is open to question. Among the sailors reeling around Valletta, few would have joined him in exploring the baroque cathedral of St John to assess its treasures – 'the noble and excellent scriptural paintings' – and to conclude in Baedeker form: 'In short, it is a church well worth a stranger's notice.'[25]

Wilson's uncommon abilities had been noted by his officers, but it took influence to raise anyone from the lower deck. In Valletta, in the summer of

1808, he was approached by Captain Nisbet Palmer of the brig *Alacrity*. Palmer, it transpired, was known to Thomas Tomkison in London, and once he saw that Wilson was every bit as bright as his mentor claimed, the twenty-two-year-old was offered a place on *Alacrity* as a midshipman.

Rejoining *Unite* for the last time after a spell on an untidy sloop, he wrote:

> It was like coming into a palace yard. Everyone on board [was] cleanly dressed, the seamen in white frocks and trousers and stockings and also white shoes with black riband for ties, black silk neck handkerchiefs and straw hats . . . Such a different sight to that we had just left.
>
> It was soon known among my shipmates that I was going to leave them. Give me leave to say that there was scarcely one who did not congratulate me, in their sailor-like manner.[26]

He left with the prospect of becoming an officer. Still in the Mediterranean a year later, he was promoted again, to acting second master. Yet nothing was as good after the *Unite* again; and another mystery hangs over his final months in a gun brig. Research by the editor of his journal suggests that a dispute among her officers had poisoned the air on *Confounder*. Off the island of Mykonos in 1811, Robert Wilson deserted and disappeared from history.[27]

As British naval power extended across the Mediterranean, Napoleon attempted to give battle by other means, to bring Britain to its knees through a European trade barrier known as the Continental System. It did more harm to his allies than his foe; British commerce stood up, then flourished. Trade and influence, soldiers and civilians continued to move across an expanding empire – and to the Eastern Seas in particular.

Which may account for why, after four years of humdrum merchant sailing off his native America, Jacob Nagle crossed the Atlantic again in 1806. A man who had seen the world always had difficulty settling; and for Nagle, memories of the Indies and Pacific were combined with a belief that at forty-five he was no longer liable to be pressed.

In Wapping the planet's diversity became accessible once more. A decade had passed since Nagle last signed on an Indiaman, the *Rose* to Calcutta, and while he gave no reason for doing so again, the combination of good pay and eastern ports where – he recalled – even sailors could enjoy 'a grand situation', probably did the trick. He joined the *Neptune*, one of a new class of Indiaman, at 1,492 tons almost twice the burden of the *Rose*, transporting 400 troops to Britain's newest possession, the Cape of Good Hope, seized from the Dutch to protect the passage to India. *Neptune*'s next destination was to be Penang, where she would take on betel nut and spices for Canton, then return home laden with tea.

No sooner had *Neptune* entered the Indian Ocean than she ran into trouble. In his thirty years at sea, 'I never saw so trimendious a gale,' Nagle wrote, 'though I had been round the Cape backwards and forwards five times':

> We kept hur before the wind during the night, our sails all being furled excepting the fore topmast staysail, to keep hur from broaching two, and the mainsail clewed up. We had about forty men on the mainsail yard, endeavouring to furl it, but it was in vain, therefore they ware call'd down. They ware scarcely down before the main yard gave way.
>
> A most trimendious see following us struck us in the stern and took both boats away as though they had been lashed with straw . . . All seamen and soldiers remained on deck during the night, expecting to meet our doom every minute.[28]

They survived but anchoring at Penang six weeks later, *Neptune* lost sixteen hands to a press gang.[29] Further turbulence awaited in Canton where drunken hands were involved in a brawl in which a Chinese official was killed, and the diplomatic fallout delayed their loading of a hugely valuable tea cargo for two months. Then, under sail for the Cape once more, the crew were infected with a 'white flux' that left scarce enough fit men to work the sails.

The ship's log tells its own story of a voyage lamented by everyone. Of her ninety-eight hands, just forty-three returned home. In addition to the sixteen pressed, ten died of the flux, including a mystery man, Julius Cesar, eleven deserted, seven volunteered for the Navy, and Bartholomew Richie fell from the maintop and was drowned.[30]

The sixteen taken at Penang may even have been thought the lucky ones – until *Neptune* reached the Cape. There it was learnt that the pressed men had been sent on the *Blenheim*, an old 74 homeward bound yet in no condition for any kind of voyage. She and the frigate *Java* had last been sighted in a gale midway across the Indian Ocean. No trace of them was ever found. Almost 900 men had died.[31]

Nagle at least had reason for a Wapping cruise. He landed in London after earning the fantastic sum of ten guineas in ten days for bringing *Neptune* up the Thames from the Downs – a third of his pay for all the dangers and hardships over the previous twenty-two months. While he was being paid off – and confronting the landlord at the White Swan who tried to cheat him – a second fleet of Indiamen was making ready to depart from Ceylon.

Among those who would be sailing with them was Robert Hay in *Culloden*.

———

Hay had been thirteen when he joined as a servant whose greatest desire was to ensure that 'no officer surpassed my master in a well-brushed coat, in the brilliancy of his shoes, and the neatness and order of his cabin'. The boy's reward was access to his officer's possessions, including a nautical almanac, a Hadley's quadrant and a chart of the Channel – and 'with what extasy did I survey these deeply interesting articles!'[32]

Hay was among the ship's most active boys, racing his friend Dennis O'Flanagan to the masthead. But it was on being placed under the tutelage of Jack Gillies that he grew. A warm-hearted Irishman, Gillies was the complete seaman – from knotting to steering, and gunnery to sail-making. 'He had learned, besides, to play on the German flute, to talk French with a tolerable degree of volubility and knew a dozen games of the cards.' His one gap was literacy. Ashore once, Gillies bought a book that caught his eye for its impressive size and presented it to Hay with an air of triumph. It was a legal manual and quite incomprehensible. On seeing his protégé's face fall, Gillies explained that he had chosen the book because 'she was the largest tonnage, and the best rigged craft in a fleet of about two hundred sail; but I had not the skill to open her hatches and examine the cargo'.[33]

Five years on, Gillies had drunk himself to death and Hay had come of age in the East Indies Squadron. From a boy 'Third Class', he was made part of the carpenter's crew.[34] His learning grew too, with the gift from another of his superiors of *Improvement of the Mind* by Isaac Watts, a philosophical tract that remained his most treasured possession. Having run away to sea to escape life as a weaver, Robert Hay acquired knowledge and skills it is hard to imagine would have come his way otherwise.

His empathy with India is striking, with views verging on the subversive. At Vellore in 1806, sepoy troops angered by a code of enforced hair-shaving turned on their British fellows in the Company's forces and killed 200 of them. The sepoys, in Hay's opinion, 'were fighting to restore their ancient laws and institutions, and wresting the patrimony of their ancestors from the greedy hands of violent, haughty and avaricious usurpers'.[35]

Still in *Culloden*, he had served two great officers, Collingwood and Pellew, now commander-in-chief of the East Indies. Early in 1809, the gallant old 74 was about to escort home a fleet of fifteen Indiamen, a voyage with a strategic element because they were carrying Bengal saltpetre, the purest form of gunpowder's principal ingredient. Hay was among thousands of hands joyfully anticipating a return home: 'We found ourselves dancing round the capstan to the tune of *Off She Goes*. Cheerily was our spreading canvas expanded. Unreluctantly were our last adieus uttered to the spicy groves of India.'[36]

The fleet had reached 23°S latitude on 14 March when strong squally breezes turned into hard gales and thick weather. That night, all hell descended.

The three-day hurricane shredded sails and carried off mastheads. Surging seas smashed boats and washed away the starboard quarter galley.[37] Topmen faced the ultimate test, climbing up and out onto the yards with the ship rising and pitching, to haul in the remaining canvas. From all around came an unearthly moaning, as if from the spirits of the departed. Hay wrote:

> Every succeeding wave as it approached us with its towering curling sumit whitened with foam, looked like a huge mountain with its top envelloped in snow threatening to overwhelm us. Several times were we thrown on our beam ends and in this terrific state remained a few secconds with no other prospect than that the succeeding billow would dash us headlong into the mighty abyss.[38]

All canvas had been hauled in bar a close-reefed main topsail, yet still they were scudding at 14 miles an hour. Seeing that Pellew was reluctant to endanger lives by ordering anyone aloft again, senior men came forward – and freed the sail to blow away into the darkness:

> The most steady, vigilant and experienced hands were placed at the helm to prevent her if possible broaching to. The rest of the hands were seen clinging to the rigging, masts and spars.

Word spread that they were near the latitude where *Blenheim* was last sighted, and a man in the maintop claimed to have seen storm petrels – Mother Carey's chickens. As superstition took hold, Hay wrote, Pellew 'laid aside all trappings of superiority' and went among the men:

> All was dread, consternation and terror, but in looking in [his] face, all was confidence and safety. Dressed in a short jacket, a pair of trowsers, a small hunting cap and without shoes or stockings he went about infusing courage and fortitude into all, but I verily believe that he himself, in his heart, thought all was over.[39]

Another night, and they must have foundered. Slowly though, late on the third day, the furies started to ease, giving way over another three days to high swells and steady breezes: but, the log noted, of the Indiamen there was no sight; and when they came in at Table Bay, four were still missing – *Calcutta, Bengal, Lady Jane Dundas* and *Jane Duchess of Gordon*.

That was not all. Just weeks earlier, another homeward-bound fleet of Indiamen had encountered an almost identical hurricane in which three ships, *Lord Nelson, Experiment* and *Glory*, disappeared. As time passed and no further word was heard, it became clear that storms had swallowed seven Indiamen and two navy ships in successive seasons in the Indian Ocean – an unprecedented loss.

Yet the hurricanes of 1808–09 brought passengers and seamen together too. As one lady put it: 'Those who spend their life on shore can have no idea of the activity, courage and presence of mind on board ship.'[40] On *Diana*, where the lower deck had been swamped, wiping out livestock and destroying the crew's possessions, the captain asked passengers to subscribe to a fund for their relief, 'and that it should be done not only out of humanity & consideration for the unparalleled exertions which they had made towards saving the ship but also as an act of policy to stimulate further exertions'. The appeal raised the impressive sum of £675, more than £10 for each man.[41]

What passed in the lost ships' final hours was and remains a mystery. We are left with the account of a rare survivor from another mid-ocean calamity:

> The people, who till this period had laboured as determined to conquer their difficulties without a murmur or without a fear, seeing their efforts useless, many of them burst into tears and wept like children . . . Some appeared perfectly resigned, went to their hammocks, and desired their messmates to lash them in; others were lashing themselves to gratings and small rafts; but the most predominant idea was that of putting on their best and cleanest clothes.[42]

Resignation at the last then, and a kind of dignity. Who lived and who died . . . it was down to caprice. Almost 500 souls had been lost with the Indiamen, along with 900 on the navy ships.

There was further whimsy. Nagle had noted how sixteen of his shipmates, survivors of one storm, had been pressed out of *Neptune* only to die in *Blenheim*. But ninety more men had been pressed from the seven Indiamen which were subsequently lost. A seemingly unkind fate had been their salvation.

Superstitious? Aye, with good reason.

21

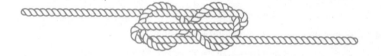

OLD FRIENDS, OLD FOES
1803-14

OF ALL Jack's foreign destinations the most favoured was a land of opportunity, conveniently located across the Atlantic. Its celebrated freedoms, common language and shared heritage have been noted before, but they made it, more than a mere destination, a sanctuary, a habitation even. No Britons had more ease of access to America than seamen: simply sign on a merchantman for Boston or Philadelphia, and step off weeks later into a new life. This vast, prosperous continent offered as much to hands with artisan skills – to carpenters, coopers and others – as to plain sailors. It welcomed them.

At a time of war, when the demand for manpower only increased, America's allure was an increasing challenge for the Admiralty. The seamen who had taken themselves off to ports like Boston were a source of exasperation for the British consul, who saw them as 'living in this Country under the Patronage of those whose Politics and principles are inimical to Great Britain'.[1] Relations between the two countries, never easy since the War of Independence, were getting a great deal worse.

At a time of rising hostility to impressment, campaigning pamphlets went to the heart of the matter: 'It was long foreseen that when the States of America should obtain their independence, our seamen would fly thither for shelter from the grasp of the Impress', declared one.[2] After a spate of attacks on press gangs in Yorkshire, another pamphlet pointed out: 'It is an incontrovertible fact that many of the best seamen, the boasted defenders of this happy country, are often induced to fly from it, in quest of an asylum in another country.'[3]

One pamphleteer's claim that 30,000 seamen had, in effect, fled Britain since 1793 appears to have been too high; but by a more tempered estimate about 10,000 had still migrated in one form or another to America by 1812.[4] Most were deserters from the Navy; and, as the authorities at home were wont to fume, they 'engage in commercial navigation where a similarity of language, usages and customs render it impracticable to trace their origin and impossible to recover their services to the mother country'.[5]

There was scant recognition of the Admiralty's own culpability in this respect – the mass demobilization of 1801 when St Vincent sent ashore more than 70,000 men without a care to their futures. The United States offered a convivial alternative. While the US Navy was still in its formative years, a booming seafaring economy provided berths for all abilities. Manning on American

New York in the 1760s. America became an increasingly appealing and convenient refuge for impressed men and deserters.

merchant vessels had surged from fewer than 10,000 before 1792 to 70,000 by 1810, many of whom were Britons.[6] America was where the leader of the *Temeraire* mutiny, James Fitzgerald, intended to seek asylum and obtain citizenship 'as soon as he was released from his bondage'. He was far from alone.

Mixed feelings were only natural in this complex transatlantic bond. We may recall the case of Joshua Davis from Boston who, during and after the War of Independence, changed sides at his own convenience and sang ballads to English and American glory with equal gusto, yet later urged American sailors to 'escape to your native country and finally get clear of these dens of horror'. Others who served in the navies of both, like James Durand and Samuel Leech, suggest that discipline was as tough and capricious in one as the other.[7] As ever, it came down to a ship's commander.

But one aspect of British naval life grated with all freethinking men like a barnacled hull on the skin. Impressment. And to citizens of a new country that worshipped its hard-win independence, it was intolerable.

Since the war's resumption in 1803, Britain had gone all piratical towards American vessels. The notional justification for intercepting them was to search for British deserters and contraband that might assist the French. On paper, the Admiralty accepted this should not happen in territorial waters and declared that American citizens would not be pressed. Who would be accepted as an American was a matter of dispute, however. Westminster held to a principle that once a British subject, always a British subject. On the other side of the Atlantic, citizenship was granted to anyone who had served two years in an American vessel; in New York citizenship papers could be bought for $2.[8]

In practice, paperwork mattered little. Abuses by press gangs were probably at their worst in the final years of the Napoleonic War when seamen were constantly being pressed out of American merchant ships. Why, it may be asked, was this the case when Trafalgar had sealed British naval supremacy? The answer is that the Navy was extended as never before in the realms it had to police, while at the same time supporting expeditionary forces being launched by the Army. Naval manpower only reached its ultimate peak of 147,087 seamen in 1813, yet even then there were ships with no crews.[9]

Meanwhile, official US records state, as many as 10,000 Americans had been impressed, some 6,250 of them in the previous five years.[10] In addition, an estimated 5,000 British subjects were taken off American vessels.[11]

One of the Americans was James Durand from Connecticut whose service for his country had decided him that its naval discipline was an outrage that 'ought not to be permitted by a government which boasts of liberty'.[12] (It appears that punishment could be just as severe in an American as a British vessel.) Durand joined a Swedish brig, which had just fulfilled a contract to carry British troops home from Spain when he was pressed off Plymouth in 1809. It was bad enough to lose £50 'and a chest full of excellent and well-chosen clothes'; but after all he had suffered in the US Navy, 'the thought of serving with the British fleet almost deprived me of reason'.[13] Serve in the frigate *Narcissus* he did, though, with twelve other pressed Americans; and she brought at least some benefit to this sensitive fellow because he preferred music to hard duty, and she had a band and a first-rate instructor. So, 'for three weeks while we chased French privateers, my chief work was blowing on a flute'.[14] By the time of his discharge, after seven years, he had learned the clarinet and violin as well; but transatlantic hostility remained intense and his memoir was chiefly intended as a tirade against 'those haughty British tyrants'.[*]

The allure of America's much-vaunted freedoms for British sailors had meanwhile been illustrated by the infamous case of the *Halifax* deserters. In the spring of 1807, dozens of men ran from at least six navy ships in American waters, some while on shore leave, some by swimming, and in the case of five men from the sloop *Halifax* by overpowering a midshipman and seizing a jolly boat. One, Jenkin Ratford, was spotted ashore by his captain and on being challenged replied that 'he was damned if he should return to the ship; that he was in the Land of Liberty; and that I had no business with him'.[15]

Soon afterwards intelligence was received that some of the *Halifax* deserters had enlisted on the US frigate *Chesapeake*. She was intercepted by the 50-gun

---

[*] Brooks, p. 75. Durand might be dismissed as more a propagandist than historical source, but Admiralty records confirm that he was pressed into the *Narcissus* on 9 September 1809. He is listed as James During of Baltimore, rated Able, aged 22 (ADM 37/2439).

Leopard and when the American captain refused to muster his hands, *Leopard* opened fire without warning. Four men died on *Chesapeake*. Jenkin Ratford, dragged from hiding below, was among four others detained as deserters. He was hanged.

Recriminations flew. The guns had been fired in American waters and the British government was eventually obliged to apologize. It still did nothing to curb impressment.

———

Not all Americans served in British ships under duress, including presumably at least some of the 373 who were at Trafalgar. Jacob Nagle had spent far the greater part of his maritime life in a variety of British merchant and naval vessels – smartly eluding the press on all but one occasion – and, as he had returned yet again to England after a spell back in America, it may even be assumed he preferred British conditions.

Like any complete hand, though, Nagle would pick and choose, being able to assess a ship before signing on, not only her mood but whither she was bound and what options awaited him there. Returning from China in 1808, he began years in the Atlantic trade, shipping from either Liverpool or Greenock for the Caribbean or America, manufactured goods outward, raw materials like mahogany and cotton home. It was exceptionally hard sailing, small crews of a dozen men handling vessels of 300 tons (the merchants did like value for their money), but Nagle earned around 27 shillings a week, almost four times naval pay, and if anything was not to his liking, or a better proposition came his way, he simply jumped ship.

Nagle was forty-six, weathered by life's storms, the loss of his wife and children especially. His journal shows it. No longer do we hear of escapades, of frolics ashore with hussies like Liddy. More common are stories of confrontation. A fraught Atlantic crossing in the *Highlander* had, as his editor pointed out, overtones of a Joseph Conrad story, with a sick captain and a dangerous crew.[16] A pair of toughs, one Danish, one German, got drunk, 'walked the deck and begin to curse and swear that they could kill the whole ships company'. Hearing the racket above, a sober Nagle came up and knocked them down.[17]

The hardened old hand was also at pains to point out the respect that he expected, and received, from those notionally his superiors. It helped that the atmosphere on these small, tightly manned vessels was informal enough for him to be invited to drink in the captain's cabin. On the 20-gun *Caledonia*, a letter of marque, he was permitted as the sole American hand to fire the guns on 4 July. Such intimacy allowed of behaviour unthinkable in a navy ship. He represented *Highlander*'s crew in a pay dispute with her owner and – because they held the upper hand in delivering her cargo – won the day. And when he thought the *Caledonia*'s chief mate was coming it high, Nagle took him aside and warned: 'I swear to you if ever you lift a hand to me, we will both go overboard together.'[18]

In 1811 he joined a Baltimore sloop, *Griffin*, bound for Rio with flour. She was low built for close coastal work – good for smuggling, Nagle observed – with the advantage that bonito soaring out of the sea in pursuit of flying fish would hit the sails and fall to the deck, providing daily fresh rations. Less palatable was the pompous supercargo, the owner's representative and therefore a figure of authority, who 'did not like to put his bum over the stern' and was seen shitting into a bucket used by the cook. Retribution came in the form of a wave that poured over the stern and swept the supercargo down into the cabin, leaving him:

> . . . pufing and blowing like a porpose up to his middel in water, crying out for help . . . we ware all ready to die a laughing.[19]

But Nagle was slowing down. On another recent voyage, while manning the helm through a bitter season, his hands and feet had been severely frostbitten. Now, on arriving in Rio, he was laid low with 'a severe cold I had got in my loines . . . and was sent to the English Hospittle'. By the time of his discharge, *Griffin* had sailed. In the normal course of events he would have had no difficulty finding a new berth as South America had become a favoured destination for British and American trade; just then, however, a conflict started that would disrupt Atlantic shipping and strand Nagle in Brazil.

In one respect he was fortunate. Born an American yet an indefatigable servant of Britain, he was spared having to choose between his two lands at a time of war.

———

Pressing American seamen had raised tension to an unprecedented level. The actual *casus belli* of 1812, however, was the related interference with American trade – the seizure of hundreds of merchant vessels destined for European ports which were thought likely to benefit the enemy. In June, Congress voted for war. An invasion of Canada a month later started it; but the next phase was a conflict at sea.

The polemics that subsequently dominated accounts on either side of the Atlantic need not detain us: in Britain, baffled fury at three successive frigate defeats gave way to haughty dismissal of what were termed irrelevant side-shows; in America, these unexpected victories against the world's supreme maritime power became, in the words of a prominent US naval historian, 'an important part of American patriotic culture'.[20] They were also subject to triumphalist hyperbole. For those at the guns, it was more complex. Rather than the usual nationalistic pride, one first-hand account reflects a rare state of confusion.

Samuel Leech was a rare case in more ways than one – a delicate English boy who hated everything about naval life yet fought on both sides, who owned up to being terrified in battle while admiring his shipmates' bravery. His memoir is another curiosity, evangelical, sometimes priggish, and patently directed at an American audience, but with observations – a number have been used here – both expressive and pertinent.[21]

Why, it may be asked, had a lad of twelve so unsuited to the life gone to sea at all? The answer is family interest. His father had been valet to Lord William Fitzroy, a naval captain, his mother was maid to the wife of Lord Spencer, a First Lord, and these connections, along with his own service as a boy in the gardens of Blenheim Palace, were expected to carry Leech to the quarterdeck. He came on board Fitzroy's frigate, *Macedonian*, 'in a complete suit of sailor apparel; a tarpaulin hat, round blue jacket and wide pantaloons'.[22]

Leech's quarterdeck airs were knocked out of him soon enough. He was tyrannized by those 'minions of power', the mids, and for his own sake had to be removed from a mess after being bullied by 'a gruff old bulldog' named Hudson. Leech learned to keep his head down, and acquired respect for the 'jocularity, pleasantry, humour and good feeling' of plain tars. But he recoiled from their profanity, and from 'the obnoxious discipline of the British navy' (for the log shows that Captain Fitzroy was an ardent flogger).[23] As recognition dawned that his interest counted for nothing here, that his best hope lay in being made servant to the surgeon, Leech cursed his decision 'to quit the quiet scenes of a native village for the noisy, profane atmosphere' of a navy ship.[*]

Rumours of war were already in the air when *Macedonian* was ordered to America, now under Captain John Surman Carden. She had thirteen American hands, some recently pressed in Portugal, and there is no reason to doubt Leech's assertion that they expressed openly their reluctance to bear arms.[24] One of them, John Card, he wrote, had gone to the captain to state his objections. Card was ordered below with a warning that he would be shot if he said another word.[25]

At dawn near the Azores on 25 October a cry went up. A large frigate lay in the north:

> Our men were all in good spirits; though they did not scruple to express the wish that the coming foe was a Frenchman rather than a Yankee. We had been told by the Americans that frigates in the American service carried more and heavier metal than ours. This, together with a consciousness of our superiority over the French, led us to a preference for a French antagonist.[26]

---

[*] Leech, p. 25. Leech's home village was Bladen, near Blenheim Palace, where he lived with his mother. The church where they worshipped, St Martin's, is the burial place of Sir Winston Churchill.

But an American she was, the *United States*, and she did indeed carry more and heavier metal – forty-four guns against *Macedonian*'s thirty-eight, with an advantage of 24-pounders over 18-pounders. Leech was on the main deck, a powder monkey, when he heard 'a strange noise, like the tearing of sails, just over our heads'.

That wind of enemy shot presaged hell:

> It was like some awful, tremendous thunderstorm whose deafening roar is attended by incessant streaks of lightning carrying death in every flash and strewing the ground with the victims of its wrath . . . I was busily supplying my gun with powder when I saw blood suddenly fly from the arm of a man stationed at our gun. I saw nothing strike him; the effect alone was visible . . .
>
> A man named Aldrich had had one of his hands cut off by a shot and almost at the same moment he received another shot, which tore open his bowels. As he fell, two or three men caught him in their arms and, as he could not live, threw him overboard.[27]

Men cheered, Leech noted, as if by instinct. 'I cheered with them, though I confess I scarcely knew for what.' Flight was not a possibility. 'What could we do but keep up a semblance of animation?' And so men became 'like tigers . . . pulled off their jackets and vests and fought like heroes'. As for Leech, 'I thought a great deal of the other world and repeated again and again the Lord's prayer.' It went on for two hours, until an order was passed to cease fire, when 'a profound silence ensued, broken only by the stifled groans of the brave sufferers'.[28]

The *Macedonian* had struck, her rigging shredded, masts toppled and sides pulverized by superior firepower. Thirty-six men were dead – among them the American protester John Card, killed by his own countrymen – and sixty-eight wounded, a severe toll for a frigate action. One man picked up the body of a shipmate and bore it to the side, weeping:

'O Bill, we have sailed together in a number of ships, we have been in many gales and some battles, but this is the worst day I have seen! We must now part!' Here he dropped the body into the deep, and then, a fresh torrent of tears streaming over his weather-beaten face, he added, 'I can do no more for you. Farewell! God be with you!'[29]

Macedonian's surrender was the second of three consecutive frigate defeats that year, a sequence of events unprecedented in British seafaring memory. The newspapers responded accordingly. 'Every individual in the country must feel humiliated at this succession of disasters which mock and render nugatory our boasted naval superiority,' raged the *Morning Chronicle*.[30] In the Commons, George Canning lamented: 'The sacred spell of the invincibility of the British navy [has been] broken.'[31]

For many years historians on either side of the Atlantic tended to their respective nationalisms; William James ascribed the Americans' success in part to the valour and ability of their British volunteers. The simple fact was that the American ships were larger and far more powerful than their opponents. There was no humiliation in the defeats of 1812.

And, according to Leech, the British prisoners harboured no recriminations. They felt themselves kindly used by their American captors and messed with them. As the two frigates sailed in company for Newport, 'all idea that we had been trying to shoot out each others' brains so shortly before seemed forgotten. We ate together, drank together, joked, sung, laughed, told yarns; in short, a perfect union of ideas, feelings, and purposes, seemed to exist among all hands.'[32]

Such was their common feeling that Leech had few qualms about going over to the enemy. Or so it appears. Many years had passed when he wrote a memoir that was, after all, directed at an American readership. Even so, his devoutness urged him to tell the truth as he saw it. The boyish gardener at Blenheim, abandoned by his aristocratic connections, had found equality and humanity in the New World.

Leech was seventeen when he landed on American soil, 'to my unspeakable delight', and – freed from 'the obnoxious discipline of the British Navy' –

joined the US Navy.[33] He was far from the only former Macedonian to change sides. Some joined the US Army:

> Others of our crew shipped and wandered in every direction; some in men of war, some in merchant vessels; some, fearful of the risk of being retaken, settled ashore . . . It was usual for our men to assume new names, and to hail from some American port on shipping in an American vessel . . . It would be an interesting task, were it possible, to trace all the results of that victory.[34]

Leech was fearful of the risks himself. Joining the US brig *Syren*, he grew his hair so it fell around his face, but crossing the Atlantic to Angola 'we had to run the gauntlet through English cruisers that hovered about like birds of prey' and he became so petrified that 'more than once I determined to run away and find a refuge among the Africans'.[35]

He was a lucky lad really. When the *Syren* was taken by the 74-gun *Medway* in July 1814 he escaped identification. Prisoners were removed to the Cape of Good Hope and a walled castle below Table Mountain which, with a sunny climate and fresh vittles, must have been among the most benign places of captivity anywhere in the world. No weevil-infested biscuit here; the worst that could be said was that the beef was 'poor, lean stuff'. The mutton, though, was excellent and the oranges 'the best in the world'.[36]

Leech was still there when Britain and the United States agreed peace early in 1815.

22

PASSAGES TO WATERLOO
1809-15

THE war's final years took some of the wind out of Jack's sails. Not that he became any the less active; quite the reverse. But the days of high glory had passed. Fighting was now largely done ashore, while the Navy's energies turned to blockading and convoying. It became the Army's amphibious ally – transporting regiments and maintaining supply lines to ensure that what eventually amounted to 420,000 soldiers and civilians across the seas were fed and equipped.[1] While naval ships were their guardians, a vast array of merchant vessels chartered by the Transport Board also joined the chain running to Portugal and Spain.

Seamen's memoirs and diaries fall relatively silent on this demanding yet less dramatic period of service. Jack Nastyface, who related his Trafalgar yarns with relish, had little to say about blockading, or 'Channel groping' as he called it, and dismissed a major expedition to support the Duke of Wellington in Portugal as no more than 'a tedious voyage'.[2] Back from India, Robert Hay dealt briefly with scouting Biscay and disrupting enemy trade in the frigate *Amethyst* before she was driven ashore in Plymouth Sound in 1811 and wrecked.

The exception was a gnarled Yorkshireman. William Richardson had come a long way since his haunting experiences on the slaveship *Spy*. He had shifted between navy and merchant vessels, surviving scurvy, hurricanes and two ship-wrecks. He knew all about being pressed. The first time he retained his compo-sure – 'I was young, did not care much and was willing to go to any part of the world' – although when it happened again, in Calcutta, and he lost all his clothes into the bargain, he did 'begin to despond'.[3] In between he returned home to South Shields, finding it much changed by years of war. 'Everyone looked gloomy and sad on account of nearly all the young men being pressed and taken away.' He married Sarah Thompson, daughter of a Portsea stone-mason and a lass plucky enough to sail with him to the West Indies. She came down with a fever and nearly died, but Mrs Richardson was among that rare species, a sailor's wife who followed her man to sea.

In 1805 Richardson was made gunner on the *Caesar*, the defining moment of his service. As befitted her name, she was an innovative and rather magnifi-cent creation: the first 80-gun two-decker, with 32-pounders on the lower deck and 24-pounders on the upper, a combination that gave her a firepower almost equivalent to a three-deck 98.[4] In his youth Richardson had rejoiced in the maintop: 'Lofty masts and square yards appeared wonderful to me, [and] we had plenty of exercise.' Now thirty-seven, he bore a far larger responsibility on a ship he loved with a mighty tenderness. Her one fault was that she rolled much, but once trimmed by the stern she did not plunge so and could outstrip any other line of battle ship.[5]

Their first action was the Battle of Cape Ortegal, where Captain Richard Strachan, 'Mad Dog' as he was known by the Caesars, set the seal on Nelson's triumph at Trafalgar a few weeks earlier, taking four French ships of the line. Richardson, commanding the guns, had the satisfaction of having 'peppered them well'.

Their final action was also the last major battle of the war.

Early in 1809, *Caesar* was off Rochefort when a French fleet was sighted coming down the coast from Brest to join a squadron at anchor in Basque Roads. *Caesar*, pursuing the rearmost vessels, blasted two frigates which were driven ashore and wrecked. The rest of the Channel Fleet arrived and, rather than simply resort to blockade, plans were laid to beard the enemy in his den.

The strategy that evolved, for fireships to go in under the batteries and set enemy vessels ablaze, was innovative and controversial: anyone captured on a fireship was bound to be executed, so notes were sent around inviting volunteers. It was divisive too: Thomas Cochrane, who was to lead the attack, spoke enthusiastically of 'using terrorism against the enemy'. Lord Gambier, the commander, declared it 'a horrible mode of warfare'.[6]

These opinions, and their echoes with modern conflict, were interestingly reflected by two men of the lower deck. Richardson had no qualms about terrorizing the foe. As the *Caesar*'s gunner, he was supervising the creation of a weapon new in naval warfare – loading a captured French *chasse-marée* with thirty-six barrels of gunpowder, each weighing 90 pounds. This floating bomb was to precede the fireships under the batteries and be detonated 'to put the enemy into confusion'.[7]

On the *Revenge*, however, one hand was appalled. While Jack Nastyface often sounded like a surly misanthrope, he believed that 'if the idea had been carried to its full extent we should not only have burnt their shipping but also the crews in them':

> And though it were an enemy, yet the thought is shuddering, that nearly ten thousand men, whilst they were harmlessly asleep in their hammocks, might be roasted to death, and perhaps without a moment to say 'Lord have mercy upon me!'[8]

At nightfall on 11 April, Cochrane led them in. He was delighted with Richardson's handiwork – an explosion that created 'one of the grandest artificial spectacles imaginable . . . the sky red with lurid glare . . . the sea convulsed as by an earthquake'.[9] The fireships followed. Most of the French were frightened into cutting their cables and drifted ashore.

Gambier's follow-up was less impressive. With the French at his mercy, he hesitated long enough for most of the stranded ships to be taken off. When he did go in, *Caesar* ran aground; and with 'shots and shells flying about us' Richardson and his shipmates gave thanks for nightfall. At dawn, having turned thirty tons of water overboard and run the after guns forward, they got her off.

Four French ships of the line were destroyed, including one that started to burn then exploded in another fireball near *Caesar*. 'Everything went upwards with such a field of red fire as illuminated the whole elements,' wrote Richardson.[10] On *Revenge*, Jack Nastyface observed wryly: 'No gala night at Ranelagh or Vauxhall could be compared to it.'[11]

The Battle of Basque Roads was acclaimed as another Trafalgar, until recognition dawned that it counted more as a missed opportunity. As a symbol of French capitulation at sea, however, it could not have been more emphatic; and British casualties were remarkably light. Richardson had concerns for a messmate, Jack Ellis, who volunteered for a fireship and had last been seen when it was swept ashore; Ellis, it seemed, must have been executed.

Years later, Richardson ran into him walking out on Portsea. Over a few tankards Ellis related that he had been repeatedly interrogated by the French, but never tortured, and stuck to his denial of having been in a fireship. As a result he had spent five years a prisoner and on coming home received his pay in full, plus prize money. He now belonged to a merchant vessel and was doing very nicely, thankee.[12]

Richardson meanwhile had stayed in *Caesar*. As part of the Channel Fleet, she joined various expeditions to launch British troops abroad. The first of these amphibious operations, to Walcheren, was a calamity. On the Iberian Peninsula, however, the tide had turned.

The rise of Britain's soldiers to a status near that of her sailors came slowly and agonizingly. But once Wellington started to advance in earnest from Portugal in 1812, the tide turned dramatically, from Ciudad Rodrigo to Badajoz, from Salamanca to Vitoria. The passage to Waterloo was accompanied, naturally, by strains of rivalry. Anecdotal accounts suggest that brawls between soldiers and sailors were common when both were closely confined at sea. Seamen were held to be mainly at fault, 'being on their own element [and] likely to be aggressive'.[13] More surprising is some evidence of mutual respect.

The Walcheren expedition showed Richardson and his shipmates how wretched military service could be. The mission began with high expectations in July 1809 – 58 men-of-war among 235 armed vessels carrying an army of 44,000 to the Scheldt estuary in Holland. 'Such a fleet and army had never left Great Britain before,' Richardson wrote, and on a fine day *Caesar* landed horses and men safely in flat-bottomed craft. 'It was a grand sight . . . so many heroes in boats extending for miles dashing along to meet their enemies on a foreign shore.'[14] In two weeks the troops occupied Flushing. Soon afterwards the first signs of 'Walcheren fever' were noted. The marshy island was seething with disease and by the time the military were evacuated, some 4,000 men had died, just 218 of them in combat, and 10,000 were ailing.[15] Naval losses were minimal, while Richardson in his rank as gunner had savoured at least one good dinner at a tavern ashore 'with claret included' for two shillings.

Once sent to join battle a British soldier was far more likely to die than his seafaring counterpart – a fact that became ever clearer during the Peninsular campaign. So, perhaps, did a common respect. Of his last voyage in *Revenge*, Jack Nastyface wrote of a stormy three-week crossing of Biscay, which:

> . . . with contrary winds and a heavy swell of sea . . . was a distressing time for the poor soldiers and their wives, who were unaccustomed to such tossing and tumbling about.[16]

Among those rolling in *Revenge*'s lee scuppers was Private William Wheeler of the Royal Surrey Militia. Wheeler's opinion of seafaring tacked as swiftly as a frigate. He had been on the Walcheren expedition and was initially captivated by the efficiency of hands at work. 'Our cutter skimmed over the waves like a seagull,' he wrote. 'I would have given the world to have been a sailor.'[17] Observing discipline on *L'Impetueux* changed all that. 'I am satisfied with the choice I made . . . What a difference is there in the treatment of men on board this ship compared to our Regiment ... I will always stop my ears when "Britons never shall be slaves" is sung.'[18]

Now, on the *Revenge*, a happy ship run with a light hand, Wheeler could appreciate again the skills displayed in a storm and 'the awful grandeur of a line of battle ship in a heavy gale rising as it were from the bottom of the deep'.[19] And how, once the gale had passed, an air of easy companionship fell on the ship:

> Two evenings each week is devoted to amusement, then the Boatswain's mates with their pipes summon 'All hands to play'. The crew instantly distribute themselves, some dancing to a fiddle, some to a fife. Those who are fond of the marvellous, group together between two guns and listen to some frightful tale of Ghost and gobblin, another party listens to some weatherbeaten tar who 'spins a yarn' of past events, until his hearers' sides are almost cracked with laughter . . . Thus my time is passed in the midst of health, pleasure and contentment.[20]

On landing at the Tagus he reflected: 'If we were pleased to get on land again, we could not [be] without feelings of sorrow at parting from men who had deprived themselves of many comforts to add to ours.'[21] Wheeler went ashore, starting a march that took him to Waterloo.

Meanwhile, two men at anchor that day in Lisbon were about to set homeward on their final voyages.

Jack Nastyface came ashore from the *Revenge* at Portsmouth in the spring of 1811. He had taken little pleasure in his trade and recent demotion to Landsman had been a humiliation. At this point he deserted and made his way back home to Surrey where he married and picked up the family shoemaking trade he had once disdained.[22] It was discovery of the booming print industry that transformed his life, however. Setting up shop as a news vendor and stationer proved so successful that the Robinsons moved to Cheapside in London. Here, more than twenty years after leaving the sea, he began the memoir which – having turned to publishing – he produced at just the right time to cash in on the status of his former shipmates and, in shaking an angry fist at the naval establishment, provide grist to the mill of a burgeoning reform movement. Moreover, at 3s 6d a copy, *Nautical Economy or Forecastle Reflections* attracted considerable publicity and proved a handsome earner for a man who had once received a similar amount for a week's work at sea.

William Richardson, on the other hand, had no desire to leave his old ship. But the *Caesar* was done for: her innovative design, loading eighty guns across just two decks, had stretched her timbers beyond endurance; and he mourned. 'She never went to sea after this, being completely worn out.'[23] Rather than find another ship, he stayed with her, so they were at rest together at Hamoaze – she used as a store ship, he living on board as a guard.

Richardson was still there when news came of Waterloo. And he was at least granted a glimpse of the objective for which Jack too had fought and died:

This was on July 27, 1815; and in passing through [Plymouth] Sound on board a sloop we went close past the stern of the *Bellerophon*, she having Bonaparte a prisoner on board. Several French officers were on her poop, but whether Bonaparte was among them or not we could not tell.[24]

Richardson never really left the sea. He kept a small boat which he called 'my hobby-horse', sailing the coast around Portsmouth into his sixties, and as friends joked that he would be buried in it, his wife Sarah appears to have seen little more of him after the war than during it. When she died, an acquaintance wrote, Richardson 'took down his bedstead and slung a hammock in his bedroom for the rest of his life'.[25]

Jack's contribution to Wellington's hard-won victories was acknowledged by the Iron Duke himself. 'If anyone wishes to know the history of this war,' he said, 'I will tell them that it is our maritime superiority that gives me the power of maintaining my army while the enemy is unable to do so.'[26] That opinion was echoed by one of his Prussian allies at Waterloo, Field-Marshal August von

Gneisenau, who, having declared it was Napoleon's folly that had 'raised England's greatness, security and wealth so high', concluded:

> They are lords of the sea and neither in this dominion nor in world trade have they any rivals left.[27]

The wars that had spanned twenty-two years are estimated to have cost the lives of about 103,660 British naval personnel. By far the largest proportion – 84,440, or 81 per cent – had died of disease or in accidents. Some 12,680, or 12 per cent, perished in wrecks, founderings or fires. Just 6,540, or 6 per cent, were killed in action. (In the Seven Years War of 1756–63, the Navy had 1,512 men killed in battle.)[28]

One pair of statistics is illuminating. The six major battles that established naval supremacy once and for all cost 1,483 lives.*

That compares with the events of Christmas Day in 1811 when the *St George* and the *Defence* were wrecked off the coast of Denmark. Just sixteen men reached the shore alive, whereas 1,380 died.[29] In the wars between 1793 and 1815, 215 British ships were lost in action and 388 in wrecks.[30]

Any suggestion that impressment diminished towards the end is challenged by the testimony of Captain Anselm Griffiths of the *Leonidas* frigate, who as late as 1811 wrote:

> By far the larger portion of a ship's company are there against their consent. Many are impressed and forcibly brought; others enter because if they do not, they will be impressed, and although they are cheerful and apparently contented, still there is that difference between them and the officers; the latter are there by choice.[31]

The question of how many of her seafarers Briton had lost by desertion must be left open. A great many, tens of thousands, had run at one point, only to

---

* Lloyd, p. 239, and Lewis, p. 362. The six battles were the First of June (1794), Cape St Vincent (1797), Camperdown (1797), the Nile (1798), Copenhagen (1801) and Trafalgar (1805).

sign on again in another guise or be impressed. Probably 10,000 but perhaps up to 20,000 had migrated to America.[32]

Another category of hands only started to reappear after the peace. Prisoners had once been exchanged, but the Revolution put a stop to that so at the end of the war men were arriving home after years in captivity. Common wisdom held that they must have been treated brutally. In fact, the lot of Britons in France was generally far better than the tens of thousands of Frenchmen confined on prison hulks in Britain. Louis Garneray's account of a brutal captivity on the *Crown* and the *Vengeance* has more than a whiff of melodrama, but conditions on these ghastly floating dungeons were certainly worse than French prisons.

Among the Britons to relate their experiences of captivity, two men stand out.

James Choyce was sixteen when he joined a vessel of the British Southern Whale Fishery. A Londoner, he had been on an oil-rich hunt off the Galapagos islands in 1797 when the crew took their fiddles ashore at Paita in what is now Peru 'for a frolic'. There, discovering that England and Spain were at war, they were taken prisoner.

Eleven years later, after a list of escapades astonishing if even only half of them were true – including various escapes, service under the flags of Spain and France, turns as a pirate and constant changes of identity – Choyce found himself on the coast of Brittany. He and another Englishman named Gilbert Watts spotted a fishing boat at the waterside and, as darkness fell, paddled out to the British blockading squadron. As dawn came up they were taken on the 74-gun *Theseus*. Mercifully, no one knew them to be traitors.

Choyce's survivalist cunning had been forged in an edgy world. The Spanish colonies of Chile, Peru and Ecuador where he spent his first four years a prisoner were lands of deserts and mountains, of blistering heat and snowy altitudes, of mud churches and goat stewed in chillies. The conditions of captivity were loose, to say the least, and Jack was able to parley his practical skills into trading. In Lima, Choyce and his fellows made straw hats and were permitted to sell them by the viceroy, an old Irishman he called Ambrose O'Hagan, thanks to whom 'we could live very comfortably'.*

Most prisoners became heroic consumers of the local *aguardiente* and were at liberty to parade around singing 'God Save the King' on mad old George's birthday. The most discomforting aspect of life was the abuse they received from the Catholic inhabitants, as 'Jews and infidels'.

They were certainly better off than their wretched families at home. Choyce's *Lydia* was just one of nine whalers seized by the Spaniards off Chile that year with 200 men whose wives, it was said, not knowing whether they were alive or dead, were 'left destitute and from their poverty open to second marriage or seduction'.[33]

Choyce led four escape attempts. All failed, he claimed, because of his fellows' thirst for *aguardiente*. 'For the first time,' he added in a voice that might have echoed one of their officers, 'I found what an unruly set of beings sailors are when under no control.'[34] Then, in 1800, they were taken to Valparaiso and set at liberty.[35]

Choyce's experiences bring to mind those in Patagonia sixty years earlier of Samuel Cooper, a survivor of the Anson expedition. The crucial difference was how British seafarers had made internationalists of themselves. Even in enemy waters, they could find a berth and take themselves to other seas. Choyce learned Spanish and worked the Pacific coast from Chile to Ecuador.

He started to live dangerously. With a band of other former prisoners he seized a local brig with the aim of sailing it home. Between his shortcomings as a navigator and his shipmates' drunkenness they were fortunate in being captured by an English letter of marque – only to be taken in turn by a Spaniard. Released on parole in Panama, Choyce was sent on a Royal Navy frigate, the *Melampus* – thus coming under the command of Graham Moore,

* Choyce, p. 37. This is plainly Ambrosio O'Higgins, the son of tenant farmers from County Sligo, who had joined the Spanish colonial service in 1770 and ended his life in Lima as the 1st Marquess of Osorno. His illegitimate son, Bernardo O'Higgins, began the long war against Spanish rule to liberate Chile, founding as an instrument of that struggle a navy, commanded by Lord Cochrane and staffed by British officers

the beau ideal of frigate captains. Choyce, however, saw himself as a victim of impressment, and deserted off Vera Cruz.

Years of surviving at the edge had shorn him of national pride, but it was after falling into French hands that Choyce really crossed the line. In 1804, back in the Atlantic, he was on a whaler captured by a French privateer and landed at Bayonne where 'I disowned the name of an Englishman, as it had always been unlucky to me'. Having assumed a Spanish identity, and being 'tired of loyalty and sick of prison', it was a relatively easy step to ask 'to enter the French navy'.[36]

Which was how he came to be in Lorient in 1808, conveniently placed on the Brittany coast and with a British squadron a few miles offshore. While one moment justifying himself in eyebrow-raising terms – 'who would not fight for so good a master as Buonaparte?' – in the next he was planning his escape.[37] So it was that on 28 June the traitor James Choyce was welcomed up the side of *Theseus* and rejoined His Majesty's Navy. This time he stayed long enough to serve at the Battle of Basque Roads but no sooner had he returned to England than he ran once again.

Whether Choyce coloured his fantastic story is hard to say. But the main facts as he wrote them are confirmed by Admiralty records, with matching dates. He used an alias, James Lyons, when taken on *Melampus* and is shown to have deserted seven months later.[38] After rowing out to *Theseus* he returned to his real name, while naturally concealing his treachery. The muster states that James Choyce and Gilbert Watts came on board off Lorient after escaping 'from a French Prison' on 29 June 1808.[39] For a combination of cunning, determination and daredevilry, few Jacks could have matched James Choyce, and in the candour of his journal, he is unique. Had he been more gifted with words, his would have been an inimitable account.[*] As it is, for a vivid picture of captivity in France we turn to the diary of John Wetherell.

---

[*] Choyce's narrative was not published during his lifetime. The manuscript was found at a lodging house in Brighton where he died in 1836 and published more than fifty years later under the title *The Log of a Jack Tar*.

Wetherell, it may be recalled, had embarked from his native Whitby in 1803 on a well-paid merchantman post only to be pressed into the *Hussar* and, within a year, shipwrecked and imprisoned in France. Eleven years had passed when he next saw home.

Everywhere a prisoner went in those days, he walked. So to reach a prison in the Ardennes from Brest, Wetherell and his shipmates marched 700 miles across France. It took eight weeks, through snow in the depths of winter, each night billeted in barracks or warehouses. Clean straw was a luxury. But for frequent acts of kindness, gifts of food and clothing thanks to the 'charity and humanity' of French civilians, many would have died. In one town 'the peasants gave us good entertainment . . . and we drank like mayors'. Of the 306 sailors who came ashore from the wreck, thirty-six still fell by the wayside. Wetherell himself struggled with acute pain from an old wound – a ball in his hip. Yet they reached their prison at Givet in comparatively good order.[40]

The first year was the worst. With sixteen men to a cell, they were as cramped as on a lower deck and equally susceptible to disease. A putrid fever carried off more than 800 men, another fifty-seven of Wetherell's shipmates among them. Hopes of a prisoner exchange rose and fell, 'and some took it to heart so they died'. It was almost out of despair, to keep himself occupied, that Wetherell started a diary.

Gradually, as year followed year, the 2,000 captives at Givet were drawn into local life. It started with employment. As usual their skills proved useful. 'Some made shoes and straw hats for sale,' Wetherell wrote, 'others got work from the people in town, shoemakers, taylors, button makers and chair bottomers.'[41] When harvest in the Ardennes brought apples, pears and potatoes to market, prisoners were allowed out to spend their earnings; and 'several blooming girls, were verry free with us'. Letters from home were also permitted. In 1809, after five years, Wetherell was able to send a letter entitling his mother to part of his pay, and to remit the rest to him through a Paris bank.[42]

As more years passed, 'we began to think it was folly to think of ever being released'. But reading helped, and once books started to come from England 'Givet Prison became Givet University'. In 1810 Wetherell wrote:

> We have become great politicians and pay great attention to the various revolutions and overturns in Europe. We are like some of the old barbars or tavern keepers that can give all the particulars of two contending armies or fleets with more punctuality than those who had been eye witness.[43]

He bought a violin for six francs, other prisoners followed, and in time 'we mustered a complete band of 24 . . . and made such progress in this delightful amusement that in a few months we could perform some verry grand pieces . . . marches, rondeaus, waltzes'.[44] The band was invited to perform in the local church and it is clear from his frequent references to music that it became Wetherell's sheet anchor.

C. S. Forester, the author of the Hornblower novels who edited the diary, believed that for food and accommodation Wetherell and his fellows were better off than in a man-of-war.[45] But Forester did not trust all his stories. One in particular does smack of an old sailor's confection. Wetherell related how a group of English hands were summoned to convey a boat with Napoleon and his wife across the Meuse, and that one forward young fellow expressed a desire for a sniff from the imperial snuffbox, whereupon it was offered to them all: 'Here,' says the Emperor, 'take each of you a snuff.'[46]

Late in 1813, following Napoleon's disastrous retreat from Moscow, prisoners were evacuated. They made knapsacks, sold possessions for brandy to celebrate, said farewells to their friends among the locals, and awaited the order to march. When it came, the band struck up 'Over the Hills and Far Away':

> I say when we parted there was not one of us could avoid shedding tears, even looking back and waving our hands as long as we were in sight of each other.[47]

Wetherell's vision of freedom gives the end of his diary a poignant twist: a French state heading towards collapse, elderly men and boys being marched off in arms; the prisoners' band complete with clarinet and cornet mustering on the square in Blois, playing popular airs, French as well as English, 'and young girls and boys hopping around like as many poppets'. But did he really find love with a French girl, Mary, the daughter of a vintner in Richelieu – she so smitten as to follow in a cart and present him with a locket, and he, torn from her embrace by the bugle to resume the march?[48]

He should be allowed some licence. Of the 306 men to escape the wreck of *Hussar*, fewer than a third survived eleven years of captivity like Wetherell and reached St Malo to be shipped home. There he jotted a few lines:

> *Each day we various scenes behold, At night in cells we sleep*
> *Should all prove true that we are told, France for thy children weep.*
> *No more beneath th'oppressive hand, Of tyrany we groan,*
> *But march to join that happy land, Which freedom calls her own.*[49]

And Wetherell's favourite yarn was, it turns out, perfectly true. Another prisoner, Edward Bonner, was a Lincolnshire villager, driven by poverty to sign on, who lost an arm in action weeks after entering the frigate *Minerve*.[50] As a prisoner with 'one flipper', as it was termed, he was among the 'aged and cripples' allowed out for a daily walk. One evening he failed to return. The gendarmes assumed he had drowned in the river; his fellows mourned a 'sober steady man'.

On Wetherell's return to England, however, he met Bonner again, who related that he had in fact hidden in woods near Givet, then made his way over ten days to Ostend where he had the luck to fall in with a band of English smugglers. They had landed him at Deal, and 'had a day's carouse'.[51] His change of fortune had continued since reaching home. He had lodged at a house 'kept by a Widow Toulson', and they were about to marry. Would Wetherell be his best man?

Thus it was that 'two days after my return, which was the 7th of June 1814, Edward Bonner and Jane Toulson were married'. Bonner was forty-five, his bride forty-six, so this was no festival of youth. But it was high summer, the setting was the noble medieval Church of All Saints in Stamford, and, after two decades of war, peace was at hand. Wetherell recalled it all with deep pleasure.

'I gave her to Bonner for better or worse,' he wrote fondly, 'but she was good.'[52]

OVER THE SIDE
1816-36

EIGHTEEN months after Waterloo a mob gathered in London to protest over the bitter fruits of victory. Among the 10,000-strong crowd at Spa Fields on 2 December was one John Cashman – a seaman, Irish and full of rage. While the great majority of protesters waved banners – 'Feed the hungry! Protect the oppressed!' – and stood to hear radical speakers denounce the betrayal of the brave sailors and soldiers now littering London's wintry alleys, Cashman was among a group who took matters further. They broke into a gunsmith's premises and armed themselves.

An Old Bailey trial heard that Cashman had distributed guns to a gang, some wearing tricolour hats, with the intention of launching an attack on Carlton House, residence of the Prince Regent. Cashman had been arrested soon afterwards – carrying a gun and a tricolour flag himself. Although shots were fired in the ensuing riots, the only casualty appears to have been a man who suffered a stab wound.

Cashman's testimony struck a chord in the air of febrile embitterment. He claimed that he had come to London to claim five years' back pay and prize money owed by the Admiralty, and question why £1 a month he had assigned to his mother in Ireland had never been paid – only to be passed from one office to another. That same day he visited a shipmate in hospital. Later, by which time he was drunk, 'I saw people running. I ran with them':[1]

> I have been at sea all my life. . . . I was reduced to the greatest distress and being penniless I have not been able even to acquaint my brave officers, for I am sure they would have come forward on my behalf.[2]

On the gallows Cashman reverted to seamanlike insubordination. He pushed the clergyman aside, saying, 'Don't bother me, I want no mercy but from God.' When the hangman tried to pull a black cap over his head, he objected, 'Let me see the last', and, turning to the crowd, urged the seamen present to give the signal for mutiny: 'Now you buggers, give me three cheers when I trip.' His last words were to the hangman: 'Come, Jack, you bugger. Let go the jib-boom.' As his body dangled from the noose, cries went up of 'Murder' and 'Shame'.[3]

Actually, the records of Cashman's trial and naval service show he was not as ill-used as was reported in the radical journals which rallied to his cause. The claim that he had been 'wounded nine times over many years of service' was untrue: a fisherman from Waterford, he entered the frigate *Iris*, rated Ordinary, in 1810, serving in her just three years but never in action; and a portion of his wages had been paid to his mother until he was discharged 'for harbour duty', where he was employed for the next two years.[4]

However, the publicity surrounding Cashman's trial and his execution on 12 March 1817 had the potential to set off unrest and create a seafaring martyr. Britain may have been victorious and, with Boney safely stored on St Helena, a world power with neither enemies nor rivals. Yet it was also in the midst of a severe depression. Put simply, the impact of peace on an economy based for more than twenty years on waging war had been disastrous in human terms. Naval and military spending were pared to the bone, affecting production in every field. Employment shrank. Food prices shot up. On the same day it reported Cashman's trial, *The Times* published details of a fund that had raised £33,533 18s 6d to relieve 'extreme distress in Spitalfields and its vicinity'.

While there were those among the well-to-do who subscribed generously to help the poor, there were also those anxious that a rising clamour for constitutional reform posed a new revolutionary threat. *The Times* saw in the Spa Fields riots 'attempts by the disaffected to incite the lower orders to acts of devastation'.[5]

Among the 'lower orders', Jack had been especially hard hit. Once again peace led to a mass payoff and seamen were said to make up the largest body

Disabled seamen were dependent on charity, and begging and the need for public benevolence rose sharply after the peace of 1815.

of London's beggars. In 1801 the number of navy hands had been cut from some 126,000 to fewer than 50,000.[6] This time, from a peak of 147,000 in 1813, manning was reduced within four years to just 23,000.[7] Moreover, this was to be a lasting peace. Through the 1820s naval manning did not rise above 25,000. Soldiers, by comparison, were demobilized at a more gradual pace and kept on in greater numbers – from 240,000 in 1815 to 103,000 in 1828.[8]

Some Jacks survived on their wits. The most recognizable figure on London's streets was Billy Waters – black, American and an early busker. Billy had lost a leg falling from the tops in *Ganymede* in 1812, and his fiddle and pegleg 'excited much mirth and attention' from theatregoers who tossed ha'pennies into his hat.[9] As well as enabling him to support a wife and two children, busking had brought him a little fame. Billy was a subject for the caricaturist George Cruikshank and a canvas attributed to Sir David Wilkie. But what he called 'an honest living by the scraping of cat-gut' did not survive harder times; his fiddle ended up at a pawnbroker and Billy's final days were spent in St Giles's workhouse, where he died in 1823, aged forty-five. Old shipmates as well as his family were said to have attended his funeral.

For a great many others it was tougher still. Just how deep in John Cashman had been with the motley collection of discarded warriors, reformers, revolutionaries and scallywags involved at Spa Fields cannot be said; sailors were commonly associated with trouble on the streets; but without the unifying element of a ship, they lacked the organization demonstrated during the great mutinies twenty years earlier. According to the radical historian E. P. Thompson, seamen with 'their riotous dispositions' became noted for an ability to rouse gatherings in post-war political turbulence.[10] The main body of dissidents, however, came from organized labour, evangelicals, the poor, and their advocates among the intelligentsia. Jack may have been as vociferous as ever, but ashore he remained a loose cannon.

Weeks after Cashman's execution, Parliament passed the Seditious Meetings Act, prohibiting unauthorized gatherings of more than fifty people. Its influence was negligible. In the summer of 1819, campaigning moved to Manchester, a centre of activism, where Henry Hunt was to address crowds on parliamentary reform. 'Orator' Hunt was a radical of peaceful intent, but he had been a speaker at Spa Fields and riotous forces remained at work.

On 21 June a speaker named Walker – reported by the newspapers as being 'rigged from stem to stern [as] a sailor' – harangued a crowd at St Peter's Field composed mainly of textile workers, a group whose livelihoods were being destroyed by mechanization and who had petitioned the Prince Regent for either poor relief or funding to emigrate to Canada. Walker's exhortation to these Luddites, as they were known, was to eschew pleading and to 'strike terror into the heart of the plundering villains wallowing in luxury while we are starving'. His speech reportedly evoked cries of 'Bravo Jack Tar!'[11]

It has been suggested that Walker was no Jack Tar at all but a government agent. Whether or not this was the case, spies had indeed been active locally, informing magistrates that agitators were at work. Tension was consequently high when a crowd estimated at 60,000, including many seamen, mustered at St Peter's Field again on 16 August to hear 'Orator' Hunt. Wild enthusiasm at his arrival set off a disastrous over-reaction by the magistrates, who ordered his arrest. In the ensuing chaos, yeomen charged to disperse the crowd, wounding more than 400 protesters and killing fifteen, including a child and a woman.

The Peterloo Massacre, as it became known, was a watershed that might have stimulated further violence and repression; but shame at the outrage ran deep, touching the nation's conscience. Ultimately, resolution of the wars with France set a new political agenda – one that culminated in the Great Reform Act of 1832.[12]

Merchant ships were busier than ever, serving the economy profitably and their owners even better. Jack fared less well. Some of those hands thrown overboard by the Navy found berths as mercantile manning rose from 132,000 in 1814 to 169,000 a year later. But it fell back to 106,000 within two years, and wages went down too.[13] If events on Tyneside are anything to go by, the reason was a straightforward case of exploitation by ship-owners.

The north-east was the one region where sailors were bound together in a communal form of seafaring. London and Liverpool were shipping centres with disparate parts. Only the conurbation of Tyneside, which dispensed coal to London, provided waters where men who shared employers and conditions could take concerted action.

Trouble started when peace led to an immediate slashing of wages. From a peak of £9 during the war, pay for a return voyage to London had been cut to as low as £3. Manning was also reduced, to the point that some vessels had insufficient hands for a safe passage. In September, in an echo of Spithead in 1797, a committee of sailors presented local shipowners with a list of demands: a standard £5 wage and a fixed man–tonnage ratio.[14] In the meantime, shipping was closed down.

Magistrates tried to mediate, without success. The strikers sent foreign seamen ashore.[15] Enough violence occurred for the mayor of Newcastle to request the Admiralty for a warship to enforce order. Lord Sidmouth, the Home Secretary, despatched an official whose report left little doubt where justice lay. Notwithstanding the strikers' violent methods:

> I feel myself compelled to bear my testimony to Yr Lordship in favour of their principles and in other respects good conduct as well as the solidity of their grounds of complaint . . . Ships from these ports have gone to sea shamefully deficient in strength to navigate them.[16]

Revulsion at the ship-owners' avarice touched the ruling class. Sidmouth told the mayor he trusted that the 'consideration and liberality which is due British seamen' would be shown the strikers. The Duke of Northumberland weighed in with criticism of the ship-owners, as did two army generals who had been involved in keeping order.

The ruthless exercise of market forces produced turbulence on the south coast too. At Lyme Regis it was reported that 'riotous sailors have determined not to proceed to sea unless they are allowed the same wages they had in the war'.[17] But the six-week Tyneside strike of 1815 was the first and last of its kind to secure its objectives. The closest otherwise was a strike four years later by keelmen, who handled the barges that ran from upriver mines to ports. It was no coincidence that the Tyne's coal industry again provided a binding factor.

One charitable initiative was intended specifically to benefit merchant sailors. During a brutal winter in 1817–18 the highly visible suffering of seamen ashore moved William Wilberforce and other philanthropists to set up a fund for their relief. The Seamen's Hospital Society was formed in 1821 and – proudly declaring that the shelter provided by the hulks *Grampus* and *Dreadnought* was for merchant sailors 'of all nations' – may even have been intended as a rebuke to that magnificent nearby establishment, the Royal Hospital at Greenwich, which was exclusively for naval hands.[18]

Overall, employment in all maritime sectors, including the Navy, is estimated to have gone from an all-time high of 270,000 in 1810 to 145,000 a decade later – a reduction of 47 per cent.[19] America became a promised land for British seamen once more. While figures for those who migrated can only be a matter of guesswork, at least one of our narrators, who had rejoiced at returning to 'that happy land which freedom calls her own', did not stay. John Wetherell, former prisoner of war, ended his seafaring life in New York.

Men who had once deserted without a care beyond their next frolic were left high and dry. From 1816 the Admiralty was receiving petitions almost daily on behalf of men who had forfeited their pension rights after being listed as 'R' – or run – from their ship. Some had the benefit restored because they had resumed service and distinguished themselves in another ship, or were able to produce letters of support from a captain, as in the case of William Thorpe, who had failed to return to the *Unicorn* before she sailed because he was at his father's funeral. More often their pleas were simply rejected.[20]

With desperate times came desperate means of survival. Levels of crime soared, from petty larceny to violent robbery. One former sailor who started out at the low end of the spectrum ended up among the most notorious figures of the time – celebrated, vilified and mysterious all at once. His story is utterly implausible while being ascertainably true.

To this day it is hard to fathom just who he was, but given that William Swallow – the name by which he is remembered in colonial folklore – was an alias, that is perhaps to be expected. A 'veritable Houdini' in the words of the Australian writer Robert Hughes, he was also known as William Brown, William Waldon and by at least three other monikers.

His real name was William Walker. While most of what he had to say about himself is open to question, he was probably born in Sunderland in around 1792 and went to sea early on; like many of the ablest seafarers, he learned the ropes on an east coast collier. He also claimed to have been impressed and served the last two war years in the Navy, although in what ship or role he did not say. In any event, by the time he was discharged, aged about twenty-three, he was an exceptional mariner. After the war he sailed in merchantmen, including a spell as master of a coastal brig, and married Susan Addison with whom he had three children. Whatever his crimes – and they were many – it is clear that he was a devoted family man.[21]

Life turned bitter for the Walkers when he was shipwrecked in 1820. Home in Sunderland a few months later but without a ship, he was arrested with stolen goods: a quilt, a tea canister, two blankets and a curtain. That was not quite enough to earn a death sentence but sufficient for seven years' transportation. It also inspired his escape instinct. While being shipped down the coast to London, he slipped over the side, swam until – miraculously – he was picked up and joined a collier under the name William Brown. Not for the last time, Walker's desire to return to Susan and the children would prove his downfall; for on reaching home he was soon recognized and in June 1821 was among 172 convicts on the *Malabar* bound for Van Diemen's Land.

Sailors made up a good proportion of Australian convicts, as is apparent from the frequency with which they crop up in Walker's story. Here, moreover, is proof that seafaring skill served even the criminal class well. He was one of six convicts who helped to sail *Malabar* to the far side of the world and were therefore identified with good behaviour. Once they reached Hobart, he was employed around the harbour.

Eight months later, two men claiming to be survivors of a shipwrecked whaler turned up 700 miles across the Tasman Sea in Sydney. Suspicions were aroused when their names could not be confirmed, and investigation showed them to be Walker and John Wilkinson, a fellow sailor-convict. They had escaped on a stolen schooner.

On the passage back to Van Diemen's Land their vessel ran into a furious three-day storm which brought her to the verge of disaster and offered Walker a lifeline. 'Remarking that his own life was of little moment', he volunteered to go aloft and hacked away the broken topmast threatening to drag them down.[22] Although given 150 lashes back in Hobart, he was spared exile to the punitive jail at Macquarie, and a few months later was among nine convicts stowed away on a departing ship. At Rio, he picked up a passage to England.

Three years after being transported, William Brown, as he now called himself, was home to celebrate Christmas in 1823 with Susan and their two children at lodgings in Bermondsey. The family was reunited but the third child had died, and from this point Walker's story starts to assume a dark Dickensian melancholy.

Over the next five years, Walker found occasional berths shipping out of Wapping, including one to the Baltic, while Susan worked for a Soho uphol-sterer, James Newton of Wardour Street. They had aspirations. But times were harder than ever. Whether from ambition or need, William Brown reverted to the thieving habits of William Walker. He had been stealing from shipping yards round Deptford – cordage, canvas and tools – when he was arrested for house-breaking. Now assuming the name of William Swallow, he was tried at Guildford and sentenced to death, commuted to transportation for life. In December 1828 he was heading to Van Diemen's Land for the second time, his paramount fear that he would be recognized as William Walker making him liable to execution.

Swallow – as we must now call him – was a man of many talents, resource-fulness and fortitude among them. That he was also plausible and likeable is evident from the times he won over figures in authority; so far as can be ascertained, he never resorted to violence. His greatest talent, however, was seafaring and on the convict ship *Georgiana* he again impressed officers in a storm and by repairing sails. On landing at Hobart he was described as 'a very good man' and employed as harbour coxswain. Six years had passed – long enough for him to avoid immediate detection.

Whatever was driving Swallow's Houdini-like escapades, he did not stop there. A few months later he was found trying to stow away again, and this time he was embarked with thirty other hardened convicts on the *Cyprus* brig for Macquarie – the punishment jail. A few days later, on 14 August 1829, *Cyprus* was at anchor in a bay. The military officer in charge and the surgeon had gone off fishing while the captain had drunk himself senseless. Late in the afternoon a group of convicts were brought up for fresh air. On being ordered below again violence broke out, guns were fired and within minutes the brig was in their hands.

Swallow, it has been claimed, was the leader of these pirates of the South Seas.[23] He certainly came to prominence subsequently, as the only mariner capable of navigating the brig, but evidence as to the leadership points elsewhere. He only appeared on deck as the officers, soldiers and crew were being cast off in a boat, along with fifteen convicts who opted to join them. 'You see, gentlemen, I am a pressed man,' he called out.[24] He certainly seized an opportunity and started to assert himself. The hard men, however, were Leslie Ferguson and Robert McGuire, both Irish farm labourers, transported for theft.[25]

Swallow's renown in Australia was as a fabulous escaper, but arguably his greatest feat was navigating a brig around the Pacific with a crew of fourteen criminals. Only two had sailing experience and one of them was soon lost overboard in a storm. To start with he had little control as heavy weather swept them south-east within 500 miles of New Zealand. There he was able to set a northerly course towards Tahiti.

The voyage of the *Cyprus* followed a pattern familiar in South Seas dramas – idyllic islands, tropical storms and turbulence aboard. Order was challenged by constant disputes. Their first anchorage, off an island east of Tonga, was identified by Swallow as Niue, where 'I was received in a very friendly manner by the king'.*

* HO17/59/18. Swallow's account is contained in his subsequent petition and is demonstrably false in places. Here he appears to have been mistaken as the island in question has been identified as one of the Tonga group.

Here a split divided those wanting to stay and the majority who opted to go on to China and Japan. When the *Cyprus* sailed again after six weeks, the turbulent Ferguson and McGuire remained among the islanders.

Reduced to a nine-man crew, Swallow took the *Cyprus* almost 5,000 miles north in less than three months. Though assisted by a following wind and the brig's hold of healthy rations, it was still a remarkable work of seafaring that he could note sighting the coast of Japan at the end of November. They did not stay, being met by a volley of fire from the shore. But by now China was within reach. After one final bust-up which split the crew in two parties, the *Cyprus* was scuttled off Whampoa.

On 7 September 1830 a seaman named William Waldon came ashore at Margate from the *Charles Grant* Indiaman. He wanted to go to London directly, he told the captain, after a long separation from his family. Waldon had been a useful hand on the homeward voyage, so Captain Everest was happy to grant his request.

After this latest bravura escape, nothing could have prepared Waldon – aka Swallow, aka Walker – for the next thunderbolt. Susan Walker, having assumed that he was gone forever from her life, had remarried. She was now Susan Flook, wife of a grocer's assistant.

Disaster was closing in. Officials at Whampoa had been suspicious from the outset of the four seamen claiming to have survived a shipwreck and who obtained berths on the homeward-bound *Charles Grant*. Once descriptions confirmed them as being escaped convicts, a fast-sailing vessel was despatched to alert the authorities. Swallow, as usual, was a step ahead in leaving at Margate, but the other three were arrested on landing in London.

The bigamous Susan, a survivor herself, stunned and confused though she must have been, was also won by her husband's devotion. Gleefully, the newspapers picked up the story:

> She was persuaded to leave Flook and remained with Swallow three days, when Flook discovered their retreat, and she returned with him. [Swallow] took another lodging and Flook, discovering that his wife was in the habit

of visiting him, gave information to a man named Taylor. He, in expectation of the reward, informed the police.[26]

So it was that on 4 November, Swallow was among five former convicts to be brought up at the Old Bailey, charged with piracy. As the nominal captain of the *Cyprus*, he was assumed to have been in charge and *The Times* had run racy stories ascribing to him a fantastic criminal past, as 'one of the most desperate thieves that ever infested the metropolis'.[27] The gallows appeared a certainty.

Then Dr Walter Williams, surgeon of the *Cyprus* and one of those sent ashore, took the stand. Swallow, he testified, had not come up on deck until after the ship was taken. Indeed, he had suffered a serious and life-threatening condition that required surgery a few days before the uprising. 'He was in a fair way of recovering but still exceeding weak.' As the longboat was about to be sent off he had leaned over the rail, saying: 'I am a pressed man. I am unarmed and surrounded by armed men.'

When the jury came back it was to find all the accused guilty – except Swallow. Two of the four, George Davis and William Watts, were hanged at Execution Dock on 16 December. The other two were granted mercy and transported again. So far as is known, the real leader, Leslie Ferguson from Carrickfergus, lived out his days among Polynesian islanders.

William Swallow was landed at Van Diemen's Land for the third and last time in 1831. The companions of his final years at the gruesome penal station at Macquarie included at least four other convicts from the *Cyprus* but not Susan, of whose later life nothing is known. He died of tuberculosis on 12 May 1834, aged forty-two, by which time his adventures had become the subject of one of the proscribed Australian convict ballads known as 'treason songs':

> *William Swallow he was chosen our commander for to be –*
> *We gave three cheers for Liberty and boldly put to sea.*
> *Lay on your golden trumpets, boys, and sound their cheerful note!*
> *The Cyprus brig's on the ocean, boys, by Justice does she float!*

It is most unfortunate, as the historian Robert Hughes has noted, that William Swallow never wrote a memoir.[28]

———

The expansion of empire helped to keep Jack afloat. Before the wars Britain possessed twenty-six colonies. In 1815 that number was forty-three.[29] It was not only new destinations that stimulated trade by sea. One solitary empire all on its own generated vast wealth for British merchants. At first China had been totally disinterested in anything British. When Jacob Nagle sailed there in 1806 with *Neptune*, a great Indiaman of 1,200 tons, she arrived virtually empty and departed with 24,000 chests of Britain's favourite consumer product – tea.[30] By the time William Swallow and his fellows entered the *Charles Grant* at Whampoa, Indiamen were delivering a product for which China had developed an insatiable appetite.

Opium production in Bengal was supervised by the Company and trafficked from Calcutta to Canton in quantities that made addicts of an estimated three million Chinese. 'Trafficked' is an appropriate term as the trade was prohibited by the emperor and the drug had to be smuggled by sharp-sailing buccaneers from the Bay of Bengal through the maze of vast and tiny islands that constitute the Malay Archipelago, inhabited by natives who could be friendly, hostile or treacherous. If the risks were high, the profits were immense, and the Company absorbed them complacently to pay for its tea. China's narcotic dependency destroyed innumerable lives before the Opium War of 1839–42 in which, it has been noted, the British went to war to defend their right to be drug traffickers.

The opium trade, though detestable, was also, in the words of the historian Cecil Northcote Parkinson, 'the parent of fast-sailing ships'.[31] Because the drug perished rapidly it had to be delivered quickly, so giving rise to a nimble, sharp-bowed vessel called an opium clipper. The later generation of high-masted, broad-sailed clippers used to transport tea appear to have been based on an American design; but the first use by British seafarers of these exquisite, innovative vessels was to smuggle narcotics.

Fast-sailing was the order of the day. No longer did Indiamen have to sail in convoy under naval protection, so the days when a dozen or more ships could only move at the pace of a single clumsy laggard were done; and as the East India Company's monopolies of trade with India and China were abolished in 1813 and 1833, the door opened to competitors.

While the skill and activity of an individual company would always set the pace, Indiaman design had moved on too. In those distant days when William Spavens sailed with the *Elizabeth*, covering the 13,900 miles to Java in 119 days counted as excellent. A study of voyaging by the next generation of Indiamen shows a good passage being reduced to 100 days.[32] In 1829 a Company ship, *Marquis of Wellington*, reached Bengal in eighty-one days.[33]

So, opium, tea, silk, spices – whatever the subject of British trade, it was being shifted faster than ever and, moreover, in all seasons. The monsoons no longer constrained sailing times. Clippers, wrote a later seafarer, had to be tall-sparred and carry the utmost spread of canvas, 'and she must *use* that sail, day and night, fair weather and foul'.[34] A dazzling new form of deep-water sailing emerged just as the heroic age had passed.

What insights of his own Jack might have brought to this era of maritime history we can only imagine. Sailors' narratives start to dry up.

Robert Hay, that earnest and genteel hand, had survived the *Amethyst* wreck of 1811 in Plymouth Sound in characteristically thoughtful manner. 'I clothed myself in my best apparel and took a few small articles which I most esteemed.'[35] These included his copy of *Improvement of the Mind*, the gift that had guided his self-education. He departed the sea with wisdom and some final insights on, for example, impressment:

Seamen who have been pressed together into one ship have usually a great affection for one another. Their trade, their habits, their misfortunes are the same and they become endeared to each other by a similarity of sufferings.[36]

Hay's naval service served him in obtaining work as a canal steersman in his native Paisley and, a week before Waterloo, he was 'united to that woman who is now the partner of my joys and cares'. Six years later he concluded the memoir he had set down for their children with a thanksgiving and a prayer:

> She possessed then neither beauty nor fortune, but as I myself possessed neither of these qualifications I had no reason to complain of the want of them on her part . . . In her company the years – during which we have been blessed with temporal prosperity and excellent health – have glided along in a happy even tenor of uniformity. Little addicted to company, I spend most of my leisure hours in company with my books.
>
> Man, we know is born to trouble, and who is so presumptuous as to expect exemption from the universal law. Whatever measure of distress may be mingled in my future, I hope my creator will endow me with fortitude to bear up under it with resignation.
>
> Paisley, November 6, 1821

In his emergence from poverty – the son of a weaver with nine children – to sagacity and a kind of serenity, Robert Hay bears comparison with our earliest subject, William Spavens. Here were two humble boys separated by more than fifty years yet both inspired to see the world, and both discovering themselves through the sea.

Hay was only thirty-two when he finished his memoir. He declined to have it published, even though it was well within his grasp. We can make that assumption because he went on to found Robert Hay & Son, Book Makers and Printers, and edit the *Paisley Advertiser*. The most improbable and self-effacing of seamen, he died aged fifty-eight in 1847.

That James Choyce's *Log of a Jack Tar* failed to reach an audience during his lifetime was not for want of trying. His concluding address to 'you gentle reader' expressed the hope that:

> This tale of my adventures, and of my many hardships when a prisoner to the Spaniards in South America, and likewise of how I was marched from one end of France to another chained like a wild beast . . . may prove of interest and advantage to you who read it.[37]

Choyce's life at the edge, as prisoner, traitor, escaper and deserter, did not end with the war. Reading between the lines of his next voyage – 'in the ship *Inspector* to Timor and other islands in the Indian seas, [where] we had many dangerous occurrences' – he might have joined in the opium trade coming out of Bengal.

Choyce's last voyage, in 1820, took him back to where he had started almost thirty years earlier, in a whaleship to the Pacific. Here the savages were of his own kind – English pirates washed up on Alexander Selkirk's Island of Juan Fernández, who he did well to escape. Other islands brought other desperados. With Chile's rebellion against Spanish rule in full spate these were perilous seas in which piracy was a survival mechanism.

When the Lizard was sighted in the summer of 1822, Choyce was suffering from the sailor's affliction, rheumatism, and 'was only fit to be laid up'. There his narrative ends. 'Now I swing idly at my moorings, though for an old shipmate I can always find a glass of grog.'[38] A tough survivor – another whose seemingly preposterous stories stand up to scrutiny – Choyce lived another fourteen years at a Brighton boarding house within sight of the sea.* He died aged fifty-nine and was buried at the church of St Nicholas. Another fifty years then passed before his manuscript came to light, along with charts, a telescope, a model of a whaleship and some items of scrimshaw.

---

* Choyce is registered in the 1837 electoral list as living at No. 2 Chapel Street. He did not bother to vote.

What then of that other great survivor, Jacob Nagle? The war of 1812 had left
Nagle stranded in Brazil. He worked in a Rio tavern and sailed local waters, but
the returns were poor and he stayed on long after the younger Nagle would have
shipped out. Poverty and bouts of a mysterious condition introduced him to
vulnerability. Once, brought low in a strange port in South America, his proud,
ebullient and heroically phonetic narrative took a startling turn. He had, as he
reflected, sailed the four quarters of the globe, seen men killed beside him in
action, twice been taken prisoner, three times cast away, had a ship founder
under him, and spent days in an open boat without food or water – and yet:

> . . . at this minute it apeared to me that I was in greater distress and missery
> than I ever had been in my life. I fell on my nees, and never did I pray with
> a sincerer hart than I did at that time . . . when the dore opened and in
> came a black woman with a bason of soop and part of a fowl, and then left
> me to reflect upon what the Lord had done for me and his merciful good-
> ness to a sinner.[39]

He duly recovered, sailing from Brazil for Virginia in 1821. And suddenly,
aged sixty, when he might have been expected to stow his sails, Nagle embarked
on a new series of transatlantic passages in brigs and sloops that continued
until 1824. His editor, John C. Dann, wrote that he seemed to be trying to
outsail the Grim Reaper, or hoping to find another Captain Bond in a new
Netley. Perhaps he was just fearful of destitution in his final years.

Acute financial need there certainly was. Having been, to all intents and
purposes, an English seafarer all his adult life, he returned to the United States for
family and economic reasons. He applied for a pension for his soldiering during
the Revolution, but that turned into a long process, so he did odd jobs – chop-
ping wood, planting potatoes. He was still often penniless and had to stay with
relatives. Aptly enough, the closest he came to a home was the town of Canton,
Ohio, where one of his sisters lived and which brought to mind his last Indiaman

voyage. After a lifetime in motion he was still on the move, now on foot, a knapsack on his back, from refuge to refuge. Nagle's transience brings to mind the observations of an old navy officer:

> Take sailors out of their ships and marshal them on shore and they will be found to be restless and unsteady, and particularly impatient of inactivity.[40]

Nagle's final voyage was on a canal steamboat, his last walk a 90-mile hike back to Canton which took ten days. He was then seventy-eight. He died a year later, in February 1841. An obituary notice in the local newspaper, which lamented the neglect of 'an old Revolutionary' left 'poor and destitute', testified that he was at least recognized:

> Of the utmost simplicity in his manners, he was nevertheless of undaunted courage. The writer of this article knew him well. Many an hour have we listened to him, recounting the privations he underwent in the continental army and the perils he encountered on the waves.[41]

The origins of *The Nagle Journal* are unclear. John C. Dann, whose meticulous research verified its authenticity and accuracy, believed that Nagle set it down in the 1830s over no more than two or three years, basing it on diaries and journals that have not survived. He hoped for income from publication – like others before in reduced circumstances. In its endearingly individual form, that was never feasible. As Dann says, however, Nagle had succeeded in preserving the chronicle of a life of which he was proud: 'It was, in a sense, his last and most memorable voyage.'[42]

24

STORYTELLERS
1810–40

YARNS always played a part in taking men to sea but one story had been enduringly potent. The novel, first published in 1719, about a sailor marooned on a tropical island, was a literary landmark that worked its magic on dreamy types from John Nicol to Robert Hay. 'I read it over and over with great avidity and delight,' Hay wrote. Like Nicol, he turned his back on a prosaic family trade in the hope of 'meeting similar adventures' to its hero. Another romantic, Charles Pemberton, was carried off on the same course: 'Every word of Robinson Crusoe I could repeat from my head; and how I longed for a desolate island and a man Friday.'[1]

Quite why the castaway narrative exerted such fascination may appear something of a mystery. Is it because readers saw a man finding a way to escape the confines of the age? The survivor making do and thereby discovering a path to self-reliance? Having overcome danger and his inhospitable environment, Crusoe had established his own domain; after being rescued he even confesses an urge to return: 'I could not resist the strong inclination I had to see my island.' Just so, John Nicol, while aware of the sea's dangers, could reflect: 'I looked upon them as an interesting part of the adventures I panted after.'[2]

Stories of the sea, maritime folklore – call the phenomenon what we will, these had carried a potent message that served naval recruitment well. So it is hardly to be wondered at that Britain's age of naval supremacy set in train a new cycle of storytelling. Celebrated in print, Jack started to relate his own yarns. As Samuel Leech saw it, old tars became the spinners of tales akin to 'the great magician' Walter Scott, feeding 'a greedy public who read as eagerly as our men used to listen'.

There is a widespread belief among maritime historians that wariness is needed. Most accounts were not published until well after Napoleon's defeat and have been associated with an age of reform when radical voices were being raised and old ways challenged. In the words of N. A. M. Rodger:

> After the great wars ideas continued to evolve – and this lays a trap for the historian for in the 1830s radical politicians (in Britain and the US) adopted naval and military discipline, and in particular flogging, as a convenient rhetorical symbol for a range of social and political targets. This created a market for polemical books and pamphlets in the form of memoirs describing naval discipline in lurid terms. Some of these memoirs incorporated genuine material but they express attitudes which were unknown until well after 1815.[3]

Which memoirs Rodger had in mind is not stated. The obvious example from the lower deck is William Robinson, aka Jack Nastyface, who was never short of a grievance and, in playing his presence at Trafalgar for all it was worth, seized the moment to give accounts of savage punishments, even those that no longer pertained. Running the gauntlet, for example, had been abolished in 1806 and the detested practice of starting in 1809 – almost thirty years before Robinson's book cited them as being in current use.[4] Samuel Leech could also be something of an axe-grinder, combining accounts of British brutality for his American readership with another trend, for devout evangelism; in other respects, however, his is a vivid and valid voice.

But most of the memoirs cited here speak without reference to the reformist attitudes of the 1830s and were not published until very long afterwards. (Initially, readers' appetites were more for stories from the quarterdeck, so midshipmen weighed in along with officers.)

William Spavens was the first into print, in 1796, with a work driven by financial need after his crippling accident at sea. John Nicol was next, in 1822, and he too had a financial objective, having been left in poverty. Neither had any discernible agenda.

Of the other memoirs related at length here, those by Jacob Nagle, Robert Hay, John Wetherell, William Richardson and Robert Wilson were – to all intents and purposes – lost and did not see the light of day until the following century when they were all long dead. Nagle evidently had hopes for his journal's publication, though in the main he was reliving, for himself, a life no maritime novelist could have invented. His memoir was overlooked for almost 150 years and did not reach the public until 1982 after it came to auction. Robert Hay wrote his memoir for family and, as we have seen, declined to have it published. It was only thanks to a descendant that it came to light finally in 1953. John Wetherell's three-volume manuscript was also lost for more than a century before being passed to C. S. Forester, who was editing it when Hay's account came out. William Richardson's memoir was published in 1908, also after editing. Robert Wilson's forgotten journal followed in 1951.

Of the lesser accounts, that by James Choyce did find a publisher in the nineteenth century, but he too was dead by then. Though George Watson's narrative was published in 1827 it received scant attention outside his native Newcastle and is far the rarest of all books by seamen.[5]

What marks all of these memoirs is how they stand up to scrutiny. True, they are the voices of individuals with human foibles; no two men will, after all, give identical descriptions of the same event. But for simple facts, recording their presence at the history to which they were witness, all are substantiated by contemporary records – ships' logs and musters. Wetherell's eye for a story may have led him to embellish detail, but his version of a prisoner's life in France rings with colour and humanity. Richardson pulled no punches in acknowledging his part in the slave trade as well as heroics in battle. And just when Choyce appears to enter the world of fantasy, with his deadpan account of coming up the side of a British ship as a traitor, the log confirms his story.

Historians do need to be wary of their sources. For all his love of a good yarn, Jack is surprisingly dependable.

There is another aspect to these accounts, of which Nagle's is in many ways the most outstanding. Those who ventured to far-flung places were always renowned as storytellers. They might be disbelieved – often were. Yet they knew their stories to be true and they could not stop retelling them. The likes of Spavens, Nagle and Hay were reviving a bardic tradition from the earliest days of seafaring, only now, having acquired the gift of literacy, they were revelling in the written word as once sailors had in song. As ever, though, everything came from their own experience of the fantastic, as common men at sea. Seafaring, it bears repeating, nourished poetry in their souls.

When it came to readership, however, publishers had to scent profit if they were to present Jack as an author. And Archibald Campbell, for one, did not look the part. At the end of the war he was to be seen with a barrel organ in Edinburgh. Both lower legs had been amputated and he 'earned a miserable pittance by crawling round the streets grinding music'.

There he would have remained had he not been noticed by a gentleman named James Smith. A highly educated merchant, Smith was intrigued to discover that the crippled musician (for he played the fiddle too) had been a seaman of an unusual sort. Campbell did not talk of battles or war, but of a South Seas paradise. On bleak days in Auld Reekie, he would tell how, thirty years after James Cook's final voyage, he had sighted 'high abrupt cliffs . . . the mountains of Owhyhee with spouting waterfalls' and come ashore with painful awkwardness on his stumps to the golden sands where the great navigator had been clubbed to death.

As Campbell related it, Hawaii had changed much since the days when pale-skinned aliens were met with axes and clubs. At King Tamaahmaah's court, 'my appearance attracted the notice and excited the compassion of the queen Tamena'. The king's interest was more practical, and it was on learning that Campbell could weave and repair sails that he had welcomed him into the royal hut.[6] There, in a circle of islanders seated on mats, the young invalid from Glasgow feasted on albacore and yams.

A few months later, having restored the sails of the king's vessels, Campbell had been given 60 acres of land where, as he was carried on men's shoulders, he marvelled at 'the beauty and fertility of the country . . . well shaded with large cocoa-nut trees'.*

The women, of course, were no less lovely. A dozen villagers were assigned to work his estate.

As a businessman, Mr Smith might have wondered whether the sad figure relating these stories was a fantasist. But Campbell could produce papers testifying to his past. As a boy apprenticed to a weaver on Clydeside, he had first glimpsed tall masts from river boats and yearned for the open sea. His sailing life followed a familiar pattern – impressment, desertion and an Indiaman voyage. The trouble started when he signed on an American bound for the Aleutian islands, was wrecked on Kamchatka and suffered frostbite, leading to the amputation of both his feet. It was only thanks to kindly Russian mariners that he had reached the South Seas.

Hawaii's white inhabitants, Campbell continued, were all seamen. Among them was a Welsh hand, Isaac Davis – the sole survivor of an attack on an American schooner who had become the king's right-hand man. The islanders' hostility, he explained to Campbell, had been rooted in fear; two men from another ship had also been killed a few years later.† But a survivor from that party, an English hand named Young, had also been taken in by the king, who discerned the power within the seafarers' gift. Davis and Young went on to help Tamaahmaah in conquering the islands of Maui, Molokai and Oahu to unite the archipelago. As a reward they were made chiefs and given large grants of land.[7] Another of the king's followers was an escaped convict from New South Wales, William Stevenson. A grand existence they all enjoyed too, from

* Campbell, p. 101. The site of his land lies a few miles west of what is now Honolulu.
† They appear to have been the astronomer William Gooch and a lieutenant of the *Daedalus*, who were among a party to come ashore on Oahu to trade for provisions in 1792 when they were separated and murdered.

fertile soil and bountiful seas, not to mention magnificent landscapes and graceful wives.

Why then, the question was posed, had Campbell not stayed?

The answer came in two parts. When he used to survey his little kingdom, Campbell said he had given thanks. He had men to bear him aloft to court, a hut below the mountains and rainforests fed by the Manoa waterfalls, and of course the company of Polynesian ladies. Peace and prosperity prevailed, thanks to Tamaahmaah's wisdom and what Campbell called the islanders' 'natural ingenuity and unwearied industry'.

But his stumps had never fully healed. They gave him constant pain. And amid the idyll, occasional, jarring episodes of violence would explode. When the king's brother died:

> The natives cut off their hair and went about completely naked. Many,
> particularly the women, disfigured themselves by knocking out their front
> teeth and branding their faces with hot stones.[8]

The rare arrival of a ship, a whaler bound for England, resolved the matter. Campbell placed his dilemma before the king, who said, 'if his belly told him to go, he would; and if mine told me so, I was at liberty':[9]

> He then desired me to give my compliments to King George. I told him that
> I had never seen King George. He expressed much surprise, and asked if he
> did not go about amongst his people, to learn their wants? I answered that he
> did not do it himself but had men who did it for him. Tamaahmaah shook
> his head and said other people could never do it so well as he could himself.[10]

Campbell had been torn ever since. As he told Mr Smith, surgery had failed to quell his pain and an Edinburgh infirmary had discharged him as 'incurable'. Now he longed once more for his sunny Arcadia.

For what followed there is scant evidence, but it appears that Smith took Campbell under his roof, gave him a desk and negotiated a contract with

Constable & Co of Edinburgh for one of the earliest sailor's memoirs.[11] In May 1816 a collaborative title was published:

A VOYAGE ROUND THE WORLD
FROM 1806 TO 1812
By Archibald Campbell

It has been suggested that Campbell's colourful version of life among castaways and bare-breasted Polynesians was bowdlerized by Smith, who edited the book with the rectitude expected of a Fellow of the Royal Society.[12] Readers – promised accounts of shipwreck and the dark paradise where Cook had met his death – still flocked to buy the book. Such were sales, it was announced that the author had acquired the funds 'to return to the friendly territory of King Tamaahmaah'.[13]

Archibald Campbell, with a wife, Isabella, and a pair of wooden legs he had fashioned himself, sailed to America in 1818. More money was forthcoming from a New York edition which sold out and attracted the attention of a mission school in Connecticut. The final piece did not fall into place. Having been recruited to take Christianity to Hawaii on the strength of his righteous text, Archibald and Isabella were dismissed when it was discovered that in fact they were 'not pious'.*

Campbell, it appears, never did return to his island in the sun. Those other sailors – the Welshman Davis, the Englishman Young – they had stayed, the first Europeans to leave a genetic trail in Hawaii; but like so many others, their stories would never be told.

Campbell's book may have been influential in other ways, though. Six years after his *Voyage* was published, another down-and-out sailor was spotted on

---

* For all its historical and cultural interest, Archibald Campbell's *Voyage Around the World* is an ascetic read, thanks to James Smith's editing. This absence of *vivre* greatly frustrated the psychologist Stanley Porteus, a resident of Hawaii himself, who conducted further research on Campbell's life in order to produce *The Restless Voyage*, a vivid but novelized version of the original. Apart from his discovery that the Campbells had been expelled for impiety, it is the original that is used here.

those same Edinburgh streets by a bookbinder and scribe. It is quite feasible that John Nicol's *Life and Adventures*, issued by William Blackwood of Edinburgh in 1822 and the prototype for subsequent seamen's memoirs, actually had its genesis in the success of Archie Campbell's now-forgotten book.

———

Publishers were particularly enthused by storytellers who were more than plain Jacks and could introduce a risqué touch. A naval report in *The Times* about 'a young and delicate female calling herself Miss T–lb–' who was languishing in hospital after serving in the *Brunswick*, twice being wounded in battle and now facing a leg amputation, piqued considerable interest.[14] The product, the *Life and Surprising Adventures of Mary Anne Talbot . . . Related by Herself*, was a bestseller of 1809.

And no wonder. Mary confessed to being the illegitimate offspring of an aristocrat who was only the first of many bad men in her life. The next, a guardian, stole her inheritance before passing the fourteen-year-old to an army officer who made her a sexual slave and carried her off to the West Indies where she joined the military as a drummer. Under the *nom de guerre* John Taylor, she returned to fight at the Battle of Valenciennes, deserted, walked across Europe and joined the Navy in time to receive the first of her wounds at the Glorious First of June. Back at sea, she was captured again, this time by the French, and spent eighteen months in prison before crossing to America. Then, on her return to England, she was impressed. By now understandably desperate, Mary revealed herself to be a woman in order to avoid further naval service and opened up a new career on the London stage. This does not even touch on the titillating aspects of her various relationships, mainly with women. As the first researcher to check the story against naval and army records concluded, the most remarkable thing about the *Life and Surprising Adventures of Mary Anne Talbot* is that it was so long accepted as a true account.[15] All that can be said with certainty is that when a ghostwriter compiled her 'autobiography', Mary was a domestic servant in the house of the book's publisher Robert Kirby; and that she died in 1808, aged about thirty.

Cross-dressing 'Amazons' had been a popular biographical subject for some time, a trend established by a life of Hannah Snell, who adopted male form as a marine named James Gray in a navy squadron off India where she really did see action and was wounded. As she too owned up to being a woman and later took to the stage, *The Female Soldier: or The Surprising Life and Adventures of Hannah Snell*, of 1750, evidently provided a model for Talbot's story. But although much embellished, it is rooted in fact.[16]

In seafaring terms, however, no transsexual fantasy matches that of William Brown. In August 1815, the war with France over, *The Times* – which had a nose for this kind of tale – revealed that among those paid off on the *Queen Charlotte* was 'a female African who had served as a seaman for upward of 11 years'. Brown plainly was the real thing – Able and captain of the foretop to boot: 'She is a smart, well-formed figure, about five foot four inches in height,' the paper reported, 'possessed of considerable strength and great activity; her features [are] rather handsome for a *black* . . . and she appears to be about 26 years of age':

> In her manner she exhibits all the traits of a British tar and takes her grog with her late messmates with the greatest gaiety.[17]

A William Brown named in the *Queen Charlotte*'s muster has been cited as substantiating the story.[18] Alas, this twenty-one-year-old from Grenada, discharged for 'being a female', had been detected within four weeks of entering, on 23 May 1815, and rather than captain of the foretop, had been a Landsman. She was promptly sent ashore.[19]

Of all seafarers' tales at that time, none so roused the press nor so discredited the naval establishment as the real-life Crusoe drama which created the scandal of 1810. On 3 April the radical MP Francis Burdett stood in the Commons to denounce a naval officer's wickedness. The Honourable Warwick Lake was guilty of a 'most atrocious, cruel and cowardly act of murder' and, Burdett declared, his dismissal in disgrace was not enough for those of His Majesty's subjects most interested in the case – seamen who had fought and bled for their country. Nothing would serve but that Lake be prosecuted as a murderer.[20]

For weeks the prints had been full of the appalling treatment of Robert Jeffery. As it appeared, Jeffery, aged seventeen, from the fishing village of Polperro, had been pressed out of a privateer off Cornwall by the brig *Recruit*. By the time she reached the Leeward Islands, he had twice been accused of stealing drink and Captain Lake announced he 'would not keep such a fellow in his ship'.[21] Jeffery had been rowed to a rocky uninhabited islet known as Sombrero, set down and marooned.

That the story had come to light at all was due to a purser who wrote to his MP describing Lake as 'this *titled murderer*'.[22] The letter was passed to the Admiralty and, because it also implicated Rear-Admiral Alexander Cochrane for having knowledge of Lake's action, response was obligatory. When the captain came to court martial, however, two years had passed and no hope could be entertained that Jeffery had survived on an atoll lacking either food or fresh water.

Reporters were present at the trial when Lake admitted blandly to having had the youth marooned. Trying to recover himself, he said he had believed the island inhabited and later sent a party back to Sombrero, which found no trace of anyone at all. Lake then brought the court up sharply again by declaring that the boy must have escaped and was probably back in England, 'concealed [so] he may be let loose upon me, to seek compensation in damages'.[23]

For crusaders like Burdett and the journalist William Cobbett, the lines were clear: on one side the Honourable Warwick Lake, heir to a viscountcy and a symbol of corrupted power, on the other an innocent Cornish youth, plucked from his native shore by a press gang and murdered in diabolical fashion. As Burdett put it: 'Why was he not simply cast into the sea? It would have been more merciful.'[24]

In the ensuing outcry the Admiralty despatched a fast-sailing vessel for Sombrero to establish Jeffery's fate.[25] There was little doubt, however, that

Burdett had been right in telling the Commons: 'He has perished.' The worst appeared to be confirmed by a report three weeks later that an American ship had found Jeffery, but only after he 'had ate off his flesh as far as he could reach'. Barely alive then, he had soon expired.[26]

By now newspaper stories were being headlined 'Jeffery The Seaman'. The next account from America was the most sensational yet. Robert Jeffery was alive and had been living in Massachusetts for almost three years. An affidavit declared that he had survived on Sombrero for nine days on limpets and rainwater until being sighted by telescope from a passing ship. Since then he had worked as a blacksmith in the town of Marblehead where he was known as 'the Governor of Sombrero'.

A month later, in October 1810, *The Times* related that 'the young man whose case has excited such extraordinary interest' had arrived safely home in Polperro. His appearance – fair-haired, slender, aged about twenty-two and roughly 5 feet 4 inches with a light complexion – was a subject of intense interest, for up to this point many had refused to believe he was still alive, including Cobbett and Jeffery's mother. Their reunion was observed by a reporter:

> At first she gazed on him with a kind of bewildered anxiety, as if doubtful whether she could trust what she saw: in a few moments she recovered herself, and they rushed into each other's arms – 'Oh! my son,' and 'Oh! my mother', interrupted by sobs on both sides, were all they could utter for some time. At length the agitation subsided, and a scene of calm endearment ensued.
>
> The village was a scene of generous tumult until a late hour in the night. Jeffery repeatedly declared that he entirely forgave Captain Lake.[27]

Such generosity of spirit may have been due to the £600 Jeffery received in compensation from his former captain – on condition that he not be pursued for damages.[28] Jeffery also had three years' back pay from the Admiralty, and profits from a racy booklet:

AN ACCOUNT OF THE SUFFERINGS OF

Jeffery The Seaman

MAROONED

DURING HIS ABODE ON THE DESOLATE ROCK OF

SOMBRERO

WHERE HE WAS LEFT

BY THE INHUMAN ORDER OF HIS CAPTAIN

Extracted From A Journal or Diary

With these proceeds Jeffery was able to buy a share in a trading schooner. Unfortunately, the venture seems to have failed as he returned to black-smithing. In 1820, two years after his marriage to a local lass at Lonsallos church, he died aged thirty.

That the market for tales by ostensibly illiterate plebeians continued to grow may in part be due to Tom Allen. In 1827 Frederick Chamier, a naval officer with literary ambitions, set out to find men who had sailed with Nelson, and was led to the Royal Hospital at Greenwich where Tom was living as an elderly pensioner. Nelson's self-styled 'wally de sham' had gone back to sea after dismissal by his master, serving in a frigate off Spain before being invalided out in 1812.[29] Tom retained his connection with Nelson's family in Burnham and was made servant to Sir William Bolton in a household that included Horatia, the admiral's daughter by Emma Hamilton. After Bolton died, Tom and his wife Jane were in poverty until their plight was brought to the atten-tion of Sir Thomas Hardy, captain of the *Victory* at Trafalgar and now governor at the hospital, who took them in. Chamier found him there, listened to his story and turned it into a novel, *Ben Brace, The Last of Nelson's Agamemnons*.

Tom lived to see this fictional account of a seaman described as 'Nelson's coxswain and valet' achieve wide popularity. Indeed, it rapidly went into a third edition which Chamier updated with a tribute to his informant, quoting a letter from Greenwich dated March 1836. It is signed 'Ben Brace', but

addressed 'to the Gentleman wot wrote my life', and may be inferred to have
come from Tom:

> As it's blowing great guns and small arms . . . I've got snug in my own
> cabbin and am about to tell you what I think of my Life. I'm much obliged
> to you, sir, that's what I am – because I think it was my due. A man that has
> served under Nelson is somebody, even now when sailors drink tea, have no
> tails, wear no buckles, and are giving over baccy – except in pipes.

He had a point. Though there are those who believe Tom's part in Nelson's
story was inflated, he attracted curious visitors to Greenwich and was seen as
representative of sailors as a body. 'If I'm out a walking,' he wrote, 'if anybody
wants to see me, they've only got to ask, for I'm in all their memories.' On his
death two years later, an obituary came close to the mark in describing him as
'a mixture of honest hardihood, untutored simplicity, pardonable vanity and
nautical prejudice . . . a fine example of the British tar'.[30] Hardy regarded Tom
well enough to arrange a memorial to 'the faithful servant of Admiral Lord
Nelson', which still stands near the hospital site.*

In the same year Chamier's novel was published, theatre audiences in fashionable Bath were being entertained by one actor's portrayals of Macbeth and
Shylock. Acclaim for Charles Pemberton was enough to bring him to Covent
Garden in 1829, where the actor-manager Charles Kemble held sway. They
may have clashed. Pemberton had run his own theatre in the West Indies, and
his passion for Shakespeare's tragic roles left no doubt that he valued his own
interpretations. The critics were less certain, and Kemble did not invite him
back. So Pemberton gave up the theatre and took to another stage, as a
campaigner.

---

* Chamier was not the only former naval officer to turn his knowledge to fiction: Captain
Marryat's novels were the biggest sellers of their time, but he wrote mainly from the
perspective of the midshipmen's berth.

Around this time he started to write for a radical journal, the *Monthly Repository*, articles about his life which he intended to turn into a memoir. So, after a night of fiery speechifying to an artisan audience, he would pick up his pen and resume the story of a boy born into 'the humblest class – the poorest of the poor', taken to sea by reading *Robinson Crusoe*. Pemberton realized he had a credibility problem. *The Autobiography of Pel Verjuice*, he wrote, was likely 'to be dismissed as a tissue of impudent falsehoods; or, at best, a specimen of my faculty of invention'.[31]

It is hard to imagine Pemberton, also known as Thomas Reece and Peregrine Verjuice, in blue jacket and canvas trowsers, and even harder to picture the figure he would have cut among his shipmates. A friend from his acting days said he had 'a handsome, intellectual face, what the French would call *spirituelle* in expression', while his writing has the moody self-indulgence of a Byron at sea, swinging between black despair and euphoria.[32] He could rail as wildly

A troubled romantic, Charles Reece Pemberton achieved success on stage and as a writer only after failing as a seaman.

against seafaring in all its aspects and characters – 'the degrading communion into which I had thrown myself' – as he would revel in the sights of foreign places and ancient worlds. There are times when he might indeed be thought to have made the whole thing up. But while his descriptions need to be treated with caution, the facts of his narrative and career are – like our other narrators – confirmed by Admiralty records.[33]

Charles Pemberton was born to a Welsh labourer and only received an education because his family moved from Pontypool to Birmingham with its Unitarian charity school where boys 'of indigent parents were fed, clothed, flogged, and taught – gratis'. He joined the legion of readers enraptured by *Robinson Crusoe* and aged seventeen fled apprenticeship at a grim brass foundry and, with a friend, walked the hundred miles to Liverpool docks.

His writing reflects a wild, possibly manic-depressive personality, and, in describing the horrors of his start in navy life, is prone to embroidery; the two youths volunteered but he suggests they had been impressed. At Spithead he was taken on the guardship *Salvador del Mundo*, which he described with an unnerving turn of phrase:

> She sat enthroned upon the glistening surface of the mirror, the Queen of magnificence and beauty! . . . Reader, she was a hell afloat.[34]

Pemberton claimed to have endured such pain at the hands of a sadistic bosun's mate that 'I should have been tried and hanged for murder had I remained a week longer on board'. But while he fell all too often into empurpled melodrama, he strived to express the paradoxes and sensations of sea life. The world changed when he left the *Salvador* and came aboard the frigate *Alceste*. She became 'my wandering habitation, my beloved and beautiful home'.

The *Alceste* had just been commissioned. Her complement of 230 included 83 Landsmen, among whom was the Welsh youth named in the muster as Thomas Charles Reece, alias Pemberton.[35] For all his populist ideas, he felt no affiliation with these fellows: 'The refuse of jails – beings whose infamy was their source of merriment.' An Irishman of his own age, Justin Moran, was 'half demented, but in the eye was a sinister knavery'.[36]

They sailed from Plymouth on a calm, clear day in September 1807, escorting a convoy bound for Gibraltar. Five years would pass before the Alcestes sighted England again and though by then they had performed service across the Mediterranean, had intercepted innumerable strange sail in quest of intelligence and taken the French frigate *Pomone* in a stirring action, these events play no part in Pemberton's narrative. The reason may be that his own record had been, to say the least, undistinguished. The truth was, he never had the makings of a seaman. After three years as a Landsman, he had still not been made up to Ordinary when Captain Murray Maxwell took pity on him and made him a clerk.

But Pemberton's world had been enlarged by foreign places – from Lisbon to Tangier, Capri to Valletta, Cagliari to Genoa – and he felt blessed: 'How truly, deeply, do I thank the God of Nature for such anodynes scenes like this have thrown on my parched spirit.'[37] More significantly, sea life had educated him in humanity. From lamenting 'the degrading communion into which I had thrown myself', he had discovered 'the quality of my comrades . . . men whose lives and characters were unimpeachable, industrious men on whose reputations the world's breath could not cast a blemish'. The *Alceste* he called 'my wandering habitation, my beloved and beautiful home, the happiest home I ever knew'.[38] With Captain Maxwell at the helm:

> . . . she was a feather in a cup of oil, floating and bending so easily and smoothly. Why was this? True, he was one of the most skilful and cool-headed seamen that ever commanded a ship. [Men] put forth their strength, skill and cheerful alacrity because he was merciful and considerate.[39]

He liked to evoke scenes of life afloat:

> Reader, did you ever see an army of bats suspended by the heels to the roof of a cavern? If you have you may form some idea of the 'tween decks of a

frigate at night, when some two or three hundred hammocks are slung up to the ceiling, the deck overhead, with half as many sleepers snoring in chorus; though my zoology does not tell me that bats snore.[40]

And he summoned a vision that had stirred him when orders were given to make sail:

> The instant flashing effect is magical and magnificent: the minute-ago-naked masts, beams and yards, the whole of the uptowering and beautiful skeleton is clothed in fifteen thousand feet of graceful drapery, so perfectly fitted and so admirably put on; then out it swells and curves in the wind. It is beauty itself . . .[41]

Pemberton left the sea in 1812, still only twenty-two. After quitting the stage he made his home in Sheffield where unionism was on the rise in the steel industry. He turned radical, inveighing against priests and Tories, impressment and the monarchy. (A special ire was reserved for 'the Mulish Moloch known as George the Third'.)[42]

Yet he remained a wanderer, with a final journey that took him to Egypt and down the Nile by boat and donkey. 'Look ye,' he wrote to a friend, 'a letter from Thebes is not to be had every day at Sheffield.' At Karnak, 'encompassed by human productions that seem impossible,' he wrote:

> Of all the temples [it] is the most extensive, the grandest, most sublime and mysterious – full of dark suggestions and concealments, remote hints and thundering proclamations.[43]

He died a year later, in 1840, leaving three plays (which show a palpable desire to emulate Shakespeare) and his 'autobiography' – a pile of papers so prolix and moody it was only rendered readable by the most rigorous editing.[44]

While he and Nagle served simultaneously it is hard to imagine the troubled romantic and the boisterous topman as messmates. Nagle's tales reflect not only his swagger but the shared humanity of encountering a terrified islander in what is now Papua New Guinea:

> I laid holt of him and helped him up alongside the boat and patted him on the shoulder to passefy him. He made motions to me that we came from the clouds, pointing up in the elements, supposing our guns to be thunder and lightning.[45]

Yet Pemberton, in his romanticized ramblings, may have caught something Nagle could only reach for – an explanation why true Jacks kept going back, from ship to ship to ship:

> She is a huge sea dragon, swimming along with her enormous wings thrown upward to the air while her copper belly curls up the hissing and boiling foam of the sea, and dashes the clipping waves as if in derision at their familiar touch . . . The proud and gorgeous mass of machinery, slowly gathering progress, glides round into her destined track. She is the engineer of her own road, and digs it up as she advances, and it closes up behind, leaving no line to denote the course of her journey . . . She is so beautiful, and she glides along with so much grace that her every motion might seem the dignity of joy. Who could have thought she was an ocean monster, destined to seek victims and devour them?[46]

SAFE MOOR'D
1820-40

IN THE autumn of 1838 an old hulk passed up the Thames to Rotherhithe on her final voyage – not under sail but steam, pulled by a pair of 'tuggers' to Beatson's breakers yard. A year later J. M. W. Turner unveiled a portrayal of the moment, rich with artistic licence; the hulk is seen as a noble old three-decker with her masts standing, when in reality they had already been stripped; and she is being carried off in her ghostly shimmering grandeur by a single, dark and dwarfish vessel under a cloud of fiery steam. The painting voted Britain's most loved work of art is heavy with metaphor; a white flag of surrender flies aloft; the heroic age is being consigned to history by technology.

Turner's *Fighting Temeraire* contains another symbolic touch which tends to be overlooked. The observer is seeing the passing not just of sailing ships but of those who worked them. And as well as glory at Trafalgar, the *Temeraire* exemplified Jack's travails against a system that decorated him with praise yet was savage in punishment and miserly with reward. The grand old 98 is remembered for coming gallantly to the rescue of Nelson's *Victory* at Trafalgar. The outrage of 1802, deplored as 'one of the most fatal blots on our naval annals' – the hanging of a dozen men from the yards 'on which they had so lately and gallantly served' – is forgotten.

So, had all the effusion – about 'brave Jack', or 'honest Tar' – had it all been a sham? In the poorhouses and from parish dependants up and down the land, many a heartfelt Aye would have been heard. Lost seamen were publicly visible enough to anger campaigners like George 'Bosun' Smith, a sailor himself before he was seized with Baptist fervour. Of stentorian voice and 'oceanic tempestuous nature', Smith had frequent run-ins with the authorities while lobbying for naval reform. But it was the blight of poverty that moved him to his greatest labours: a fund for shipwrecked and distressed men and their families in 1824; and founding the Destitute Sailors' Asylum in London in 1827. The 'Bosun's' zeal did not stop there. With a crew of boys in nautical outfits singing hymns, he helped to found a refuge for seamen's orphans and another for repentant Polls. Unfortunately, his dedication was not matched by management skills and four times he ended up in a debtors' prison; he won prominent supporters, including naval officers such as Captain George Gambier, only to fall out with most of them. But Smith was a seaman who made an outstanding contribution to the welfare of old shipmates.[1]

That many remained in acute need was recorded by the journalist Henry Mayhew. A solicitor's son but a chaotic boy, Mayhew ran away to sea at twelve and made a single voyage to India before returning to London where 'shipwrecks [had] got so common in the streets that people didn't care for them'.*

Among the shipwrecks was one John Roome, found 'crying watercress and herrings' on a street in Blackfriars' in the 1840s. Roome had been *Victory's* signalman at Trafalgar, had raised the flags that informed every hand what England expected of them that day.[2] He was now broken, destitute and, at sixty-eight, near the end of his life.

This account would have been the richer for evidence from those who felt betrayed, those who 'having been sucked like oranges, were thrown into the gutter like the peel'.[3] Yet the voices we do have, ranging from William Spavens to William Richardson, speak with a common characteristic – pride. And

---

* Thompson, pp. 293–4. Mayhew went on to co-found *Punch* magazine in 1841.

warfare had been their binding mechanism. It is no coincidence that from 1740 Britain had been at war for thirty-seven of the years up to Waterloo. In her account of the forging of Britain, Linda Colley sees the wars with France as having had the support, broadly speaking, of the entire nation. 'For all classes and for both sexes, patriotism was more often than not a highly rational response and a creative one as well. Patriotism in the sense of identification with Britain served . . . as a bandwagon on which different groups and interests leaped so as to steer it in a direction that would benefit them.' Being a patriot, as she says, was a means of gaining a much broader access to citizenship.[4] Still more so was this in Jack's case. What may now be thought patronizing clichés, like 'honest Tar', were at the time badges of status. He had been the nation's survival mechanism, and over a century of wars from which no generation was exempt had prized his honour in a way that left little room for ambivalence.

As to whether seafaring contributed to the creation of a national identity, the evidence is mixed. Scots, the third-largest contingent on the lower deck, had invested as boldly and devotedly in British patriotism as the English and Welsh. Ireland's incorporation into a United Kingdom by the Act of Union in 1800 and Catholic Emancipation in 1829 could never really shake the identity of a separate island, and, as we have seen, Irish hands, the second-largest group, retained nationalist instincts which had led to significant rebellions. A seaman named George Watson, English himself, saw them as enduringly distinctive components of the lower deck:

> The Irish are daringly bold and impetuous but need to be led. They are generous and kind-hearted when they are at peace, but the turbulent passions in them often cause them to violate every tie of friendship. The Scot is sullenly brave and proud of the memory of his ancestors. He fights to maintain their ancient glories . . . In battle a lion or a vulture, but when victory crowns his arms he becomes a lamb or a dove. John Bull is a mixture of both . . . resolute and coolly courageous . . . but he has prudence enough not to urge an hopeless warfare and manly submits to his fate.[5]

For the survivors – and there were many – benefits were still to be had.

Navy hands made contributions throughout their service towards pension funds that provided for them in the event of disability, sickness or after long or distinguished service. These funds had been amalgamated in 1814 under the roof of the Royal Naval Hospital at Greenwich, which sheltered a fixed number of in-pensioners and disbursed payments to a far larger number of out-pensioners with homes or families. That year 5,491 men aged between eighteen and seventy-four were registered as out-pensioners. In 1815 a further 7,596 were added to the list and in 1816 another 2,922. Following demobilization numbers continued to decline – to 2,166 in 1818 and 635 in 1820.[6] A large majority were aged between thirty and fifty, but the youngest was seventeen, the oldest eighty-four. One seventy-three-year-old granted his pension in 1814 was still alive in 1821.[7]

These men received annual amounts ranging from £7 for, say, a damaged hand, to £16 for the loss of a leg. The latter figure was also paid to John Southey, who had 'lost an eye and all his teeth', and John Hancock, who was simply 'worn out'.[8] It was not until 1831 that clear rates of pay for disability were laid down:

> An able seaman having lost two limbs or being otherwise so severely wounded as to require the care of some other person shall have from 1/6 to 2s a day; for less injury & not requiring care from 1/- to 1/6 a day . . . if able to contribute to some small degree of his livelihood, from 9d to 1/- a day.[9]

Generally pensions were for life, although the Admiralty seemingly wanted to reduce the dependency of those it had made alcoholics as payments for 'diseased liver' could be limited to three years. Out-pensions for lengthy or meritorious service were more generous: a typical intake of fifty-three men in the month of September 1815 were approved payments of between £12 and £21 for life.[10] (By comparison, lieutenants received £50 a year, captains £80.)

More fortunate still was another category of pensioner.

John Roome, having been observed begging on the street in Blackfriars, was questioned by a local doctor who, informed that this dishevelled figure had been the Jack who hoisted the signal at Trafalgar, 'could scarcely refrain from a demonstration of reverence towards the old embarrassed man who sat uneasily before me'.[11] As it turned out, the doctor discovered the reason Roome had no pension was not down to neglect by the state, but because he had deserted from *Victory*. Presented with the facts, the Admiralty did the decent thing and granted Roome a place at Greenwich where he lived for a further thirteen years.

The Royal Naval Hospital beside the Thames was, in fact, no medical facility but the world's most magnificent almshouse, a showpiece of English Renaissance architecture by Sir Christopher Wren, with facilities for up to 2,710 resident pensioners. The number of in-pensioners and the 21,260 out-pensioners registered between 1814 and 1820 are no grounds for complacency, set against the 140,000 hands who served at the height of the war. Still, those granted a berth at Greenwich received a blessing available to none others of the common order besides their smaller number of army equivalents at Chelsea. Nearby stood the school for the children of dead shipmates – those killed in action or disabled.

George King, a man of twenty-four years' service with battle honours, joined about 300 old hands who presented themselves at the Admiralty on a winter's day in 1832 in the hope of a Greenwich berth. Each came bearing a 'ticket', a certificate of his service, and, if he could, a letter of commendation from a former officer. Thirteen were accepted. King was among the hundreds to be dismissed. He was already an out-pensioner and for the time being he got by, his income supplemented by casual labour in and around Wapping – 'two days' work at St Katharines Dock just before Christmas Eve'. The next time, he was one of 100 men applying for nine places:

> At eleven their lordships arrived . . . I did not expect to be admitted but one of the lords asked me my service and also my pension to which I answered him 24 years service and £16 pension when he ordered my ticket to be taken away and I was ordered into the outer office to sit down.[12]

At four o'clock that afternoon, King landed at Greenwich and entered the splendid sanctuary where he would spend the last fifteen years of his life.

The inhabitants were issued with a blue suit, a tricorn hat and four pairs of blue hose – a uniform, in effect, that foreshadowed the regime introduced for seamen in 1857, but which must have struck as odd a group of men who had dressed at sea in whatever slops were at hand. Paintings, lithographs and cartoons of Greenwich pensioners in their long coats and tricorn hats almost invariably include one figure with a wooden leg, and we may observe among their number our first storyteller, William Spavens, a pegleg himself, eulogizing the retreat where:

> The park is delightful . . . the clothing for the pensioners comfortable, and the provision wholesome and plentiful; all of which conspire to render life, loaded with infirmities, tolerable if not happy in its decline, 'when safe moor'd in Greenwich tier'.[13]

By all accounts, the 'Greenwich Geese' remained an awkward crew. The nickname is said to have been coined because of raids on a local farmer's fowls. One pensioner was expelled after fathering his ninth illegitimate child in Greenwich.[14] Another character who acquired a measure of fame was Arthur Hardy, who quitted the hospital 'without leave' three times, despite being a double amputee. Hardy was noted without irony in the hospital records as having 'Run' in 1805, 1808 and 1811 – although he had lost both legs below the knee on the sloop *Hawke*. The third time he found another sanctuary, in Windsor, and remained there for sixteen years before writing to beg re-admission. He returned on Christmas Day, 1830, dying nine months later aged seventy-five.[15] (As to the reasons for his 'deserting', it is possible that Hardy, like a number of other pensioners, did so to be reunited with family. Wives were not allowed to live at Greenwich, which explains why John Nicol did not apply for entry until after his wife died. By then, as we have seen, the Admiralty ruled that he had left it too long.)

Fights and drunkenness were more common transgressions and delinquents had to wear a yellow coat with red arms – a stigma that the pensioners turned to smart advantage. The hospital had started to attract visitors, and as most questioners' interest related to Trafalgar, they would be directed for an answer to one of the yellow-coated 'Canaries' – he being described as a veteran who could give a dramatic first-hand account of those events for a small fee. The grateful visitors' largesse would then be shared around.

Most hobby crafts at sea had a practical aspect, but scrimshaw, the engraving of whales' teeth, was a decorative art.

What the pensioners made of their noble surroundings – Corinthian pilasters, cupolas and vestibules, not to mention canvases by Sir Peter Lely, Sir Godfrey Kneller and Thomas Gainsborough – is not recorded. On a practical level, four great buildings contained the wards housing typically between twenty and forty men. Each ward was divided into individual cabins which, with a bed, table and chair, afforded more private space than the occupant had ever enjoyed at sea. Rations were better too – beef three times a week, mutton twice, with pease soup and cheese the other two, plus drink in the form of four pints of small beer a day. (Agricultural and factory workers were doing well if they ate meat more than once a week.)[16] Meals were taken in the most resplendent space of all – the Painted Hall, with its chiaroscuro ceiling *The Triumph of Peace and Liberty over Tyranny* by Sir James Thornhill. Although the diners may not have realized it, there in this grand allegorical work, among the kings and queens, the Greek and Roman gods, is one of their own. John Worley, admitted in 1705 and reputed to have been among the hospital's most disruptive residents, gazed down with bearded, saint-like benevolence on his successors.

Other facilities included a library with more than 1,400 volumes and a bust of Charles Dibdin inscribed with lines from 'Tom Bowling'. An officer resident noted with regret, however, that 'few of the pensioners avail themselves of the privileges thus extended to them; not more than twenty or thirty [use] the library'. More common was it to find a group of Falstaffian figures, 'as melancholy as lugged bears' after a night's carouse.[17]

Of those lucky to be 'safe moor'd in Greenwich tier', George King perhaps found himself on a bench with another old hand, George Watson, two bluecoats, with clay pipes and stone beer flagons at hand.[18] There one might say, 'Tip us a yarn', and accounts – of ships, of voyages, of wrecks, of shipmates and tyrants, mutinies and battles – would begin.

———

George King had been in the frigate *Melpomene* with the Baltic fleet off Finland in '09 when volunteers were asked to come forward for a raid on Russian gunboats. They rowed several miles through the dark and seized the first boat before coming under point-blank fire. 'The coxswain was close alongside of me,' King related. 'His head was blown clean off his shoulders, part of his head took off my hat, and his brains flew all over me.' Another man, both legs severed, lay in the bottom of the boat, trying to open his knife 'to cut his belly, but we took the knife from him'. He begged to be heaved overboard, then died.

Casualties were heavy – 54 of 270 volunteers from four ships killed or wounded. One Russian gunboat had been burned and six taken.[19] When the smoke cleared, King recalled, 'we commenced upon the grog and in less than an hour some of our chaps were singing one of Dibdin's songs'. Back on *Melpomene* there was more grog:

> The captain asked us if we could guess at our loss. We said no. He then ordered us a glass of grog each and the purser took us all down and gave us each a tumbler of Hollands gin. I drank it off and went and laid down in my berth under the table and was soon fast asleep.[20]

Here George Watson picked up the thread, for he too had been on a cutting-out caper – in the year '12 in the Adriatic. George was an unusual cove, something his fellows remarked on. He left a well-paid merchantman because he preferred the Navy, you see, had never been pressed and never left, right up to when Johnny Crapaud gave him a broadside. Navy ships were, well, so *lively*. Take the *Eagle* and her farmyard below where the livestock 'were spared slaughter and had names given to them':

> There was Billy the goat, Jenny the cow, Tom the sheep, Jack the goose and many others; Jenny the cow, after being two years on board, ran dry, and therefore was killed; poor Tom the sheep was killed by lightening and I know not what became of Billy; as for Jack the goose, he saw them all out . . . he would come out of his coop and join the forecastlemen and seemed quite at home amongst them. This sociality of the goose made every body notice and some would exclaim in his perambulations, 'Well done, Jack!' 'Bravo, old Turko!'[21]

Of *Eagle*'s captain, Charles Rowley, who once thrashed him with a stick, ordered him aloft, then gave him a dozen for good measure, Watson said: 'There could not be a better commander when the ship was in port and duty done. You might indulge in every merriment and festivity with impecunity.' After all, as he saw it, 'there is such diversity of characters in a ship that it is necessary to deal harshly with some for the comfort and security of others'.[22]

Then came the night – 17 September it was – he volunteered for an operation to cut out enemy gunboats on the River Po. In barges, they raced upriver as Johnny opened fire. Coming up the side, George 'felt the true ferocious characteristics of war fire my bosom, though in general I was naturally averse to it' – and ran straight into an explosion of cannister shot from a gun a few feet away which hurled him and two others back into their boat. One ball 'went through my right thigh, and shattered the bone just below the hip':

> The pain was not poignant, but a kind of indescribable sensation which benumbed me all over. I concluded from it, that to be shot dead would be a very easy way to be sent out of this world.[23]

Watson spent months in a Malta hospital, then another two years at Plymouth. Laid up, his right leg useless and surrounded by nurses, he admitted to great frustration because he was 'fond of the society of women'. That took him off to recall the devout harlots of Palermo 'going on shore every morning to confess their sins', and back on board, 'at it again at night, as fresh as ever'.[24] Mind you, George went on, those Plymouth nurses with 'several husbands' at sea were also 'exceedingly bold and audacious':

> I had a great deal to do to repulse the temptations I met with from these syrens.[25]

He was a windy old cully, Watson, but he had a way with a story and held his listeners' attention even when he started to explain how he came to God. Over those years in hospital, he related, he passed the time in writing and drawing, and helped one of the more virtuous nurses by sewing clothes for her son, which she repaid with flagons of wine. But for books there was only the Bible and, as he read, 'gradually I got triumph over the follies of my youth and resolved if ever I reached home to be another man'. When a young fellow came to hospital after losing both his arms, Watson had another revelation:

> I said to myself 'Take a view of that poor youth and own that nothing ails thee!' and cheerfully hopped about with my crutches.[26]

At this point he was inclined to quote lines he attributed to Milton's *Paradise Lost*, which added a few words of his own but conveyed the general sense of the thing:

> *God, nor to time nor place doth pay respect, Unless holiness be there,*
> *Or thither brought By those that frequent there.*[27]

George Watson was granted his berth for being crippled in action, George King for meritorious service. Both 'rejoiced in the goodness of the Almighty' for carrying them 'through troubles and uncouth adventures' to be Greenwich pensioners.

Images of these characters abounded, especially in caricature form – squiffy-eyed old soaks, lacking in teeth as well as the odd limb. A notable exception is John Burnet's *Greenwich Hospital and the Naval Heroes* marking Trafalgar Day: Burnet knew his subjects well and represented them individually in this panoramic work, celebrating their finest moment with lasses and children on Observatory Hill in 1832 as a frigate passing downriver fires a salute. There, a wee girl on his shoulder, is Joe Brown, captain of the foretop in *Victory*, while the grizzled ancient carving a beef joint is Frank Cowen, who was ashore with Cook at Hawaii. And there, beside him, is none other than a curly-haired Tom Allen. It is a lyrical piece, of a kind with romantic portrayals of the *Sailor's Return* by Thomas Stothard.

What makes Burnet's work remarkable, however, is that it was painted not for an admiral or official but the Duke of Wellington, who hung it at Apsley House as a companion to *Chelsea Pensioners reading the Waterloo Dispatch* by David Wilkie. The Iron Duke's respect for Jack has been noted before. This tribute gave rise, moreover, to the only true portraits of our seamen. In preparing his canvas, Burnet painted nine pensioners. No satires these, but recognizable humans, thoughtfully presented. Thus they are brought to the modern eye, from a strong-featured (and surprisingly youthful-looking) Tom Allen, to a man known only as Joseph Miller, pensive, wise – a reflective face that has seen the world and everything in it, and is prepared for the end.

———

Those denied naval pensions faced a more whimsical fate, being thrown back onto the mercy of their parishes or local charities. Not all were quite what they appeared. Owen Roberts declared himself 'born under an unlucky planet' when he was sighted, on the streets of Liverpool in the 1820s, selling copies of a pamphlet about his seafaring life. The local press took up his cause, a man 'in his 87th year, totally blind, and led about by his wife, nearly as aged as himself . . . a very interesting couple'. It was soon pointed out that Roberts was not exactly destitute, receiving 4s a week from the parish and a further 4s a week as an out-pensioner of the merchant sailor's charity, the Seamen's Hospital Society.[28] Nor had he been unlucky, having survived no fewer than fourteen slaving voyages from Africa and two years in a French prison. Owen Roberts got by for another four years, to become that rarest of sea creatures: one who had been afloat for almost half a century – in men-of-war and privateers as well as slaveships – and lived into his nineties.[29]

Prosperity in a lengthy era of peace enabled the nation to express its gratitude more practically through a range of charitable institutions. In the wake of 'Bosun' Smith's Destitute Sailors' Asylum and the Seamen's Hospital Society, launched by Wilberforce's campaigning, came the Sailor's Home, founded by two evangelical naval captains, which opened in Stepney in 1835. Other

Christian sponsors came forward until virtually every major port had a seamen's refuge.[30]

For those still in naval service, a pension scheme was introduced in 1831 to replace the whimsical system of calculating and approving individual pensions. At sea, an easing of discipline was visible. Flogging round the fleet was abolished in 1824, and punishment became more regulated as the Admiralty responded to radical politicians like Joseph Hume, who decried a system that favoured the 'arbitrary caprice of commanding officers' over the rule of law. Use of the lash was reduced.[31] The total number of naval hands flogged fell from 2,007 in 1839 to 860 seven years later.[32]

Yet in one area, naval statute remained impervious to the age of reform. While the need for impressment had passed, and would not return in the long peace of the nineteenth century, successive governments had shied away from abolishing it, as if tampering with the past might threaten challenges from the future. Abolition, in fact, was an increasingly discomforting cry at Westminster – not in regards to slavery, which had been outlawed as a trade in British territories in 1807, but to impressment.

In a letter to William Wilberforce from Lloyd's Coffee House in 1816, a seaman turned activist, Thomas Urquhart, related how during the war he and his wife, out walking in London, had been manhandled and beaten by a press gang before being rescued by passers-by. On taking their case up with the Lord Mayor, they were granted £50. Urquhart's point, however, was to urge Wilberforce and other philanthropists 'to act with the same ardour and zeal in the cause of British seamen' as they had over slavery. He concluded: 'The sufferers have a much stronger title than the African to your sympathy.'[33] (This may indeed have inspired Wilberforce to launch his charity for distressed hands.)

The cause was taken up in less challenging terms by a true seaman's friend, Captain Anselm Griffiths, who had campaigned long and hard for reform and in 1826 published a treatise *Impressment fully Considered with a View to its Gradual Abolition*. After more than ten years of peace, he believed, the nation had forgotten its debt:

Remember that by carrying the war into every country, every clime, every quarter of the globe, they kept you free . . . Let us purchase their affection and freedom, and no longer have hundreds of these fine open-hearted fellows (for such they intrinsically are) skulking about during the impress, degraded as well as disguised.[34]

Lobbying by an MP, John Silk Buckingham, a former sailor himself, produced a motion for abolition in 1833, but even the Great Reform Act climate that year failed to secure its passage. Another old seaman, the actor Charles Pemberton, was beside himself, 'sick and pale with the shame which every Englishman ought to feel' and bitterly quoting Shakespeare: 'This other Eden, demi-paradise.'[35] An elderly admiral returned fire at these 'babbling blockheads'; if impressment were discontinued and seamen could not be 'brought together *instantly* on the burst of war, there is nothing to prevent *invasion*'.[36]

Though debate went on, press gangs had disappeared from the streets, never to return. The Royal Navy's manning system, of 'sign-on and discharge', was gradually but also fundamentally affected by the coming of steam, and the requirement for smaller, more qualified crews. Tradition gave way finally in 1853 to the creation of a standing force of the Crown.[37]

In the meantime, while comparisons with slavery were being trotted out again, it happened that Jack was fighting and dying once more – this time in the cause of suppressing that inhuman traffic. What one historian has called 'the longest and hardest campaign the Royal Navy ever waged' – against the Atlantic slave trade – had reached a turning point.[38]

PAX BRITANNICA
1819-40

DAVID Bartholomew must have known he was dying as *Leven* passed yet again through the islands off West Africa early in 1821, but he knew too he had done his duty and that may have eased acceptance of his fate. He had shown that old brute St Vincent what a humble hand might achieve – and, in rising from lower deck to command, given his lordship a terrific licking. He could reflect too that his final and most valuable service would be to the lasting benefit of other plain seamen like himself.

The Congress of Vienna had provided Britain with a diplomatic platform to rally the post-war world to the cause of abolishing slavery. Negotiations did not succeed, however, and in 1819 a naval squadron was posted off West Africa with orders 'to use every means to prevent the continuance of the traffic in slaves'. How that laudable objective was to be achieved would tax commanders of the Preventative Squadron for decades, but as a starting point a survey was commissioned of a space of which the Navy remained remarkably ignorant – the coast off Senegambia and in particular the chain of islands directly to the west through which some 60,000 slaves were still being filtered annually, the Cape Verde islands. The officer appointed was Captain David Bartholomew, his ship the frigate *Leven*.

Among naval surveyors and hydrographers, Bartholomew is a forgotten man; yet the qualities that so suited him for that task, single-mindedness and a refusal to countenance failure, are indelibly stamped on his career. Precious little is known of his early years beyond that he hailed from Linlithgow in West Lothian and had spent years in the Baltic and Atlantic trade before being swooped up in a hot press at Wapping in 1795. His skill was soon spotted. Weeks after coming aboard the *Scipio* as a Landsman, he was made Able.[1] A quick mind brought further promotion – to carpenter's mate, coxswain, master's mate and midshipman – and, crucially, the patronage of an influential officer, Sir Home Riggs Popham.[2] By the peace of 1801, Bartholomew was an acting lieutenant making lunar observations by chronometer to establish longitude. One captain was astonished to find this rare skill in 'a person in his situation'.[3]

Bartholomew distinguished himself in action more than once, but by far his bravest act was to challenge the terrifying St Vincent. When war resumed, the lowly officer wrote to the First Lord petitioning for a placement. He was ignored. He wrote again, and then again. He did not stop writing – until finally, perhaps because he knew St Vincent detested his patron Popham, had the temerity to imply in his eighth and last letter that he was being passed over out of spite. The First Lord promptly proved the point by ordering that Bartholomew be impressed as a common seaman for a second time.

Justice came comparatively swiftly. Bartholomew's captain on the *Inflexible* made him master's mate, thus starting him up the ladder once more. St Vincent was brought to book by his enemies in a new government who had him censured for 'an arbitrary and violent act which must disgust all young men who had nothing but their merits to recommend them, and [is] likely therefore to be highly injurious to his Majesty's service'.[4] Within a year Bartholomew was promoted lieutenant. For a captaincy he waited another ten years. By then he was forty-eight, but with service in various roles sufficiently distinguished to earn him the Order of the Bath.

Bartholomew's experience with chronometers brought his final commission. With the Navy about to embark against the slave trade, mapping the Cape Verde islands assumed urgency when the sloop *Erne* was wrecked on Sal owing to 'that island being laid down in the Admiralty chart very incorrect'.[5]

On Christmas Eve of 1818, Captain Bartholomew sailed from Portsmouth in *Leven* with orders 'to use all possible diligence in making a correct survey of the space between these islands of the Coast of Africa'.[6]

All possible diligence he duly exercised for more than two years. Mostly *Leven* cruised between Bonvista, Sal and the other six main islands of Cape Verde, but the captain also spent weeks ashore taking lunar observations with what – to judge from the frantic scratchings of his journal – fell little short of obsession. Such indeed was necessary as the moon's relatively rapid movement made the calculation of longitude from lunar distances intricate, and frustrating too thanks to cloud and weather conditions. Bartholomew's fretful care for the well-being of his chronometers, sextants and astronomical quadrants is also evident. Hardship is occasionally glimpsed: 'The thermometer stands at 95°. Not a piece of bread nor a glass of water all day.' Safe anchorages are described in minute detail. The king of Dakar was a genial host. Otherwise the journal offers few personal insights and of slaves and slavers there is barely a mention.

But then Bartholomew passed over even his own tragedies. A year into *Leven*'s mission, a nineteen-year-old midshipman from Edinburgh died. The circumstances leave little room to doubt that George Bartholomew was the captain's son.[7] When Bartholomew himself fell ill, the dangers as well as the difficulties of taking on the slavers had become all too clear.

The Slave Trade Act of 1807, abolishing human trafficking in British colonies, failed to significantly deter a rampant Atlantic trade and within four years a further Act had to be passed, introducing more severe penalties for what was now deemed a felony. From the peace of 1815, Britain exerted pressure to extend the ban through treaties with its new allies, Spain, Portugal and the Netherlands. These too had negligible impact, while other states, notably old enemies such as France and the United States, had no desire to cooperate with what they saw as a now-overweening Britain. By the time the Preventative Squadron was formed in 1819 it was clear that efforts to suppress trading to British territories had led to a boom in markets elsewhere.

Glory always eluded the West Africa squadron, which accounts for why it is a comparatively neglected subject.[8] There were no grand battles or decisive moments – rather interminable labours in brutal conditions, along with profound suffering, relieved by moments of pride and humanity. Britain's seamen led the way in an act of national redemption, and they paid an accordingly high price.

Broadly, the operation bore some similarity to the wartime blockade of France, only now the objective was to intercept slave ships emerging from Africa into the Atlantic. Initially, the squadron consisted of a frigate, three sloops and two brigs. It was slightly increased from time to time, though always composed of smaller vessels. But there were never enough of them and because they were in pursuit of innumerable quarry operating along 2,400 miles of coastline, the task was impossible. As for rules of engagement, confusion reigned.

Within a year it was clear the Admiralty had failed to comprehend the scale or expense of the task, let alone the dangers. The enemy, from slave masters ashore to traders at sea, were cunning, heavily armed, violent and impossible to police; and thanks to the vast profits to be made, traders from new maritime states, such as Brazil, were following in the wake of the Spaniards, Portuguese and French.

In 1820 a party from the gun-brig *Thistle* came ashore at Guinea with an ultimatum for a slaver named Curtis, son of a British trader. On approaching Curtis's settlement they came under fire. One was killed, nine were captured. Survivors reported that on Curtis's orders the captives were 'stripped and exposed to a vertical sun' before being shot, mutilated and left 'to be devoured by wild beasts'. Among those listed in *Thistle*'s muster as 'Massacred by African traders' were William Woodgate from Tunbridge Wells, and twenty-three-year-old William Daniels from York.[9]

Yet the greatest risk came not from hostiles afloat or ashore, but miasmas in the air. Ships off West Africa encountered all the diseases of the Bight of Benin – and all year round. They rolled heavily in the offshore swell, decks roasting, swept periodically by tropical storms and malignant fevers in the form of malaria and dengue. Between November and March they were afflicted by the

Harmattan, a dust-laden wind blowing off the Sahara that infected men's eyes. Regular contact with rescued slaves introduced dysentery and diarrhoea.

The *Leven*'s first commission was relatively untroubled, the captain's son George a rare fatality. The start of 1821 found her off the island of Sal, but at this point Bartholomew fell ill and his journal ends. The sole surviving record is the master's log. A seaman named Martin died a few days before they came to single anchor off Maio on 19 April, when, at 3.30:

> Departed this life Captain D.E.Bartholomew, CB. Struck the colours & pendant half mast.
> Sent boat with the body of the deceased captain to be interred.
> Received one live bullock. Fresh breezes and fine.[10]

Earl St Vincent may have taken some interest in the news. Recently made Admiral of the Fleet, he always claimed to have the interests of seamen at heart – despite his zeal in hanging them. He outlived by two years the common sailor who dared to stand up to him.

Bartholomew's legacy was a map of the islands and Africa between the longitudes of 23.7° W and 17.2° W and 10° to 20° N latitude, along with surveys of the Azores, Madeira and parts of the Persian Gulf; and the gift of two young officers he had cultivated on *Leven*, Alexander Vidal and William Mudge, both of whom became accomplished hydrographers themselves; Vidal added to his mentor's work by surveying the slaving coast from Gambia to the Congo – a service that proved invaluable in the events that lay ahead.

Mortality figures for the early years of the Preventative Squadron were not collated. It would appear, however, that the risks were well known to seamen on the sloop *Bann* as she prepared to sail from Chatham early in 1822. They were a solid company – seventy-two hands who had been together a year and recently returned from Jamaica. News that their next voyage would take them to Africa started an exodus. Seventeen men ran within weeks.[11]

On 2 March, William Hales and Charles Welch received a dozen lashes apiece for trying to follow the deserters.[12] That opportunity was lost when, trimming and setting topgallants in light breezes and fine weather, they glimpsed the church at Folkestone for the last time before peeling away into the Channel. Eight weeks later they came to off Sierra Leone and it would appear that Hales was still bitter. A Gosport man, born to his trade and rated Able, he had been flogged again, for drunkenness and neglect.

The squadron was based at Sierra Leone, the colony founded by Britain for liberated slaves. Since then slaving had surged along the coast on either side; and however noble the British objective, results had so far been unimpressive – from fifteen suspected slavers intercepted in 1820, the number dropped the following year to nine.[13]

The *Bann* was a 20-gun ship-sloop, nimble enough for navigating close inshore yet well armed to defend herself and with sufficient men and boats to run up the swampy creeks where traders mustered their cargo for loading. Her first foray was not a success – the Spanish schooner they boarded in the Bight of Benin had yet to take on slaves. To the east a month later in the Bight of Biafra they netted a small fish, a Portuguese vessel with thirty-three slaves. As was standard practice, they were taken to Sierra Leone to join the growing population of freed slaves, while the schooner was returned to her owners.

A week later *Bann*'s log records:

Saw a stranger on the starboard at 10. Bore up and made sail in the chase. Brought her to at 3. Boarded the St Antonio polacre under Portuguese colours with 336 slaves.[14]

So atrocious were conditions for those on the polacre that Captain Charles Phillips, to his lasting credit and at considerable risk to his ship, brought 102 of them onto the *Bann*, 'there being so many as to render their removal necessary'.[15] As to how they were received by hands who had to share their own limited space, the log is silent. But lesser concerns were shed. William Hales had not been flogged for months, nor had anyone else. If *Bann*'s record speaks of anything, it is dedication to the task in hand. In her short, tragic service, she epitomized a sacrificial crusade.

The freeing of 336 slaves was followed by further successes. By the end of 1822 the *Bann* had taken five vessels in three months and liberated 813 men, women and children.[16] Her exertions required an extensive refit at Freetown, a port where anecdotal evidence suggests church attendance by seamen was unusually high and records show desertion was virtually unknown. While anchored here the first signs of illness appeared. On 30 March, William Cole, a nineteen-year-old Landsman, died and was committed to the deep.

The initial symptom was a high temperature, but sweating bodies were nothing unusual in airs of 40° between decks. It was when black vomit poured from men's mouths that the yellow fever became unmistakable. Captain

Disease, always the cause of most deaths among seamen, reached epidemic levels
during the anti-slavery operations off West Africa.

Phillips sailed for the nearest refuge, Ascension. Bedding was aired, decks were washed. Nothing else could be done. From 12 April men died almost daily: Edwards Poole, John Kirby, William Franklin, Richard Cox.[17] Seven more were cast over the side before they anchored at Ascension on 25 April:

> Sent hands on shore to rigg tents for sick. Sent sick on shore. Departed this life George Coney, boy.

The deaths of almost half her ratings, thirty-one men and two boys, and the loss of Captain Phillips, who was invalided home, removed *Bann* from the squadron for the rest of 1823 and caused the number of slaving vessels captured that year to fall to just three.

In January she returned with a few men from *Swinger* – and a curious list of characters who appear in the muster like the cast of a pantomime. Among them were Bottle of Beer, Jack Boo, Half a Dollar and Black Wil. All were rated Ordinary, besides King George and Prince Will – both of whom were Able naturally. These were Kroomen – members of an ethnic group in what is now Ivory Coast, and experienced seamen in their own way. One, Jack Freeman, made this clear by deserting.[18]

On 31 January, off the River Lagos, four slavers were sighted – empty while their companies were in the interior conducting trade. Four of *Bann*'s boats departed upriver in pursuit, armed and victualled. William Hales and Charles Welch were with them; two years had passed since their painful attempt to desert; Portsmouth was a lifetime away.

The next morning, heavy firing was heard from beyond the mangroves. It lasted an hour and soon afterwards three boats were seen hastening out over the bar. They had, the log stated, been 'attacked by Natives and Portuguese'. A lieutenant, a mid and six men were wounded. William Hales was dead, 'killed in action'.

The Kroomen were paid off before *Bann* sailed for England, even King George having found the Navy was not for him. Of her seventy-two hands originally mustered, just nineteen remained when they came home on 2 June.

Among those cheering the sight of British isles in summer was Charles Welch. He had been a latecomer to seafaring – aged twenty-eight and from Newry when he signed on as a Landsman and tried to desert with Hales. Four years on, having survived a flogging, yellow fever, attack by natives and now rated Able, he had cause to celebrate a windfall payoff of almost £50.

Africa evidently held no terrors for Welch. Ten years later he was back at Sierra Leone in the survey vessel *Aetna*, and this time willingly. He did take the precaution, though, of naming his mother Phoebe as the beneficiary in the event of his death.[19]

Of the consequences of their endeavours beyond Africa men were oblivious. Britain's bilateral negotiations to secure treaties against slavery passed them by, as did an acrimonious debate over the operation's merits. While the government persevered with an intrinsically noble policy – albeit without adequate resources – *The Times* was among those to rail against the decision 'to send Englishmen to such a pest house'. A mixture of 'quackery and hypocrisy' had created 'a costly grave for British subjects by nicknaming it a school for the civilization of negroes'.[20]

One captain's description of service conditions can only have fanned the debate. 'You can form no conception of what they have to undergo – for months at anchor, rolling terribly, the thermometer 86 degrees: no supplies of fresh stock, except at long intervals and not sufficient vessels to ensure certain reliefs.' Another wrote that the 'effect even upon the best organised mind is sometimes distressing'.[21] Witnessing human barbarity may have had further impact. A slaver awash with shit could be smelt to leeward before it was sighted.

Even after a slave ship was taken and her cargo notionally freed, legal proceedings at Freetown could frustrate the final objective. The squadron operated under treaty jurisdiction and formal hearings delayed condemnation of a slaver. In one case, the Brazilian schooner *Umbelina*, captured off Lagos with 377 slaves, lost 194 of them on the voyage to Freetown where another twenty died in harbour during the two-month wait for condemnation.[22]

Testimony from the lower deck about this dire saga is lacking. The presence of Charles Welch and perhaps 8,000 other men who served off Africa between 1820 and 1840 is, as ever, stated in the musters, along with their origins and ages. There they assume some human form, along with the notes indicating whether or not they survived. Otherwise, however, they are mute. In that respect, we have come full circle back to where this narrative started, with the epic of Anson's voyage.

Ascribing noble intentions to them would be fanciful. West Africa was the Navy's most deadly station and the desertion rate from ships in home waters once men learnt that they were bound for the Bight of Benin speaks for itself. Over Christmas in 1826, the frigate *Sybille* lost forty-nine men from a complement of 275 before she sailed from Portsmouth.[23] As usual in conflict, however, victory meant prize money. The Treasury had placed a £10 bounty on each emancipated man, woman or child. By 1830 this had become too costly to sustain and was reduced to £5.[24] But prize money and the effort needed to secure it may have brought some of the satisfaction that had rewarded British seafarers in storm and battle for centuries.

Slave ships often offered resistance, especially those with superior firepower. As in the case of the 18-gun sloop *Primrose*, however, which intercepted a Spanish vessel of twenty guns, fought her side-to-side before boarding, and suffered three dead and twelve wounded against fifty-two dead and fourteen wounded among their opponents, it was the slavers who took most casualties; the superiority of British seamanship and gunnery remained indisputable.

Perhaps in the logs of such ships can be seen the dedication and activity that kept these skills at a pitch. On the *Sybille*, for example, off Lagos in March 1828, along with entries recording the routine washing and scrubbing of clothes, the arrival of provisions from Santa Cruz and the lightning storms that beset them, it was the daily exercise of 'Boys and Boarders at the Broadsword', the sight of a strange sail to set her haring off in pursuit, that kept these companies on their toes – and alive.

The *Sybille* was among the squadron's most successful cruisers. But it was her small, quick companion that first attracted notice, and eventual fame in the newspapers at home. She was called *Black Joke*.

———

Built in America, the *Black Joke* started her career as a slaving brig, the *Henriquetta*, and was on her sixth voyage to Brazil when *Sybille*'s captain, Francis Collier, hunted her down, freeing 542 slaves. Collier, impressed by the brig's speed, bought her for £900, manned her with fifty-five of his hands, and came up with her unnerving name.

The Black Jokes were no band of boys. Richard Holt was fifty-seven, William Fielder fifty and at least six other Able hands were in their forties. Fielder, from Portsea, was in addition a smuggler who had been offered naval service as an alternative to prison. So was one of the younger hands, Thomas Atkinson, aged eighteen from Liverpool. The Black Jokes also included a quota of Kroomen. They had no King George, which was unusual; the name appears to have been given to the most senior Krooman, either for his ability or standing among tribal fellows. But they did include Pea Soup, Jack Snapper and Sea Breeze.[25]

A Krooman endured the fatigue, the heat and, above all, the fevers, better than Jack. He was vital to the operation and, it is apparent, the two groups rubbed along like most shipmates. Black seamen had long been equals, and accounts of the odd fracas have a ring of the usual lower-deck tensions rather than any racial overtones. When Edward Fitzgerald, for example, knocked overboard Jack Fryingpan's hat, containing his £12 pay, he claimed he'd 'only paid him what he owed [me]'; and Fryingpan's loss was deducted from Fitzgerald's wages.[26] That Kroomen were excluded from prize money was down to an Admiralty decree. This was challenged by Collier, who pointed out that they 'preserved many European lives'.[27] His appeal was ignored, but otherwise black and white served as equals.

It is hard to imagine that this proximity did not touch the way seamen saw Africans as a whole. All were constant witnesses to the harrowing treatment of slaves – sights like that which greeted men boarding the fiendishly misnamed *Dos Amigos Brazilieros*:

> [Her] filthy and horrid state beggars all description. Many females were in an advanced state of pregnancy & several had infants of from four to twelve months of age. All were crowded together in one mass of living corruption.[28]

Many slaves died at the point of liberation. Brazilian vessels were especially terrible places; in addition to the earlier atrocity of the *Umbelina*, a schooner captured with 361 slaves lost 122 by the time they reached Freetown; in another case, children composed almost a third of a human cargo of 320. When a hard twenty-eight-hour chase by the schooner *Hope* of a heavily armed Brazilian brig ended in a blaze of guns that killed eleven of her crew and liberated 608 slaves, any seaman would have taken satisfaction.[29]

The Black Jokes and the Sybilles made an effective team. Early in 1828, soon after being commissioned, *Black Joke* rescued 155 slaves from a Spanish vessel. Four months later she brought the campaign its biggest coup so far, the freeing of 645 souls from a Brazilian brig in the Bight of Benin. That year 6,630 slaves were saved. The start of 1829 brought even more spectacular success. In the first three months *Black Joke* took 900 slaves out of two vessels, *Sybille* a similar number from four more.

Collier was delighted, particularly with *Black Joke*'s smugglers who, he informed the Admiralty, had 'conducted themselves with the greatest gallantry' and deserved to be freed once the ship reached home. He repeated his request that Kroomen receive prize money. One other concern had, however, assumed disturbing form.

The squadron's mortality figures were first collated in 1825 and, at forty-eight of the 663-man force, or a loss of 7.2 per cent, would have been officially regarded as acceptable for so sickly a station.[30] That year 3,615 men, women and child slaves were emancipated. Over the next two years these figures remained at a roughly equivalent level. In 1828, while the number of slaves freed almost doubled, deaths in the squadron also rose – to eighty-four in a force of 958, or almost 9 per cent.[31]

The first sign of a new epidemic was observed at Freetown the following May. Alerted to the peril, Collier kept *Sybille* clear of Sierra Leone while cruising the Bight. His log retains an air of activity: 'Exercised Boys at the Broadsword'. 'Trimmed and made all sail in chase.' The first sign of disaster appears on 17 August:

> At 11, Departed this life, James Felland. At 2.20, Committed Body of the Deceased to the Deep.
>
> At 10, Departed this life, Geo. Lewis.[32]

So the roll call began. Two days later, James Doland, one of the boys recently exercising his broadsword, died. Within a week, twelve more men and another boy had been buried at sea. On 30 August a new entry appears: 'Conducted Divine Service.'

A south-westerly course had been set for St Helena. Reduced and sickly, unable to make the most of the light breezes and fine weather, *Sybille* covered no more than 90 miles a day. Men were still dying, though at a slower rate. Divine service was again being conducted as the island was sighted. Fresh supplies were taken on board. Deaths slowed, then ceased. Divine service continued.

Black Joke meanwhile had been at Freetown when the yellow fever broke out and her losses were even more severe – twenty-three out of a company of forty-five, including two of her smugglers; William Fielder and Thomas Atkinson would never enjoy their hard-earned freedom.

The *Eden*, yet another ill-named ship, was the worst affected. Out of her nominal 160-man company, 110 including thirteen Kroomen died by December.[33] A letter home from one of her officers was printed in *The Times*:

> Imagine a set of poor wretches lying upon gratings on the deck, some dying, some dead, some delirious, some screaming for water to quench

their parched tongues, and no one to attend to their call; others calling on their wives and children to bestow on them their last blessing.[34]

A desperate outfit was devised from blankets in an effort to seal men's skins from contact with damp air, leading one mid to observe: 'All hands looked like so many polar bears.'[35] It had no effect, of course. The year of 1829 was far and away the squadron's worst. Two-hundred and four men were lost to disease and two died in accidents out of a force of 792 – a mortality rate of almost 26 per cent.[36]

The *Black Joke* recovered to strike a few last blows for freedom. In 1831 her new crew of forty-five, including a few more smugglers, were responsible for emancipating 1,304 slaves. Among the four ships she took that year was a Spanish brig. The *Marinerito* was fast and new with intimidating firepower while *Black Joke* was falling to pieces. She still outstripped the Spaniard, and when the Black Jokes swooped, boarded and seized her, Lieutenant Peter Leonard watching from the *Dryad* acclaimed 'one of the most spirited actions on this coast'.

Even the most hardened of hands were overwhelmed by what they found. Almost 500 slaves, grossly overloaded, terrified and maddened by dehydration, made 'a picture more distressing,' Leonard wrote, 'than anyone can conceive who has not felt the cravings of a burning thirst for many hours under a tropical sun'. Trying to relieve their torment, the Black Jokes distributed water liberally and the slaves went wild – 'they madly bit the jugs with their teeth . . . drops that fell on the deck were lapped and sucked up with the most frightful eagerness.'[37] Fifty-seven died before they reached Freetown.

A few months later, Leonard and others (including some of the slaves she had freed) mourned as *Black Joke* – 'which has done more towards putting an end to the vile traffic than all the ships of the station put together' – was hauled ashore at Freetown and set ablaze.

Leonard's account passes discreetly over one aspect of her final operation. The *Marinerito*'s 'inhuman crew' had been deemed 'not to be pitied' and landed on an island to fend for themselves. They included, Leonard noted, 'several Englishmen'. In their case, being cast away may have been considered a merciful option; British subjects engaging in the slave trade faced execution.[38]

That a significant number of British seamen did serve in slave ships there can be no doubt. Hands on navy vessels putting in at Rio were offered huge bounties to desert. The frigate *Galatea* lost six men there in 1830. The *Leven*, after her vital survey work off West Africa, and bound for Mozambique where she was to carry the crusade against Arab slavers, had twenty men run – though they were rounded up and flogged.[39] Few Jacks were actually brought to book. It is likely that a blind eye was turned to some while others were quietly accepted back into the fold.

An exceptional case involved two Britons found in a Havana slaver in 1829. The *Midas*, as she was named, had reached the West Indies before being taken in a brisk exchange of fire. Along with 580 slaves, those on board included James McDonnell and Daniel Martin. Their trial in London was chaotic. McDonnell, a Scot, and Martin, from the West Country, claimed to be Americans. A jury still found them guilty of slave dealing, while recommending them for mercy.[40] They were duly sentenced to transportation.

The war on slave-trading did not end with a defining victory. It ground on, year after year. Slaves were freed in increasing numbers and bilateral treaties were signed, but the number of cruisers allotted to the squadron remained hopelessly inadequate, especially after its theatre of operations was extended south of the Equator in 1830. The profits to be made from human trafficking, then as now, kept illicit trade alive.

Progress of a sort was signalled in May 1833 when the *Pluto*, paddling off the River Bonny, became the first steam-powered vessel to capture a slave ship. That year only 3,293 men, women and children were emancipated, but in 1834 the number rose to 4,947 and in 1835 it reached 7,128, the highest figure yet.[41] These statistics still have to be compared with the estimated number of slaves imported to Cuba and South America. For 1833 it has been put at 30,500, rising to 38,200 in 1834 and 66,600 in 1835 as trading shifted from West Africa mainly to the Portuguese territory of Angola.[42] As an overall percentage, the Preventative Squadron was only rescuing some 10 per cent of those being taken from Africa.

Mortality among seamen fell, then shot up again to 12 per cent in successive years from 1837. The campaign had lasted longer than the Napoleonic War, yet still could not be deemed a success.[43] Disillusionment at times touched an idealistic generation of young officers and men alike.

The year of 1840 marked further innovation as more steamships were introduced in an operation for which they were notionally suited – flat-bottomed for shallow waters and with the manoeuvrability to cruise upriver and close inshore. Other battles continued meanwhile at diplomatic and legal levels. The negotiating table was ultimately where victory would be won as initially reluctant or hostile states signed up to more than treaties and gradually began to support restrictions and ultimately suppression.

That Jack would fight to the end was never doubted by one officer of the Preventative Squadron whose tribute, blending admiration and patronization, could have come from any point in the hundred years of this narrative:

> It is gratifying to think that Jack is still the same – that he fights for the love of it just as he was wont to do – for it is not to be supposed that any notions concerning the inhumanity of slave-dealing or the boon of emancipation he is about to confer on so many hundreds of his fellow-creatures enter his thoughtless head when he begins the conflict. He is ordered – it is his duty: and besides this, he likes it, being a pugnacious kind of animal, fond of a little excitement to vary the monotony of his life, hebetated [sic] by seclusion from the rest of the world, and to add another tale to the string of yarns he has to spin.[44]

A revolution in seafaring was meanwhile giving rise to an age-old concern – where to find the next generation of able hands. One officer put his finger on the essential problem:

It is very evident that the nursery for seamen has been greatly injured and broken up by the introduction of steam navigation.[45]

Here, with Pax Britannica in place and the steam age in ascent, is an appropriate moment for Jack to depart. He had been the making of the first and never really belonged in the second – at least in his original incarnation. He was no philanthropist and his level of success in suppressing the slave trade has been defined as modest. It is perhaps a matter of regret that his story should conclude here on a note of decline.

Yet the nature of the endeavour surely speaks for itself. Between 1825 and 1840 the Preventative Squadron liberated 65,720 men, women and children and restored them to their own. In a force that usually ran to no more than 900 in any year, and never exceeded half a dozen smaller vessels, almost 1,000 British seamen died.[46] They had shared the privations of this bleak crusade with the enslaved, a group of fellow humans with whom they were often seen as synonymous. While their labours received scant recognition at the time, the only comprehensive study of the war against the Atlantic slave trade rings true in its verdict: 'Posterity should conclude that few episodes in the history of the Royal Navy have been more deserving of true glory.'[47]

EPILOGUE

THE age of sail did not end with the coming of steam; it simply assumed new forms. Wisdom had it that some things were still best done by sail and for decades they were. Charting the seas was one. Charles Darwin's voyage in the *Beagle* is remembered for shaking perceptions on the very nature of human existence, but it started with a commission to survey the southern tip of America. Another charting expedition, by the *Rattlesnake* to the Great Barrier Reef and New Guinea, followed a few years later. Fast-sailing remained the domain of canvas even longer. Britain's most famous ship after the *Victory*, the *Cutty Sark*, was only built in 1869.

Love of the old ways endured of course, as evidenced by a yearning that runs through British culture from Turner to Ralph Vaughan Williams, from the shanties sung up and down the coast to the poetry of John Masefield. The sea was actually a troubled habitat for Masefield, who was an indifferent sailor, being once shipped home in distress. Yet *Salt-Water Ballads* set him on the path to the poet laureateship, and the combination of his lyrics and John Ireland's setting rendered 'Sea Fever' a much-loved condition.

But with change came a sense of loss. An old captain lamented that in 1839 there was not a single vessel sailing out of Dover. The same story was told up and down the coast, where 'the packets are all steamers'. The Navy had been pared down to 30,000 men, and the hands of old replaced by ratings who joined, often as boys. 'The spirit of the men is broken,' the captain went on. 'You no longer hear a ship's company boasting with pride of the dexterity and quickness of their evolutions.' Gone was the contest, 'for a joke or a wager', between foretop men and maintop men.[1] The tribe had been dispersed.

Ultimately, the sea would always draw a certain type of character. The tribe had been dispersed but aspects of tribal living survived – a rude equality, simplicity, a sense of identity and belonging. Thomas Hodgkin, a Quaker physician who campaigned against impressment, observed that seafaring appealed to the adventurous because it was 'spirit-stirring and not dull and deadening, like throwing a shuttle or twisting a cotton thread'.[2] There would always be those like Henry Jervis of the *Pylades* who, in irons for disobedience, shook a fist at a master's mate, saying if he caught him ashore 'he would give him a Bloody Thundering good Walloping', and might eat him too but supposed he should be 'a very tough bit'.[3]

What was lost with the passing of sail was a culture, and a language. Elements of Jack's lingo have been absorbed into the mainstream, from 'taken aback' to 'cut and run', from 'by and large' to 'at loggerheads'. But instructions on, for example, how 'To Furl a Royal' from *The Seaman's Friend* of 1841 by Richard Henry Dana, author of *Two Years Before the Mast*, might as well be in a foreign tongue: 'Make a skin of the upper part of the body of the sail, large enough to come down well abaft, and cover the whole bunt when the sail is furled. Lift the skin up and put into the bunt the slack of the clews (not too taut) the leech and foot-rope and body of the sail.'

Somewhere, in that blend of canvas and words, may lie an answer to one mystery. Jack, this narrative has tried to show, had been nourished by encounters with distant lands and strange people. It did not take a voyage to the South Seas, however, for a plain seaman to glimpse and reach out for the sublime. Something about his immense environment and his labours imbued poetry. A sailor might be illiterate yet still describe his ship as: 'Snug as a duck in a ditch, never straining as much as a rope-yarn aloft and as tight as a bottle below.'[4]

Visions from aloft may have been part of it. Men have always ascended the heights for a perspective of life and the world. In biblical times, it was to encounter God. Since what the Romantics described as the discovery of mountains in the nineteenth century, climbers of the Alps and fell walkers in the Lake District have sought to master 'the mount sublime' and put the sensation into words, Samuel Taylor Coleridge among them. Risk, striving, attainment, exhilaration – these were also the experiences of the topman. Samuel Kelly, a mariner of the eighteenth century, saw it thus:

> I have read somewhere that seamen are neither reckoned among the living nor the dead, their whole lives being spent in jeopardy. No sooner is one peril over, but another comes rolling on, like the waves of a full grown sea.[5]

Today the vast majority of world trade is moved by sea, so ships and sailors are more vital to the international economy than ever. Yet it is hard to see the crewman of a container vessel reflecting with Robert Hay: 'The qualities of a ship are to a seaman what the charms of a mistress are to a poet.' Or with Aaron Thomas, on entering a stormy bay:

> All is calm, there is no uproar, nor no voice heard but the man heaving the lead. Every soul thinks what a slender barrier there is between them and eternity. They pause, the ship still driving on . . . The sea roars, the masts crack, the winds whistle, the elements in tumult, but the man at the lead, lashed to the chains, sings, 'By the lead, five'.[6]

Jack could be moved, as we have seen, to try to convey these sensations – working above an elemental space that shifted from a quiet eternal majesty to buffeting madness, from blue serenity to black peril. He and his fellows failed of course, though it is testimony to the power of this binding force that they felt such a compulsion. It took a Polish seaman, born Konrad Korzeniowski, who found his true calling under canvas in British clippers and became one of the greatest writers in the English language, to note that a passion for the sea was 'something too great for words'.[7]

Joseph Conrad did, however, late in life, decide 'to lay bare with the unreserve of a last hour's confession the terms of my relation to the sea'. This was 'the best tribute my piety can offer to the ultimate shapers of my character, convictions and, in a sense, destiny – to the imperishable sea, to the ships that are no more, and to the simple men who have had their day'.[8] These, as he wrote elsewhere, were:

> Men who knew toil, privation, violence, debauchery – but knew not fear, and had no desire of spite in their hearts. Men hard to manage, but easy to inspire; voiceless men – but men enough to scorn in their hearts the sentimental voices that bewailed the hardness of their fate. It was a fate unique and their own; the capacity to bear it appeared to them the privilege of the chosen! Their generation lived inarticulate and indispensable, without knowing the sweetness of affections or the refuge of a home – and died free from the dark menace of a narrow grave. They were the everlasting children of the mysterious sea.[9]

The last word rightly belongs to one of those who shared a berth with the likes of Jacob Nagle and John Nicol. A seaman of the *Minotaur*, William Thorpe kept a record of Trafalgar which he passed late in life 'to my Dear Sarah as a memorial'. Thorpe ended with a verse, a medium for which Jack had a special fondness. It came from a song, one of obscure origin, which he set down as a valediction for his shipmates:

> *Heedless of danger, to the Scene*
> *Of War, the lowly hero came*
> *There fell unnoticed and unknown –*
> *The World's a stranger to his name.*
> *Scorn not to think on one so Poor;*
> *Worth oft adorns the Humble mind;*
> *Oft in a common sailor's breast*
> *Dwell virtues of no common kind.*[10]

NOTES

PROLOGUE

1. Rodger, *Safeguard*, p. 270.
2. Ibid, pp. 269, 314.
3. Quoted in ibid, p. 315.
4. Earle, p. 13.
5. Walvin, *Black Ivory*, p. 318; Earle, p. 10.
6. Earle, p. 130.
7. Meyerstein, p. 25.
8. Ibid, p. 51.
9. Ibid, p. 109.
10. Barlow, *Journal*, vol. 1, p. 21.
11. Barlow, *Journal*, vol. 2, p. 452.
12. Quoted in Wilson, *Empire*, pp. 227–8.
13. Barlow, *Journal*, vol. 1, p. 213.
14. Quoted in Rodger, *Command*, p. 214.
15. Ibid, Appendix VI, pp. 636–9.
16. Voltaire, *Letters on the English*, Chapter 10.

CHAPTER 1

1. The widespread neglect of navy musters as a research tool, noted by Lloyd in *The British Seamen*, p. 111, no longer pertains. For individual ships in Anson's squadron, see, for example, ADM 36/1385, muster of the *Gloucester*.
2. For routine see, for example, Robinson, *Nautical Economy*, pp. 5–10, and for the life of a mess Leech, p. 20.
3. For seamen's dress, Rodger, *Wooden World*, p. 64; Williams, p. 156; Earle, p. 34; Clayton, p. 34.
4. Hay, p. 72.
5. Morris, p. 62.
6. ADM 36/4456, muster of the *Wager*.
7. ADM 36/1385, muster of the *Gloucester*; and ADM 36/554, muster of the *Centurion*.
8. Hay, p. 86.
9. These figures relate to seamen, and do not include those other men of the lower deck, the marines.
10. Williams, *The Prize of All the Oceans*, is the definitive account.
11. ADM 51/888, log of the *Severn*, records Bubb's death. Insofar as his personal details presented here are concerned, he is a composite figure drawn from various sources.
12. Leech, p. 22.
13. Thursfield, p. 28. The description comes from a later time, but is typical enough of the conditions.

14. Quoted in Rodger, *Command*, pp. 238–9.
15. Williams, p. 74.
16. ADM 51/402, log of the *Gloucester*, 23 July 1741.
17. See Jonathan Lamb, *Scurvy: The Disease of Discovery.*
18. Isaac Morris, a midshipman, wrote the only first-hand account of this extraordinary episode, *A Narrative of the Dangers and Distresses which Befell Isaac Morris and Seven more of the Crew Belonging to the Wager.* See pp. 16–17 and 38.
19. Ibid, pp. 52–3.
20. Ibid, p. 55.
21. Ibid, p. 62.
22. ADM 51/402, log of the *Gloucester*, 23 July 1741.
23. Williams, p. 104.
24. Quoted in Williams, p. 165.
25. ADM 36/554, muster of the *Centurion*.
26. In addition to seamen, this number includes officers, marines and soldiers. The most appalling statistic of all concerns this latter 'army' of invalids. Virtually every one of the 260 soldiers died.
27. Williams, p. 206.
28. Rodger, *Command*, p. 239.
29. Williams, p. 208.
30. Ibid.

CHAPTER 2

1. Rodger, *Spavens*, p. 28.
2. ADM 53/593, log of the *Medway*, 4 July 1755.
3. Rodger, *Spavens*, p. 28. Spavens is normally a reliable chronicler, but on this occasion he was carried away by his fondness for a tale or his memory played him false. In fact, the *Medway's* log tells us, just one man, William Cook, was killed, and that three days before the review.
4. See Rodger, *Spavens*, p. 23, for his early life. His dissertation on geography in which he confesses his former belief that the world was flat is on p. 117.
5. Ibid, p. 27.
6. Quoted in Williams, *Prize*, p. 18.
7. Gradish, pp. 29–30.
8. Ibid, p. 32.
9. Ibid. The ports were King's Lynn, Bristol, Newcastle, Liverpool, Whitehaven, Yarmouth, Edinburgh, Hull, Gravesend and Pembroke; the towns were Shrewsbury, Gloucester, Winchester, Leicester, Reading and Leeds.
10. See *Poseidon's Curse* by Christopher Magra and *The Myth of the Press Gang* by J. Ross Dancy. Both authors are American academics.
11. Gradish, p. 55.
12. Earle, p. 180.
13. The officer responsible was brought to trial but acquitted. See ADM 12/25, Court martial of Lieutenant Sax.
14. Rodger, *Spavens*, p. 46.
15. Nicol, p. 205.
16. Childers, p. 67.
17. Rodger, *Command*, p. 277.
18. Leech, p. 24.
19. Lavery, *Nelson's Navy*, p. 201.
20. Robinson, *Nautical Economy*, p. 9.
21. Thursfield, p. 257.
22. Gradish, p. 141.
23. ADM 36/5126, muster of the *Blandford*.

24. Thursfield, p. 243.
25. Quoted in Taylor, *Storm and Conquest*, p. 84.
26. Rodger, *Spavens*, p. 35.
27. ADM 36/5126, the muster of the *Blandford*, shows that he was raised from Ordinary to Able in January 1757.
28. Quoted in Lavery, *Nelson's Navy*, p. 134.
29. Rodger, *Spavens*, p. 161.
30. This is based on a study of the skeletons of navy seamen. See Boston et al.
31. Thursfield, p. 245.
32. Leech, p. 141.
33. On a 24-gun frigate like the *Blandford* each man would receive some 0.18 per cent of the total. See Rodger, *Wooden World*, p. 129.
34. Rodger, *Spavens*, p. 163.
35. Ibid, p. 164.
36. ADM 12/23, Court martial of J. Dowick.
37. Rodger, *Wooden World*, p. 206.
38. ADM 1/5297, Court martial of Captain Penhallow Cuming.
39. ADM 1/5297, Court martial of Thomas Halsey, Patrick O'Hara, Charles Elliott and Thomas Johnson.
40. Ibid.
41. W. E. May, *The Mutiny of the* Chesterfield, in *The Mariner's Mirror*, 47:3, 1961.
42. ADM 12/22, ff. 11–12.
43. Gradish, p. 111.

CHAPTER 3

1. Rodger, *Spavens*, p. 45.
2. ADM 51/1029, log of the *Vengeance*, 29 May, 26 July, 30 July, 1 August 1759.
3. Rodger, *Spavens*, p. 46.
4. Ibid.
5. ADM 36/6970, muster of the *Vengeance*.
6. Rodger, *Spavens*, p. 73.
7. Ibid, p. 63.
8. Ibid, p. 48.
9. Ibid.
10. Ibid, p. 46.
11. Gradish, p. 42. The total number brought into service during the war was 85,665, but that included marines.
12. Rodger, *Spavens*, p. 48.
13. *The Sailors Advocate*, p. 4, online edition.
14. Gradish, p. 69.
15. Fort, pp. 3–4.
16. See Bundock.
17. Gradish, p. 79.
18. *The Interesting Narrative of the Life of Olaudah Equiano*, chapter 4, online edition.
19. Ships' boys are of course also a staple of maritime fiction. Jim Hawkins, the best known, has more to do with piracy and adventure than the sea; but Peter Simple and Jack Easy are the creations of Frederick Marryat who went to sea at fourteen himself. Like his characters, however, Marryat belonged to the school of young gentlemen who entered as midshipmen, with money or influence behind them; another was twelve-year-old Horatio Nelson. Though these lads might have visited the seamier parts of a ship, they did not dwell there.
20. Pietsch, p. 18.
21. Ibid, p. 5.
22. Quoted in Colley, *Britons*, p. 97.

23. Clayton, p. 172.
24. Quoted in Rodger, *Wooden World*, p. 37.
25. Thursfield, p. 252.
26. Garstin, pp. 19–20.
27. Leech, p. 21.
28. Ibid, pp. 37, 63.
29. Byrn, *Crime and Punishment*, p. 123.
30. ADM 12/26, f. 13.
31. Burg, pp. 75–6.
32. ADM 1/5300.
33. Burg, p. XI.
34. ADM 1/5300.
35. Ibid.
36. It should be added that there is some doubt as to whether the disdainful description of navy tradition as 'no more than rum, sodomy and the lash' was properly attributed to Churchill.
37. This figure is based on ADM 12/26 in the Digest of Courts Martial series.
38. ADM 1/5355, Court martial of John Ware and John Douglas, 14 June 1800.
39. ADM 1/5350, Court martial of George Reed and Thomas Tattershall, 4 July 1795.
40. Wareham, p. 68.
41. ADM 12/26, f. 27.
42. ADM 1/5297, Court martial of John Blake. In the index of court martials ADM 12/21, this is the only case recorded under Buggery, as distinct from Sodomy or Sodomitical Practices, for the fifty years 1756–1806. There is no category for bestiality.
43. Peitsch, pp. 22–3.
44. Ibid, p. 33.
45. Carretta, p. 41.
46. Ibid, p. 60.
47. Ibid, p. 63. This biography gives a comprehensive account of Equiano's seafaring career. If there is an element of exaggeration in Equiano's own memoir, the key facts of his service on the *Roebuck*, *Royal George* and *Namur* are confirmed by his listing in the respective musters.

CHAPTER 4

1. Thursfield, p. 255. Robert Wilson's description of setting sail is on pp. 252–3.
2. See Rodger, *Spavens*, pp. 114–15.
3. Thomas, p. 196.
4. Lavery, *Nelson's Navy*, p. 300.
5. See Gradish, pp. 164–9.
6. Quoted in Rodger, *Command*, pp. 280–1.
7. ADM 51/1029, log of the *Vengeance*.
8. Rodger, *Spavens*, p. 49. He was in error about the date. They came to in Quiberon Bay on 19 November.
9. ADM 51/1029, log of the *Vengeance*.
10. Rodger, *Spavens*, p. 50.
11. Thursfield, pp. 252–3.
12. *The Interesting Narrative of the Life of Olaudah Equiano*, chapter 4, online edition.
13. Quoted in Adkins, p. 273.
14. Hay, p. 181.
15. Rodger, *Spavens*, p. 52.
16. Rodger, *Command*, p. 290.
17. Hay, p. 172.
18. Rodger, *Spavens*, p. 55.
19. ADM 51/1029, log of the *Vengeance*.
20. Lloyd, *Health of Seamen*, p. 265.

21. Carretta, p. 85.
22. Ibid, p. 82. This biography includes a comprehensive account of Equiano's life at sea.
23. Bundock, pp. 78–97.
24. Ibid, p. 82. A claim that a quarter of crew on Royal Navy ships in the late eighteenth century were black has been dismissed as 'fanciful' in Nicholas Rogers' study, *The Press Gang*.
25. Quoted in Rodger, *Wooden World*, p. 119.
26. Ibid.
27. Rodger, *Spavens*, p. 64.
28. There are no reliable figures for the number of desertions. Gradish suggests on p. 111 that the figure may have been 40,000, but this seems too high.

CHAPTER 5

1. Quoted in Colley, *Elizabeth Marsh*, p. xxii.
2. Sutton, p. 29.
3. Quoted in Rodger, *Wooden World*, p. 183.
4. ADM 106/1144, f. 132.
5. Fielding.
6. Lloyd, *Health of Seamen*, pp. 265–7.
7. Sutton, p. 82, Woodman, *Neptune's Trident*, p. 156.
8. Lincoln, *Trading*, pp. 11–13.
9. Quoted in Clayton, p. 164; the remark is attributed to the London magistrate, Sir John Fielding, brother of the author Henry.
10. Ackroyd, p. 553.
11. Earle, p. 155. A sample comparison of logs of navy and company ships confirms this to be the case.
12. Reading seems to have been surprisingly common among seamen. Rodger, *Wooden World*, p. 45.
13. Rodger, *Spavens*, p. 72. Pursers were unpopular figures, regarded as corrupt profiteers who sold off seamen's rations.
14. Ibid, p. 75.
15. ADM 12/21. The actual category under which these offences occur is Assault at Sea. My observation is also based on a fairly wide study of ships' logs and punishment records.
16. Nicol, p. 191.
17. Bromley, p. 125.
18. Rodger, *Spavens*, p. 74.
19. Ibid, p. 82.
20. Ibid, p. 113.
21. British Library, *Catalogue of the East India Ships' Journals and Logs*, 1600–1834, by Anthony Farrington.
22. Rodger, *Command*, p. 316.
23. Taylor, *The Caliban Shore*, p. 13.
24. Earle, p. 130.
25. ADM 36/6817, muster of the *Tyger*.
26. ADM 1/5296, f. 449, Court martial of John Carter.
27. All extracts as above.
28. ADM 36/6817, muster of the *Tyger*.
29. ADM 12/24, f. 37, Court martial of John Newson.
30. Hay, p. 100.
31. Ibid, p. 98.
32. Rodger, *Spavens*, p. 207.
33. Hay, pp. 111–12. The word shampoo is, in fact, of Hindi origin.
34. Rodger, *Spavens*, pp. 207, 206, 198.

35. The quotation actually reads: 'If thou art he, but Ah! How chang'd from him, Companion of my Arms! How wan! How dim! How faded all thy Glories are! I see myself too well, and my own change, in thee.'
36. Rodger, *Spavens*, p. 222.
37. Ibid, pp. 98–9.

CHAPTER 6

1. Quoted in Colley, *Elizabeth Marsh*, p. xxv.
2. Hough, p. 86.
3. Ibid, p. 66.
4. ADM 36/8569, muster of the *Endeavour*.
5. Holmes, *Age of Wonder*, p. 39.
6. Cook's Journal, 12 May 1769.
7. Glyndwr Williams, *Seamen and Philosophers in the South Seas*, in *The Mariner's Mirror*, 65:1, 1979.
8. Holmes, *Age of Wonder*, p. 17.
9. Cook's Journal, 3 June 1769.
10. Hough, p. 154.
11. Cook's Journal, 13 April 1769.
12. Brown, *Poxed and Scurvied*, pp. 81–2.
13. Cook's Journal, *Person of the Natives of Tahiti*.
14. Nicol, pp. 3–4. Strictly speaking, Nicol was not a Foremast Jack, much of his time at sea being spent as a cooper, a maker of casks. However, he was a man of the lower deck and speaks with intimate knowledge of life there.
15. Nicol's scribe was an Edinburgh bookbinder named John Howell, who might be thought as his authorial voice. However, a comparison with Howell's other work as a ghostwriter indicates that Nicol's *Life and Adventures* was his own distinctive narrative.
16. Nicol, p. 52.
17. Ibid, p. 19. Nicol never spells out his carnal appetites, but his fondness for women is explicitly stated, as is the fact that he was troubled by his failings as a former man of faith.
18. Ibid, p. 15.
19. ADM 55/84, log of the *King George*.
20. Nicol, pp. 73–5.
21. ADM 55/84, log of the *King George*, 20 December 1786.
22. Nicol, pp. 90–1.
23. Ibid, pp. 96–7.
24. Ibid, pp. 99 and 102.
25. ADM 55/84, log of the *King George*, 25 December 1787.
26. See Andrew Cook, *Establishing the Sea Routes to India and China*, in Bowen, Lincoln and Rigby.
27. See Taylor, *The Caliban Shore*, p. 73.
28. Nicol, pp. 106–7.
29. ADM 55/84, log of the *King George*, 21 August 1788.
30. *A voyage round the world but more particularly to the north-west coast of America: performed in 1785, 1786, 1787, and 1788, in the King George and Queen Charlotte.*
31. Nicol, p. 109.

CHAPTER 7

1. McCullough, p. 135.
2. Nicol, p. 32.
3. Ibid, p. 28.
4. *The Narrative of Joshua Davis*, p. 12. This pamphlet is published on The Navy Department Library (US).
5. Ibid, p. 14.

6. Sherburne, p. 81.
7. Colley, *Elizabeth Marsh*, p. 163.
8. Sherburne, p. 70.
9. Gilje, pp. 104–5. The most famous American disturbance, the Knowles riot of 1747, incurred no fatalities.
10. Magra, *Poseidon's Curse*. A fellow American academic, Paul Gilje, believed Magra pushed his evidence too far. Their respective arguments can be found only in *Reviews in History*.
11. Rodger, *The Naval World of Jack Aubrey* in Cunningham, p. 51.
12. The figure of 900 ships is in Pasley, p. 8.
13. Gilje, p. 119.
14. James, p. 117.
15. ADM 12/22 contains an index of court martials for desertion.
16. Ibid.
17. ADM 1/5309, f. 448. Court martial of Francis Roderick, 22 May 1778.
18. ADM 1/5310, f. 373. Court martial of William Pearce, 24 October 1778.
19. Gilje, p. 114.
20. ADM 1/5309, f. 129. Court martial of Stanley Cooper and James Read, 13 January 1778.
21. Ibid, f. 519. Court martial of William Dominey, 17 October 1777.
22. ADM 12/24.
23. ADM 12/23, f. 501. Court martial of Thomas Wood, 26 October 1779.
24. Quoted in Rodger, *Command*, pp. 402–3.
25. ADM 36/8378, muster of the *Scorpion*, gives what little personal detail is known of Swift: that he was twenty-four, rated Able, and joined the ship on 4 July 1777. Whether the date was coincidental, only he ever knew.
26. ADM 1/5309, f. 351, Court martial of William Swift and Edward Power, 16 March 1778.
27. Ibid.
28. Davis, pp. 36–7.
29. Rodger, *Command*, p. 399.
30. Davis, p. 64.
31. Dann, p.17. Nagle's phonetic way with language is eloquent in its own way but it can be distracting, and in places I have altered his spelling for clarity's sake.
32. Ibid, p. 70.

CHAPTER 8

1. Colley, *Britons*, p. 352, and Carretta, p. 19.
2. Walvin, *Black Ivory*, pp. 57, 233 and 16.
3. Earle, p. 130.
4. Woodman, *Neptune's Trident*, p. 191.
5. Caretta, p. 7.
6. Ibid, pp. 33–4.
7. Ibid, pp. 31–2.
8. Ibid, p. 34.
9. Gilje, p. 109.
10. Carretta, pp. 72–3.
11. Ibid, p. 98.
12. Ibid, pp. 101 and 106.
13. Knight, *Pursuit of Victory*, p. 31.
14. Carretta, pp. 152–3 and 159. The author points out that while Equiano claimed to have kept his own journal of the expedition, it has not survived and in his memoir he drew on Phipps's published account verbatim in places. For this reason, his own writing is largely passed over here.
15. Ibid, p. 151.
16. Ibid, p. 202.

17. Ibid, pp. 116–17.
18. Childers, p. 41.
19. Ibid, p. 52.
20. Carretta, pp. 31–2.
21. Childers, p. 50.
22. Woodman, *Neptune's Trident*, p. 189.
23. Childers, p. 51. This is another instance where the original was edited.
24. Ibid, pp. 54 and 58.
25. Robert S. Levine, *The Cambridge Companion to Herman Melville* (Cambridge, 1998), p. 24.
26. Leech, p. 42.
27. Childers, p. 63.
28. Ibid, p. 73.
29. Ibid, p. 111.
30. Ibid, pp. 292–3.

CHAPTER 9

1. Dann, p. 143.
2. Meyerstein, p. 51.
3. Nicol, p. 196.
4. Leech, p. 62.
5. Robinson, p. 56.
6. Goodall, p. 26.
7. Leech, pp. 63–4.
8. Robinson, p. 58.
9. Ibid, p. 57.
10. Thursfield, pp. 131–2.
11. Quoted in Adkins, p. 164.
12. Ibid, p. 159 (Goodall, p. 24).
13. Quoted in Ackroyd, p. 554.
14. Quoted in Lincoln, *Naval Wives*, pp. 140–1.
15. Rodger, *Wooden World*, p. 136.
16. Hay, p. 190.
17. ADM 1/5319, ff437, Court martial of George Arnold.
18. Dann, pp. 154–7.
19. Ibid, p. 186.
20. Quoted in Adkins, p. 162.
21. Garstin, p. 60.
22. Ibid, p. 62.
23. ADM 51/950, log of the *Surprise*, 15 January 1783.
24. ADM 1/5322, f. 132, Court martial of Thomas Mullogn alias Murray.
25. Ibid, f. 481, Court martial of Thomas Sneden and others.
26. The case is mentioned by Byrn, *Crime and Punishment*, p. 167.
27. Childers, p. 187.
28. Nicol, pp. 40–2.
29. Ibid, pp. 44–6.
30. Moorey.
31. Lloyd, *Health of Seamen*, p. 267.
32. Porter, pp. 145 and 162.
33. Richard Greenhalgh's letters (84/546) are held at the Royal Naval Museum in Portsmouth but have been incorporated in Watt and Hawkins, *Letters of Seamen in the Wars with France*. They are dated between 1793 and 1802. They are incorporated here for their relevance to the chapter subject.
34. Ibid, Letter dated December 1794.

35. Ibid, 17 October 1797.
36. Ibid, September 1797.
37. Ibid, 12 August 1798.
38. Ibid, April 1800.
39. ADM 1/5355, Court martial of Thomas Hubbard and George Hynes, 10 December 1800.
40. Ibid.
41. ADM 51/1309, log of the *St George*, 22 December 1800.
42. Rogers, pp. 1–2.
43. Old Bailey online, 11 September 1771.
44. Rogers, p. 2.
45. Quoted in Colley, *Britons*, p. 145.
46. ADM 12/24, Court martial of Daniel Stewart, 17 November 1785.
47. Rodger, *The Naval World of Jack Aubrey*, in Cunningham, p. 53.
48. Garstin, p. 72.

CHAPTER 10

1. Rodger, *Command*, pp. 358–9.
2. Ibid, pp. 361–2.
3. ADM 1/5118/10.
4. These figures are compiled from an analysis of Appendix 9 in Sutton's *Lords of the East*.
5. Hay, pp. 43–4.
6. Dann, pp. 73–4.
7. Quoted in Hughes, p. 79.
8. Keneally, pp. 98–9.
9. Dann, p. 86. In some places I have edited down Nagle's prose for the sake of brevity.
10. Ibid, p. 92.
11. Keneally, p. 73.
12. Hughes's account of the founding of Australia remains a wonderfully evocative and compelling read.
13. Dann, p. 99.
14. Ibid, p. 96.
15. Hughes, p. 92.
16. Dann, p. 107.
17. Ibid, pp. 122–3.
18. Hughes, pp. 100–1.
19. Nagle's will, leaving all his possessions to 'my beloved friend Terence Burne', is at the National Archives, ADM 48/67/14.
20. Dann, pp. 144–5.
21. Ibid, p. 150.
22. Nicol, p. 111.
23. Ibid, p. 119.
24. Hughes, p. 143.
25. Nicol, p. 117. See also Rees, *Floating Brothel*, pp. 50–1. Forging of seamen's wills was common, especially among publicans and brothel-keepers.
26. Nicol, p. 119.
27. Ibid, pp. 125–6.
28. Rees, *Floating Brothel*, p. 169.
29. Nicol, p. 115.
30. Ibid, p. 130.
31. Ibid, p. 146.
32. Ibid, p. 132. Detail of convicts' later lives comes from *The Second Fleet: Britain's Grim Convict Armada of 1790* by Michael Flynn.

CHAPTER 11

1. Caroline Alexander's *The Bounty* is a lucid account of the mutiny and its aftermath.
2. Ibid, p. 112.
3. Leech, p. 22.
4. Robinson, pp. 40–2 and 72.
5. Hay, pp. 66 and 156.
6. Dann, pp. 237–8.
7. Ibid, p. 74.
8. Ibid.
9. Ibid, p. 45.
10. Nash, pp. 31–2 and 29.
11. Nicol, p. 46.
12. Nash, p. 41.
13. Ibid, pp. 43–4.
14. Ibid, p. 68.
15. Ibid, p. 45.
16. Ibid, p. 46.
17. Ibid, p. 72.
18. Ibid, p. 74.
19. Ibid, p. 81.
20. See Riou's journal of the voyage in Nash, pp. 60–112.
21. Nash, p. 83.
22. Ibid, pp. 126–7. Pardons for the twenty-one men were granted only after they had embarked for Australia and in the course of this further voyage six of them died.
23. Dann, pp. 74–6.
24. Ibid, pp. 152–3.
25. Ibid, pp. 158–60.

INTERLUDE

1. Murray, p. 34.
2. Thursfield, p. 14.
3. Thompson, p. 62. Marsden is recorded as deserting after the *Amethyst* was wrecked at Alderney in 1795 (ADM 36/11301).
4. Goodall, pp. 50–1.
5. Fowler, pp. 99–100.
6. Ibid.
7. Earle, pp. 130–1. This survey may be treated with caution. It is based on a study of musters up to 1775 and concludes that out of every thousand merchant seamen, five would die in accidents, ten in shipwrecks and forty-five of disease, all of which appear singularly low.
8. Taylor, *Storm and Conquest*.
9. Dann, p. 120.
10. Ibid, p. 108.
11. Leech, p. 128.
12. Adkins, p. 119.
13. See Jean Hood, *Marked for Misfortune*.
14. Nicol, p. 46.
15. See Nathaniel Philbrick, *In the Heart of the Sea*.
16. Lloyd, *Health of Seamen*, p. 266.
17. Leech, pp. 70–1.
18. Carrington, p. 257.

CHAPTER 12

1. Lewis, p. 16.
2. From the start of war in 1803, for example, out of government spending of £38,956,916, the Navy cost £10,211,373 while the Army cost £8,935,753. See Holmes, *Redcoat*, p. 86.
3. Summerville, p. 26.
4. See Urban.
5. Ibid, pp. 136–9.
6. Bromley, pp. xvi–xvii.
7. Ibid, p. 125.
8. Ibid, p. 173.
9. Taylor, *Commander*, p. 25.
10. Ibid.
11. Dann, p. 173.
12. Ibid, pp. 179–80. Nagle evidently saw the term 'negro' as interchangable for people of dark complexion.
13. Nicol, p. 160.
14. Ibid, p. 164.
15. L/MAR/B 287K, log of the *Nottingham*, 23 July 1795.
16. Nicol, p. 171.
17. Ibid, p. 173.
18. Lloyd, *British Seaman*, p. 263.
19. Ibid, p. 121.
20. Ackroyd, p. 170.
21. ADM 1/5119/16, Petition to Lord Hood, 23 April 1791.
22. Lincoln, *Naval Wives*, p. 42.
23. Knight, *Britain Against Napoleon*, p. 76.
24. Bromley, p. 185.
25. Childers, p. 111.
26. Lewis, p. 118; Lloyd, *British Seaman*, pp. 177–8.
27. Rodger, *Command*, pp. 443–4.
28. Lewis, p. 122.
29. ADM 106/1144, f. 284.
30. Lloyd, *British Seaman*, p. 171.
31. Ibid, pp. 178–9, and Lewis, p. 139.
32. J. Ross Dancy, *The Myth of the Press Gang*. This revisionist argument has stimulated debate and further study. It is right to challenge what the author calls 'the myth that most men in the Royal Navy served against their wills'; as the present work has shown, seamen regarded impressment as an inescapable adjunct of their trade. That is not to say it did not generate significant resistance, and the point bears repeating that although ships' musters are a valuable resource for research, they are not absolute records. Contrary evidence simply illustrates the inconsistency of statistics.
33. ADM 1/5357, 22 July 1801.
34. Lavery, *Nelson's Navy*, p. 143.
35. Rogers, pp. 42 and 106.
36. L/MAR/B 59D, log of the *Rose*, 22–23 July 1795. Nagle said twenty-three men had been pressed but the log says thirty.
37. Dann, p. 169. In editing the journal, Dann points out that Lincoln was Nagle's grandmother's name.
38. Ibid, p. 186.
39. Ibid.

CHAPTER 13

1. Taylor, *Commander*, p. 65.

2. Hay, p. 49.
3. Taylor, *Commander*, pp. 59–60.
4. Hay, p. 156.
5. Taylor, *Commander*, p. 77.
6. For Tom Allen's life I have drawn on the research generously made available online by Joan and Adrian Bridge. See www.joadrian.co.uk/TomAllenStory.htm
7. Lewis, p. 93.
8. Parsons, p. 241.
9. Fowler, p. 88.
10. Quoted in Lewis, p. 105.
11. ADM 36/11358, Muster of the *Agamemnon*.
12. ADM 51/1104, Log of the *Agamemnon*.
13. Knight, *Pursuit of Victory*, pp. 157–62.
14. Parsons, p. 241.
15. Lloyd, *British Seaman*, p. 10.
16. Rodger, *Command*, p. 448.
17. Watson, p. 88.
18. Old Bailey online, trial of John Chilton, 30 October 1805.
19. Murray, p. 54.
20. Ibid, p. 150.
21. Goodall, p. 45.
22. Ibid, p. 14.
23. Murray, p. 186.
24. Quoted in Rodger, *Wooden World*, p. 250.
25. Quoted in Lewis, p. 25.
26. Murray, p. 190.
27. Thursfield, p. 246.
28. Parsons, p. 247.
29. Ibid, p. 242.
30. Sugden, p. 42.
31. *United Service Journal & Naval & Military Magazine*, February 1836.
32. Parsons, p. 250.
33. Sugden, pp. 289–90.
34. Ibid, p. 311.
35. *United Service Journal & Naval & Military Magazine*, February 1836.
36. Parsons, pp. 249–50.
37. Ibid, pp. 247–8.
38. Sugden, p. 863.
39. Cunningham, p. 60.

CHAPTER 14

1. Quoted in Dugan, pp. 14–15. Paine's brief career as a privateer is analysed in *Thomas Paine – Privateersman*, by Alyce Barry, accessible online.
2. Forester, Introduction to *The Adventures of John Wetherell*, p. 13.
3. Dann, p. 293.
4. Leech, p. 28.
5. Nicol, p. 36.
6. Thursfield, p. 36.
7. Dann, pp. 109–10.
8. E. P. Thompson's *The Making of the English Working Class* covers this ground from a radical perspective.
9. Leech, p. 34.
10. This analysis is based on ADM 12/24, the Digest of Courts Martial.

11. Ibid, 13 September 1774.
12. Ibid, 19 January 1781.
13. Ibid, 18 August 1783.
14. Ibid, 17 November 1785.
15. Ibid, 6 December 1785.
16. ADM 1/5331, f. 736.
17. Ibid, evidence of Thomas Pakenham.
18. ADM 51/1130, log of *Culloden*.
19. See Hamilton and Laughton, p. 51. and Pasley, p. 73.
20. These figures are based on entries in ADM 36/12169, the muster of *Culloden*.
21. Neale, p. 96.
22. ADM 1/5331, f. 679, evidence of Samuel Bostock.
23. ADM 1/5331, f. 712, evidence of Jeremiah Collins.
24. ADM 51/1130, 8 December 1794.
25. ADM 1/5331, f. 685, evidence of Thomas Pakenham.
26. Ibid, f. 689, evidence of John Edwards.
27. Ibid, f. 699, evidence of Thomas Pakenham.
28. Rodger, *Command*, p. 445.
29. ADM 12/24, Court martial of William Parker etc., 20 January 1796.
30. Robinson, p. 105.
31. Dann, pp. 196–7.
32. ADM 1/5125, 8 November 1795. This pre-dated Nagle's arrival in the ship by some months, so he was not the author.
33. Dann, pp. 192 and 204.
34. Knight, *Pursuit of Victory*, p. 208.
35. Dann, p. 209.
36. Knight, *Pursuit of Victory*, pp. 214–15.
37. Nagle's is the only account of this event in Nelson's career. A year later, on returning to Portsmouth, the Blanches requested another ship, 'as we did not like the capt'. Ibid, p. 211.
38. Quoted in Wilson, p. 404.
39. ADM 51/1199, log of *Culloden*.
40. Ibid, 28 and 31 March 1796.

CHAPTER 15

1. Gill, pp. 7–8.
2. Coats and MacDougall, p. 23.
3. Manwaring and Dobree, pp. 9–10.
4. Leech, p. 59.
5. Vale, *The Post Office, The Admiralty and Letters to Sailors in the Napoleonic Wars.*
6. Coats and MacDougall, p. 28.
7. Ibid, p. 8.
8. Dugan, p. 33.
9. Coats and MacDougall, p. 80.
10. Ibid, p. 214.
11. Ibid, p. 130.
12. Gill, p. 12.
13. Coats and MacDougall, p. 24.
14. Ibid, p. 33.
15. Ibid, pp. 57–8. Ann Coats's research has rescued Joyce from centuries of misrepresentation which portrayed him as either a quota man once imprisoned for sedition or an Irish subversive.

16. Rodger, *Command*, p. 452.
17. Manwaring and Dobree, Appendix I.
18. Coats and MacDougall, p. 24.
19. Taylor, *Commander*, p. 139.
20. Gill, p. 32.
21. Ibid.
22. Coats and MacDougall, p. 31.
23. Gill, p. 43.
24. Rodger, *Command*, p. 448.
25. Gill, p. 37.
26. Ibid, pp. 41–2.
27. Coats and MacDougall, p. 78.
28. Mostert, p. 201.
29. Rodger, *Command*, p. 441.
30. Gill, p. 56.
31. Ibid.
32. Coats and MacDougall, pp. 76–7.
33. Baynham, p. 27.
34. Coats and MacDougall, p. 73.
35. Gill, p. 70.
36. Ibid, p. 71.
37. Coats and MacDougall, p. 140.
38. Gill, p. 76.
39. Mostert, p. 208.
40. *Dictionary of National Biography*.
41. Rodger, *Command*, p. 450.
42. Ibid.

CHAPTER 16

1. ADM 51/1195, log of the *Director*, 12 May 1797.
2. ADM 1/5340, evidence of Lt Thomas Pampe.
3. ADM 51/1195, log of the *Director*, 13 May 1797.
4. Manwaring and Dobree, pp. 123–4.
5. Despite the importance of the mutinies of 1797 to Britain's social as well as naval history, the subject has been strangely neglected and at the time of writing still lacks a definitive account. *The Naval Mutinies of 1797: Unity and Perseverance* by Ann Coats and Philip MacDougall comes closest but is a collection of studies that lacks an overarching narrative. A PhD thesis from 1998, *Mutiny and Sedition in the Home Commands of the Royal Navy, 1793–1803* by Christopher Doorne is a close examination. Another academic thesis, *The Nore Mutiny – Sedition or Ships' Biscuit?*, by Anthony Brown, is a fine and detailed study of its subject. *The Great Mutiny* by James Dugan is overlooked because, as popular history, it lacks footnotes, but it is the product of close research.
6. It has been claimed that while in London on their return journey McCarthy and Hollister imbibed not only ale but rhetoric from the London Corresponding Society, a group of artisan activists; McCarthy could be something of a firebrand himself. But even prosecution witnesses agreed that he had argued in favour of the Spithead terms. It appears likely, however, that the society had links with other groups of mutineers.
7. ADM 1/5340, evidence of Lt George Forbes.
8. ADM 1/5486, evidence of Richard Parker.
9. Ibid, evidence of Admiral Charles Buckner.
10. Brown, *The Nore Mutiny*.
11. ADM 1/5340, evidence of Charles McCarthy.

12. Ibid, evidence of William Bray.
13. Ibid, evidence of Thomas Hewson.
14. Ibid.
15. Ibid, evidence of William Wilson.
16. DNB. Ann Coats's research of Parker's life matches her study of Valentine Joyce in bringing to light new material that sets both men in context, shorn of the polemics that have characterized previous treatments.
17. Brown, *The Nore Mutiny*.
18. Gill, p. 128.
19. See Philip MacDougall, *The East Coast Mutinies*, in Coats and MacDougall.
20. ADM 1/5486, evidence of Richard Parker.
21. Manwaring and Dobree, pp. 273–6.
22. ADM 51/1195, log of the *Director*, 19 May 1797.
23. Coats and MacDougall, pp. 152–3.
24. ADM 3/137.
25. ADM 1/5486, evidence of John Snipe.
26. Watts and Hawkins, p. 436.
27. ADM 1/5340, evidence of Thomas Hewson.
28. Ibid.
29. Gill, p. 10.
30. ADM 36/12741, muster of the *Inflexible*.
31. ADM 1/5486, evidence of William Welch.
32. ADM 1/5349, evidence of John Taylor.
33. ADM 1/5340, evidence of Captain Knight.
34. ADM 1/5486, evidence of Captain Parr.
35. Watts and Hawkins, p. 456.
36. ADM 1/5486, evidence of Captain Wood.
37. Watts and Hawkins, p. 410.
38. Ibid, pp. 421–2.
39. Ibid, p. 420.
40. Ronald, p. 130.
41. Watts and Hawkins, pp. 452–3.
42. Ibid, p. 455.
43. Manwaring and Dobree, pp. 188–9.
44. Coats and MacDougall, pp. 188–9.
45. Ibid, p. 260.
46. Manwaring and Dobree, p. 216.
47. Coats and MacDougall, p. 157.
48. ADM 1/5486, evidence of William Levington.
49. Ibid, evidence of Thomas Barry.
50. AMD 1/5340, evidence at the trial of twelve men of the *Montague* identified the three escapees as key figures in enforcing oaths.
51. ADM 51/1202, log of the Inflexible, 15 June 1797.
52. Dugan, pp. 322–3.
53. Manwaring and Dobree, pp. 102 and 250.
54. Brown, *The Nore Mutiny*.
55. ADM 1/5486, evidence of Richard Parker.
56. Manwaring and Dobree, pp. 273–6.
57. Ibid, p. 271.
58. Thursfield, p. 357.
59. ADM 1/5340.
60. Kennedy, p. 246.
61. ADM 3/137 and ADM 36, 12781.
62. ADM 51/1195, log of the *Director*, 10 July 1797.

CHAPTER 17

1. Rodger, *Command*, pp. 450–1.
2. Pope, *The Black Ship*, p. 67.
3. Ibid, pp. 154–9.
4. Ibid, pp. 174–7.
5. ADM 1/5348.
6. Pope, *The Black Ship*, pp. 22 and 330.
7. Mostert, p. 229.
8. Rodger, *Command*, p. 455.
9. ADM 36/12755, muster of the *Montagu*.
10. Dugan, p. 409.
11. Ibid.
12. Ibid, p. 411.
13. Padfield, *Nelson's War*, p. 105.
14. Manwaring and Dobree, p. 245.
15. ADM 51/1195, log of the *Director*, 12 October 1797.
16. Ibid.
17. RNM 1984/546, 17 October 1797.
18. Bayley, *In Which We Serve*, in Cunningham, p. 33.
19. Dugan, p. 414.
20. Holmes, *Redcoat*, p. 154.
21. Nicol, p. 179.
22. Ibid.
23. Kemp, pp. 171–2.
24. Rodger, *Officers and Men of the Navy*, in Fury, p. 67.
25. Nicol, pp. 186–7.
26. Watt and Hawkins, p. 159.
27. Ibid, p. 160.
28. Nicol, p. 188.
29. Knight, *Pursuit of Victory*, p. 297.
30. Fraser, p. 112.
31. Lavery, *Shipboard Life*, pp. 355 and 357.
32. Hay, pp. 156–7.
33. Ibid, p. 66.
34. Ibid, p. 76.
35. Ibid, pp. 67 and 77.
36. Fraser, p. 17.
37. Wareham, p. 69.
38. ADM 51/1366, log of the *Melampus*, September–December 1800.
39. Wareham, p. 69.
40. Thursfield, p. 144.
41. Hamilton and Laughton, pp. 104 and 182.
42. Leech, p. 41.
43. Rodger, *Command*, p. 504.
44. Taylor, *Commander*, p. 85.
45. Dann, pp. 237–8.
46. Ibid, p. 214.
47. Ibid, p. 220.
48. Ibid, p. 239.
49. Earle, p. 49.
50. Nicol, p. 197.
51. Ibid, pp. 199–207.
52. Ibid, p. 208.

53. In his introduction to the modern paperback edition of Nicol's memoir, Tim Flannery cites the judgement of Alexander Laing in an earlier republication that 'the passages of terse grandeur . . . lifts Nicol's story, from time to time, to the level of great English prose'.
54. Nicol, p. 211.

CHAPTER 18

1. Robinson, *The British Tar*, p. 418.
2. Thursfield, p. 35. The Rev Mangin was only too pleased to quit the sea and rejoin Hester Thrale and her company in Bath. His writing is not very original, echoing the opinion of Dr Johnson, another of Mrs Thrale's friends, that a ship was 'a prison within whose limits were to be found Constraint, Disease, Ignorance, Insensibility, Tyranny, Sameness, Dirt and Foul air: and the dangers of Ocean, Fire, Mutiny, Pestilence, Battle and Exile'.
3. Lloyd, *British Seaman*, pp. 224–5.
4. ADM 36/14639, muster of the *Temeraire*.
5. Goodall, pp. 25–7.
6. Ibid, p. 28.
7. Knight, *Britain Against Napoleon*, p. 217.
8. Padfield, *Maritime Power*, p. 196.
9. Childers, p. 72.
10. Bromley, p. 156.
11. *The Times*, 1 December 1802.
12. Dann, p. 248.
13. Fraser, p. 171.
14. Tom Allen website.
15. Conrad, *The Mirror of the Sea*, p. 78.
16. Goodall, p. 36.
17. Conrad, *The Mirror of the Sea*, p. 79.
18. Goodall, p. 39. Goodall's account is largely echoed by the account in the *Naval Chronicle*.
19. Willis, pp. 158–9.
20. Goodall, p. 46.
21. Ibid, pp. 44–5.
22. Ibid, p. 40.
23. Mostert, p. 425.
24. Ibid, p. 426.
25. Goodall, p. 47.
26. Ibid, p. 47.
27. Ibid, p. 49.
28. ADM 36/14639, muster of the *Temeraire*.
29. *The Times*, 24 October 1800.
30. *The Times*, 27 January 1801.
31. Ibid, 12 May 1802, and Lloyd, *British Seaman*, p. 229.
32. Kemp, p. 181.
33. *The Times*, 11 March 1803.
34. Ibid.
35. Rogers, *Sea Fencibles, Loyalism and the Reach of the State*, in Philp, p. 45.
36. Ibid, pp. 41 and 44.
37. Rogers, *The Press Gang*, p. 5.
38. ADM 1/4366, Letter from John and Alexander Anderson, 12 November 1803.
39. Stephen Jones, 'Blood Red Roses', in *The Mariner's Mirror*, 58:4, 1972.
40. ADM 51/1417, log of the *Hussar*.
41. Forester, p. 34.
42. Davey, p. 23.
43. Forester, p. 28.

44. Lloyd, *British Seaman*, p. 241.
45. Balladry and recruitment is the subject of James Davey's *Singing for the Nation*, in *The Mariner's Mirror*, 103:1, 2017.

CHAPTER 19

1. Robinson, *Nautical Economy*, pp. iii–iv.
2. Rodger, *Command*, pp. 485–6.
3. Ibid, pp. 532–3.
4. Watt and Hawkins, pp. 217–18.
5. Ibid, p. 221.
6. Ibid, p. 224.
7. Robinson, *Nautical Economy*, p. 12.
8. http://www.joadrian.co.uk/TomAllenStory.htm: In a reference to a clergyman to whom Tom had applied as a steward, Nelson wrote two weeks before sailing that he 'would not be able to perform such a service well'.
9. Robinson, *Nautical Economy*, pp. 12–13.
10. These numbers are of ratings, excluding petty officers, marines and supernumeraries.
11. Cordingly, *Billy Ruffian*, p. 212. This is based on a survey conducted by a captain of the *Bellerophon*.
12. Hay, p. 44.
13. Rodger, *Command*, p. 498. Based on the Ayshford Complete Trafalgar Roll.
14. ADM 36/16545, muster of *Revenge*.
15. Thursfield, p. 364.
16. Nicolson, p. 51.
17. Robinson, *Nautical Economy*, pp. 17–18.
18. Ibid, pp. 15–16.
19. Thursfield, p. 364.
20. Ibid, p. 227.
21. Ibid, p. 226.
22. Robinson, *Nautical Economy*, p. 20.
23. Fraser, p. 215.
24. Thursfield, p. 364.
25. Knight, *Pursuit of Victory*, p. 515.
26. Thursfield, p. 251.
27. Cordingly, *Billy Ruffian*, p. 83.
28. Fraser, p. 271.
29. Ibid, p. 256.
30. Thursfield, p. 365.
31. Watt and Hawkins, p. 250.
32. Robinson, *Nautical Economy*, p. 84.
33. Ibid, p. 28. Robinson does not identify the mid, who is named in ADM 36/16545, the muster of *Revenge*. It may be, however, that Nastyface was following a trend in narratives of the time to portray mids as little monsters of the lower deck.
34. Fraser, p. 259.
35. Leech, p. 82.
36. Robinson, p. 21.
37. Wilson, p. 456.
38. Robinson, p. 35.
39. Knight, *Pursuit of Victory*, p. 524.
40. Cunningham, p. 33.
41. Watt and Hawkins, pp. 247–8.
42. Ibid, p. 241.
43. Ibid, p. 252.

44. Ibid, p. 237.
45. Ibid, p. 238.
46. Nicol, pp. 205–6.
47. Lavery, *Shipboard Life*, pp. 255–6.
48. Rodger, *Command*, p. 543.
49. Knight, *Pursuit of Victory*, p. 520.
50. *Dictionary of National Biography*.
51. ADM 37/2829, muster of *Revenge*.
52. Robinson, *Nautical Economy*, p. 42.
53. Ibid, pp. 104–5.

CHAPTER 20

1. Captain Robert Corbet of the frigate *Nereide* ordered 924 lashes to be inflicted on the backs of 22 men over just two weeks in the Indian Ocean in 1809. The nightmare of the *Nereide* has some echoes with the *Hermione*, both being solitary frigates in distant seas, but whereas Hugh Pigot was an irrational brute, Corbet's natural zeal descended in isolation into a form of insanity. His savagery triggered a peaceful mutiny for which one man was hanged. Corbet himself was tried for cruelty but acquitted and a year later killed in action. For a full account see *Storm and Conquest* by the present author.
2. In his memoir, Watson referred only to 'my townsman W M'K'. He is identified in ADM 37/2095, muster of the *Fame*.
3. Watson, pp. 64–5.
4. Ibid, p. 70.
5. Ibid, p. 83.
6. Ibid, pp. 89–90.
7. Ibid, p. 71.
8. See Thursfield, pp.121–6.
9. Ibid, p. 140.
10. Ibid, p. 133.
11. ADM 51/1559, log of the *Unite*, 29 October 1805.
12. Thursfield, p. 136.
13. ADM 51/1559, log of the *Unite*, 22 January 1806.
14. Thursfield, p. 144.
15. Ibid, p. 168.
16. Ibid, p. 255.
17. Ibid, p. 245.
18. Ibid, p. 164.
19. Ibid, p. 185.
20. Ibid, p. 159.
21. Ibid, p. 226.
22. Ibid, p. 228.
23. Ibid, p. 213.
24. Ibid, p. 240.
25. Ibid, p. 215.
26. Ibid, p. 237.
27. See Thursfield's notes, pp. 125–6.
28. Ibid, pp. 263–4.
29. Nagle wrote that twenty-five men had been pressed but Neptune's log gives the number as sixteen. L/MAR/B/98.
30. L/MAR/B/98, log of the *Neptune*.
31. While the total disappearance of navy vessels was rare, four ships had foundered in 1804. The loss of life in the 64-gun *York*, a sloop, a schooner and a cutter in 1804 probably exceeded the deaths at Trafalgar a year later.

32. Hay, pp. 61–3.
33. Ibid, p. 74.
34. ADM 36/17388, muster of the *Culloden*.
35. Hay, p. 134.
36. Ibid, p. 162.
37. ADM 51/1866, log of the *Culloden*.
38. Hay, p. 166.
39. Ibid, p. 167.
40. Taylor, *Storm and Conquest*, p. 65.
41. Ibid, p. 72.
42. Adkins, p. 119.

CHAPTER 21

1. Derriman, pp. 35 and 101.
2. Bromley, p. 160.
3. Ibid, p. 158.
4. Lewis, p. 437.
5. Bromley, p. 160.
6. Toll, p. 271.
7. Leech, pp. 102 and 135–6. Brooks, pp. 18 and 33.
8. Lloyd, *British Seaman*, p. 195.
9. Knight, *Britain Against Napoleon*, p. 437.
10. Gilje, p. 157, Davey, *In Nelson's Wake*, p. 256.
11. Rodger, *Command*, pp. 565–6.
12. Brooks, p. 18.
13. Ibid, p. 49.
14. Ibid, p. 59.
15. Toll, pp. 292–3.
16. Dann, p. 262.
17. Ibid, pp. 262 and 275.
18. Ibid, pp. 292, 278, 288.
19. Ibid, p. 302.
20. John B. Hattendorf, 'Changing American Perceptions of the Royal Navy since 1775', in *International Journal of Naval History*, 1 July 2014.
21. The veracity of Leech's memoir can be tested against surviving records. ADM 51/2538, the *Macedonian's* log, matches his narrative and shows floggings were frequent, though Captain Fitzroy usually limited the number of lashes to between twelve and eighteen. The muster, ADM 37/2609, confirms that James Stokes, who Leech described as having 'cared for my interests with the faithfulness of a parent', had deserted and was captured.
22. Leech, p. 19.
23. Ibid, p. 90.
24. ADM 37/2609, muster of the *Macedonian*.
25. Leech, p. 72.
26. Ibid.
27. Ibid.
28. Ibid, pp. 75–7.
29. Ibid, p. 82.
30. Davey, p. 261.
31. John B. Hattendorf, *The Naval War of 1812 in International Perspective* in *The Mariner's Mirror*, 99:1, 2013.
32. Leech, p. 83.
33. Ibid, pp. 89–90.
34. Ibid, pp. 93–4.

35. Ibid, p. 110.
36. Ibid, p. 115.

CHAPTER 22

1. Rodger, *Command*, p. 561.
2. Robinson, p. 103.
3. Childers, pp. 67 and 97. The original 'I did not care much' was changed on editing to 'fret much'.
4. Lavery, *Nelson's Navy*, p. 46.
5. Childers, pp. 209 and 212.
6. Davey, pp. 282 and 284.
7. Childers, p. 244.
8. Robinson, *Nautical Economy*, p. 77.
9. Davey, p. 284.
10. Childers, p. 249.
11. Robinson, *Nautical Economy*, p. 79.
12. Childers, p. 250.
13. Parkinson, *Trade*, p. 298.
14. Childers, pp. 262–3.
15. Holmes, *Redcoat*, p. 18.
16. Robinson, p. 102.
17. Liddell Hart, p. 23.
18. Ibid, p. 25.
19. Ibid, p. 48.
20. Ibid, p. 47.
21. Ibid, p. 49.
22. ADM 37/2829, muster of *Revenge*.
23. Childers, p. 306.
24. Ibid, p. 308.
25. Ibid, p. vii.
26. Knight, *Britain Against Napoleon*, p. 427.
27. Rodger, *Command*, p. 574.
28. Pope, *Life in Nelson's Navy*, p. 131.
29. Hepper.
30. Ibid.
31. Adkins, p. 154.
32. Lewis, pp. 437–8.
33. Maxworthy.
34. Choyce, p. 107.
35. Ibid, p. 97.
36. Ibid, p. 172.
37. Ibid, p. 177.
38. ADM 36/14601, muster of *Melampus*.
39. ADM 36/1189, muster of *Theseus*.
40. Forester, pp. 113–36.
41. Ibid, p. 141.
42. Ibid, p. 152.
43. Ibid, p. 156.
44. Ibid, pp. 177–8.
45. Ibid, p. 21.
46. Ibid, p. 173.
47. Ibid, p. 191.
48. Ibid, pp. 233–58.
49. Ibid, p. 275.

50. ADM 36/15530, muster of the *Minerve*.
51. Forester, p. 181.
52. Ibid, p. 183. The marriage of Ann (not Jane) Toulson to Edward Bonner is confirmed by parish records. The date was actually 4 July, not 7 June as stated by Wetherell.

CHAPTER 23

1. *The Times*, 12 December 1816.
2. *Morning Chronicle*, 31 January 1817.
3. Dugan, pp. 469–70, website ExecutedToday.
4. See ADM 37/4325, ADM 51/2467, ADM 27/15. Trial report, TS 11/1031/4431.
5. *The Times*, 3 December 1816.
6. Knight, *Britain Against Napoleon*, p. 217.
7. See David J. Starkey, *Britain's Seafaring Workforce*, in Fury, pp. 170–2.
8. Knight, *Britain Against Napoleon*, p. 469.
9. ADM 37/4656, muster of *Ganymede*, confirms that William Waters of New York entered the ship in December 1811.
10. Thompson, p. 663.
11. Walmsley, p. 64.
12. Knight, *Britain Against Napoleon*, p. 470.
13. David J. Starkey, *Britain's Seafaring Workforce*, in Fury, pp. 170–2.
14. For a full account, see Norman McCord, *The Seamen's Strike of 1815 in North-East England*, in the *New Economic History Review*, 21:1, 1968.
15. ADM 12/174, 24 July 1815.
16. McCord, *The Seamen's Strike*.
17. ADM 12/174, 10 April and 8 September.
18. Conrad Dixon, *Seamen's Sixpences*, in *The Mariner's Mirror*, 70:4, 1984.
19. David J. Starkey, *Britain's Seafaring Workforce*, in Fury, pp. 170–2.
20. ADM 2/1714 contains letters of response to petitions in 1816 and 1817.
21. All information about Walker's career is taken from Warwick Hirst's *The Man Who Stole the Cyprus*, unless otherwise indicated.
22. Hughes, p. 215.
23. Hirst.
24. *The Times*, 4 November 1830.
25. As stated, the key information about the *Cyprus* piracy is taken from Hirst's diligent research of the subject.
26. *The Times*, 18 October 1830.
27. Ibid.
28. Hughes, p. 216.
29. Knight, *Britain Against Napoleon*, p. 474.
30. Dann, p. 273.
31. Parkinson, *Trade*, p. 354.
32. Henry Wise, *Analysis of a Hundred East India Voyages*, 1839 (downloadable).
33. Parkinson, *Trade*, p. 375. Whether the destination was Java, Madras, Bombay or Calcutta made surprisingly little difference.
34. From Wikipedia, quoting Alan Villiers's *Men, Ships and the Sea*.
35. Hay, p. 186.
36. Ibid, pp. 220–1.
37. Choyce, pp. 214–15.
38. Ibid.
39. Dann, pp. 312–13.
40. Crawford, p. 213.
41. Dann, p. 348.
42. Ibid, p. xxiv.

CHAPTER 24

1. Fowler, p. 45.
2. Nicol, p. 6.
3. Rodger, *The Social History of English Seamen 1650–1815*, in Fury, p. 64.
4. Robinson, p. 114.
5. Watson's *Narrative of the Adventures of a Greenwich Pensioner* cannot be seen even at the British Library, and it seems the Newcastle Library has the only public copy.
6. Campbell, p. 91.
7. Ibid, p. 97.
8. Ibid, p. 101.
9. Ibid, p. 105.
10. Ibid, p. 106.
11. These conclusions are drawn from Stanley Porteus's research for *The Restless Voyage*.
12. Ibid.
13. Campbell, p. 198.
14. *The Times*, 4 November 1799.
15. Stark, pp. 107–10.
16. Ibid, pp. 102–7.
17. *The Times*, 2 September 1815.
18. Stark, pp. 86–7.
19. ADM 37/5039, muster of the *Queen Charlotte*. This research was conducted by the National Archives and is available on the NA website.
20. *The Times*, 4 April 1810.
21. Derriman, p. 15.
22. Ibid, p. 42.
23. Ibid, p. 60.
24. *The Times*, 4 April 1810.
25. Ibid, 17 April 1810.
26. Ibid, 1 May 1810.
27. Ibid, 31 October 1810.
28. Derriman, pp. 112–13.
29. http://www.joadrian.co.uk.
30. *The Norwich Mercury*, 12 October 1839.
31. Fowler, p. 33.
32. George Holyoake, *Sixty Years of an Agitator's Life*, vol. 1, p. 44.
33. Pemberton was present on all three vessels he mentioned – taken aboard the *Friendship*, listed as Thomas Charles Reece, alias Pemberton, a volunteer Landsman, transferred to the *Salvador del Mundo*, and sent into the frigate *Alceste* of Captain Murray Maxwell. Curiously, he states that he was registered as Peregrine Verjuice, the name he adopted in his memoir, when he was actually named in the musters as Thomas Reece.
34. Fowler, pp. 106–7.
35. ADM 51/2477, muster of the *Alceste*, and ADM 51/2105, log of the *Alceste*.
36. Fowler, p. 127.
37. Ibid, p. 129.
38. Ibid, p. 166.
39. Ibid, p. 156.
40. Ibid, p. 120.
41. Ibid, p. 118.
42. Ibid, p. 157.
43. Ibid, p. 478.
44. *The Life and Literary Remains of Charles Reece Pemberton* (1843) edited by John Fowler was followed by another version ten years later, *The Autobiography of Pel Verjuice*, edited by George Phillips. The edition cited here is the first of these.

45. Dann, p. 136.
46. Fowler, pp. 118–19. Pemberton could not restrain his fondness for words and I have edited his prose.

CHAPTER 25

1. *Dictionary of National Biography.*
2. Fraser, p. 325.
3. Stephen Jones, *Blood Red Roses*, in *The Mariner's Mirror*, 58:4, 1972.
4. Colley, *Britons*, p. 5.
5. Watson, p. 166.
6. ADM1/5122/19.
7. Ibid.
8. ADM 2/1145, ff. 107 and 496.
9. ADM 1/5245.
10. ADM 2/1146.
11. Fraser, p. 325.
12. Adkins, p. 387. George King's original manuscript was once held at the Caird Library in Greenwich, but has been withdrawn by the holder.
13. Spavens, p. 99.
14. Martin Wilcox, *The Poor Decayed Seamen of Greenwich Hospital*, in the *International Journal of Maritime History*, June 2013.
15. Hardy's record is contained in ADM 73/45. He came from rural Rutland and with a trade listed as 'Husbandry' would have been responsible for the ship's livestock; his legs were amputated as a result of illness rather than action.
16. Vale, p. 33.
17. *The Greenwich Pensioners*, published in 1838 under the pseudonym of Lieutenant Hatchway, is a novel but contains enough detail to stand as a fair record.
18. Author's confession: George Watson was in fact an out-pensioner who returned to his native Newcastle; I have placed him at Greenwich as a device to bring together the voices of two pensioners.
19. Cordingly, *Billy Ruffian*, p. 222.
20. Adkins, pp. 240–2.
21. Watson, pp. 125–6.
22. Ibid, pp. 113–14.
23. Ibid, pp. 178–80.
24. Ibid, p. 83.
25. Ibid, p. 202.
26. Ibid, pp. 186–91. The conclusion that George Watson was long-winded is drawn from his narrative style.
27. Watson, p. 102.
28. Anthony Tibbles, *Born Under an Unlucky Planet*, in *The Mariner's Mirror*, 99:3, 2013.
29. Ibid. Roberts's journal, unfortunately, gives little detail of the events to which he was party.
30. Stephen Jones, *Blood Red Roses*, in *The Mariner's Mirror*, 58:4, 1972.
31. Vale, p. 37.
32. Lloyd, *British Seaman*, p. 248.
33. Thomas Urquhart, *Letters on the Evils of Impressment*, 1816.
34. Robinson, *The British Tar*, p. 143.
35. Fowler, pp. 205–6.
36. Bromley, p. 176. The pamphlet's author was Sir Thomas Byam Martin.
37. R. Taylor, *Manning the Royal Navy*, in *The Mariner's Mirror*, 44:4, 1958.
38. Andrew Lambert's Foreword in Grindal.

CHAPTER 26

1. ADM 36/11510, muster of *Scipio*.
2. Conrad Dixon, *To Walk the Quarterdeck: The Naval Career of David Ewen Bartholomew*, in *The Mariner's Mirror*, 79:1, 1993.
3. Ibid.
4. *Dictionary of National Biography*.
5. Grindal, p. 217.
6. ADM 55/86, Bartholomew's Journal.
7. ADM 37/6235, muster of the *Leven*.
8. *Sweet Water and Bitter* by Sian Rees (2009) presented the subject to a general readership, but *Opposing the Slavers* by Peter Grindal (2016) was the first detailed history.
9. ADM 37/6776, muster of *Thistle*.
10. ADM 52/3947, master's log, *Leven*.
11. ADM 37/7044, muster of *Bann*. A few years later, *Sybille* had 49 of her 275 complement desert at Portsmouth before she sailed (ADM 37/7737).
12. ADM 51/3070, captain's log, and ADM 37/7044, muster of the *Bann*.
13. These figures are taken from the list in Grindal of suspect vessels detained (pp. 763–83).
14. ADM 51/3070, log of *Bann*, 6 October 1822.
15. Ibid, 10 October 1822.
16. Grindal, p. 770.
17. ADM 51/3070, log of *Bann*.
18. ADM 37/7044, muster of *Bann*.
19. ADM 37/7842, muster of *Aetna*, and ADM 27/23.
20. *The Times*, 17 November 1827.
21. Rees, *Sweet Water*, p. 203.
22. Grindal, p. 365.
23. ADM 37/7737, muster of *Sybille*.
24. Grindal, p. 371.
25. ADM 37/7737, muster of *Sybille*.
26. Grindal, p. 462.
27. Ibid, p. 378.
28. Ibid, p. 288.
29. Ibid, pp. 296, 299 and 309.
30. Ibid, p. 799.
31. Ibid, pp. 773 and 799.
32. ADM 51/3466, log of *Sybille*.
33. Grindal, pp. 357–8.
34. Rees, *Sweet Water*, p. 142.
35. Ibid.
36. Grindal, pp. 358–9.
37. Ibid, pp. 134–5.
38. Ibid, pp. 132 and 212.
39. Grindal, p. 402, and Rees, *Sweet Water*, p. 129.
40. *The Times*, 25 October 1830.
41. These figures are compiled from the table in Appendix A of Grindal.
42. See Appendix H in Grindal.
43. Grindal, p. 463
44. Leonard, pp. 131–2.
45. Bromley, p. 197.
46. From Appendix A and Appendix G of Grindal.
47. Grindal, p. 758.

EPILOGUE

1. Bromley, p. 197.
2. Rogers, p. 133.
3. ADM 1/5357.
4. Pope, *Nelson's Navy*, p. 177.
5. Garstin, p. 138.
6. Murray, p. 99.
7. Conrad, *The Mirror of the Sea*, p. 38.
8. Ibid, p. 39.
9. Conrad, *The Secret Sharer and Other Stories*, p. 22.
10. JOD41, Caird Library, Greenwich. Thorpe evidently misremembered a couple of words, but not so as to alter the sense, nor the last three lines.

BIBLIOGRAPHY

MANUSCRIPT SOURCES

The National Archives, Kew: Repository for all Admiralty papers. The musters of navy ships (ADM 36 series) have been an essential resource, providing information about seamen's backgrounds and data for testing the veracity of individual accounts. Captains' logbooks (ADM 51 series) offer further insights into shipboard life and punishment records. Court-martial hearings (ADM 1 series) taken down in the shorthand of the day give voice to seamen's conduct and grievances.

British Library, London: East India Company records

Caird Library, National Maritime Museum, Greenwich

The Library of the National Museum of the Royal Navy, Portsmouth

SEAMEN'S MEMOIRS

Primary

Campbell, Archibald: *A Voyage Around the World from 1806 to 1812*. Edinburgh, 1822

Childers, Spencer (ed.): *A Mariner of England – An Account of the Career of William Richardson, 1780 to 1819*. London, 1908 (reprint)

Choyce, James: *The Log of a Jack Tar*. Maidstone, 1973

Dann, John C. (ed.): *The Nagle Journal – A Diary of the Life of Jacob Nagle, Sailor, from the Year 1717 to 1841*. New York, 1988

Forester, C. S. (ed.): *The Adventures of John Wetherell*. London, 1994

Fowler, John (ed.): *The Life and Literary Remains of Charles Reece Pemberton*. London, 1843 (online)

Hay, M. D. (ed.): *Landsman Hay – Memoirs of Robert Hay, 1789–1847*. London, 1953

Leech, Samuel: *A Voice from the Main Deck – Being a Record of the Thirty Years' Adventures of Samuel Leech*. London, 1999

Nicol, John: *The Life and Adventures of John Nicol, Mariner*. Edinburgh, 1822 (online, or in paperback, edited by Tim Flannery, Edinburgh, 2000)

Robinson, William: *Nautical Economy; or Forecastle Reflections of Events During the Last War*. London, 1832 (online, or in paperback, titled *Jack Nastyface, Memoirs of an English Seaman*, London, 2002)

Rodger, N. A. M. (ed.): *Memoirs of a Seafaring Life – The Narrative of William Spavens*. Bath, 2001

Watson, George: *A Narrative of the Adventures of a Greenwich Pensioner*. Newcastle, 1827

Secondary

Barlow, Edward: *Barlow's Journal of his Life at Sea from 1659 to 1703*. London, 1934

Brooks, George, S. (ed.): *James Durand an Able Seaman of 1812 – His Adventures in 'Old Ironsides' and as an Impressed Sailor in the British Navy*. New Haven, 1926

Bulkeley, John, and Cummins, John: *A Voyage to the South Seas in the Years 1740–41*. London, 1757 (online)

Davis, Joshua: *A Narrative of Joshua Davis, an American Citizen who was Pressed and Served on Six Ships of the British Navy*. Baltimore, 1811 (online)

Garstin, Crosbie (ed.): *Samuel Kelly – An Eighteenth-Century Seaman*. London, 1922

Goodall, Daniel: *Salt Water Sketches – Being Incidents in the Life of Daniel Goodall, Seaman and Marine*. Inverness, 1860 (reprint)

Hamilton, Richard, and Laughton, John Knox (eds): *Above and Under Hatches – Recollections of James Anthony Gardner*. London, 2000

Knight, Roger, and Frost, Alan (eds): *The Journal of Daniel Paine, 1794–1797*. Sydney, 1983

Meyerstein, E. H. W. (ed.): *Adventures by Sea of Edward Coxere*. Oxford, 1945

Morris, Isaac: *A Narrative of the Dangers and Distresses which Befell Isaac Morris and Seven more of the Crew Belonging to the Wager*. London, 1751 (online)

Murray, Jean (ed.): *The Newfoundland Journal of Aaron Thomas, 1794*. London, 1968

Parsons, George: *I Sailed With Nelson*. Maidstone, 1973

Price, George: *Pressganged – The Letters of George Price of Southwark*. Royston, 1984

Sherburne, Andrew: *Memoirs of Andrew Sherburne, a Pensioner of the Navy of the Revolution*. Long Island, 1831 (online)

OTHER PUBLISHED WORKS

Ackroyd, Peter: *London, the Biography*. London, 2000

Adkins, Roy and Lesley: *Jack Tar – Life in Nelson's Navy*. London, 2008

Alexander, Caroline: *The Bounty – The True Story of the Mutiny on the Bounty*. London, 2003

Anon.: *The Sailors Advocate*. London, 1728 (Download)

Baynham, Henry: *From the Lower Deck – The Navy, 1700–1840*. London, 1972

Blake, Richard: *Evangelicals in the Royal Navy, 1775–1815*. Suffolk, 2008

Bolster, W. Jeffrey: *Black Jacks – African American Seamen in the Age of Sail*. Cambridge, MA, 1997

Boston, Ceridwen, Witkin, Annsofie, Boyle, Angela, and Wilkinson, David: *Safe Moor'd in Greenwich Tier – A Study of the Skeletons of Royal Navy Sailors and Marines Excavated at the Royal Hospital, Greenwich*. Oxford, 2008

Bowen, H. V., Lincoln, Margarette, and Rigby, Nigel (eds): *The Worlds of the East India Company*. Suffolk, 2002

Bromley, J. S.: *The Manning of the Royal Navy – Selected Pamphlets, 1693–1873*. Navy Records Society, 1976

Brown, Kevin: *Poxed and Scurvied – The Story of Sickness and Health at Sea*. Barnsley, 2011

Bundock, Michael: *The Fortunes of Francis Barber – The True Story of the Jamaican Slave Who Became Samuel Johnson's Heir*. London, 2015

Burg, B. R.: *Boys at Sea – Sodomy, Indecency and Courts Martial in Nelson's Navy*. Basingstoke, 2007

Byrn, John D.: *Crime and Punishment in the Royal Navy – Discipline on the Leeward Islands Station, 1784–1812*. Aldershot, 1989

Byrn, John D. (ed.): *Naval Courts Martial, 1793–1815*. Navy Records Society, 2009

Carretta, Vincent: *Equiano, the African – Biography of a Self-Made Man*. London, 2006

Carrington, Richard: *A Biography of the Sea*. London, 1965

Chatterton, E. Keble: *The Old East Indiamen*. London, 1914

Clayton, Tim: *Tars – The Men Who Made Britain Rule the Waves*. London, 2007

Coats, Ann Veronica, and MacDougall, Philip (eds): *The Naval Mutinies of 1797: Unity and Perseverance*. Martlesham, Suffolk, 2011

Colley, Linda: *Britons – Forging the Nation, 1707–1837*. London, 1992

Colley, Linda: *Captives – Britain, Empire and the World, 1600–1850*. London, 2002

Colley, Linda: *The Ordeal of Elizabeth Marsh – A Woman in World History*. London, 2007

Conrad, Joseph: *The Mirror of the Sea & A Personal Record*. London, 2008

Conrad, Joseph: *The Secret Sharer and Other Stories* (formerly entitled *The Nigger of the Narcissus*). London, 2014

Cordingly, David: *Heroines and Harlots – Women at Sea in the Great Age of Sail*. London, 2001

Cordingly, David: *Billy Ruffian – The Biography of a Ship of the Line*. London, 2003

Cotton, Sir Evan, and Fawcett, Charles: *East Indiamen – The East India Company's Maritime Service*. London, 1949

Crawford, Captain A.: *Reminiscences of a Naval Officer*. London, 1999

Cunningham, A. E. (ed.): *Patrick O'Brian – Critical Appreciations and a Bibliography*. Wetherby, 1995

Dancy, J. Ross: *The Myth of the Press Gang – Volunteers, Impressment and the Naval Manpower Problem in the 18th Century*. Martlesham, Suffolk, 2015

Davey, James: *In Nelson's Wake – How the Navy Ruled the Waves After Trafalgar*. London, 2015

Derriman, James: *Marooned – The Story of a Cornish Seaman*. Emsworth, Hampshire, 1991

Dugan, James: *The Great Mutiny*. London, 1966

Earle, Peter: *Sailors – English Merchant Seamen, 1650–1775*. London, 2007

Eder, Marckus: *Crime and Punishment in the Royal Navy of the Seven Years' War, 1755–1763*. Aldershot, 2004

Fielding, Henry: *Journal of a Voyage to Lisbon* (online)

Fort, Tom: *The Village News – The Truth Behind England's Rural Idyll*. London, 2017

Fraser, Edward: *The Sailors Whom Nelson Led – Their Doings Described by Themselves*. London, 1913

Fury, Cheryl (ed.): *The Social History of English Seamen, 1650–1815*. Martlesham, Suffolk, 2017

Garneray, Louis (translated by Richard Rose): *The Floating Prison – Nine Years of Captivity on the British Prison Hulks*. London, 2003

Gilje, Paul: *Liberty on the Waterfront – American Maritime Culture in the Age of Revolution*. Philadelphia, 2004

Gill, Conrad: *The Naval Mutinies of 1797*. London, 1913

Gradish, Stephen: *The Manning of the British Navy during the Seven Years' War*. London, 1980

Grindal, Peter: *Opposing the Slavers – The Royal Navy's Campaign against the Atlantic Slave Trade*. London, 2016

Hatchway, Lt.: *The Greenwich Pensioners*. London, 1838

Hepper, David: *British Warship Losses in the Age of Sail, 1650–1859*. Rotherfield, East Sussex, 1994

Hirst, Warwick: *The Man Who Stole the Cyprus – A True Story of Escape*. New South Wales, 2008

Holmes, Richard: *Redcoat – The British Soldier in the Age of Horse and Musket*. London, 2001

Holmes, Richard: *The Age of Wonder – How the Romantic Generation Discovered the Beauty and Terror of Science*. London, 2009

Hood, Jean: *Marked for Misfortune – An Epic Tale of Shipwreck, Human Endeavour and Survival in the Age of Sail*. London, 2003

Hough, Richard: *Captain James Cook*. London, 1994

Hughes, Robert: *The Fatal Shore – A History of the Transportation of Convicts to Australia, 1787–1868*. London, 1987

Inglefield, Captain J.: *The Loss of His Majesty's Ship* Centaur, in Archibald Duncan (ed.), *The Mariner's Chronicle*, 1834 (online)

James, Lawrence: *The Rise and Fall of the British Empire*. London, 1994

Kemp, Peter: *The British Sailor – A Social History of the Lower Deck*. London, 1970

Keneally, Tom: *The Commonwealth of Thieves – The Story of the Founding of Australia*. London, 2006

Kennedy, Gavin: *Captain Bligh – The Man and his Mutinies*. London, 1989

Knight, Roger: *The Pursuit of Victory – The Life and Achievement of Horatio Nelson*. London, 2005

Knight, Roger: *Britain Against Napoleon – The Organization of Victory, 1793–1815*. London, 2013

Lamb, Jonathan: *Scurvy: The Disease of Discovery*. Princeton, 2016

Lambert, Andrew: *The Challenge – Britain Against America in the Naval War of 1812*. London, 2012

Land, Isaac: *War, Nationalism, and the British Sailor, 1750–1850*. New York, 2009

Lavery, Brian: *Nelson's Navy – The Ships, Men and Organisation, 1793–1815*. London, 1989

Lavery, Brian: *Shipboard Life and Organisation, 1731–1815*. Navy Records Society, vol. 138, 1998

Leonard, Peter: *Records of a Voyage to the Western Coast of Africa . . . etc.* 1833 (online)

Lewis, Michael: *A Social History of the Navy 1793–1815*. London, 1960

Liddell Hart, B. H. (ed.): *The Letters of Private Wheeler, 1809–1828*. London, 1951

Lincoln, Margarette: *Naval Wives and Mistresses*. London, 2007

Lincoln, Margarette: *Trading in War – London's Maritime World in the Age of Cook and Nelson*. London, 2018

Lloyd, Christopher (ed.): *The Health of Seamen*. Navy Records Society, 1964

Lloyd, Christopher: *The British Seaman*. London, 1968

McCullough, David: *1776 – America and Britain at War*. London, 2006

Magra, Christopher: *Poseidon's Curse – British Naval Impressment and the Atlantic Origins of the American Revolution*. Cambridge, 2016

Manwaring, G. E., and Dobree, Bonamy: *Mutiny – The Floating Republic*. London, 1987

May, Trevor: *Smugglers and Smuggling*. Oxford, 2014

Moorey, Peter: *Who Was the Sailor Murdered at Hindhead?* Haslemere, 2000

Morriss, Roger: *The Channel Fleet and the Blockade of Brest, 1793–1801*. Navy Records Society, 2001

Mostert, Noel: *The Line Upon a Wind – An Intimate History of the Last and Greatest War Fought at Sea under Sail, 1793–1815*. London, 2007

Nash, M. D.: *Last Voyage of the Guardian, 1789–91*. Cape Town, 1990

Neale, Jonathan: *The Cutlass & The Lash – Mutiny and Discipline in Nelson's Navy*, London, 1985

Nicolson, Adam: *Men of Honour – Trafalgar and the Making of the English Hero*. London, 2006

Padfield, Peter: *Nelson's War*. London, 1976

Padfield, Peter: *Maritime Power and the Struggle for Freedom, 1788–1851*. London, 2003

Parkinson, C. Northcote: *War in the Eastern Seas, 1793–1815*. London, 1954

Parkinson, C. Northcote: *Trade in the Eastern Seas, 1793–1813*. London, 1966

Pasley, Sir Thomas: *Private Sea Journals, 1778–82*. London, 1931

Philbrick, Nathaniel: *In the Heart of the Sea*. London, 2000

Philp, Mark (ed.): *Resisting Napoleon – The British Response to the Threat of Invasion, 1797–1815*. London, 2006

Pietsch, Roland: *The Real Jim Hawkins – Ships' Boys in the Georgian Navy*. Barnsley, 2010

Pope, Dudley: *Life in Nelson's Navy*. London, 1981

Pope, Dudley: *The Black Ship*. Barnsley, 2003

Porter, Roy: *English Society in the 18th Century*. London, 1991

Rediker, Marcus: *Between the Devil and the Deep Blue Sea*. Cambridge, 1987

Rees, Sian: *The Floating Brothel*. London, 2001

Rees, Sian: *Sweet Water and Bitter – The Ships that Stopped the Slave Trade*. London, 2009

Richmond, H. W.: *The Navy in India, 1763–1783*. London, 1931

Robinson, Charles: *The British Tar in Fact and Fiction*. London, 1909

Rodger, N. A. M.: *The Wooden World – An Anatomy of the Georgian Navy*. London, 1988.

Rodger, N. A. M.: *The Safeguard of the Sea – A Naval History of Britain, 660–1649*. London, 1997

Rodger, N. A. M.: *The Command of the Ocean – A Naval History of Britain, 1649–1815*. London, 2004

Rogers, Nicholas: *The Press Gang – Naval Impressment and its Opponents in Georgian Britain*. London, 2007

Ronald, D. A. B.: *Young Nelsons – Boy Sailors During the Napoleonic Wars*. Oxford, 2009

Stark, Suzanne J.: *Female Tars – Women Aboard Ship in the Age of Sail*. London, 1996

Sugden, John: *Nelson – The Sword of Albion*. London, 2012

Summerville, Christopher (ed.): *Regency Recollections – Captain Gronow's Guide to Life in London and Paris*. Welwyn Garden City, 2006

Sutton, Jean: *Lords of the East – The East India Company and its Ships, 1600–1874*. London, 2000

Taylor, Stephen: *The Caliban Shore – The Fate of the Grosvenor Castaways*. London, 2004

Taylor, Stephen: *Storm and Conquest – The Battle for the Indian Ocean, 1809*. London, 2007

Taylor, Stephen: *Commander – The Life and Exploits of Britain's Greatest Frigate Captain*. London, 2012

Thomas, Hugh: *The Slave Trade – The History of the Atlantic Slave Trade, 1440–1870*. London, 2006

Thompson, E. P.: *The Making of the English Working Class*. London, 1980

Thursfield, H. G. (ed.): *Five Naval Journals, 1789–1817*. Navy Records Society, 1951

Toll, Ian: *Six Frigates – The Epic History of the Founding of the US Navy*. New York, 2006

Uglow, Jenny: *In These Times – Living in Britain Through Napoleon's Wars*. London, 2014

Urban, Mark: *Rifles – Six Years with Wellington's Legendary Sharpshooters*. London, 2003

Urquhart, Thomas: *Letters on the Evils of Impressment*. London, 1816

Vale, Brian: *A Frigate of King George*. London, 2001

Vickers, Daniel: *Young Men and the Sea – Yankee Seafarers in the Age of Sail*. London, 2005

Walmsley, Robert: *Peterloo – The Case Reopened*. Manchester, 1986

Walvin, James: *Black Ivory – A History of British Slavery*. London, 1993

Walvin, James: *An African's Life – The Life and Times of Olaudah Equiano, 1745–1797*. London, 2000

Wareham, Tom: *Frigate Commander*. London, 2004

Watt, Helen, and Hawkins, Anne (eds): *Letters of Seamen in the Wars with France 1793–1815*. Martlesham, Suffolk, 2016

Williams, Glyn: *The Prize of All the Oceans – The Triumph and Tragedy of Anson's Voyage Around the World*. London, 2000

Willis, Sam: *The Fighting Temeraire*. London, 2009

Wilson, Ben: *Empire of the Deep – The Rise and Fall of the British Navy*. London, 2013

Woodman, Richard: *The Sea Warriors – Fighting Captains and Frigate Warfare in the Age of Nelson*. London, 2001

Woodman, Richard: *Neptune's Trident – A History of the British Merchant Navy, 1500–1807*. Stroud, 2008

ARTICLES AND THESES

Brown, Anthony: *The Nore Mutiny – Sedition or Ships' Biscuit? A Reappraisal*, in *The Mariner's Mirror*, 92:1, 2006

Davey, James: *Singing for the Nation: Naval Recruitment and the Language of Patriotism in Eighteenth-Century Britain*, in *The Mariner's Mirror*, 103:1, 2017

Dixon, Conrad: *Seamen's Sixpences*, in *The Mariner's Mirror*, 70:4, 1984

Dixon, Conrad: *To Walk the Quarterdeck – The Naval Career of David Ewan Bartholomew*, in *The Mariner's Mirror*, 79:1, 1993

Doorne, Christopher: *Mutiny and Sedition in the Home Commands of the Royal Navy, 1793–1803*. PhD thesis, University of London, 1998 (online)

Foy, Charles: '*Unkle Sommerset's Freedom': Liberty in England for Black Sailors*, in *Journal for Maritime Research*, May 2011

Hattendorf, John B.: *The Naval War of 1812 in International Perspective*, in *The Mariner's Mirror*, 99:1, 2013

Hattendorf, John B.: *American Perceptions of the Royal Navy Since 1775*, in *International Journal of Naval History*, July 2014

Hunt, William R.: *Nautical Autobiography in the Age of Sail*, in *The Mariner's Mirror*, 57:2, 1971

Jones, Stephen: *Blood Red Roses*, in *The Mariner's Mirror*, 58:4, 1972

Land, Isaac: *New Scholarship on the Press Gang* (Download from Port Towns & Urban Cultures website)

McCord, Norman: *The Seamen's Strike of 1815 in North-East England*, in *The New Economic History Review*, 21:1, 1968

McCord, Norman: *The Government of Tyneside, 1800–1850*. Cambridge University Press, 1970

Macleod, Norman: *History of the Royal Hospital School*, in *The Mariner's Mirror*, 35:3, 1949

Maxworthy, Christopher: *British Whalers, Merchants and Smugglers on the Pacific Coast of South America, 1783–1810* (Download from *Derreteros de la Mar del Sur*)

May, W. E.: *The Mutiny of the* Chesterfield, in *The Mariner's Mirror*, 47:3, 1961

Taylor, R.: *Manning the Royal Navy*, in *The Mariner's Mirror*, 44:4, 1958

Tibbles, Anthony: *Born Under an Unlucky Planet*, in *The Mariner's Mirror*, 99:3, 2013

Vale, Brian: *The Post Office, The Admiralty and Letters to Sailors in the Napoleonic Wars*, in *The Mariner's Mirror*, 105:2, 2019

Watt, James: *The Health of Seamen in Anti-Slavery Squadrons*, in *The Mariner's Mirror*, 88:1, 2002

Wilcox, Martin: *The Poor Decayed Seamen of Greenwich Hospital*, in *The International Journal of Maritime History*, June 2013

Williams, Glyndwr: *Seamen and Philosophers in the South Seas*, in *The Mariner's Mirror*, 65:1, 1979

Willis, Sam: *The High Life: Topmen in the Eighteenth-Century Navy*, in *The Mariner's Mirror*, 90:2, 2004

ACKNOWLEDGEMENTS

THIS book had its genesis in a conversation I had more than ten years ago with Julian Loose. He had been the editor of my first two works with maritime themes and, over a celebratory lunch, planted the seed for a third. Although it took a decade to evolve, in form, scope and direction, he indulged me when I needed time to stand back and engage with other subjects, published those too, and all the time sustained the loyalty which finally carried the finished product to Yale University Press. Our fifth book together is a tribute to his vision and perseverance.

Few areas of Britain's history have been subjected to such rigorous examination as its maritime past, and it follows that as a relative latecomer to these waters I have been a beneficiary of the hard research carried out over many years by academics and amateurs alike. Above all, however, for his help in finding my way, his guidance towards original sources and for saving me from errors of fact and judgement, I owe a special debt to Roger Knight.

Throughout the preparation of this work it has been my intention to have the men who were at the centre of British maritime endeavour speak in their own voices. In some cases this required copyright permissions, and for granting theirs I must express particular gratitude to two leading naval historians. N. A. M. Rodger generously approved usage of his edited version of William Spavens's narrative and extensive quotation from his own seminal work, *The Command of the Ocean*. With similar generosity, John C. Dann allowed free usage from Jacob Nagle's treasure of a journal which, as readers will have observed, forms a central strand of my own narrative.

Others to whom I am pleased to extend my thanks for their open-handedness in granting relevant permissions are Ben Jones of the Navy Record Society, for the five naval journals edited by H. G. Thursfield; Tom Walker at the Folio Society, for the Spavens journal; and Michael Leventhal and Chatham Publishing, for Samuel Leech's memoir. Joan and Adrian Bridge conducted extensive research into the life of Tom Allen, which they have made freely available online.

Another copyright holder from whom relevant permission was obtained was the Estate of C. S. Forester, who edited *The Adventures of John Wetherell*. I was unable to find a holder associated with *Landsman Hay*, the memoir of Robert Hay; the publisher, Rupert Hart-Davis, was dissolved in 1993.

Seamen's letters were a rich resource. Margaret Newman guided me to the correspondence of Richard Greenhalgh at the National Museum of the Royal Navy at Portsmouth. I am also happy to acknowledge my use of *Letters of Seamen in the Wars with France*, edited by Helen Watt and Anne Hawkins.

The National Archives in Kew is the repository for Admiralty records. These were essential, both for testing the reliability of seamen's memoirs and for finding the stories of other long-forgotten individuals within court-martial records, ships' musters, logbooks and wills. As anyone who has conducted research there knows, the National Archives, run by the staff with efficiency and courtesy, is a national treasure. Other libraries where I had the pleasures of discovery and the help of staff were the Caird at the National Maritime Museum and the British Library.

One resource proved especially elusive. George Watson's *Adventures of a Greenwich Pensioner*, published in 1827, is so rare even the British Library does not have a copy. Possibly the last in a public collection was traced to Newcastle Library where Fiona Hill was kind enough to send it for study at my own local library.

Illustrating the seaman's life has posed a challenge. The contemporary artists so prolific in turning out canvasses of gold-braided officers and their magnificent ships did little to portray the men who sustained both. In searching for images of Jack Tar other than hackneyed caricatures, I sought the advice of

Pieter van der Merwe of the National Maritime Museum, and acknowledge his help.

I wish to express my gratitude to Caroline Dawnay, who has been my agent for almost twenty years – a happy and fruitful time for the writing of non-fiction. Those who read early texts and offered illuminating comments included my daughter Juliette and my friend Tom Fort.

Two anonymous specialist reviewers of the final product observed some factual errors and gave this author reason to be thankful for the rigorous procedures followed by Yale. Clarissa Sutherland steered the production meticulously; my thanks too to Marika Lysandrou for her editorial advice, to Percie Edgeler for the handsome design, to Katie Urquhart for arranging use of the pictures, to Richard Mason for copy-editing and to Lucy Buchan for work on the proofs.

Throughout my writing life, one person has been a constant inspiration – an insightful reader, a forthright critic, a warm supporter, an indomitable fellow traveller. From our first steps together, over many years of adventures and storms, my wife Caroline has helped to shape what I wrote and how I did it as only a true and loving soulmate can.

INDEX

Burke, Edmund, 81, 249, 252
Burkett, Thomas, 163
Burne, Terence, 151–2, 153, 154–5, 176
Burnet, John (artist), 415–16
Burney, Fanny, 87
Burnham, 210, 398
Bury, Lancs, 138, 140
Byng, Admiral John, 53
Byrn, Michael, 163

Cadiz, xx, 45, 313
Caesar, Julius (seaman), 75
Calaway, James, 228
Calcutta, 71–3, 75, 77, 93, 196, 201, 204, 337, 355, 381
Calder, Admiral Sir Robert, 313
calenture (ailment), 83
Campbell, Archibald, 390–4
Campbell, Rear-Admiral George, 300–3
Campbell, Isabella, 393
Campbell, Captain Patrick, 332–4
Camperdown, Battle of, 139, 278–81, 361
Canada, 60, 63, 349, 373
Canning, George, 352
Canton, China, 15, 71, 91–2, 337, 381, 385–6
Canton, Ohio, 385–6
Cape Finisterre, xxii, 290
Cape of Good Hope, 35, 70, 93–4, 147, 150, 152, 158, 166, 170, 173, 175, 197, 337, 338, 353
Cape Horn, 11, 12, 13, 14, 81, 89, 147, 152, 159, 181
Cape Ortegal, Battle of, 355
Cape St Vincent, Battle of, 214, 219, 220, 236, 244, 282–3, 291, 361
Cape Verde islands, 419, 420, 421
Card, John, 350, 351
Carden, Captain John, 350
Caribbean Sea, xix, xxi–xxii, 29, 34, 55, 107, 109, 111, 117, 119, 131, 181, 268, 347
Carlton House, 369
Carter, John, 75–6
Carteret, Captain Peter, 34–5
Casey, Michael, 137
Cashman, John, 369–70, 372
Cass, Stephen, 139, 141
castaways, 93–5, 153–4, 163, 173, 184, 292, 387, 393, 396–8
Cawsand Bay, 325
Cesar, Julius (seaman), 338
Ceylon, 338
Chamier, Frederick (author), 398–9

Channel (English), xix, 4, 9, 52, 53, 55, 135, 177, 193, 200, 204, 242, 272, 300, 312, 314, 338, 424; wrecks in, 181
Channel Fleet, 195, 210, 226, 228, 238, 242, 243, 263, 355, 357
Chapman, James, 45
charities, for seamen, 304–6, 371, 375, 406, 416, 417
Charles, John, 275
Charles II, King, 243
Chatham, 135, 200, 211, 212, 262, 423
Chatham Chest (pension fund), 32, 80
Chelsea Pensioners reading the Waterloo Dispatch (painting), 416
Chesapeake Bay, 107
Chile, 13, 15, 362–3, 384
Chilton, John (highwayman), 215
China, xxiv, 66, 89, 98, 159, 196, 291, 297, 325, 347, 379, 381–2; as observed by a seaman, 91–2
Choyce, James, xvii, 362–4, 389
Christian, Fletcher, 162–3
Churchill, Winston, 47, 350
Ciudad Rodrigo, 357
Clements, Thomas, 167–70
clippers, 381–2
Clive, Colonel Robert (later Lord), 53
Cliveden, 8
Clydeside, 39
Coad, Theophilus, 209
Cobbett, William (campaigner), 144, 396, 397
Cochrane, Rear-Admiral Alexander, 396
Cochrane, Captain, Lord Thomas, 356, 363
Cole, William, 425
Coleridge, Samuel Taylor, 438
Colley, Linda, 407
Collier, Captain Francis, 429, 430, 431
colliers and coal trade, xix, 49, 120, 121, 199; as nursery for seamen, 210, 215, 297, 308, 328, 374, 375, 376
Collingwood, Captain (later Vice-Admiral Lord) Cuthbert, 164, 175, 210, 242, 286–7, 288, 313, 318, 325, 339
Collingwood, Captain Luke, 113
Collins, Jeremiah, 230–2
Colpoys, Vice-Admiral Sir John, 228, 250
Conflans, Comte Hubert de, 58
Congo river, 114, 423
Congress of Vienna, 419
Conrad, Joseph, 110, 178, 194, 299–300, 347, 438–9
Constable & Co (publisher), 393
Constantinople, 330